Meaning, Language, and Time

Meaning, Language, and Time

Toward a Consequentialist Philosophy of Discourse

Kevin J. Porter

Parlor Press
West Lafayette, Indiana
www.parlorpress.com

Parlor Press LLC, West Lafayette, Indiana 47906

SAN: 254-8879

Library of Congress Cataloging-in-Publication Data

Porter, Kevin J., 1970-
   Meaning, language, and time : toward a consequentialist philosophy of
   discourse / Kevin J. Porter.
      p. cm.
   Originally presented as the author's thesis (Ph. D.)--University of Wis-
   consin-Madison.
   Includes bibliographical references (p.   ) and index.
   ISBN 1-932559-78-7 (pbk. : alk. paper) -- ISBN 1-932559-79-5 (hard-
   cover : alk. paper) -- ISBN 1-932559-80-9 (adobe ebook) 1. Meaning
   (Philosophy) 2. Consequentialism (Ethics) 3. Time--Philosophy. 4.
   Language and languages--Philosophy. I. Title.
   B105.M4P67 2006
   121'.68--dc22
                           2006006626

Printed on acid-free paper.

Original cover art by Colin Charlton.

Parlor Press, LLC is an independent publisher of scholarly and trade titles
in print and multimedia formats. This book is available in paper, cloth
and Adobe eBook formats from Parlor Press on the World Wide Web
at http://www.parlorpress.com or through online and brick-and mortar
bookstores. For submission information or to find out about Parlor Press
publications, write to Parlor Press, 816 Robinson St., West Lafayette,
Indiana, 47906, or e-mail editor@parlorpress.com.

For my son, Connor—the most consequential person in my life

Contents

consciousness
201

read later

Table and Illustrations

Acknowledgments

I cannot mention all of the people who have made this book possible by supporting me in my efforts to become someone who could write it. But I would like to pay some of the debts of gratitude that have accumulated during the past ten years. The first person I must thank is Martin Nystrand, for his ready ear and sound advice and for allowing me the latitude to write what would prove to be a rather un-dissertation-like dissertation. I must also thank the other members of my PhD committee at the University of Wisconsin-Madison, who pressed me on points where I needed to be pressed: Michael Bernard-Donals, Deborah Brandt, David Fleming, and Robert Asen. Michael was and remains a source of encouragement; to him, I also owe much gratitude, not only for helping me to develop a book proposal, but for making me believe that such a proposal should be written in the first place. Deborah was a great help during the early stages of my writing the essay, eventually published, that I reexamine in Chapter 8. Jon Fowler, a good friend, generously gave of his time to talk about and through my ideas, even the most counterintuitive, in a way that was rigorous and serious, yet also fun; I'm not sure how many afternoons we spent in restaurants on State Street. Frank Walters steered me toward analytic philosophy—especially the work of Donald Davidson—and encouraged me during my earliest attempts, in my MA thesis, to construct a theory of meaning; had he dwelt on its many flaws instead of seizing upon a few spots of brightness, this book would not have been written. A special thanks goes to Lynn Worsham for publishing two essays of mine—"Literature Reviews Re-Viewed: Toward a Consequentialist Account of Surveys, Surveyors, and the Surveyed" *JAC* 23 (2003): 351–377; and "Composition and Rhetoric Studies and the 'Neglected' Question of Meaning: Toward a Consequentialist Philosophy of Discourse" *JAC* 23 (2003): 725–764—that, in modified form, constitute the nucleus of Chapter 1; in doing so, she twice granted me a forum through which to address my colleagues. And her acceptance of my essay, "The 'Neglected' Question of Meaning: Toward a Consequentialist Philosophy of Discourse," provided me with a timely sense of validation for my work during a time when I was in doubt as to whether I should, or even could, continue. I wish to thank David Blakesley for his encouragement and patience and for providing this book a home during a time of crisis in academic publishing that has forced many university and scholarly presses to take fewer chances on genre-stretching, interdisciplinary research. I also wish to thank John Muckelbauer, whose review of the manuscript was thorough and thought-provoking; his comments have helped shape the "final" version of this book in ways that, although they will remain forever invisible to readers, are quite obvious to me. And I very much appreciate the work of copyeditor Colin Charlton.

And finally, I wish to thank my son, Connor, who has seen me sitting in front of a computer more often than I would like. I dedicate this book to him, paradoxically, because he has the miraculous ability to make me forget all about my work.

Meaning, Language, and Time

1 The Neglected Question of Meaning

The only solution is to reject the traditional formulation of verbal behavior in terms of meaning.

— B. F. Skinner

Preoccupation with the theory of meaning could be described as the occupational disease of twentieth-century Anglo-Saxon and Austrian philosophy [. . .]. When he [Wittgenstein] said 'Don't ask for the meaning, ask for the use,' he was imparting a lesson which he had to teach to himself.

— Gilbert Ryle

INTRODUCTION

In *Being and Time*, Heidegger (1927/1962) contends that Western philosophy has neglected the ontological question of Being and its temporality in favor of ontic questions about beings; according to Heidegger, it is disastrous to conflate beings with Being. Similarly, researchers in contemporary rhetoric and composition studies, as well as those scholars who were working during its institutional formation in the early 1970s—although they make frequent mention of *meanings*—have neglected to provide a coherent, explanatory account of *meaning* and its temporality. In some published research, meaning is treated, if at all, intuitively and unproblematically, as if it were already well understood and, consequently, not in need of any definition. At other times, meaning is seen by researchers within rhetoric and composition through lenses provided by other disciplines, generating the seemingly endless stream of articles and books adhering to the formula of "An *X*ian or *Y*ical approach to composition theory," where *X* refers to some particular thinker and *Y* to some particular intellectual move-ment.[1] Or, still more problematically, the term *meaning* is occasionally effaced entirely in discussions of language, as if language could be ad-equately explained without reference to it; for some theorists, the *question of meaning* may be too burdened with metaphysical or essentialist baggage to be worth asking.

This Heideggerian sense of neglect should be kept in mind through-out this introduction. I am not treating the term *neglecting* merely as a synonym for *ignoring:* The field of rhetoric and composition stud-ies has not ignored meaning in the sense that meaning has not been theorized about or discussed at all, no more than theorists of ontology have ignored what constitutes existence. But, at the same time, *neglect* is not simply synonymous with, say, *inadequacy* (i.e., that meaning has been inadequately treated by researchers within rhetoric and compo-sition studies): We cannot overlook the fact that this neglect is also manifested in discussions of language that efface meaning entirely. For me, the neglect of the question of meaning extends over the full range of ways in which the temporality of meaning, language, and dis-course have been inadequately conceptualized (i.e., by treating mean-ing, language, and discourse in ways that violate their temporality) or disregarded entirely.

It is too easy to cite numerous texts in which meaning or vari-ants upon it (e.g., *meaningful, meaningfulness, mean, meant,* etc.), if not entirely absent, are used only in token fashion and/or without further comment or definition.[2] I find this ease puzzling: The fact that papers with such abbreviated handlings of meaning are routinely written, published, read, and cited raises questions about why a term like *meaning* does not require further comment, especially given our disciplinary penchant for deconstructive interrogation and given the prominence of meaning as a subject of philosophical, rhetorical, and empirical research. Rather than a single reason for this baffling treat-ment of meaning, several possible reasons suggest themselves: (a) the question of meaning is not the focus of the study; (b) the question of meaning is tacitly assumed already to have an *answer;* (c) the question of meaning is deliberately set aside; and (d) the question of meaning is unintentionally omitted. Let us explore each of these possibilities in turn.

First, the absence of the question of meaning in a given text may be pragmatic—that although the question has not been answered satisfactorily, the asking of the question would raise too many obstacles for the work of the text to proceed. For the purposes of the text, then, meaning may be treated as a *primitive* term (i.e., a term that cannot be decomposed further by being defined by other terms but must, in some sense, be accepted as is). Language is assumed to be meaningful (and *it is* meaningful, which lends credence to this setting-aside of meaning); therefore, the researcher proceeds to discuss particular meanings as they present themselves to him or her without investigating why they are presentable as meaningful in the first place. This is risky, especially if a researcher operates on only a tacitly accepted theory of meaning that may not withstand careful scrutiny; but it is also almost inevitable, for to say that we must understand something completely before we may speak of it is absurd. It must be the case that language-users—researchers included—may *assume* meaning analogously to the way physicists assume that gravity is attractive in calculable ways even if they cannot explain exactly how gravity works: To say that gravity is attractive because it exerts a gravitational force is akin to saying, as Molière's (1673/1950, "Finale," pp. 48–65) celebrated example of a circular argument goes, that opium induces sleep because it has soporific powers. Clearly, any piece of research must make many assumptions about what it can safely leave out, or no research could be conducted at all; and whether a particular piece of research abstains from asking the question of meaning is certainly not the only criterion by which it should be judged. The omission may be telling, but not necessarily so.

Second, the question of meaning in a given text may be set aside, not because it is too heavy for the text to bear its weight, but because the author believes that the question has already been satisfactorily addressed, if not completely resolved. For example, such seems to be the view of Heilker and Vandenberg (1996), who do not list *meaning* as one of their *Keywords in Composition Studies*. This is a staggering omission in a book purporting to speak about the "hot topics" of a field heavily invested in the study of discourse—although the omission may in the end say more about the *field* than about the *book*.

An important clue for differentiating whether the absence of the question of meaning can be attributed to the first possibility or the second is the way that the author advocates or rejects, explicitly or implicitly, various traditions of thought about language. Does the author appear to rigidly embrace and echo thinkers or slogans associated with

Derridean poststructuralism, or Chomskyan linguistics, or Heideggerian phenomenology? With what confidence are these attitudes toward meaning expressed? Does the credibility of the evidence and the analysis ultimately depend upon the assumed validity of the particular tradition within which the text attempts to situate itself? I cite a brief example: When Nancy Welch (1998) speaks without hesitation of "the surplus" (p. 384) of a student's first draft or of "the latent surplus of a present moment" (p. 385) that the technique of "sideshadowing" is intended to release, her claim that there is in fact this surplus depends upon the validity of Bakhtin's philosophy, upon which Welch draws. As Bakhtin goes, so goes Welch.

Third, the question of meaning may not be addressed in a given text because meaning is not considered problematic in the first place. The question *never arises* because the author operates with tacit, intuitive notion of meaning without appeal to any specific theory of meaning. That the question may not arise is understandable, for people often look "through" language to meaning as opposed to looking at language (or, it should be added, meaning) itself, a process enabled by its potential for *transparency* (cf. Gadamer 1966/1977c, p. 65; Nystrand 1982c, pp. 75–76). People frequently attend to language only when it becomes problematic or *opaque*—when it resists being, as Heidegger (1927/1962) would put it, *ready-to-hand*. A person does not require a conscious, formalized theory of meaning in order to participate in meaningful discourse—and this is fortunate, for there would be no discourse otherwise! As even Chomsky (1986) would concede, a child does not acquire his or her language through encounters with formalized instruction in transformational grammar; the theory is not and was never intended to be a pedagogical tool for language-learning.

Finally, the question of meaning may be neglected in the belief that such a question is not worth raising in the first place because it suggests (a) a *metaphysics* that flies in the face of empirical validation (i.e., that in addition to the mundane objects that comprise the physical world there are non-physical entities—*meanings*—which must be accorded a quasi-ontological status) or (b) an *essentialism* that refuses to acknowledge the historical contingency of language as a *bruta factum* because claims about meaning-in-general would be of necessity ahistorical. In a postmodern age in which we distrust metanarratives to such an extent that we are, as Nystrand and Duffy (2003) suggest, no longer inclined to ask "big questions," addressing the question of meaning may seem misguidedly nostalgic. But I would argue that the very act of rejecting the question of meaning requires that one has already *answered* it to one's own satisfaction.

Let us look more closely at three specific rejections of meaning—at least as "meaning" has, from the authors' perspectives, been theorized. First, in a critique of the work of Ann Berthoff, Winterowd (2000) dismisses the importance of "the foundational notion that composition is the making of meaning" (p. 304). Meanings are made in composing, says Winterowd, but they are more the byproduct than the focus of the process: "Now, it is certainly the case that when we use language we make meaning—willy-nilly, inevitably—but no one begins to write (or talk) with the *purpose* of making meaning. That is, language is symbolic action, and action implies motive or purpose, and that is the foundation of a valid theory of composition and of an effective composition pedagogy" (p. 304). For Winterowd, questions of use/action and purpose/intention should be brought to the fore, and questions of meaning necessarily fade away because the making of meaning happens "willy-nilly, inevitably," *unmysteriously.* This stance has implications for Winterowd's pedagogy: "As a teacher of writing, my first question to a student about his or her text is this: 'What do you want this piece of writing to *do?*' That question generates a dialogue that allows both me and my student to read and critique the text as a piece of real-world discourse. It allows us to treat the text rhetorically" (p. 305). Presumably, a question about the meanings of the text would not lead to so productive a dialogue or would inevitably treat the text as a piece of unreal-world, *arhetorical* discourse (a notion to which I will return in the final chapter).

Eleven years earlier, Susan Miller (1989) proposed a historicist, textual rhetoric that would provide "a way to account for the variability and even the accidental conditions that actually determine the practical impact (as opposed to the 'meaning') of writing" (p. 10). Like Winterowd, Miller appears to assume that "impact" is separable from meaning, but later she moves closer to my own understanding of meaning—with the caveat that *understanding* refers not to an instantaneous grasp of fully-formed concepts waiting patiently for linear explication in this book, but to my experience of the temporally distended strands of thought that have run concomitant to the non-linear writing of it—when she articulates her resistance only to definitions of the term *meaning* that "do not include in that term the prominent or inconsequential fate of the written text, its writer's motives toward the textual world it enters, or its historical precedents" (pp. 36–37).

In a similar reversal, Worsham (1991) describes the work of radical French feminists on *écriture féminine* as "one of the most dramatic developments in recent writing theory and pedagogy, not only because it may reformulate our notion of literacy and its consequences but also because it could produce a crisis in composition's self-understanding" (p. 83). This projected crisis would result from the resistance of *écriture féminine* to the mastery of meaning that phallocentric academic discourse, which many composition instructors have attempted to (re)produce in their students, seeks to achieve. Discussing the work of Julia Kristeva (1982/1986), Worsham claims that the "desire to give meaning, to explain, to interpret [. . .] is rooted in our need for meaning when confronted by meaninglessness, our need for mastery when confronted by what we fear most: the enigmatic other that exceeds and threatens every system of meaning, including individual identity" (p. 83). *Écriture féminine,* on the other hand, "arises not from the desire to give meaning but from the desire to go beyond meaning to a topos of pure invention where discourse becomes more radically political to the extent that it approaches the heterogeneous in meaning" (p. 84). But we later learn that "to go beyond meaning" is only to go beyond meaning that could be totalized: reminiscent of Miller, meaning does not ultimately disappear because meaning is not *essentially* phallocentric, but can be made heterogeneous (p. 90). *But if one accepts the heterogeneity of meaning as a starting premise, there is no reason to reject the term or even to change it.*

I find myself sympathetic only to the first reason for neglecting the question of meaning, which is a pragmatic concession to the limitations inherent in the processes of research. The approach is, perhaps, incrementalist, attempting to resolve local problems in discourse in the hope that answers to more general questions will emerge later. Thus, the question of meaning is a question *deferred,* not *ignored.* The remaining explanations, however, seem to me to be, respectively, *misguided,* in that insufficient accounts of meaning are treated as sufficient; *insular,* in that the question of meaning is alive enough in discussions of language and discourse for a contemporary researcher to have encountered it; and *dogmatic,* in that the question of meaning need not necessarily be a metaphysical question. And it also may be the case that a rigorous metaphysics could contribute much to the question of meaning and so should not be rejected out of hand. As Waismann (1956/1959) argues in response to criticisms of the logical positivists that the only meaningful statements are those which could be confirmed or denied through empirical methods: "To say that metaphysics is nonsense *is* nonsense" (p. 380).

SOME CONSEQUENCES OF NEGLECTING
THE QUESTION OF MEANING

An appropriate question to ask at this point is this: *So what?* What undesirable consequences arise from the general neglect of meaning (or, the neglect of meaning-in-general) in rhetoric and composition studies? And what undesirable consequences arise from the neglect of meaning in particular texts? *Do we really need yet another theory of meaning?* Responding to the first question, I contend that understanding how discourse works requires understanding what makes discourse meaningful; that answer, of course, is dangerously close to committing a *petitio principii*. For this claim to express something other than a tautology (that is, for this claim to be informative), we must find specific cases in which meaning, treated as a given, is non-explanatory or even obfuscatory. I will examine two instances: William J. Vande Kopple's (1994) essay on grammatical subjects in scientific discourse and Scott Lyons's (2000) essay on what he terms *rhetorical sovereignty*.

A brief aside: I am not treating the work of Vande Kopple or Lyons as representative anecdotes of "the field" in the sense that their work somehow encapsulates all of the ways in which researchers within rhetoric and composition have handled meaning. In fact, my own understanding of meaning destabilizes the very notion of "the field" as something that could be so represented (cf. K. Porter, 2003). But since a complete enumeration of texts is impossible (and an extended enumeration in this chapter impractical), I am merely providing a few concrete examples of the neglect of the question of meaning that set the stage, so to speak, for the lengthy critique of theories of meaning, within and beyond rhetoric and composition studies, that this book undertakes. I am not asking readers to make the inductive leap from two examples to a generalization about "the field" (no more than I would make that leap based on a reading of these texts only), but only to accept the premise that *some researchers* have neglected the question of meaning as I have formulated it.

The foci of Vande Kopple's (1994) study, as he notes in his succinct title, are "Some characteristics and functions of grammatical subjects in scientific discourse." His central finding is that these grammatical subjects tend to be unusually long, due to the use of expletive constructions, compounds of keywords in parallel or antithetical structures, premodifications of keywords, and postmodifications of keywords with relative clauses (p. 541). Promoting the use of extended subjects, argues Vande Kopple, are pressures on scientists to be precise in terminology, economical in expression, and efficient in conveying the vast accumulation of given information on a subject (pp. 546–555). Vande Kopple speculates that the writing of scientists "reflect[s]" a mode of thinking—labeled "paradigmatic or logico-scientific" by Bruner (1986)—which emphasizes explicitness of reference, universal and objective truth conditions, and description and explanation (pp. 556–557).

This is curious: Surely Vande Kopple does not mean that texts which *reflect* scientific thinking—if we will allow that science is unified enough to have a uniform way of *thinking*—reflect that thought in the sense of *mirroring* the thought processes of the author-scientist: Scientific articles are not spontaneous free-writings, but carefully crafted pieces of prose (cf. Schilb, 1999, for a critique of similar claims about the mind-mirroring properties of personal essays). The scientific article, despite being purported to be the reflection of a mode of thought, is never actually the thought of any person; consequently, the texts do not *reflect* or *mirror* a mode of *thought,* but rather are used by authors in an attempt to evoke a *thinking* (a process, not an instantaneously apprehended *thought* that grasps a fully describable *content)* in a particular way.

A second curiosity is that Vande Kopple does not explicate what he means by *meaning,* despite his stated interested in the meaning of grammatical features of discourse (p. 535). By questioning the meaning of particular, formal properties of texts, Vande Kopple has already *bypassed* the question of meaning in general, just as much of the work in linguistics—the tradition in which he mainly operates, judging from his bibliography—does. That is, Vande Kopple's analysis of the data—which is quite rigorous on its own terms—already *assumes* a formalist theory of meaning and simply *operates within it,* enabling him to count words and taxonomize them into various functions (e.g., noun, verb, adjective) and to identify more extended structures (e.g., phrases, clauses, sentences). Nouns are not constituents of the physical universe, even if they are used to refer to those constituents: One does not ever simply encounter a noun. However, Vande Kopple tends to speak of linguistic entities as carriers of intrinsic meaning; thus, *sentences* can have a "main focus" (p. 543), *scientific discourse* can "refer" (p. 538), and *nominalizations* can "convey" information (p. 554), even if he mentions in passing the intentions and strategies of authors in constructing the texts (and either way, the meaning of the text is fixed, whether by grammar or by intention). In fact, Vande Kopple (1985) elsewhere describes one of the functions of metadiscourse as helping "readers grasp the appropriate meaning of elements *in* [italics added] texts" (p. 84). This may simply be an ill-chosen expression on his part, but the choice is telling nonetheless, for by defining metadiscourse in this way, he must allow that a text may *contain* at least one *inappropriate* meaning, whatever that may be. How might this inappropriate meaning insinuate itself *into* the text? Why does discourse require metadiscourse to act as a guide for the unwary? And what guides the reader through metadiscourse?

Barton (1995) critiques the textualist nature of Vande Kopple's analysis of metadiscourse markers, finding instead that they serve interactional or interpersonal functions; in her study, she suggests that non-contrastive and contrastive connectives emphasize agreements and blunt disagreements between members of a discourse community. For Barton, interactional meaning can override semantic meaning. However (to use a contrastive connective), Barton's analysis again *assumes* the meaningfulness of the metadiscourse markers; to speak of metadiscourse markers is already to have identified particular marks *as* metadiscourse markers as opposed to markers of something else (discourse?).

Lest the reader think I am being unfair to Vande Kopple, or even hypocritical, I concede that, to quite a large extent, locutions like "this text refers to" are unavoidable (in the sense that I haven't yet found a satisfactory way of avoiding them), perhaps because of the profound sway of what I will define later as *meaning apriorism* (i.e., the assumption that the meaning of an utterance or text is always to be found in or grounded by something prior to that utterance or text or to any interpretation of that utterance or text) over intuitive and theoretical understandings of meaning. Similar expressions appear "in" this book, but they should be read in consequentialist terms, not aprioristic ones.

That is, according to what I will term later as *meaning consequentialism* (i.e., the assumption that the meaning of an utterance or text is the consequences that it propagates), to say that "this text refers" is not to make an essentialist claim about the contents of the text but a pragmatic claim about a particular consequence or subset of consequences of the text, one that I presume, but cannot guarantee, accords with consequences that text has evoked or would evoke in other readers. In this way, I make claims "about" texts with the understanding that their meanings are *real* insofar as I experience them, but also *contestable* insofar as others encounter those texts; a text will mean only what I think it means only if I am its only reader. However, because Vande Kopple offers no comparable disclaimer, I read his use of these expressions as manifestations of the formalist dimension of meaning apriorism.

It is important to note that I am not disputing Vande Kopple's data, which no doubt emerged from his careful interactions with the texts he studied, or even his general conclusions. Clearly, Vande Kopple did not require an articulated theory of meaning in order to gather his data: He simply gathered the meanings he perceived as ready-to-hand in the text. And equally clearly, Vande Kopple did not need to spell out a theory of meaning in order to have his paper favorably reviewed by peers and published in a major journal. In fact, I readily see those very divisions and distinctions in grammatical structures that Vande Kopple uses in his analysis; but my agreement with Vande Kopple that discourse as I experience it is amenable to such an analysis explains neither why it is amenable, nor why we agree that it is so amenable. And, as Wittgenstein (1922/1981, 6.341, 6.342, 6.35) might suggest, pointing to his analogy of the mesh, the fact that discourse can be segmented in various ways that are internally consistent is not proof that discourse *really* is segmented in those ways. Rather, what I am trying to emphasize is the familiar notion that data are not innocently gathered from the page, available for all to encounter as meaningful, and therefore conclusions based upon that data are not innocent or objective, either (cf. Fish, 1970/1980e, 1976/1980b, 1980d, 1980g); what makes them seem innocent or objective is that they are not challenged (i.e., they are intersubjectively held to be valid), at least by those whose opinions matter. (Of course, why such intersubjective agreement occurs is an important issue for a theory of meaning to explain.)

If, as I asserted earlier, nouns cannot be objectively measured in the way that the quantity of ink on a page could, then whatever meaning people ascribe to the text—or, as I would prefer to put it for reasons to be made clearer later (and I use *later* to emphasize the temporality of the gap between that future discussion and *current* one, instead of using a term like *below* that would treat the gap in terms of spatial separation within the same instant of time), whatever consequences that text evokes in and through people—is not *contained* in the text, pace Vande Kopple. This is a key point: To my mind, the claim that a text is meaningful in itself (i.e., that it has an intrinsic or objective meaning) is akin to the claim that the sun intrinsically exerts a gravitational pull. An intrinsically meaningful utterance or text, if one existed, could not help but be meaningful in the same way that the sun cannot help but be gravitationally attractive. But meaning does not operate in this way, for utterances and texts clearly do not consistently produce a certain consequence or uniform set of consequences. By not attending to this fact, Vande Kopple ascribes powers to the texts he studied that they do not have. Does that matter? Only if we wish to understand how texts actually operate.

Far removed from the theoretical orientation of Vande Kopple's work, Scott Lyons's (2000) essay is a critique of the ways that Native Americans have been colonized and controlled through white American discourses that purport to speak of and for Native Americans. White culture, according to Lyons, has been able to exercise *rhetorical imperialism,* which is "the ability of dominant powers to assert control of others by setting the terms of the debate. These terms are often definitional—that is, they identify the parties discussed by describing them in certain ways" (p. 452). Examples of such imperialism would include the incorporation of Native Americans into U.S. government treaties, textbooks, and scholarly research written by whites. Lyons argues that rhetorical imperialism should be overthrown and replaced by what he calls *rhetorical sovereignty,* which is "the inherent right and ability of *peoples* to determine their own communicative needs and desires in this pursuit [of agency, power, community renewal], to decide for themselves the goals, modes, styles, and languages of public discourse" (pp. 449–450). And, in the abstract to his paper, rhetorical sovereignty is defined as "a people's control of its meaning" (p. 447), though it is unclear in the abstract and remains unclear throughout the essay exactly what *meaning* might be, how it operates in discourse, and how peoples (to use Lyons's preferred term) might control it

The ethical force of Lyons's essay is compelling, but I am troubled both by the implicit theory of meaning that must underlie this doctrine of rhetorical sovereignty and by the unexamined essentializing of terms like "Native Americans" (p. 461), "Indians" (p. 449), "American Indian experience" (p. 449), "Native discourse" (p. 449), and "a people" (p. 454). Let us take each of these problems in turn. First, it is unclear what leads Lyons to believe that meanings can be controlled by anyone or that "a people" has an "inherent right" to exercise that control. But what if a people (or peoples, or persons) may only *attempt* to control, fix, or set(tle) meanings, yet such control—however so much we may agree with the motivations behind the attempt—can never be final because the consequences of utterances and texts cannot be indefinitely contained? And if we think of meanings in terms of the consequences that result from encounters with utterances—rather than assuming that meanings regulate or in some sense validate or authenticate those consequences—then these consequences, however unruly or random they appear, can never be *perversions* or *contaminations* of a privileged, pure, primary meaning that people "own" (cf. Adler-Kassner, 1998, p. 221), for *the meanings of an utterance are its consequences*. As Yarbrough (1999) argues, "It is impossible to maintain or protect the 'integrity' of another's discourse or our own for the simple reason that 'meaning' and 'truth' and 'value' are consequences of discursive interaction, not antecedents" (p. 167). In fact, Lyons says as much when he concedes that "sovereignty" is a "contested term" with "shifting meanings" (p. 449) and when he acknowledges that "discourses of resistance and renewal have never ceased in Indian country" despite the pressures of "hegemonic versions of the American Indian story" (p. 453). To say that a people can and should control meanings is to say that a people can and should forever remain isolated and static, immune from the consequences of contact with outsiders. Of course, this realization about meaning doesn't excuse the ways in which certain texts and utterances have produced horrifying consequences; but we should note that the problem isn't that the "natives" are deprived of words entirely, but that their words are often *inconsequential* for their oppressors or produce *undesired consequences*.

This brings us to the second problem: Lyons's peculiarly nostalgic vision of "culture" or "a people" as pure, peaceful, consensual, Edenic.

According to Lyons, "A people is a group of human beings united together by history, language, culture, or some combination therein—a combination joined in union for a common purpose: the survival and flourishing of the people itself. It has always been from an understanding of themselves as a people that Indian groups have constructed themselves as a nation" (p. 454). Different peoples can even form confederations, such as the Haudenosaunee (i.e., the Iroquois League), that are "based upon the principle of peaceful coexistence" (p. 455)—so peaceful, in fact, that "Haudenosaunee sovereignty is probably best understood as the right of a people to exist and enter into agreements with other peoples for *the sole purpose* of promoting, not suppressing, local cultures and traditions, even while united by a common political project—in this case, the noble goal of peace between peoples" (p. 456, emphasis added). This is a noble goal, indeed, but the absence of any tension between these "local cultures and traditions," which curiously interact with each other *only* to promote each other's different cultures and traditions, seems to imply that the goal was always already achieved.

There is a vast difference between treating "a people" as a fragile construct—what Benedict Anderson (1983/1996) calls an *imagined community* and Carolyn R. Miller (1994) terms a *rhetorical community* that cannot be realized except through the relentless but ultimately quixotic effort to *manufacture* and *maintain* a shared history, a shared language, a shared culture—and treating it, as Lyons consistently does, as an actual collective of people welded together by history, language, and/or culture. This latter treatment assumes that history, language, and culture exist monolithically enough, purely enough, and substantially enough to bind persons together across space and time; but the *assumption* that history, language, and culture can do this is neither proof *that* they can, nor an explanation of *why* they can.

Does Lyons's failure to theorize key terms like *history, language, culture,* and *meaning* matter? Yes, but only if one rejects his main arguments because they are grounded on implicit and, more importantly, faulty assumptions about spatialized and homogeneous history, language, and culture and about fixed meanings that peoples possess by inherent right. In short, I am hoping, through a propagation of the consequences of this book, to *inaugurate* and *promote* an always partial, always transient community in which arguments such as these are rejected.

Toward a Consequentialist Philosophy of Discourse

Just link. Just link. Just link.

—Victor Vitanza

This project arises from my sense that ending the neglect of the question of meaning is crucial for rhetoric and composition (and beyond); that our field must develop a rigorous, explanatory theory of meaning, one capable of avoiding the pitfalls which attend classical, modern, and contemporary treatments of meaning; and that rhetoric and composition is uniquely positioned to pursue such a theory because of its interdisciplinarity. These are three admittedly provocative claims, in several ways, for they suggest (a) that the field does not currently have a well-developed, coherent understanding of meaning; (b) that questions about the meanings of texts or the construction of those meanings cannot be addressed adequately without an understanding of meaning in a more general sense; (c) that the theorization of meaning should be prominent in contemporary inquiry until such an understanding is achieved; and (d) that as members of a field of research noted, perhaps even celebrated for its eclecticism (cf. Bizzell, 1992d; Gates, 1993; A. Lunsford, 1991; Worsham, 1999), we have the potential for *constructing* such a theory rather than *importing* one from other domains of inquiry because we need not have obstructing disciplinary commitments to any particular theory or methodology. In my own case, even though I have learned much from the work of others regarding meaning, language, discourse, and time, the philosophy of discourse that I am developing is not Austinian, Bakhtinian, Davidsonian, Derridean, Wittgensteinian, etc. Not considering myself a disciple of any of these thinkers, I have no need to defend them at all costs or close myself to alternative theories or my own arguments—not so incidentally, I do not feel the need to be dogmatic about my own ideas, either.

Of course, the explicit or implicit conceptualizations of meaning that appear in rhetoric and composition cannot be isolated from the larger, historical propagation of ideas about this elusive term. To understand why meaning is treated as it is variously treated within our field, we must take a wider perspective, tracing as far as possible the myriad ways meaning has been theorized—a project that this book can only initiate, not complete. What emerges from this necessarily partial investigation—and I have yet to encounter reasons for thinking otherwise—is the inadequacy of treatments of time in considerations of meaning. Most of the important and intractable problems confronted by theorists—e.g., accounting for the stability of discourse *and* its elasticity; the conventions of language *and* their misappropriations; the materiality of discourse *and* its temporality; its systematicity *and* its anomalousness; its memory *and* its forgetting; even the question of whether "it" should be referred to as an "it"—can be traced to inadequate theorizations of the connections between time and meaning that fall under the rubric of what I call *meaning apriorism*. The central tenet of meaning apriorism, which informs in one way or another every approach to meaning with which I am familiar, even those that struggle against it, is that the meaning of an "utterance"—which, following Bakhtin (1986/1996), I use in an extended sense that includes written texts—is to be found always in some sense, logically and/or temporally, prior to that utterance or to any interpretation of that utterance—that if we are to look for meaning—as a speaker or writer, listener or reader—we must look *behind* us in time.

Meaning apriorism involves a relation of some kind—or, better, *sets* of relations—between meaning and time, even if they are relations only of *negation* or *denial.* Three such relations may be formulated as follows: meaning apriorism (a) locates meaning outside of time entirely in a transcendent, panchronic, eternal realm of divinity or of logic; (b) flattens time and its relationship to meaning by rendering time in spatial or absolute (Aristotelian or Newtonian) terms; and (c) distorts the temporality of discourse by treating the movement of discourse as evolution and the movement of time as duration. In each case, the play of time and meaning is poorly conceived; and one of my central arguments is that distorted conceptions of the relationship between meaning and time necessarily lead to distorted conceptions of discourse: We cannot be clear about meaning if its relationship to time is already opaque in our thinking. As I will attempt to demonstrate, such opacity has led theorists into unnecessary dilemmas that force them to dismiss some quite meaningful linguistic phenomena as *secondary, parasitic,* or even *meaningless.*

What I hope to offer, then, is the groundwork for a coherent philosophy of discourse, one that conceptually integrates meaning and time by fusing the meaning of a sign to its consequences (what I term *meaning consequentialism*), a claim that itself has evoked and will continue to evoke manifold consequences which, as they emerge, will illustrate the unfolding or, as I prefer to call it, the *propagation* of meanings. Pursuing this project requires drawing upon the insights and dilemmas of many fields frequently opposed to or substantively isolated from one another: cognitive science and psychology (including artificial intelligence); communication theory; composition and literacy studies; critical theory; cultural studies; dialogism; discourse and conversation analysis; hermeneutics; history; linguistics; literary theory; philosophy of language, mind, and time; rhetoric; semiotics; sociology/social theory; and theoretical physics. I am convinced that isolationist currents of thought in these disciplines lead to impoverished conceptions of discourse; but I also see important connections between these disciplines through overlapping concerns about (a) the production, dissemination, and consumption of meanings and/or discursive practices through time; (b) the proper theorization of formalized and decontextualized abstractions such as *culture, society, language,* and *discourse communities,* as well as critiques of their feasibility as analytic terms; (c) the acquisition and use of "language" by individuals through time and the connections between individual "language" users and social formations; (d) the relationships between past, present, and future, especially as they are represented (or created) through discursive practices; and (e) the construction of appropriate methodologies for studying discourse and/or time.

Of course, the balancing act must be subtle, excruciatingly so, in order to defuse common and, in some ways, quite understandable concerns about interdisciplinary research. I realize that by injecting this book into so many conversations and linking one to another—perhaps akin to the way that Vitanza (1997) conceives of linking, which is always in danger of being seen as "irresponsible" (p. 5)—I risk satisfying no one. Some readers may think that I glide too easily through key texts; these are readers who want some kind of reassurance ("Show me your papers, please!"), visibly demonstrated in the text and not merely assumed, that I *understand* these texts as they really are as well as the contexts that make them intelligible. Some readers may think that I get bogged down in unnecessary digressions, elaborations, and overcomplications; these would be readers who want me to speak plainly and directly ("Get to the point, please!"), who don't want to reread a single paragraph, and who, if their wants are left wanting, will suspect me of being unclear in my own thinking and, perhaps, of trying to disguise that fact with lots of distractions, irrelevancies, and jargon—and with syntax that would confound the best sentence-parsing computer program yet designed. And still other readers may think that I move too quickly, rushing from one proposition to the next without providing enough scaffolding to support any of them ("Connect the dots, please!"); these would be readers who want a text that conveys a (mostly) finished thought, as opposed to a text that traces a thinking through of meaning consequentialism which is more a soft weave of strands than a single thread or tightly bound rope. Sometimes, probably very often, perhaps always, these different kinds of readers will be found in a single reader, perhaps every single reader. And I'm a reader of this book, too.

How does one write to so many different kinds of readers? At what moment does the concatenation and juxtaposition of texts drawn from such variegated traditions and disciplines become abstruse, perhaps senseless? So many voices, often speaking past each other, unaware of each other—and these voices are not mere stylistic peculiarities in the text, for they inform the ways in/by/through which I think about meaning, language, and time. As I reread some passages, I hear echoes of Wittgenstein's epigrammatic elusiveness; in others, the down-to-earth sensibility of Davidson, or the dull flatness of Skinner, or the systematicity of Carnap. *I speak like all of them so as not to speak like any of them.* The task, I suggest, is not to find a common language—for there is none to find, anywhere—but to construct a text that opens up new possibilities for, in no order of priority, thinking and speaking and writing about meaning and language and time without the pretense that these "possibilities" are in some sense already there, waiting. This book simply does not map onto the neat disciplinary categories which I—and most if not all of my eventual readers—have been trained to recognize and respect; it doesn't do anything *simply*.

But that's the point.

An Outline of This Chapter

The overarching purpose of this introductory chapter, of course, is to present my case for pursuing meaning consequentialism as a philosophy of discourse. However, because meaning consequentialism immediately raises numerous challenges to current (and often tacit) ways of conceptualizing meaning, language, and discourse, that case cannot be made in as straightforward way as I would wish or as readers likely expect. Like Heidegger (1927/1962), I find myself repeatedly needing to digress in order to advance the argument (note, too, that a digression is not a regression, not a return to something already there). For example, consider the next section of this chapter: Whereas readers might expect the first chapter of a book to contain an extensive literature review on the central topic, I find myself forced to confront fundamental questions about what a literature review actually does and theorize it in terms acceptable to my formulation of meaning consequentialism—*but before readers have had any chance to encounter more extended comments on the premises of meaning consequentialism and well before that theory has been fully developed (for it doesn't happen here).* Readers, then, are in a sense being thrown, unavoidably so and perhaps with a feeling of disorientation, into the theory *in media res*—a sense magnified by the fact that the theory itself is always underway, branching, propagating, so that I feel at times no less disoriented than readers.

The second section defers again the expected literature review, instead propagating some of the insights of the first section through an analysis of published surveys of the "field" of rhetoric and composition. Although this section, as a byproduct of its analysis, discusses how meaning has been conceptualized in the field—or, more precisely, how treatments of meaning in the field and the field itself have been conceptualized—my main purpose is to demonstrate the problems that attend these literature reviews, especially the ways that they and the field they purport to describe conceptualize meaning. In sum, the first two sections are an attempt to justify my *not* writing an ordinary, *expected* literature review.

The third section provides a broad overview of meaning apriorism. Reacting against the taxonomies that fragment the field of rhetoric and composition into impermeable "factions" with oppositional views of meaning, I offer my own taxonomy, not of theories of meaning per se, but of the principles of meaning apriorism that I see made manifest in classical, modern, and contemporary theories of meaning. Thus, the way that I conceptualize and discuss theories of meaning in the chapters that follow does not divide them into rival camps, but illuminates—and even manufactures—unsuspected commonalities in consequences of theories often thought to be incommensurable.

The fourth section provides a programmatic sketch of meaning consequentialism that attempts to highlight the ways in which a consequentialist philosophy of discourse distances itself from theories that manifest elements of meaning apriorism not only in its premises, but also in the way it answers the question, "What is a theory of meaning supposed to *do?*"

Finally, the fifth section presents a detailed outline of and rationale for the arguments and organization of the chapters that follow; and it also explains why—once more against likely reader expectations—this book, despite its length, can serve only as a prolegomenon to the critique of meaning apriorism and to a satisfactory theorization of meaning consequentialism.

A "Digression" on the Treatment of Prior Research

> The use of citations is intrinsic to scientists' story making because it contextualizes local (laboratory) knowledge within an ongoing history of disciplinary knowledge making. Such contextualization is essential because it is only when the scientist places his or her laboratory findings within a framework of accepted knowledge that a claim to have made a scientific discovery—and thereby to have contributed to the field's body of knowledge—can be made.
>
> —Carol Berkenkotter and Thomas Huckin

Because of my deep commitment to notions of the temporality—especially the *futurity*—of meaning (that is, the necessarily temporally distended and futural consequences of utterances and texts) it would be insufferably ironic for me to begin with an ordinary survey of antecedent research within rhetoric and composition studies on the topic of meaning. Such a survey—the ubiquitous literature review—is customary in contemporary scholarship, though hardly an essential feature of scholarly work, which has no fixed essence (cf. Bazerman, 1988; Connors, 1998, 1999). However, I find myself forced to theorize the *literature review* in terms that harmonize with my own advocacy of premises of meaning consequentialism before I can offer my own extended review of antecedent research—all the while conceding that, from the opening page of this book, I have already "cited" antecedent research. I begin with a philosophical speculation about why a scholarly book (or an article, or a dissertation, or a conference paper, etc.) without a literature review of some kind would likely be treated as inappropriate, if not outright transgressive.

Let us start with what we might consider a brief, standard(ized) reading of the purposes for a literature review: The literature review is primarily the vehicle through which authors (a) acknowledge debts to their predecessors; (b) demonstrate their familiarity with research on the topic, including the most *current* (thereby demonstrating that the researcher is "up to date"[3]); (c) place their work in relation to the work of others, thereby hoping to gain credibility and enhance relevance through association with work that was at least at some point in time deemed credible and relevant enough to be published or presented publicly; and (d) offer evidence for the originality of their work, which fills a significant gap—not just any gap—within the existing (and usually *contemporary*) corpus of scholarly material.

But we might also consider another interconnected set of purposes for literature reviews. First, it is primarily the vehicle through which authors are required to submit to the priority of the past, acknowledging "predecessors" that occasionally, perhaps frequently, are known only *after the fact;* for example, a reviewer may demand the inclusion of a particular citation in a paper to be published that does not in any other way affect the development of the piece (cf. Berkenkotter and Huckin, 1993, p. 119). In this way, the literature review acts against the possibility of invention occurring *more than once:* Priority is granted to the earliest inventor, and all others are mere copiers, even if they "copied" in complete ignorance of or possible connection to the "original" invention. According to Rees (1997), such a process occurs in the physical sciences, where the first "discoverer" of a phenomenon is always accorded the professional prestige, even if a second "discoverer" acts independently of the first.[4]

It should be noted that my claim about the literature review acting against invention occurring more than once precludes neither the citation of a single, collaboratively written work (i.e., an invention can be the result of a collaboration, yet still be treated as a having a single source), nor the citation of multiple works in relation to the development of a particular concept. But notice that, in the latter case, the point of the citations is to give credit where credit is due for the stages of development of that concept (e.g., source *Y* would not be credited at all if it simply reiterated source *X*, but only if it differentiated itself from *X* in some significant way).

Second, the literature review presents the illusion of a past that can be mastered,--i.e., that is, fully knowable—if one has the requisite intelligence and perseverance. Although not every single work is—or is expected to be—cited, authors are presumed to be treating the most relevant work selected from the entire corpus; the criteria for relevance are not conceded to be works that the author and his or her audience are aware of, or prefer, or actively reject, but rather are somehow demanded by the subject matter itself—what we might, following the tradition of German hermeneutics, refer to as the *Sache* (Bruns, 1992, p. 62). In other words, relevance is presumed to be determined topically (i.e., by the text containing certain material), not socially (i.e., by the collective interests and knowledge of a group of researchers) or psychologically (i.e., by the idiosyncratic interests and knowledge of the author). For example, when raised by a reviewer, the question "Why isn't *X*, which is highly relevant, included in this paper?" should not be taken as a criticism of the completeness of the research, for no literature review can be definitively complete (or, if it is, that fact cannot be empirically verified, except in extremely unlike cases), but rather as a criticism that the author hasn't properly acknowledged that bit of the past valued or at least recalled by the reviewer.

And finally (*final* only in the sense that this is the last purpose I will discuss, not that could be discussed), when treated as an academic exercise, the literature review guarantees that students must *confront* antecedent research, which—along with the entire set of institutional apparatuses founded upon it—might otherwise slip into oblivion, just as classical languages in the eighteenth and nineteenth centuries and English literature in the twentieth century slowly waned in prestige and faded from the memories of generations of students (cf. T. Miller, 1997).

In sum: The literature review speaks *of* the past (i.e., it refers to and can only refer to prior work), *by* the past (i.e., prior work provides the launching point or germinating seed for all that follows), and *for* the past (i.e., it represents the claim of prior work on our present attention and demands that we do not forget). It is a past that is paradoxical in its ponderous weight and its crystalline fragility—deterministic, yet inefficacious. It is a past that fears for its existence if it is forgotten and clamors for us to feel obligated to it (cf. Struever, 1985, p. 268), even as it claims to be the inescapable foundation for the present and future; for as Lyotard (1979/1993) puts it, "never forget" is the "golden rule" of the Western conception of knowledge (p. 22).[5]

But there is another way to view the literature review besides that of an account of the past on its own terms, hermetically sealed and hermeneutically alienated from the present (i.e., the past requires interpretation precisely because we are alienated from it), like looking through a fantastically acute telescope at a community on a distant planet beyond all possibility of contact because it has long since expired. We may conceive of the literature review not as a way to *acknowledge* an antecedent community, but as a way to *constitute* or *inaugurate,* through a re-viewing of the past, an *imagined community* (B. Anderson, 1983/1996) or *world* (Heidegger, 1960/1993a), however fleeting. This re-viewing is enacted by stitching together and synchronizing particular texts and authors and then by inviting readers to pretend that that quilt is a reality, to act as if Aristotle, Descartes, Locke, and Quine are (note the presence of presentness here) engaged in *the,* or at least *a,* "Conversation of Mankind" (cf. Oakeshott, 1959/1962). When that pretense is lost—when an author, in effect, claims that Aristotle, Descartes, Locke, and Quine belong to a discourse community and therefore *are* engaged in real dialogue with each other simply by having their texts juxtaposed (cf. Halasek, 1999, p. 66) or, even more fantastically, that this persistent conversation is in some sense more *alive* than we, who hope to join that conversation, are, finding ourselves fleetingly yet inescapably caught in "the interment of the present" (Bruns, 1992, p. 198)—then the temporality of discourse has been effaced. *The meaningfulness of the links made in a literature review does not extend into the past, but only into the future:* To add Quine to the list has no consequences for Aristotle (or for Quine, after his death on December 25, 2000), but only for those of us who read that list and who may subsequently think about Aristotle differently as a result. What these consequences are or might be cannot be fully known or exhausted (though not because they possess hidden, unsuspected depths or a mysterious, imperishable vitality); in fact, at the time of writing, *these consequences do not exist, nor can they be deterministically predicted.* The text at the time of its inscription does not contain the seed of all that follows, *even if all that follows would not have occurred had the text not been written.*

The goal of a literature review, on this proposed alternative account, is not *knowledge:* one does not read a literature review in order to comprehend the works in-themselves, for although the citations in the review may stand in for the texts, they cannot substitute for them (i.e., the citation does not serve as a microdot of the cited text). Rather, it is *edification* (cf. Rorty, 1979): By juxtaposing and synchronizing texts in certain ways, can we say *interesting*—if not *original*—things about them?

Muckelbauer (2000) is close to this position when he advocates *productive reading,* a way of engaging texts that "demonstrates a greater concern for producing different concepts than for reproducing a preexisting program" (p. 74). In fact, for Muckelbauer, "invention is the *telos* of an encounter with a text—invention of both concepts and subjects. To read productively means not only to attempt to alter the question, but to alter oneself through the question, to encounter a text hoping to think differently through an engagement with it" (p. 92). In short, a reader's encounter with a text should be consequential, transformative. Muckelbauer's concept of productive reading is consonant with my own understanding of meaning consequentialism to the extent that he does not presume to know or depict a true or essential Foucault, but only wants to construct an interesting and consequential way of talking about Foucault. However, notice that Muckelbauer hopes this way of talking will be interesting and consequential *despite the following remarkable concession on his part:* "I need not claim a more accurate or complete understanding of Foucault than other readings. It would, no doubt, be relatively easy to produce elements of his corpus that contradict the claims I will advance" (p. 73). I read this as an admission by Muckelbauer that he has encountered passages in Foucault's texts the consequences of which for Muckelbauer contradict claims that he wants to make and subsequently does make despite his own experiences with the texts.

I suggest that Muckelbauer misses a key distinction between a *true* Foucault, who does not exist and never existed because what Foucault's texts *mean* can never be definitively fixed, and a *consequential* Foucault, the manifold concrete ways in which Foucault's texts have affected and presently affect readers, Muckelbauer included. Whether Foucault's corpus would really or objectively yield these contradictions is besides the point: To intentionally set aside contradictions to one's own preferred reading of a text is *not* reading productively—even on Muckelbauer's own terms—for doing so entails that one is not open fully to thinking differently *even if one does end up thinking differently about a text after engaging it* (cf. Dasenbrock 1991/1993, 1999). Obviously, even the most programmatic reader must think differently about a text in some respects after reading it! If not, why read at all? But Muckel-bauer rejects certain consequences of his engagement with Foucault's texts, thereby attempting to make these consequences inconsequential, even non-consequential, in time, especially if Muckelbauer's reading eventually *forgets* the Foucault who resists it. Any theory of reading in particular or of interpretation in general that suppresses certain *unde-sirable* consequences of an encounter with a text or utterance or sign misunderstands how texts and utterances are encountered, even if, as Sartre (1943/1956) might say, *nothing* can prevent Muckelbauer from doing what he does, certainly least of all the text, which, as we have seen, can be rendered almost inconsequential by a determined, pro-ductive reader like Muckelbauer in this particular instance.

I should add that I find Muckelbauer entirely correct when he sug-gests that there are different styles or strategies for engaging texts and that these methods will produce different effects or, as I prefer, conse-quences, in the course of reading. But the initial act of interpretation or understanding cannot discard the consequences of reading precisely because it is comprised of those consequences; however, our further as-sessment of and response to those consequences share no similar con-straint. What this means is that Muckelbauer's strategy of resisting some of the consequences of his encounter with Foucault's work isn't a method for *reading* Foucault, because resistance can emerge only in response to the consequences of what has been read, but of *rewriting* him after the fact of reading.

The literature review that follows—and, indeed, all of the uses to which I put texts throughout this book—will not be productive in Muckelbauer's sense, though I suggest that they will not transmit *a priori* meanings either. My goal is to be *faithful*, if not to the *texts-in-themselves*, then to the *consequences* evoked in me during my en-counters with these texts and with the texts of other researchers who have encountered them. That is, I try to be sensitive to the effects that these texts evoke within me—in short, to adhere to Peirce's pleas (a) for sincerity in philosophical inquiry: "Let us not pretend to doubt in philosophy what we do not doubt in our hearts" (1868/1991c, p. 56); and (b) for integrity in the response to his own work: "I require the reader to be candid; and if he becomes convinced of a conclusion, to admit it" (1869/1991a, 87).

Problematic Surveys of Rhetoric
and Composition Studies

A disclaimer: This section will not survey treatments of meaning
in the field of rhetoric and composition studies (throughout this book,
the work of researchers and theorists in rhetoric and composition studies will be positioned beside, not segregated from, the work of cultural
critics, linguists, literary theorists, philosophers, etc.); rather, this section will review how the field has been surveyed (particularly in terms
of underlying theories of meaning) and, consequently, configured and
reconfigured. The justification: I contend that an examination of the
ways in which the field has been taxonomized will illuminate important differences in how I will formulate my own taxonomy theories of
meaning within and beyond rhetoric and composition studies.

So we begin, again, with questions, rather than exposition: What
is a survey? How is it conducted? For what purposes? And is rhetoric
and composition studies an object of some sort—a "field"—that is,
in fact, surveyable? These are not unimportant questions for a project
concerned with meaning because it may be that surveys bring into
being/meaning what they purport to describe.

These questions are inseparable because one cannot separate the
surveyor from the act of surveying—no more than one can separate, as
Yeats (1927/1988a) put it, the dancer from the dance. What do surveyors do? They use instruments to determine distances, clarify boundaries, and map uncertain terrain; and they talk and write about the
results of their work, objectifying, abstracting, and mastering space
through what Cintron (1997, p. 24) terms *discourses of measurement.*
Surveys can be conducted on various scales, from the particulars of a
single plot of land to the entire globe, with resulting losses in acuity as
the ratio of scale expands. The lack of resolution of a survey is problematic if the purposes to which one puts the survey demand greater
resolution (e.g., I cannot use a map of the interstate system of the U.S.
to travel through the back-roads of rural Wisconsin). It is also problematic if one believes and acts upon the belief that a survey is more
fine-grained than it actually is (e.g., I would be foolhardy to sail along
the coastline of Norway relying upon a pocket-sized globe for guidance in navigating the fjords, or to trust the apparent dimensions of
countries on a Mercator map).[6]

But it would be equally foolhardy to adhere without qualification
to Augustine's (trans. 1997) claim that "the historian does not him-

self produce the sequence of events which he narrates, and the writer on topography or zoology or roots or stones does not present things instituted by humans, and the astronomer who points out the heavenly bodies and their movements does not point out something instituted by himself or any other person" (II.121). The historian may not produce the events that prompt her narrative, but she does produce the narrative that sets those events into language, that highlights particular elements at the expense of forgetting others, that perhaps even "depicts" events that never occurred as concrete facts. And land formations, animals, plants, rocks, and stars do not sort themselves into the categories of stable scientific taxonomies, but are sorted in categories of shifting stability by professionals in various disciplines (cf. Foucault, 1966/1970, 1969/1972a; C. Goodwin, 1994; Journet, 1993, 1999). Surveys (maps, narratives, and so on) may even precede or constitute that which they purport to describe, what Baudrillard (1983) has termed the "precession of simulacra" (p. 2).

The political dimension of a performative (or precessional) survey, whether map or narrative, should not be overlooked, either. For example, Benedict Anderson (1983/1996) argues that, at least in the case of Siam, the map of that country preceded its political reality (p. 173). And he contends that Harrison's invention of the chronometer in 1761 conceptually transformed the entire surface of the earth into a "geometrical grid which squared off empty seas and unexplored regions in measured boxes" to be "'fill[ed] in' by explorers, surveyors, and military forces" (p. 173). Similarly, Ryan (1994) argues that "the cartographic practice of representing the unknown as a blank does not simply or innocently reflect gaps in European knowledge but actively erases (and legitimizes the erasure of) existing social and geo-cultural formations in preparation for the projection and subsequent emplacement of a new order" (p. 116). For Ryan, the survey of an explorer, "by recording and imposing reality, is not merely *reflecting* a material arrangement, but *enabling* it" (p. 128).

Narratives, too, can be productive, inaugurating a world or part thereof rather than representing it. In a much more contemporary context, Dunmire (1997) has studied the ways in which "projected events"—in her case, Gulf War print media reports of an "imminent" Iraqi attack on Saudi Arabia—create virtual events treated as *present* facts that demand *present* response. Dunmire claims that the media construction of this projected event "suppresses the hypothetical and interested status of the Iraqi/Saudi Arabian projected event and represents it as a discrete, autonomous event unfolding within the context of the Persian Gulf conflict" (p. 222).

Surveying the Surveyors

Rhetoric and composition studies has not suffered from a lack of surveys and surveyors; and the enormous effort put into repeatedly surveying the field and disseminating the results is entirely predictable if one thinks of meaning and discourse operating in consequentialist terms, for without sustained effort, there would be no field at all. One survey published during the formative years of rhetoric and composition studies as an independent academic discipline, Richard Fulkerson's (1979/1996) "Four Philosophies of Composition," finds inspiration for its taxonomy in Abrams's (1953) four-part schema of theories of literature and literary criticism. Abrams argued that each approach emphasizes "one of the four elements in the artistic transaction" (Fulkerson, 1979/1996, p. 551): the *pragmatic* focuses on the reader and evaluates literature according to its effects; the *mimetic* focuses on a shared universe and evaluates literature on its success in mirroring that reality; the *expressive* valorizes the subjective feelings of the artist; and the *objective* emphasizes the text as an object with internal properties (p. 551). Fulkerson contends that Abrams's approach, suitably tweaked by changing *pragmatic* to *rhetorical* and *objective* to *formalist*, can highlight the differences in various approaches to the theory and praxis of rhetoric and composition studies. These competing approaches, according to Fulkerson, "give rise to vastly different ways of judging student writing, vastly different courses to lead students to produce such writing, vastly different textbooks and journal articles" (pp. 551–552). Fulkerson does not hesitate to name names, placing, for example, Hirsch (1977) in the formalist camp, Macrorie (1970) and Stewart (1972) in the expressivist camp, Beardsley (1976) in the mimetic camp, and Corbett (1965) in the rhetorical camp. Fulkerson does not seem so much concerned with advancing a particular approach to composition—though he admits to using journal-writing "in the service of a mimetic set of values" (p. 554)—as he is concerned with what he see as the "mindlessness" of many instructors who "either fail to have a consistent value theory or fail to let that philosophy shape pedagogy" (p. 554). For example, he excoriates instructors who assign what appear to be expressivist assignments (i.e., express your opinions on a subject), but who then evaluate them according to rhetorical criteria (i.e., would this paper persuade a reader?).

Although Fulkerson does not appear to have a particular axe to grind—or, at least on my reading of his essay, is successful enough concealing it—Nystrand, Greene, and Wiemelt (1993, p. 268) correctly point out that the field of rhetoric and composition studies has frequently been sketched in terms of competing theoretical factions with an explicit "hero" lauded by the author. If this is an offense, then one of the chief offenders is Berlin (1982/1996, 1988). Like Fulkerson, Berlin (1982/1996) uses the four-part schema of elements frequently identified in the rhetorical situation (writer, reality, audience, and language), but he disagrees with Fulkerson that

> differences in approaches to teaching writing can be explained by attending to the degree of emphasis given to universally defined elements of a universally defined composing process. The differences in these teaching approaches should instead be located in diverging definitions of the composing process itself—that is, in the way the elements make up the process—writer, reality, audience, and language—are envisioned. (p. 556)

The four factions of rhetoric and composition studies, by Berlin's reckoning, are the *Neo-Aristotelians* or *Classicists* (e.g., Corbett, 1965), who hold that there is a "happy correspondence" between the structure of the mind and the universe, with "language serving as the unproblematic medium of discourse" to communicate pre-existing truths about reality (p. 557); the *Positivists* or *Current-Traditionalists* (e.g., authors of standard composition textbooks), who maintain that the universe is knowable, but only through a rigorous, scientific method of inductive reasoning, with language used to adapt "what has been discovered outside the rhetorical enterprise to the minds of the hearers" (p. 559); the *Platonists* or *Expressionists* (e.g., Coles, 1978), who believe that truth is incommunicable, a property of individuals who can only approximate—because language "can only deal with the realm of error, the world of flux, and act" (p. 560)—this personal truth through writing that channels the writer's unique voice; and the *New Rhetoricians* or *Epistemic Rhetoricians* (e.g., Berthoff, 1978), who posit truth not outside of or prior to language, but constituted by it, with rhetoric serving "as a means of arriving at truth" and as a means of creating meaning and shaping reality (pp. 562, 564). Berlin announces his preference for the fourth approach, though, like Fulkerson, he is especially concerned about the confusion caused in the composition classroom when instructors fail to have an articulated, consistent praxis.

Six years later, Berlin (1988) revised his map of the field, reducing it to three dominant factions: *cognitive rhetoric* (e.g., Emig, 1971), the "heir apparent of current-traditional rhetoric" grounded in the methods of individualistic cognitive psychology and built upon the premise that "the structures of mind correspond in perfect harmony with the structures of the material world, the minds of the audience, and the units of language" (p. 480); *expressionistic rhetoric* (e.g., Elbow, 1981), with its focus on the authentic "experience of the self, an experience which transcends ordinary non-metaphoric language but can be suggested through original figures and tropes" (p. 485); and, again the hero of the narrative, *social-epistemic rhetoric* (e.g., Bartholomae, 1985/1996), which holds that knowledge comes into existence through discursive interactions comprised of "social constructions [. . .] inscribed in the very language we are given to inhabit in responding to our experience" (p. 488). The motivation for Berlin's taxonomy is not simply descriptive, but political: He faults both cognitive rhetoric and expressionistic rhetoric for their failure to provide effective critiques of what he portrays as the dominant, oppressive ideology of Western capitalism; in fact, he finds these rhetorical approaches to be complicit with the status quo.

Nystrand, Greene, and Wiemelt (1993), in their rigorous "intellectual history" of the field, discern only four major categories as well: *formalism,* in which language is an objective, static system and meanings are encoded within the formal properties of texts; *constructivist structuralism,* in which language operates in accordance to underlying mental structures and in which meaning emerges through the cognitive processes of individuals; *social constructionist structuralism,* in which these underlying structures and meanings are removed from individual minds and located in shared social practices; and *dialogism,* in which language and meaning emerge through the collisions between "the forces of individual cognition, on the one hand, and social ideology and convention, on the other" found in concrete communicative interactions (p. 295).

Table 1.1. Taxonomies of Rhetoric and Composition Studies.

Berlin (1982/1996)	*****	Classicist	Positivist	Expressionist	Epistemic	Epistemic
Berlin (1988)	*****	*****	Cognitive	Expressionist	Social-Epistemic	Social-Epistemic
Bizzell (1982/1992a)	*****	Outer	Inner	Inner	Outer	Outer
Faigley (1985)	Textual	Social	Individual	Individual	Social	Social
Fulkerson (1979/1996)	Formalist	Rhetorical	Mimetic	Expressive	*****	*****
Greene (1990)	*****	*****	Cognitive	*****	Social	Socio-Cognitive
Kent (1992)	*****	*****	Cognitive	Expressionist	Social Construction	*****
Knoblauch (1988/1996)	*****	Ontological	Objectivist†	Expressionist	*****	Dialogism
Nystrand et al. (1993)	Formalist	*****	Constructivism	Constructivism	Social Constructionism	Dialogism

† Knoblauch's (1988/1996) category of "objectivist" is marked by an asterisk because its inclusion of social constructionism is wildly at variance with the other terms in the column, even though much of his description of the category does overlap with them. Of course, this failure to produce clear-cut, stable categories is hardly surprising and certainly is not the goal of this survey of surveys of composition and rhetoric studies.

As Table 1.1 indicates, other important taxonomies of the field overlap comfortably, if not precisely, with the schemas already discussed.

For example, Knoblauch (1988/1996) offers four rhetorical approaches underlying writing instruction: the *ontological*, with a clear-cut distinction between language and reality, resembles Fulkerson's mimetic and Berlin's Neo-Aristotelian approaches; the *objectivist*, which "locates knowledge in human intellectual activity as it acts upon experiential information" (p. 586), corresponds to positivism, current-traditional rhetoric, cognitive rhetoric, and strong versions of social constructionism; the *expressionist*, which claims that knowledge is constituted by the imagination rather than given by sense data, is analogous to the expressive and the Platonic; and the *sociological* or *dialogical*, with its focus on language as a social practice "rooted, as are all social practices, in material and historical processes" (p. 589), corresponds to the epistemic or social-epistemic approaches. And so on: there are Bizzell's (1982/1992a) *inner-directed* and *outer-directed* approaches; Faigley's (1985) categories of the *textual*, the *individual*, and the *social;* Greene's (1990) call for a dialectical interplay between the *social* and the *cognitive* trends in writing research, forming a *socio-cognitive* approach; and Kent's (1992) *expressivism, cognitivism,* and *social constructionism.*

A qualification: It should be noted that Kent's (1992) contribution both accepts and surpasses earlier characterizations of rhetoric and composition studies. He accepts three of the standard divisions: *expressivism,* which holds that "innate mental categories function as a scheme either to represent reality or to frame reality" (p. 59); *cognitivism,* which "claims that the mind can be reduced to physical components or psychological states that account for human action," so that writing processes can be reduced to "mental activity" (p. 59); and *social constructionism,* which assumes that "we manufacture our subjectivity through the social conventions we share with fellow human begins" (p. 60). His innovation, however, is his contention that these three approaches fall under a common category: *internalism.* According to Kent (1992),

> The internalist imagines that a conceptual scheme or internal realm of mental states—beliefs, desires, intentions, and so forth—exists anterior to an external realm of objects and objects. In relation to mean-

> ing and language, the internalist thinks that we have
> ideas in our head, a kind of private language, and
> then we find a public language to help us communi-
> cate these ideas. Because meaning and language are
> located within our conceptual schemes—within the
> wiring of our brains, or within the transcendental
> categories of our thought, or within our communal
> social conventions—human subjectivity becomes, for
> the internalist, the starting place for every investiga-
> tion of meaning and language use. (pp. 57–58)

Kent rejects internalism in favor of *externalism,* which maintains "that no split exists between an inner and outer world and claims that our sense of an inner world actually derives from our rapport with other language users, people we interpret during the give and take of communicative interaction" (p. 62). But where Kent sees only a pro-found disjunction between theories of externalism and internalism, I perceive an unsuspected commonality: They both manifest premises of meaning apriorism.

A second qualification: Although the researchers discussed demar-cate no more than four categories, their categories are not perfectly iso-morphic (especially those covering the social dimension of discourse), which explains the omissions and the overlaps found in Table 1.1. In fact, because scholars must make a case for the originality—however slight—of their work, it would be quite surprising if essays whose main contribution to the field is surveying the field were to be in uniform agreement about how to carve it!

Categorization and Its Discontents

> The mind is fond of starting off to generalities, that it may
> avoid labor, and after dwelling a little on a subject is fatigued
> by experiment.
>
> —Francis Bacon

There can be no doubt that these surveys perform useful tasks, not the least of which is the disciplining of the limitless heterogeneity of the past into the finite span and duration of an essay or book for peda-gogical purposes: Imagine the promise of over 2000 years of thought about truth, language, and meaning condensed into an easily digested and regurgitated form! Who wouldn't prefer that to the impossible task of reading through that entire corpus? Quine (1960), then, might call surveys such as these *useful myths*—narratives or theories which work well enough pragmatically to navigate or manage reality even if they do not actually describe it. But at what cost are these myths told and retold and these maps drawn and redrawn? What errors do they commit that we should try to avoid? I suggest that these surveys are problematic in five ways: (a) they conceive of the field of rhetoric and composition largely in terms of theories; (b) they sort theories and theorists into discrete, atemporal categories; (c) they fail to provide a larger context for the operative ideas within the field; (d) they mistake their work in constituting and maintaining "the field" as an imagined community with which readers are invited to identify and perpetuate for work that describes a unified, stable (enough) entity that exists apart from the spatially and temporally dispersed people and texts who comprise "it"; and (e) they are all vested in the notion that meaning must have some definable *locus,* even if the specific locus to be privileged is contested.

As Nystrand, Greene, and Wiemelt argue, while surveys of the field such as those discussed earlier "usefully contrast various conceptions of writing," they nevertheless "neglect the emergence of scholarly thinking and empirical research about writing qua writing, the emergence of a writing research community, and the question of why composition studies started when they did" (p. 270). In short, surveys of the field are too focused on published research, overlooking the impact of newly-founded PhD programs, open admissions policies, and empirical research methods.[7] The latter two neglected influences seem indisputable to me: The surveys discussed earlier escribe a field already assembled into opposed camps, and they have little, if anything, to say about how rhetoric and composition studies was institutionalized in higher education in the early 1970s—which does not imply that no one has discussed this institutionalization The first point about the neglect of "the emergence of scholarly thinking and empirical research about writing qua writing," however, seems on shakier ground. Perhaps Fulkerson can be faulted for neglecting the formative empirical dimension of composition research, but the other surveys all include references to some version of cognitive research into writing processes. None of the authors would dispute that empirical research has been an influential paradigm for scholars within the field or that this kind of research program was helpful in establishing rhetoric and composition studies as a *respectable* discipline within higher education—even if their depictions of empirical research lack breadth and even if some authors, Berlin especially, would ultimately reject it.

A second objection raised by Nystrand, Greene, and Wiemelt is the tendency for surveys to "treat each of these phases [theoretical approaches] discretely and atomistically," rendering them unable to account for "important connections between evolving trends, that is, how one builds on another, at once responding to and conditioning the positions of those who come both before and after" (p. 271).[8] It is easy to criticize as simplistic these four-part schemas, but it is more difficult to escape the urge to simplify complexity (i.e., the urge to offer a complete picture) via categorization. Just how difficult is exemplified by the fact that Nystrand, Greene, and Wiemelt *retain* the impulse to taxonomize trends in composition studies into discrete categories, though in this case the components are distributed across five decades, with formalism (1940s-mid-1960s) slowly replaced as a dominant school of thought by constructivism (late-1960s-early 1980s), which is in turn replaced by social constructionism (1980s), which is in its turn challenged and enriched by dialogism (late 1980s)—forming a progression that, as Phelps (1999) warns us about in relation to Berlin's work, too easily allows for the subsumption of theoretical differences into "successive moments in the inevitable march toward an intellectually and morally superior stance" (p. 42).

The irony of this resemblance between their approach and that of their predecessors is not lost on Nystrand, Greene, and Wiemelt, yet they contend that "it is only through an articulation of differences in formalist, structuralist, and dialogical approaches that we can begin to see important connections among them" (p. 274). However, the clearest connections defined by Nystrand, Greene, and Wiemelt are those between the structuralisms of constructivism and social constructionism, with formalism and dialogism standing at either end as incommensurable approaches to language and meaning. There is no discussion of how formalism might be operative in dialogism, or how particular underlying principles might be operative in both of them. Thus, possible similarities remain obscured, tending to (re)produce the impression of conceptual atomism.

Nystrand, Greene, and Wiemelt state that their intention is not to "define hard boundaries or set strict chronologies between the evolving intellectual positions" (p. 274), but Knoblauch hedges his own schema in the same way (p. 584), and I'm certain that every surveyor of the field would agree with Britton et al.'s (1975) maxim, "We classify at our peril" (p. 1), and would distance themselves from a reification of their categories to the extent that particular scholars need not occupy only a single category. And no doubt readers, too, would, if directly asked, reject reified categories as well. But with *what* conceptual tools would they replace them? It seems to me inevitable that these subtleties and hedges are lost as these surveys are read, taught, and cited—i.e., as their meanings propagate through time—to the point that certain researchers become exemplars—even caricatures—of particular, separate, and pure approaches (e.g., Flower as Cognitivist, Elbow as Expressivist, Bartholomae as Social Constructionist, etc.). These surveys provide little sense of tensions, contradictions, and traces of other perspectives *within* the thinking of individual researchers, precisely because acknowledging them would of necessity disrupt the neatness—however carefully hedged—of the pre-fabricated, oppositional categories that the surveys construct.

A third problem, again presciently noted by Nystrand, Greene, and Wiemelt, is the failure of surveys to "situate the evolution of these debates [between theoretical approaches] in an ongoing, general intellectual context" (pp. 271–272). This provincialism, they suggest, prevents a proper understanding of *where* rhetoric and composition studies has come from: "the advent of composition studies needs to be understood less as a local weather disturbance in departments of English and more as part of a fundamental climate change involving the evolution of general epistemologies animating thought about discourse" (p. 273). This is a powerful criticism, and it is precisely the substance of this objection that prompts the interdisciplinary approach of my own research. However, the "wider historical context" offered by Nystrand, Greene, and Wiemelt is not wide enough (nor could it possibly be wide enough) to meet their ambitious goal, for what scholarship it cites beyond the field of rhetoric and composition studies—aside from the work of Austin, Bakhtin, Durkheim, and a few others—is from twentieth-century work within linguistics or sociolinguistics. If Nystrand, Greene, and Wiemelt ask how we *arrived* at dialogism from formalism, they do not ask how we *started* from formalism. The nets they use simply aren't large enough to answer that question.

Nor can there be an exhaustive answer. The dangers of *conceptual holism*—the attempt to link in a single, coherent, albeit unimaginably complex, atemporal (because panchronic) intertextual web—are as perilous as *conceptual atomism*. We must resist the temptation to think of "the field" (or the supposed factions of the field—e.g., constructivism, constructionism, and so on)—as a unified entity (i.e., as a term with a determinate extension) composed of a completely interlocking, seamless web of researchers who read the same texts (presumably, all of them) at the same time (presumably, immediately after they are published), who discern the same meanings (presumably, stable) and subsequently replicate and retain them with the same fidelity (presumably, perfect). We must question our tendency to conceive of "the field" at all as something that exists apart from the fragile—and therefore necessarily continuous—efforts through literature reviews, taxonomies, citations, classroom instruction, doctoral programs, etc., to manufacture and sustain links between researchers and texts and thereby to (re)constitute "the field" as a normative ideal or a myth, something to which we are continually hailed to identify (cf. Barthes, 1957/1982; Burke, 1950/1969). We must allow for readers who read differently, apply differently, and forget; for texts that are lost, delayed, dormant, or deliberately ignored; for authors who make similar claims that do not share common origins; for a past littered with "conflicting elements, multiple causes, and loose ends" (Phelps, 1999, p. 52).[9]

In short, we must acknowledge—despite our *sense* of the continuity of past research and its connections to an interlocking body of current work—the inherently aporetic nature of both; and we must abandon, with Einstein (1916/1961), the notion of *instantaneous effects*—in this case, that consequences of texts are immediately felt by everyone—as an atemporal fiction. I prefer to think of "the field" as a convenient fiction, a shorthand for the multitude of ephemeral and always partial clusters of synchronized researchers, practitioners, students, texts, and utterances—with each individual (human or nonhuman) a focal point of transient links that vary in scope but that do not extend into infinity, either spatially or temporally. That is, by knowing person *X*, I am not necessarily connected to every person that *X* knows, has known, or will ever know, ad infinitum: My understanding of meaning consequentialism does cohere with a "small world" or "six degrees of separation" theory of social connections.[10]

Perhaps a visual metaphor will help: Instead of a single grid in which all objects are situated and interconnected, think of "the field" as a *colloidal laminate,* each separate layer of which is solid enough to map a particular cluster of synchronized people and utterances that extends through time, yet which is fluid enough to change shape as the cluster changes (like the image on a liquid crystal display screen) or evaporate entirely if it loses its members. The field is a non-totality because, although it is comprised of a finite number of finite consequential networks of people, utterances, and texts, each network is not composed of selections from the same total number of objects (i.e., there is not a single, master-set from which each network chooses particular elements), precisely because how the field is defined changes its shape (i.e., extension is not separable from intension). In this way, the field should not be considered as a set of layers of equal size extending over the same surface. Adding to the instability of the field, the boundaries of the networks are continuously changing as people come and go and as utterances and texts are produced and forgotten and as their meanings propagate.

A person, utterance, or text will occupy points in multiple layers, but membership in one layer does not extend to membership in others (i.e., two people connected in one layer are not necessarily connected in any other, though they may be), preventing the laminate from being a thoroughly interconnected totality, even if one could view the laminate with a panoptic gaze that compresses—like the final product of an overlay of successive sheets on an overhead projector—the multiplicity of patterns into a single constellation, an illusion of thorough interconnection. Invocations of "the field," then, can be used to produce that illusion, to persuade us that only particular layers legitimately constitute it, to invite us to widen our memberships to other layers, or to prompt us to rethink our notions of the ways in which rhetoric and composition studies is configured.

As I mentioned earlier, the various "factions" within rhetoric and composition studies have been portrayed as antagonistic; and certainly some advocates of particular "camps" have been rather dismissive, even caustic, in their treatments of the ideas of standard bearers of other "camps." But if, as I suggest, each camp actually overlaps with its presumed competitors, what commonalities do they share? One crucial area of agreement is the claim that meaning has a particular *locus,* even if there is much disagreement about which locus should be privileged (implicitly or explicitly) as foundational—or antifoundational, as the case may be—from the set of all possible loci (e.g., formal properties of texts, logical structures of propositions, intentions, social practices, cognitive processes, physical objects and properties, etc., or perhaps even located only in intersections between two or more loci). The opposition between meaning apriorism and meaning consequentialism is not merely another way of (re)labeling the tensions between foundationalist and antifoundationalist theories of language. The general proposition that meaning has a particular locus or set of loci falls under the rubric of *meaning apriorism,* and the particular loci themselves I will treat conceptually as *principles of meaning apriorism.* None of these loci, I suggest, even when combined in subtle ways, can provide a suitable location for the grounding of meaning—not because meaning lacks a *place* (i.e., meaning does not occur apart from space), but because it resists *placement* (i.e., a settling or grounding in a particular location or kind of location). To try to freeze meaning in this way is to do violence to its temporality.

Toward A Consequentialist Conception of the Survey

What, then, might a consequentialist survey of theorizations of meaning within rhetoric and composition studies and beyond look like? My answer is: Read this book. (And then imagine what the book *looks like,* if you can; or think about how this book physically and conceptually resists being *flattened* into an image.) However, I can discuss four strategies that inform what follows. First, theorists and their theories will not be sorted into discrete, impermeable categories, but rather will have particular elements highlighted that manifest the principles of meaning apriorism: No argument will be made or implied (a) that the theorists and their theories fall within only the single principle or set of principles of meaning apriorism to which I explicitly connect them; (b) that the theorists and their theories are in perfect conformity to that principle (i.e., that there are no tensions, contradictions, or gaps in their theories); and (c) that the principles of meaning apriorism are mutually exclusive. The goal of proposing the interlocking categories of meaning apriorism is not differentiation per se (though I do not deny substantive differences between theories), but integration: To see, *despite* these substantive differences, the fundamental—and quite problematic—commonalities that underlie classical, modern, and contemporary theories of meaning.

Second, although a much wider context for the variations of meaning apriorism manifested in rhetoric and composition studies and beyond it will be supplied by Chapters 2 through 6, I will not attempt to provide a neat chronology that traces causal connections from, for example, philosopher X to rhetorician Y, or to describe how compositionist Z responds to Y. There are attempted borrowings, to be sure—and disagreements as well that will be noted—but my purpose is not to trace the influences of particular thinkers, as if the *origin* of meaning apriorism could be found in a single text whose meaning has been faithfully transmitted reader to reader, generation to generation; rather, my purpose is to grasp as far as possible in a project of necessarily limited scope the dispersion and ubiquity of meaning apriorism within the classical, modern, and contemporary thought about meaning, language, and discourse.[11]

Third, I will not pretend to fully describe already existing fields or disciplines—i.e., to provide a panoptic gaze that compresses and freezes the laminates of philosophy, rhetoric, linguistics, etc. On the contrary, by discussing *particular* texts, this book—even as it is being written, read, revised, and so on—alters the *non-totality* of these fields by changing the ways in which people and texts are situated, by creating new layers of the laminates, and by widening the memberships of old ones—even though these fields in manifold respects remain totally unchanged because what happens in one or several networks need not affect all of the others. It is in this sense that all description of fields is constitutive—in the same way, to invoke Heidegger (1960/1993a) once more, that a work of art inaugurates a world. One of the ways that the collectivity of a field is *enacted*, not *found*, is through researchers "hailing" other researchers as "fellow travelers with separate itineraries who stop to meet common needs" (Clark, 1998, p. 14)—in this case, the need to theorize meaning.

And fourth, I will not attempt to treat meaning apriorism as a Procrustean bed onto which every aspect of classical, modern, and contemporary theories of meaning must fit; quite the contrary, for I do not wish to replace caricatures of theorists and their theories with other caricatures, but to resist the impulse to caricaturize. As I hope will become clear in time (and *because* of it, for time is a necessarily condition for something's becoming clear), manifestations of meaning consequentialism that appear in the literature of rhetoric and composition studies and other fields will be quite germane to my development of the theory of meaning consequentialism. If, as I suggest, meaning consequentialism represents a more adequate theorization of meaning than meaning apriorism, then it would be quite surprising indeed if no other thinkers in their deliberations on meaning had ever struck upon at least some of its tenets. Peirce (1868/1991c) once wrote that "if disciplined and candid minds carefully examine a theory and refuse to accept it, this ought to create doubts in the mind of the author of the theory itself" (p. 56). Whether my admittedly counterintuitive theory in fact persuades disciplined and careful minds remains to be seen, but I can at least find solace in the fact that some of its key premises are not unprecedented.

A final note about my own preoccupation with theory: I am not writing a history of meaning apriorism, nor am I reporting on the findings of an empirical study intended to test the merits of meaning consequentialism. This project from the start is set within a framework of philosophical argumentation (even if some philosophers would not recognize it as such).[12] Some passages will no doubt be read as meta-physical speculation, perhaps even as poetry. *So be it.* However, I take seriously Condillac's (1746/1982c) criticism of the arm-chair philosophy of rationalists: "Imagine people waking from a deep sleep and, seeing themselves in the middle of a labyrinth, proposing general principles for discovering the way out. What could be more ridiculous? Nevertheless this is how philosophers behave [. . .]. A philosopher suddenly becomes a sage, a man for whom all nature holds no secrets, and that through the magic of two or three propositions!" (pp. 8–9). My study will not be limited to an invocation of and response to the work of philosophers (still less to the work of individuals whose credentials as philosophers seem to be universally acknowledged), but will invoke—and be evoked by—research, including some empirical studies, from many different fields. Purely rationalist speculation risks leading to sterility tautologies—i.e., to theoretical premises that are true analytically, not synthetically; my goal is not to construct a philosophical system that is true by definition, but rather, as Popper (1934/1959) would put it, to propose a *bold conjecture* that may be falsified by the test of experience. Although beyond the scope of this book, I conceive of the overall project of developing meaning consequentialism along of lines of Dennett's (1991) attempt to merge philosophical and empirical approaches to the mind, even if I lean by inclination more toward the former than the latter.

MANIFESTATIONS OF MEANING APRIORISM:
LOCATIVE AND TEMPORAL PRINCIPLES

For the concept of probability or uncertainty is simply not applicable to the acts of giving meaning which constitute philosophy. It is a matter of positing the meaning of statements as something simply final. Either we have this meaning, and then we know what is meant by the statement, or we do not possess it, in which case mere empty words confront us, and as yet no statement at all. There is nothing in between and there can be no talk of the probability that the meaning is the right one.

—Moritz Schlick

The truth is that the discourse should have a meaning immediately evident, or it will never have one.

—Henri Bergson

When a sentence is called senseless, it is not as it were its sense that is senseless. But a combination of words is being excluded from language, withdrawn from circulation.

—Ludwig Wittgenstein

I have already characterized the central premise of meaning apriorism as the assumption that the meaning of an utterance or text (or any sign) is to be found always in some sense prior to that utterance or text or to any interpretation of that utterance or text. In other words, meaning is always (at some point) grounded in the past and bounded by it, or it is grounded in and bounded by things (i.e., objects, entities, events) that are themselves panchronic, essentially atemporal.

This central premise, however, can be made manifest in a variety of ways: (1) the belief that if the meaning of an utterance changes for an interpreter, that change necessarily evolves out of the previous meaning(s) (what I term the *principle of evolution*); (2) the belief that the listener *completes* or *finishes* the construction of meaning, so that the meaning becomes a bounded and isolated historical fact or event (*principle of completion*); (3) the belief that the meaning of an utterance is a single unit (*principle of unity*) or (4) a *bounded* multiplicity or ambiguity (*principle of scope*) and is (5) static (*principle of stasis*); (6) the belief that the meaning of an utterance is housed within the mind of the speaker and/or fixed by his or her intentions prior to the production of that utterance (*principle of ideation*); (7) the belief that meanings, constrained by phonological, orthographical, morphological, syntactic, and pragmatic *structures,* form an immense lattice-work (i.e., a *language*)—whether conceived as totalizable or open-ended— that may be simultaneously studied holistically and diachronically, within an individual speaker (*principle of linguistic holism*) or (8) a social unit of varying sizes (*principle of linguistic spatialism*), without or with only minimal or uninteresting distortion; (9) the belief that meanings may exist entirely apart from concrete utterances or, in some important sense, from language users (*principle of formalism*); and the belief that these meanings ultimately derive from some foundational origin, whether (10) innate biological endowments (*principle of innatism*), (11) the laws, objects, processes, and events of the physical universe (*principle of empiricism*); (12) the immutable laws of logic and reason (*principle of rationalism*), or (13) a mystical order of nature or the divine mind of God (*principle of mysticism*).

A general pattern emerges from these thirteen principles; there is a clear sense of movement in this series, but it is marked by *retrogressivity.* The movement of meaning is a movement backwards in time. We begin, in (1: principle of evolution), with a Peircean or Bakhtinian chain of interpretations, each one linked to the preceding one; we can arrive at the most recent or final interpretation—for Peirce concedes the pragmatic necessity of an end to interpretation—*only* in light of what precedes it. This is the *limit* of meaning apriorism, the extent to which this doctrine may be stretched before unraveling entirely. These interpretations, it should be noted, occur within the individual mind as part of the *processes* of semiosis, interpretation, and/or discourse. This succession of interpretations has an origin, a first interpretation, which is formed *in response* to the speaker's material utterance (2: principle of completion); this first interpretation is an attempt to decode or decipher the meaning already within the utterance, and that interpretation is considered successful or meaningful only insofar as it duplicates this prior meaning. But for this duplication or reduplication or reproduction to operate, the meaning of the utterance must be assumed to be either unified or at least bounded in size and frozen in time to allow for complete (or sufficient) mapping (3, 4, 5: principles of unity, scope, and stasis). The meaning of the utterance becomes an unalterable historical fact, set in place by the semantic concrete of an originary and organizing principle (e.g., intentions, literal meanings, conventions, genres, reference, context, etc.). The mistake is to assume that the meaning(s) of an utterance mirror the unique particularity, materiality, inalterability, and duration of that utterance.

But meaning apriorism cannot rest here with the meaning of the utterance as the starting point, for what caused or generated this meaning in the first place? Why is the utterance meaningful? The answer offered by meaning apriorism is, once again, to look further back in time. It is presumed that the speaker has full control even before that meaning is instantiated in a concrete utterance (6: principle of ideation); the thought precedes and constructs the utterance, so we cannot account for the meaning of that utterance without in some way incorporating this thought into our interpretation: The meaning of the thought explains, guarantees, authorizes, or fixes the meaning of the utterance. However, thoughts are intelligible only within an *a priori web* of thoughts (cf. Quine, 1960)—the meaning of the thought is explicable only in terms of a choice made within that pre-existing network called a *language,* which the speaker has *in toto* at any given moment (7: principle of linguistic holism) and which is also—mostly or imperfectly—shared by members of a larger discourse communi- ty (8: principle of linguistic spatialism) (cf. Saussure 1916/1959). In- dividual meaning is an internalization of communal meanings (e.g., Luckmann, 1990; Schutz 1962/1990; Vygotsky, 1962/1986), perhaps learned even as a complex, conditioned reflex (Skinner, 1957).

This system of meanings can be explained in terms of already ex- isting pragmatic language games with expressible or inferable rules (e.g., J. L. Austin, 1962; Searle, 1969; Searle and Vanderveken, 1985) or in terms of an abstract, formalized system—a calculus of mean- ing (9: principle of formalism) (e.g., Carnap, 1947/1988; Chomsky, 1957/1969; Saussure, 1916/1959; Tarski, 1956); the regularity of lan- guage-use (discourse/performance/*parole*)—a product of *linguistic competence* that is always liable to misfires in *linguistic performance*—is simply an unfolding of the *a priori* rules of language-as-system (lan- guage/competence/*langue*), which would be comprised of well-ordered pragmatic, semantic, syntactic, morphological, orthographical, and/ or phonological rules. Meaning apriorism explains this orderliness of language-as-system in three ways, which, in any given theory, may be separate or may overlap. First, it is a result of *innatism* (10: principle of innatism), with the biology of cognition as master code (e.g., Fodor, 1987; Pinker, 1995). Second, it is a result of *logical atomism* (11 and 12: principles of empiricism and rationalism), which posits timeless propositions that underlie supposedly synonymous sentences in different languages and that exist or at least subsist even if never thought of by a subject of consciousness; and these propositions form the web of a universal logic that underlies different modes of representation, with meaning coded into the timeless, mindless—but also rational—logic of the physical universe (e.g., Frege 1918–1919/1984a, 1918–1919/1984b, 1923–1926/1984c; Wittgenstein, 1922/1981). And third, it is a result of *mysticism* (13: principle of mysticism), in which all meanings are contained within the omniscient mind of a divinity or some other kind of spiritual entity and subsequently revealed to human beings (e.g., Aquinas, trans. 1947; Augustine, trans. 1997; Emerson, 1836/1985c, 1844/1985d).

I suggest that my taxonomy of thirteen major principles is better suited to handle the nuances of and highlight some unsuspected parallels between theoretical approaches to meaning than, for example, the familiar taxonomies offered by the surveyors of rhetoric and composition studies (e.g., the categories of expressivist, cognitivist, constructivist, social constructionist, formalist, etc.). However, each of these principles in its own way is *locative:* Each principle places meaning in certain privileged locations—whether they be transcendental, abstract, or virtual dimensions (i.e., mysticism, rationalism, formalism, scope); physical reality (i.e., innatism, empiricism); social groups or practices (i.e., spatialism, evolution, completion, scope); cognitive processes (i.e., ideation, holism, completion); or contexts (i.e., stasis, unity).

Although these locative principles imply conceptions of time, none of them is welded to a particular conception; thus, what we require is a set of temporal principles for meaning apriorism that *cut across* the locative ones. These temporal principles are: (14) the *principle of panchronism,* which denies the temporality of time by denying its movement (i.e., though experienced sequentially, time does not progress: Past, present, and future have equal reality); (15) the *principle of simultaneity,* which denies the temporality of time by denying its relativity (i.e., treating time as an absolute standard shared by all objects and regions of the universe); and (16) the *principle of durativity,* which denies the temporality of time by denying its accidents, discontinuities, and losses. Consequently, meaning apriorism is made manifest through thirteen locative principles and three temporal principles.

No doubt, the "pie" of theories of meaning could be cut in many other ways, too, either by shrinking the number of principles still further or by multiplying them greatly. For example, it is possible to combine these thirteen major principles into a set of more generalized principles. Consider this higher-ordered set of six principles: (I) the *principle of transcendence* (encompassing mysticism and rationalism), which grounds meaning in a transcendental otherworld constituted by divinity or logic; (II) the *principle of integrity* (stasis, unity, scope), which assumes that meanings are treatable only as individuated wholes; (III) the *principle of physicalism* (innatism, empiricism), which locates the foundation of meaning in an objective reality; (IV) the *principle of structuralism* (formalism, spatialism), which posits that meanings form an abstract system—whether conceived as an independent entity (*langue*) or the underlying logic that regulates discursive practices (languages, genres)—and that the meaningfulness of a linguistic sign depends upon the placement of that sign in relation to other signs; (V) the *principle of constructivism* (ideation, holism), which grounds meaning in an individual's intentions or other cognitive states and processes; and (VI) the *principle of interactionism* (evolution, completion), which treats meaning, not as a private possession of individuals, but as an outcome of interactions between speakers, listeners, writers, and readers.

Other arrangements can be made as well. But my own desire is to avoid not only reducing meaning apriorism into a few principles that risk blurring away the subtleties of the analysis, but also amplifying meaning apriorism into so many principles that they lose their sense of connection and appear merely ad hoc. I think that the six higher-order principles, though they have limited usefulness, are too blunt to carve the intricacies of meaning apriorism;[13] therefore, I will rely upon the locative and temporal principles already discussed, which are sufficiently differentiated yet still integrated both internally, in terms of the various theories of meaning subsumed under the principle, and externally, in terms of the differences and connections between the principles. That is, these principles highlight important distinctions within theoretical approaches to meaning, yet they are not autonomous axioms. Not only can a single theory of meaning manifest multiple principles without contradiction, but also each of these principles can be intimately linked to others almost to the point of being indistinguishable. For example, there is a strong connection between *variations* of innatism and constructivism to the extent that psychological models of the mind often include the biological "machinery" of cognition. Does it make sense to draw a hard line, then, between innatism and constructivism, even if innatism need not entail constructivism?

Although much more detailed work will follow, I would like at this point to offer an analogy to concretize some of this very abstract discussion. Consider an *a priori* account of interpretation in terms of photography. The faster the camera speed, the shorter the time interval *depicted* in the image; a fast shutter speed *slows* the movements of the depicted objects relative to the perception of the camera, thus reducing the *smearing* produced by the movements of objects in the camera's visual field. If the camera speed is sufficiently fast, the objects crystallize into the perfect clarity of immobility—a perfect duplication. (I am reminded here of Bergson's claim that form is frozen movement.) The point is this: For interpretation to duplicate meaning, it must outpace meaning to such an extent that meaning appears frozen in place; in some sense, the meaning of the utterance must be *left behind* so that it might be reconstituted. Further, the camera must remain fixed in relation to the depicted objects; were the camera also to move, this would create additional distortions in the image. But, paradoxically, this *absolute immobility* also connotes *infinite speed,* for the meaning is everywhere simultaneously. This is an illusion created by a flattening (or spatializing) of time. Note also that the spatial dimensions of the image remain constant: Time diminishes until only purely spatial considerations are relevant. We can further extend the metaphor of photography for interpretation in meaning apriorism to include the relationship between thought and utterance: In order for the utterance to duplicate without distortion the meaning of the thought, this thought must itself be locked into place, at once immobile and omnipresent. By treating time in progressively smaller increments, meaning apriorism shaves away layer by layer the relevance of time *qua* time (e.g., in terms of change, unpredictability, otherness, perspectivity) for considerations of meaning.

I end this overview of meaning apriorism with a cautionary note: One would search in vain for a theory that labels itself *meaning apriorism,* and I am not asserting that any particular theory fully articulates—or that any particular theorist fully commits herself—to meaning apriorism. Rather, I think of meaning apriorism as an analytic construct or useful myth that illuminates important similarities in the *consequences* of classical, modern, and contemporary treatments of the relations between meaning and time, without suggesting that such consequences were inevitable, incontestable, and self-propagating.

A Brief Sketch of Meaning Consequentialism

We can scarcely expect a general account of linguistic communication to yield more than schematic outlines, which may also be lost to view when every qualification is added which fidelity to the facts requires.

—P. F. Strawson

I suffer from an embarrassment: I have no workable theory of meaning in hand. This is, however, an embarrassment that my antagonists share; nobody has a workable theory of meaning in hand. [. . .].

—Jerry A. Fodor

Before sketching my own consequentialist philosophy of discourse, I think it necessary to address the question, "What is a theory of meaning *supposed* to do?" I take this to be a normative question, rather than an essentialist question (as if a theory of meaning could have only one goal), so I can only offer some of the key assumptions that have guided and continue to guide my project of theorizing meaning:

- I will not treat—as research in a wide range of disciplines does—meaning and meanings as givens, but will investigate the conditions that create the experience of givenness;
- I will not offer—as might classical, modern, or contemporary rhetorics in the handbook tradition—advice regarding how to propagate certain desired meanings, but will theorize why and in what ways meanings propagate in accordance to and apart from our intentions, desires, etc.;
- I will not provide—as would certain traditions in philology, hermeneutics, and textual criticism—a method for determining the meaning(s) of an utterance, but will demonstrate why such

determinations can only be provisionally made (and, therefore, aren't really determinations at all); 14

and, most importantly,

- I will not assume *a priori*—as various antifoundationalist approaches to language must—that meaning has no essential properties, but will explain why these properties do not prohibit, but in fact result in, the propagation of contingent, even contradictory meanings. That is, I will not rest with the assertion that meaning is contingent or that meanings proliferate or that meanings may even be contradictory, but will attempt in a principled way to explain why meaning and discourse operate as they do: *To understand why the meanings of an utterance or text may be contradictory does not require an explanation that is itself self-contradictory.*

I realize that this last bulleted item is likely to be especially contentious because of the embrace of antifoundationalism—at least in terms of meaning or language—within rhetoric and composition studies and beyond it.[15] I do not reject antifoundationalism because it is self-refuting (i.e., in the sense that advocates of relativism are often accused of treating claims about relativism as objective truths), which it may be (cf. Dasenbrock, 1995), but because I find antifoundationalist theories to be, in the end, unsatisfactory and unproductive ways of conceptualizing language, meaning, and discourse—and not simply because, as we shall see, they fall comfortably under the rubric of meaning apriorism. Antifoundationalist theories not only fail to provide an explanatory account of the origin of meaning or language (cf. Hirsch, 1976; Hirsh-Pasek, Golinkoff, and Reeves, 1994), *but they also prohibit the very raising of questions about those origins.*

This prohibition, it should be pointed out, *conveniently* absolves antifoundationalist theorists from tackling some very perplexing and perhaps ultimately unanswerable questions not only about meaning and language, but also, more importantly, about their own theoretical constructions. For example, consider Fodor and Lepore's (1993) criticism of antifoundationalist thought within the philosophy of science: "To reject foundationalism in the philosophy of science is precisely to reject the notion of a 'first scientist' in favor of the idea that science begins *in media res*," producing a puzzling "steadystate [*sic*] picture of the physical sciences" (p. 65). I find this a persuasive objection, and I argue that antifoundationalist theories of language exhibit this kind of steady-state, *a priori* thinking: Languages, meanings, social formations, etc., are treated as if they have always already existed.[16] For example, Rorty's (and Oakeshott's) "Conversation of Mankind," mentioned earlier, has been characterized as a process that "has no beginning or end [. . . but] keeps rolling of its own accord, reproducing itself effortlessly, responsible only to itself" (Trimbur, 1989, p. 606). And Bakhtin (1986/1996) claims that "any speaker is himself a respondent to a greater or lesser degree. He is not, after all, the first speaker, the one who disturbs the eternal silence of the universe. And he presupposes not only the existence of the language system he is using, but also the existence of preceding utterances—his own and others'—with which the given utterance enters into one kind of relation or another" (p. 69). This position, of course, conforms to Bakhtin's dialogic, social-interactionist conception of language and meaning, but does it account for *all* of the phenomena of discourse? Was there *never* a *first speaker?* Only if discourses have no beginnings; only if Language was spoken prior to there being speakers. Note that Bakhtin's exclusion of a first speaker isn't *accidental,* for the existence of a first speaker—or even multiple "first" speakers—would throw into doubt his generalizing *dialogic* features of discourse as *constitutive* features of discourse.

"The eternal silence of the universe" has been disturbed so thoroughly and for so long—at least on the mote on which we reside—that it is perhaps difficult to conceive of that silence ever having been or, even if it had been, of that fact having any bearing on questions about contemporary phenomena of discourse. But I suggest that a theory which can avoid a steady-state, *a priori* treatment of meaning and discourse by explaining in a principled way how meanings and discourses could *begin* in addition to accounting for the phenomena that occur *afterward* would be the more fruitful and useful—because the more inclusive—theory. I am not claiming that meaning consequentialism already provides answers about the origins of meanings, but at least it has the potential to do so by not excluding them *a priori*.

As I have argued elsewhere, rejecting antifoundationalism need not entail a return to a modernist or positivist conception of Truth, even if we cannot or should not dispense with *truths* entirely (K. Porter, 1998). What remains of truth, then, is pragmatic concept, a standard to be sought even if never achieved with complete certainty (James, 1907/1981; Peirce, 1868/1991c, 1878/1991b; Popper, 1962).

Although people must of necessity hold many true beliefs (Davidson, 1970/1980d, 1973/1984d, 1986a; Fodor, 1987), no single belief, however strongly held, is beyond the possibility of falsification (Popper, 1934/1959; Sellars, 1956/1997); as Putnam (1978/1983c) puts it, "we never have an absolute guarantee that we are right, even when we are right" (p. 96). My hope, then, is to say things that are "right" about meaning, language, and discourse, even if I cannot provide absolute proofs.

But what are these "things" that I hope to say? What is meaning consequentialism? What would a full explication of a consequentialist philosophy of discourse look like? The latter two questions cannot be answered because in a very real sense meaning consequentialism does not yet "fully" exist and will not ever "fully" exist: Meaning consequentialism is not waiting patiently for its articulation into language. And I am also well aware that it is beyond the scope of this book to call meaning consequentialism into being because of the complexities involved. My construction of meaning consequentialism must be incremental, conducted through a patient explication and analysis of key concepts that have emerged already and those which might still emerge; this is the task I have set for Chapters 2 through 7.

However, this "failure" to provide a full articulation of meaning consequentialism should not be taken as an indication of the paucity of my current conceptions of it. The central premise stands as a bold conjecture: The meaning of a sign is its consequences. But I have only begun to realize the innumerable consequences, those that are already and those that are yet to be, inaugurated by that premise. Note that I say *already* because I am writing this section of the introduction well after the fact of having written completed drafts of the chapters that follow; that is, I am here engaging in what Serres (1979) calls the *wolf's game,* in which the author/researcher appears "to be there first in the past and calling the shots for downstream and future events" (p. 87). This section, then, is my attempt to highlight some of those consequences (only some of which can and will be pursued further in this book), thereby providing readers with a sense of the substantive yet fluid development of my theorization of meaning consequentialism; of necessity, the entries will be brief, with some concepts presented only aphoristically. My hope here is not to persuade readers that the premises of meaning consequentialism are valid or true, but only that they have been rigorously construction and are intriguing enough to merit inquiry within and, more importantly, beyond this book.

As I conceive of it, meaning consequentialism currently extends over such claims as the following:

- Being consequential is "inherent to the notion of signs" (Freadman, 1998; cf. Peirce, 1931/1960, I.213); something that is not consequential cannot be a sign.
- Utterances, not sentences, are the primary units of discourse (cf. Bakhtin, 1986/1996).
- An utterance has meaning only after its use.
- Each utterance is a unique particular.
- Meanings are consequences of utterances.
- An utterance or text is polysemic if it propagates more than one consequence. An utterance or text does not propagate more than one consequence because it is polysemic: *Polysemy is dependent upon consequentiality, not consequentiality upon polysemy.*
- Interpretations are consequences of utterances; but the consequences of utterances extend beyond human cognition and into the material world. In this way, I wish to avoid grounding meaning in an anthropocentric constructivism in which "only people can mean" (Halliday, 1978, p. 207). For the purposes of this book, meaning consequentialism will be treated only as a philosophy of discourse; however, as indicated by occasional references to signs, the premises of meaning consequentialism extend to signs of all types. Perhaps meaning consequentialism would be better characterized as a *philosophy of semiotics.*
- From the vantage point of any interpreter, an utterance may already have meanings; but these meanings are only anterior to, not pre-given for, any subsequent act of interpretation (cf. West and Olson, 1999, pp. 246, 248).
- An utterance has as many meanings as it has consequences. These consequences may be conflicting and even contradictory: The principle of non-contradiction does not determine what meanings are *permissibly* propagated.
- An utterance cannot be exhausted of meanings until it no longer generates consequences.
- We may think of the Meaning of an utterance as the total set of all its actual consequences; but this Meaning cannot be conceptualized because (a) the total set of all actual consequences

is inherently open-ended, (b) the Meaning of each consequence itself is open-ended, (c) the total set of all actual consequences does not form a amalgamated consequence that can be cognized, and (d) the very act of compiling a complete list of consequences for the expressed purpose of compiling a complete list would itself produce at least one more consequence of the targeted utterance, ad infinitum. One cannot interact with an utterance without propagating additional consequences. This conception of Meaning, I suggest, preserves the question of Meaning without invoking a metaphysics: Meaning is ineffable, not because it is transcendent, but because its ceaseless propagation into a manifold of concrete consequences necessarily outpaces any attempt to contain or quantify it. As Emerson (1841/1985a) once wrote, "Every ultimate fact is only the first of a new series [. . .]. There is no outside, no inclosing wall, no circumference to us" (p. 227). Please note that I introduce the capitalization of Meaning now, rather than at the commencement of this chapter, in order to prevent the propagation of undesired consequences (i.e., that readers believe the capital letter signals a return to metaphysics). Only at this moment am I prepared to differentiate Meaning-in-general or the Meaning of an utterance from particular meanings of utterances.

- The Meaning of an utterance is neither an average of all its particular meanings (i.e., a point of overlap of all utterance-circles on a Venn diagram), nor a court of final appeal for resolving disputes about meanings; for the Meaning is not a foundation, but a temporally (and spatially) distended outcome.
- The only way that the Meaning of an utterance could be fully experienced would be if that experience constituted the first actual consequence of the utterance; but it is not clear—and I highly doubt—whether an utterance can produce only a single consequence.
- An utterance is *thrown* or *projected* into the world (cf. Heidegger, 1927/1962). Speakers and writers can only predict or hypothesize meanings, not master them: The meanings of an utterance always exceed our grasp. The consequences of an utterance are unknowable in advance because they are not determined in advance: An utterance does not contain its consequences which the passage of time subsequently reveals (like the unfurling of

[handwritten margin note: Chase it but never win]

an already made flag; cf. Bergson, 1946, p. 21). We are always confronted by the physical—as well as phenomenological—uncertainty of the event horizon of meaning.

- There can be no purely synchronic language, whether conceived of in terms of international or national languages, regional dialects, local language games, or formalized, autonomous systems (cf. Bloomfield, 1933/1961; Humboldt, 1836/1988; Lyotard, 1979/1993; Saussure, 1916/1959). Discourse must always be temporally distended. There isn't one single unbroken chain connecting all past, present, and future utterances, but innumerable strands (some interweaving, some dispersed, some terminated); these strands propagate at different speeds and with different scopes. No utterance affects society "as a whole"—as Foucault (1971/1977g) observes, "'The whole of society' is precisely that which should not be considered except as something to be destroyed. And then, we can only hope that it will never exist again" (p. 233)—and most only produce immediate, local effects (cf. Kaufer and Carley, 1994, p. 25).

- Time is not an added dimension to space that exists all-at-once (i.e., as a panchronic timescape) even if experienced sequentially, a flat plane of simultaneity spanning the entire universe, or an unfolding continuity. Rather, time is relative, granular, discontinuous, yet also productive: Time is traumatic, but also fecund—a dispersion of localized, contingent continuations and disjunctions without an essential, *a priori* continuity.

- Communication is less a matter of sharing space (proximity) than of *sharing time* (synchronicity). Interlocutors—even proto-interlocutors such as infants interacting with their parents (cf. Butterworth and Grover, 1988)—cannot simply be in spatial proximity; they must also be reciprocally "attuned" to each other in what Rommetveit (1974, p. 78) has called a *temporarily shared social reality* (TSSR). This creates an unfolding phenomenological space or a textual space (Nystrand, 1982c). For example, even though a book may sit for years on a shelf in my office, I am not synchronized to the author's text until I finally pull it off the shelf and start reading. And I must resist the lure or annoyance of distractions if I want to stay in synchrony with the text.

- To keep discourses relatively stable (i.e., to keep people relatively synchronized through discourse) requires a massive, sustained effort carried out by educational institutions, media outlets, political institutions, religious institutions, etc.; and researchers have discussed how the mass distribution of documents made nation-building possible because people could be synchronized or imagined by and through texts in ways not available before the printing press. Because discourses are not perpetual motion machines, they must be sustained by people with vested interests who are willing to enforce these official discourses through schools until they become almost automatic for people to use and accept without question (Bourdieu, 1982/1991, p. 45). This is the part of the human cost, the violence of a system in which "the speech of the few has drowned out the bitter silence of the many" (Spellmeyer, 1993b, p. x; cf. Chase, 1926, p. 14, and T. Johnson, 2001, p. 632). As Nietzsche (1887/1992b) once remarked, "pain is the most powerful aid to mnemonics" (p. 497).
- Utterances and their consequences are subjected to discipline—that is, they must be made docile, useful, and predictable, as must human beings (cf. Foucault, 1975/1995; Nietzsche, 1887/1992b). Thus, discourses are sites of constant struggle and negotiation (Vološinov, 1929/1986).
- There is a tyranny in associating meanings only with communication—as if there cannot be meanings in the absence of communication.
- Whatever stability of meanings an utterance has over time is a result of, not the cause of, the stability of its consequences.
- The utterances with the most stable meanings, then, may be those that are the least consequential (i.e., that propagate the fewest number of consequences).17

As much as I would like this list to persuade readers that meaning consequentialism has "more to it" than will be manifest in this book, I also want to avoid the possibility that it will persuade readers that meaning consequentialism has "more to it" than it actually has (at the time of this book's publication). One significant lacuna—the most significant of all lacunae that I confront—is my inability *at this time* to provide a crisp analytic definition of *consequences*. The meaning of an utterance or text is its consequences—OK, but what are these consequences? By what criteria do we identify them? And how do we avoid misidentifying them? Or does meaning consequentialism entail that whatever consequences are *ascribed* to an utterance or text *are* meanings of it? And, if so, doesn't this lead us into the abyss of subjective meanings and unbreachable solipsism?

I take some comfort in the fact that I am not the first person to confront questions such as these and find myself without ready, straight-forward answers. For example, consider Wittgenstein's (1953/1968) repeated (and cryptic) references to consequences in *Philosophical Investigations:*

- For when should I call it a mere case of knowing, not seeing?— Perhaps when someone treats the picture as a working drawing, reads it as a blueprint. (Find shades of behaviour.—Why are they important? They have important consequences.) (II. xi.202)
- Why can't my right hand give my left hand money?—My right hand can put it into my left hand. My right hand can write a deed of gift and my left hand a receipt.—But the further practical consequences would not be those of a gift. When the left hand has taken the money from the right, etc., we shall ask: "Well, and what of it?" And the same could be asked if a person had given himself a private definition of a word; I mean, if he has said the word to himself and at the same time directed his attention to a sensation. (I.268)
- Does it follow from the sense-impressions which I get that there is a chair over there?—How can a proposition follow from sense-impressions? Well, does it follow from the propositions that describe sense-impressions? No.—But don't I infer that a chair is there from impressions, from sense-data?—I make no inference!—and yet I sometimes do. I see a photograph for example, and say "There must have been a chair over there" or again "From what I can see here I infer that there is a chair over there." That is an inference; but not one belonging to logic. An inference is a transition to an assertion; and so also to the behaviour that corresponds to the assertion. 'I draw the consequences' not only in words, but also in action. (I.486)

Each instance seems to refer to consequences that are not, in themselves, linguistic, but either practical or behavioral: (a) seemingly indistinguishable actions are found to be quite different if one considers the different consequences they produce (i.e., these actions are meaningful because they are consequential, and they are distinguishable from each other—are recognized to be/mean different actions—because they have different consequences); (b) one cannot perform actions that do not have consequences, but this does not preclude that one acts—in a way that itself has consequences—in order to perform another action, which is not actually performed and, so, is not consequential and, so, is not meaningful; and (c) whatever consequences may be, they cannot be reduced to relations that are purely logical (e.g., if *s,* then *p; s,* consequently, *p*) or lexicogrammatical (e.g., if Tom is a bachelor, then Tom is an unmarried man), but must include the concrete effects of utterances and texts.

But we seem no closer to understanding *consequences* by calling them *effects;* for all of our questions remain. Which effects? All of them? By what criteria can we know what constitutes a *real* effect? Wittgenstein recognizes the dilemma:

> When I say that the orders "Bring me sugar" and "Bring me milk" make sense, but not the combination "Milk me sugar," that does not mean that the utterance of this combination of words has no effect. And if its effect is that the other person stares and gapes, I don't on that account call it the order to stare and gape, even if that was precisely the effect that I wanted to produce. (I.498)

But it is a dilemma that he does not satisfactorily resolve, unless one is willing to agree with Read and Guetti's (1999) claim that the absence of "explicit treatment[s] of these consequences" in Wittgenstein's work results, not from his ongoing struggle to understand the consequences of utterances, but from "the magnitude or, perhaps better, the 'depth' of his conception of them: because such consequences are fundamentally *'presumptive'* both to Wittgenstein's descriptions of meaningful linguistic practice and to that practice itself, any general account of them has quite literally gone without saying" (p. 290).

Whether Wittgenstein is prompted by profundity or the fear of absurdity (or by something else entirely), I agree with Read and Guetti that a consequence of Wittgenstein's thinking is the preservation of the familiar distinction—to be discussed in Chapter 3—between the meaningful *consequences* of words "from the various non-communicative, non-meaningful *effects* that words may have on us: for example, effects of nuance and connotation consequent upon non-communicative particularities of expression in poetry" (p. 304, emphasis added). For Read and Guetti—and for Read and Guetti's Wittgenstein—the difference between the meaningful consequence and the non-meaningful effect is that the former "is immanent to language-in-action, to language interwoven with non-linguistic action and with the world, but not, in either case—and this is crucial—as any kind of outside to that language" (p. 302), whereas the latter is outside of it:

> But the obvious, measurable, and special "consequences" of meaningful linguistic developments—what such developments always accomplish, unless there is some drastic failure in communication—is a continuing change to grammar [i.e., conceived, not as a static structure of rules that stand apart from linguistic usage, but as "*a description of our interleaved linguistic and nonlinguistic actions in all their dynamism, used—presented—as a description of a set of inter-relations of the sentences, etc., in question*" (pp. 298–299)]. We may see, think, and act from these expressions; but as we do so they work to adjust what *might* always be said anywhere to what *may*—what properly can—be said here and now. So when Wittgenstein insists that meaningful expressions must make a "difference," we should understand that this difference is initially and always indicated in the development of our empirical assertions *into local and timely* presumptions *that enable further assertion.* The consequences that meaningful developments have—which no "process" could have, be it as "dynamic" as one cares, still it cannot "process" its own rules as language-in-action continually does—are in this sense well described as *grammatical* consequences. (And such grammatical consequences—meaningful consequences—must, we repeat, we distinguished from the "grammatical effects" and the mere psychological associations and effects which attend particular verbal formulations, and which are so vital in literature,

and in relation to the difficulty of adequately translating one natural language to another.) (p. 305)

grammar

✱

Much of this discussion I find attractive: that a grammar is not a *set
of abstract rules* that govern linguistic behavior, but a *description* of our
amalgamated linguistic and nonlinguistic actions; that our linguistic
and nonlinguistic actions always have "local and timely" consequences
for and made manifest by subsequent linguistic behavior; that meaning
is not reducible to physical, neurological, or psychological processes.

However, I find it quite interesting that Read and Guetti and
the Read-Guetti Wittgenstein, although they wish to think through
meaning in terms of consequences, cannot embrace—cannot account
for, do not wish to account for—all of the consequences of utterances and texts. Some consequences, it seems—especially those "so vital
in literature" but otherwise so inert for Read and Guetti (and many
other theorists)—aren't merely less consequential than other consequences; rather, they aren't *really* consequential at all. They are affective—hence, *affecting*—but not consequential. I see no other motivation for making this distinction than a desire to avoid the messiness of
these consequences that confound categorization; and the motivation
is only stronger if this messiness isn't conceived of as just *messiness,* but
misrule. Thinking through meaning in terms of consequences can lead
to consequences that, charitably, are counterintuitive and that, not-so-
charitably, are patently absurd; and we do not pursue patently absurd
ideas (otherwise, they would not be patently absurd!).

At some level, I also think that Read and Guetti recognize that this
distinction is not as clear-cut as they might wish: the clue is in their peculiar parenthetical comment. Consider what Read and Guetti do *not*
write: "and which are so vital in literature, and in relation to the difficulty of translating *literary texts from* one natural language to another."
If these psychological effects, etc., are of importance only for those
who study literary texts, not those who study *grammar* (in Read and
Guetti's sense) or language generally, why would these effects have any
bearing on the translation of one natural language into another—assuming, *as I do not,* that there are such things as *natural languages*—if
what is being translated is a non-literary utterance or text (e.g., a mathematical equation)? Wouldn't this kind of *translation* be primarily a
search for synonymous words or phrases or sentences *between* the two
languages? If so, why would psychological effects have any more bearing on this process than it would for those more mundane instances in

which people convert or equate, or, dare I say, translate words into synonymous words or phrases *within* their own natural language, if such
synonyms are even to be had? And if these psychological effects must
be taken into account when discussing synonymy, then the only kind
of language that would meet Read and Guetti's criterion of conse-
quentialness would be that which is resistant to synonymy, that which
is immune to synonymy, that which cannot be put into other words,
that which cannot be paraphrased. But, then, Read and Guetti's effort
to avoid absurdity leads them right into it, for the kind of discourse
which most resists translation—if one takes seriously the complaints
of translators—is literary discourse, especially when its effects (consequences? meanings?) depend upon the peculiar properties of specific
words (e.g., rhyme schemes, stress patterns, puns, etc.).

    However, even if Read and Guetti's argument itself ends in absur-
dity, I readily admit that the absurd consequences of their argument—
which is obscured by the fact that they do not see any absurdities—are
far less counterintuitive than my own. Some absurdities may be more
absurd than others. After all, isn't it obvious that we should carefully
distinguish (meaningful) consequences from (meaningless) correlations? Who would reasonably think otherwise? If, as a consequence of
reading a text, I decide that I regret spending $25 for it, is *that* con-
sequence a meaning of the text? Or the fact that I blinked, say, 3026
times while reading it? And isn't this kind of absurdity precisely the
kind that Wittgenstein (1953/1968) confronts when he decides that
"Milk me sugar" cannot be an "order to stare and gape, even if that
was precisely the effect that [he] wanted to produce"? Surely meaning consequentialism, if it leads to such absurdities, must be rejected!
But, (always) against expectations—this is a very *unexpected* project,
surprising and repeatedly *surprised*—I embrace this absurdity, which
I think is only apparently absurd (as opposed to Read and Guetti's
absurdity, which I think is only apparently reasonable); for I suggest
that Wittgenstein's account holds only to the extent that this (hypothetical) utterance does not result in someone's coming to believe that
the speaker, in fact, was ordering the other person to "stare and gape."
Had someone, however unlikely, actually done so (i.e., had the utterance actually propagated that particular consequence), *then the utterance "Milk me sugar" would have that meaning,* whether we want it to
or not; but that meaning would not comprise the total Meaning of the
utterance, which would include the consequences for both speaker and

intended listener. Similarly, if someone came to believe that the text I read said something to the effect that "You should regret purchasing this text," or if someone believed that the text represented some kind of elaborate *score* for a series of blinks—perhaps constructed by an eccentric devotee of Gilbert Austin's (1806) *Chironomia*—then these would in fact be meanings of the texts. In short, the Meaning of a text has no *a priori* constraints that can rule out even the most *absurd* readings, but only *a posteriori* constraints: *We should rule out meanings of a text (from our own vantage at a given point in time and space) not by identifying meanings that are impossible for it to have had, have, or ever have, but by identifying consequences that it has not (yet) had.* (Notice that this claim is normative, for it is quite obvious that people can exclude and have excluded meanings—exclusions that, if one has the power to do so, are enforced.)

This discussion hardly settles what consequences are, but my hope is that it at least provides readers with some kind of direction for following along a thinking through of meaning in terms of consequences that is not so much *dis*oriented as *non*-oriented because its counterintuitiveness entails that very little of substance can be taken for granted. And I also hope—this is a very *hopeful* project, oriented toward the future, the *futural*—that readers will find that I do not take my own arguments for granted, either. What I have already argued, and what I will argue, I assert with confidence, not with certainty; what I offer is a series of bold conjectures to be examined, not a list of dogmas to be defended at all costs. I agree with Orr's (1990) critical-rationalist stance that "bold and creative theoretical variations are required for epistemological progress" (p. 118) and that we can learn from even a failed conjecture; but at the same time, I believe that we should not reject a theory immediately for failing particular tests or for failing to provide ready-made answers to all questions. In short, what I am asking for is not an indefinite immunization of meaning consequentialism from critique, but, as Feyerabend (1975/1993) might put it, a *period of grace* in which an inability to immediately answer all questions or reconcile all initial refutations does not immediately consign meaning consequentialism to the scrap heap of theories; for if we cannot discuss or propose what we do not *know,* then we should all be reduced to the stillness of Cratylus or of Wittgenstein at the end of his *Tractatus Logico-Philosophicus:* "Whereof one cannot speak, thereof one must be silent" (7). Eternal silence would enshroud the universe once more.

CHAPTER OUTLINE

Books are often expected to be, if not definitive studies, then at least studies with a significant degree of closure. Unfortunately, if one wishes to engage topics as ancient and profound as meaning and time substantively, even the lengthiest book will be largely incomplete, especially if the theory of meaning and its relationship to time one advocates resists in varying degrees and for various reasons some consequences of (possibly) every classical, modern, and contemporary theory of meaning. Because meaning consequentialism can take so little for granted, its critique of meaning apriorism must be extensive and its theory building incremental. To do otherwise would open me to the charges of making hasty generalizations, gross oversimplifications, and deliberate obfuscations. However, the critique and theory-building, though they will be laboriously developed, cannot be pursued without providing readers with some sense of where they might be headed, which is why I provided an overview of meaning consequentialism in the previous section. Incrementalism is not blind groping, even if the outcome is underdetermined. Not every assertion I make about meaning apriorism or meaning consequentialism can be supported with arguments without swelling this book beyond all limits, which makes it all the more necessary that those issues which I do address in depth be handled adroitly.

Chapters 2 through 6 are organized around the three temporal principles of meaning apriorism, exploring the implications of these temporal principles and illustrating them through an extended investigation of their intersections with one or more locative principles; these chapters also propose careful arguments supporting particularly important premises or sets of premises of meaning consequentialism that complicate and reconfigure some of the issues raised in antecedent chapters.

Chapters 2 and 3 interrogate the limitations of theories of meaning that assume a panchronic conception of time. More specifically, Chapter 2, "The Principle of Panchronism: Eternity, Mysticism, and Interpretation," presents a critique of atemporal conceptions of time implicit in metaphysical and mystical treatments of meaning (e.g., Augustine, trans. 1992; Bhaktivedanta, trans. 1972; Leibniz, 1840/1968b; Plotinus, trans. 1956/2000; Siorvanes, 1996), including their links to the panchronic "block universe" of physicists and philosophers (e.g., Barbour, 1999; Einstein, 1916/1961; H. Price, 1996). This chapter also briefly explores the atemporality of rationalism (e.g., Frege, 1918–1919/1984a, 1918–1919/1984b; Wittgenstein, 1922/1981) and some of the manifestations of both mysticism and rationalism in rhetoric and composition studies, particularly in the attempt to conceptualize texts as containers of intrinsic content or underlying propositional structures (e.g., Bracewell, 1999; D. Olson, 1977; van Wijk and Sanders, 1999). And in Chapter 3, "Panchronism and Consequentialism: The Labor of Meaning and the End of Interpretation," I advocate abandoning the conception of interpretation as an intermediary between the meaning of an utterance and its listeners or readers and for replacing the inertia and determinism of the principle of panchronism with a consequentialist account of the immense *effort* (i.e., *the labor of meaning*) expended in the ultimately quixotic attempt to control and perpetuate meanings through time.

Chapters 4 and 5 shift the explication and analysis to a consideration of the second temporal principle of meaning apriorism. Chapter 4, "The Principle of Simultaneity: Absolute Time and the Spatialization of Society, Language, and Mind," begins with a critical examination of *discourse community, interpretive community, language, idiolect, intentions,* and other theoretical constructions that, operating within a framework of absolute time, treat language and its meanings as a flattened, fully present totality; it also briefly discusses the connections between absolute time and the principle of formalism. Key theorists discussed and critiqued include J. L. Austin, Lloyd Bitzer, Leonard Bloomfield, George Campbell, Noam Chomsky, Donald Davidson, Daniel C. Dennett, Stanley Fish, M. A. K. Halliday, Roy Harris, Martin Heidegger, Ferdinand de Saussure, and Patrick Suppes. In response to this analysis, Chapter 5, "Simultaneity and Consequentialism: The Distensions and Discontinuities of Mind and Community," proffers a consequentialist account of mind and community that incorporates and explicates their necessarily temporal distension. The central argument of this chapter is that one does not first have a language, community, idiolect, or mind and then have meanings added onto them, but that, on the contrary, the potential for meaningfulness serves as a precondition for language, community, idiolect, and mind; and this potential for meaningfulness—i.e., what it means for something to be meaningful, not what particulars are meaningful and in what ways—is not determined by languages, communities, idiolects, or minds.

Chapter 6, "The Principle of Durativity: Duration, Evolution, Intertextuality, and the Problem of Surplus Meaning," presents an extended critique of holistic, (strongly) intertextual, and developmental theories of meaning, and it examines links between the principle of evolution and durative and absolute conceptions of time. It also investigates in what ways the principle of durativity extends into conceptions of mind in terms of continuity and the multiplicity of meanings in terms of polysemy. Important figures in this chapter include Mikhail Bakhtin, Roland Barthes, Henri Bergson, Michel Foucault, Saul Kripke, Hilary Putnam, and Paul Ricoeur.

Having explicated the three temporal principles of meaning apriorism, I am finally positioned, in Chapter 7, "Meaning and Time," to provide a detailed sketch of a consequentialist theorization of time that replaces the inadequately conceived "times" of panchronism, simultaneity, and durativity with a positive account of time and its relationship with meaning in terms of *asymmetry, aperiodicity, indeterminacy, granularity, relativity, discontinuity,* and *fecundity.* Such a positive account of time is necessary, I argue, because meaning consequentialism is a positive account of meaning in which meaning is not hampered by or extraneous to time, but constituted within in. In this chapter, the phenomenology of Emmanuel Levinas and the theoretical physics of Ilya Prigogine and Isabelle Stengers figure prominently.

In Chapter 8, "Severity, Charity, and the Consequences of Student Writing: Toward a Consequentialist Writing Pedagogy," I speculate about the potential usefulness of meaning consequentialism for current issues within rhetoric and composition studies, particularly in the resolution of problems created by an unnecessary bifurcation of texts and writers into the categories of *academic* or *nonacademic;* in the enhancement of the "consequentiality" of student writing; and in the exploration of the ethical implications, if any, for writing and writing pedagogy of a consequentialist philosophy of discourse. Some of the researchers whose work is discussed in this chapter include Arthur Applebee, Deborah Brandt, Linda Flower, Bruce Herzberg, David Kaufer and Kathleen Carley, Joseph Petraglia, Aaron Schutz and Anne Ruggles Gere, W. Ross Winterowd, and Stephen Witte; I also extend and complicate my analysis of writing instruction in terms of "pedagogies of charity" and "pedagogies of severity" (K. Porter, 2001).

Finally, the book *ends* not so much with a conclusion, but an acknowledgment of the lack of closure to this (or any) book.

2 The Principle of Panchronism: Eternity, Mysticism, and Interpretation

Brahman is indestructible and eternally existing, and there is no change in its constitution.

—A. C. Bhaktivedanta

The grass may wither, the flower may fade,
but the word of our God will endure for ever.

—Isaiah

You are unchangeably eternal [. . .]. Just as you knew heaven and earth in the beginning without that bringing any variation into your knowing, so you made heaven and earth in the beginning without that meaning a tension between past and future in your activity.

—St. Augustine

Attir'd with Stars, we shall for ever sit,
    Triumphing over Death, and Chance, and thee O Time.

—John Milton

This chapter will critique what might be called *metaphysical* manifestations of meaning apriorism that invoke as locus of or foundation for meaning a panchronic, transcendental, steady-state dimension either of pure spirit and divinity or of pure logic and rationality (though these need not be mutually exclusive dimensions). In the first two sections, I examine attempts to postulate God as the certain foundation of meaning for *linguistic* and *natural* signs. The third section explores the limits of that foundation, for mystics have feared that an effable

God is no God at all; consequently, God is both the ground of expression and its limit. In the fourth section, I make clear the atemporality of mystical conceptions of meaning, an atemporality that correlates to the atemporality of God and the universe itself; and I argue that the atemporal panchronism of semantic mysticism is analogous to the atemporality of logic and the "block time" model of contemporary physics and philosophy of time. The fifth and sixth sections apply the arguments of the preceding sections to a consideration of the special problems, and the equally problematic efforts to resolve them, that attend the interpretation of sacred writings presumed to be infallible. The seventh and eighth sections discuss the role of panchronism outside of semantic mysticism, particularly its prominence within theories that manifest the principle of rationalism and its limited play within rhetoric and composition studies.

GOD AS THE FOUNDATION OF MEANING

> Yet nobody should regard anything as his own, except perhaps a lie.
>
> —St. Augustine

Beset by the complexities of discourse, some theorists, philosophers, and theologians, unable otherwise to secure the meaning and truth of representations, have in the last resort appealed to the God, who serves—directly, in the form of the Holy Spirit (Corner, 1990, p. 218) or Christ (McEvoy, 1995, p. 7), or indirectly, through the institutions of the Church (Corner, 1990, p. 218; cf. Fischer and Abedi, 1990, p. 141) or even of Plato's (trans. 1871/1964a) essences—as foundation and arbiter of linguistic and non-linguistic signs (Baudrillard, 1983, p. 10). For example, twentieth-century theologian Schubert Ogden argues that "the word spoken in Jesus Christ [is] the norm of all other words" (Funk, 1966, p. 97). Without such an anchor, communication seems unthinkable: Augustine, in *De Magistro,* denies "the possibility of human communication through rational signs (words) without a knowledge of reality (God)" (G. Kennedy, 1980, p. 152). One might think of this as yet another transcendental "proof" of God's existence: If communication is impossible without God, then the fact of communication confirms the existence of God.

Language has been construed as a direct gift from God bestowed upon humanity by, among others, Thomas Hobbes (1668/1994) and George Berkeley (cf. Land, 1985), or it has been thought, insofar as it is rational, to provide "an intimation of the divine scheme of things," so that, for twelfth-century philosopher John of Salisbury, understanding language and grammar—that is, for John, understanding *Latin*—is tantamount to understanding God's plan for the world (Pattison, 1982, p. 80).[1] One need not assume so provincial a perspective: Eighteenth-century philosopher James Harris, for example, attributed linguistic universals to "the logical structure of the word and the common dependence of all minds on the divine mind" (Land, 1985, p. 198). God has even been supposed to assume a much more active stance, speaking and writing through people and even determining how audiences react to those utterances and texts (G. Kennedy, 1980, p. 122, 127)—a God who is, in this extreme case, both speaker and audience, ceaselessly reading aloud to Himself from a script He has written in advance.

DIVINITY, LANGUAGE, NATURE

Things admit of being used as symbols because nature is a symbol, in the whole, and in every part. Every line we can draw in the sand has expression; and there is no body without its spirit or genius.

—Ralph Waldo Emerson

But language is more than a gift of God for reserved for humanity; rather, according to the Bible, the world itself was brought into existence through performative acts of naming: "God said, 'Let there be light,' and there was light" (Gen. 1:1). Or, as the creation appears in its New Testament incarnation: "In the beginning the Word already was [. . .]. He [the Word] was with God at the beginning, and through him all things came to be; without him no created thing came into being" (John 1:1–3).[2] As Barthes (1971/1977i) observes, naming is a "suzerain" act (p. 136): God's names are not descriptions of existence, but commands that bring entities into existence. Names precede the objects to which they refer, constitute them, and determine them fully. In this mythology of the word, objects appear immaterial and ephemeral in comparison to the immutability of divine words or concepts or meanings, so that, as Burke (1962/1966b) would put it, instead of words being the signs of things, things become the signs for words. God subsequently taught Adam the proper names of things, but this knowledge was lost with the downfall of the tower of Babel (Hobbes, 1668/1994, I.iii.1–2); and this first language, the *lingua Adamica*, was thought to be "a language which did not consist merely of conventional signs but which expressed rather the very nature and essence of things" (Cassirer, 1944/1972, p. 130).

Reality, then, from the perspective of the principle of semantic mysticism, is structured by a language and, consequently, is structured like a language: Nature has a "grammar" (Reid, 1937/1989, p. 48). Thus, it could be said that human beings dwell within the divine language, or *Logos* (Pattison, 1982, p. 21). Each physical object, as Augustine thought, would literally be an inherently meaningful sign from God (Murphy, 1974, p. 287), not a purely physical object with an inessential meaning merely attributed to it by someone; and, according to Berkeley, the sum total of these visible objects comprise the "universal language" of God (Ryan, 1994, p. 126).[3] For the eighteenth-century Puritan Jonathan Edwards, reality is

> essentially communicative, a system of signification in which everything is united as signifier to signified, type to antitype. Even inanimate things "communicate" this movement of intentionality, for their very existence and intelligibility depends upon their place in the divine discourse. Every pronouncement is an invitation to ontological revision, and every being obtains but tenuous grasp on reality as a fleeting anticipation of something else in terms of which it will be fulfilled. (Daniel, 1994, p. 2)

If one could perceive objects with perfect—*godlike*—vision, "there would be no meaning distinct from reality perceived; understanding would be equivalent to perceiving" (Levinas, 1972/1987, p. 75). From this perspective, God is knowable—insofar as God is knowable—through a careful study of the natural world: Sacred writings aren't the only path leading to the divine because "the universe is an observable effect of God and, therefore, a means of understanding God" (Glejzer, 1998, p. 333).

Those thinkers involved in the (pre-positivist) scientific study of nature did not necessarily sense a conflict between the natural and the spiritual. For example, Isaac Newton, who pursued alchemy with as much intensity as mathematics,

> looked on the whole universe and all that is in it *as a riddle,* as a secret which could be read by applying pure thought to certain evidence, certain mystic clues which God had laid about the world to allow a sort of philosopher's treasure hunt [. . .]. He regarded the universe as a cryptogram set by the Almighty—just as he himself wrapt the discovery of the calculus in a cryptogram which he communicated with Leibnitz. (Keynes, 1947/1956, p. 279).[4]

Similarly, the sixteenth-century physician Paracelsus could comfortably mix the study of medicine with astrology, believing that God had inscribed useful medical knowledge in the "firmament" (D. Olson, 1994, p. 162). And for Berkeley, science is nothing other than the "study of the grammar—the structural rules—of the divine language (the 'analogy' of its signs). Everyday learning is *understanding* the language of ideas; science is the *formulation of its grammatical rules*" (Land, 1985, p. 117). Speculations such as these became untenable within the scientific community, of course, as scientists increasingly considered their intellectual work to be in opposition to any kind of metaphysical inquiry, culminating in the argument by logical positivists, such as Ayer (1946/1952), that statements that cannot in principle be subject to empirical verification—such those of religion, ethics, and metaphysics—are *meaningless.*

THE INEFFABILITY OF THE DIVINE

God is unspeakable.

—St. Augustine

If God serves as the Alpha of meaning, He may also serve as the Omega—both ground and limit. For Augustine (trans. 1997, I.13), God is ultimately unspeakable, unnamable—as if being able to name God or contain Him within meaning would somehow exercise some kind of control over Him. According to Glejzer (1998, p. 336), some medieval thinkers assumed that God could not be represented; and several non-orthodox sects, such as the Nestorians of the fourth century, the Paulicians of the seventh century, and the Iconoclast heresies of the eighth and ninth centuries, acted on such beliefs by destroying religious symbols and icons and by persecuting idolaters (Fortescue, 1910/1999). The Word of God was ultimately unknowable as well for Origen (185–254 A.D.) because "the inspiration of Scripture contains far more meaning than [interpreters] can ever succeed in fathoming" (G. Kennedy, 1980, p. 139). Not only do the scriptures contain far more meaning than human beings can ever know, but, according to the hermeneutic principle of the "sensus plenoir," they also contain far more meanings than any "human author could have consciously intended" (Hirsch, 1967, p. 136). Similarly, Qur'anic exegetes can only with humility complete their exposition by saying *"wa Allahu a'lam,"* or, "God knows best" (Fischer and Abedi, 1990, p. 142). God, then, makes language and meaning possible, but also marks the point at which they become impossible—that is, God marks the *a priori* point at which language and meaning collapse.

PANCHRONISM, ETERNITY, AND BLOCK TIME

That which neither has been nor will be, but simply possesses being; that which enjoys stable existence as neither in process of change nor having ever changed—that is Eternity. Thus we come to the definition: the Life—instantaneously entire, complete, at no point broken into period or part—which belongs to the Authentic Existent by its very existence, this is the thing we were probing for—this is Eternity.

—Plotinus

[T]here are no basic ontological differences between past, present, and future events. All events exist tenselessly in the network of earlier, later, and simultaneity temporal relations.

—L. Nathan Oaklander

If God is a theorist's choice for the foundation of meaning, then one would expect, for that theorist, that the temporality of meaning would be intimately connected to the temporality of God. And this expectation is not disappointed. For example, according to Augustine (trans. 1992, XI.13), God resides not in time, but outside of it, in eternity, in which the whole of time is present; and temporality—i.e., the apparent flow of time—is a lack, an imperfection, a failure of finite human beings to experience the wholeness of time. God made time itself: There was no time before the creation of the world (XI.15), and time will come to an end when God ends the world (XI.36). The present, in which human beings live, is paradoxically a *uchronia* (i.e., a *no-time*), for, argues Augustine, if the present had a duration, however fleeting, that duration could be further subdivided into a past and future (p. XI.20). The experience of time is, rather, a "distension" of the soul into its tripartite aspects of *memory, awareness,* and *expectation* (XI.26).

Because past, present, and future already exist and have always existed, there are no surprises for God: He is panchronic and omniscient. All truths for God are *a priori* truths, even though they are "facts which [human beings] can learn only through history [a posteriori]" (Leibniz, 1840/1968b, p. 14). God sees the entire universe, extended temporally and spatially, in its unity, in its true form as a single structure, such as Benedict de Spinoza's *facies totius universi* (i.e., "the face of the whole universe") (E. Harris, 1988, p. 38) or Dante's vision of a *vertical,* atemporal hell, purgatory, and paradise, in which

> everything that on earth is divided by time, here, in this verticality, coalesces into eternity, into pure simultaneous coexistence. Such divisions as time introduces—"earlier" and "later"—have no substance here; they must be ignored in order to understand this vertical world; everything must be perceived as being within a single time, that is, in the synchrony of a single moment; one must see this entire world as simultaneous [. . .] [i.e., as] an environment outside time altogether [. . .]. (Bakhtin, 1975/1981, p. 157)

We must keep this understanding of atemporality in mind when encountering passages that appear to allow for an openness or indeterminacy to meaning. For example, Aquinas argues that the meaning of New Testament events will not be exhausted until the return of Christ at the end of the world, in an analogous fashion to the *exhaustion* of the meaning of Old Testament events by the first coming of Christ (Preus, 1969, p. 58). For Aquinas, the meaning of events "can only be revealed—indeed, can only be constituted outside of God's mind" after the fact, a posteriori, embodied in history, and, consequently, all historical events, even those involving Christ, are "subject to further interpretation" because "'things passing through their course signify something else'" (*res cursum suum peragentes significant aliquid aliud*) (Preus, 1969, pp. 55, 56). However, the openness of the meaning of these signs is illusory, for one could fully know their meaning if one could perceive them from the panchronic and omniscient perspective of God. From the vantage of eternity, the second coming—and the exhaustion of meaning entailed by it—is as real and present as the creation of the world: Like Leibniz's (1720/1968c, 1840/1968b) monads, each sign of the Bible seems imprinted with the entirety of the past and the future.[5] Further, in eternity, the causality from antecedent to consequent does not hold; one could argue that the events of the Old Testament "prefigure" Christ not by setting the terms by which Christ must and in fact does subsequently act but by their necessarily *echoing* the yet-to-occur actions of Christ. Christ could even be seen teleologically as the Aristotelian final cause for the events of the Old Testament—or, as we shall see, as the *backward cause* of those events.

From the perspective of meaning apriorism, Old Testament events prefigure the New Testament in the sense that OT events are already "laden" with their NT meaning even as they occurred during the OT era. In contrast, I argue that events can *prefigure* other events only after the fact—i.e., prefiguration is, in essence, manufactured by a retrofitting a subsequent event onto the antecedent event so that the former appears to prophesize the latter. For meaning consequentialism, then, for one sign to prefigure another sign requires a *future effort* on the part of those interpreting the signs.

The mystical visions of eternity perhaps surprisingly resemble the ironically named *block time* of modern physics and philosophy of time (Davies, 1995, p. 72). The name is ironic because, in block time, the time that we experience as passage or flow, with boundaries between past, present, and future, disappears. Time becomes only one more coordinate to be plotted for the positions of objects in a 4-dimensional space-time continuum, with each dimension simply a "degree of freedom" or "variable" that is "needed to describe a topological manifold" (Ray, 1991, p. 82). For Einstein (1916/1961), the 3-dimensional world that humans experience "happens," whereas 4-dimensional reality merely "exists" (p. 140), resembling Plotinus's (trans. 1956/2000, III.3) stable eternity and his fellow Neo-Platonist Proclus's "imparticipable time" immune to change (Siorvanes, 1996, p. 134). Events do not *happen* in space-time, but are only *encountered* (Whitrow, 1972/1975, p. 103), and time is reduced to a "differentiation of space" (E. Harris, 1988, p. 58; cf. Alexander, 1920). In block time, the "events in the past and future have to be every bit as real as events in the present [. . .]. Events and moments have to exist 'all at once' across a span of time" (Davies, 1995, p. 72). In its most extreme form—and certainly controversial within physics—time disappears entirely:

> The world is to be understood, not in the dualistic terms of atoms (things of one kind) that move in the framework and container of space and time (another quite different kind of thing), but in terms of more fundamental entities that fuse space and matter into the single notion of a possible arrangement, or configuration, of the entire universe. Such configurations, which can be fabulously richly structured, are the ultimate things [. . .].
>
> Space and time in their previous role as the stage of the world are redundant. There is no container. The world does not contain things, it is things. These things are Nows that, so to speak, hover in nothing. (Barbour, 1999, p. 16)

It would be improper to say that in block time the universe exists *simultaneously*—i.e., Bakhtin's "synchrony" mentioned earlier—because simultaneity is the point of intersection of objects *in* space-time, just as it would be improper to say that all objects occupy the same position on any of the other three dimensions[6]; rather, to conceptualize block time, we must do so from an atemporal perspective, what Huw Price (1996) refers to as "the view from nowhere" (p. 3).[7] For Price, an atemporal perspective places no priority on the past or the future in causal explanations, so that "the state of a system may depend on its future as well as its past" (p. 75). Correlations exist not only between objects that interacted in the past, but also between those that will interact in the future (p. 126); thus, there is no independence of objects from "incoming influences," no matter how remote their origins (p. 117). Price acknowledges that most physicists and philosophers of time, however much they might claim adherence to the block time universe, still find notions such as backward causation unpalatable; but, he argues, only from this atemporal perspective can certain peculiarities of quantum mechanics, in which systems seem to defy relativistic prohibitions on simultaneous action-at-a-distance by behaving as if they had advanced knowledge of future events, be reasonably explained.

Price sums up his argument thus: "[we] bear the marks of [our] future as [we] bear the marks of [our] past" (p. 242). But it is a summation of a view from a nowhen, a uchronia, that could apply equally well, I suggest, for those who subscribe to one variant or another of the principles of semantic mysticism and panchronism. From such a vantage, one might say, then, (a) that whatever verbal or written responses this very sentence—i.e., this section of my book that I am writing now—will generate are as *real* now, in the moment of its typing, as is this sentence itself, (b) that this sentence, even as I type it, invisibly *bears the marks* of its future consequences, and (c) that this very sentence was already waiting for me to encounter it twenty years ago, before even my birth, before even the creation of the world.

INERRANT SCRIPTURE

There is nothing so clear, and sure, and certain, as the Gospel.

—Samuel Mather

It cannot be that God's word has proved false.

—St. Paul

When the word of God which is really true, is false literally, it is true spiritually.

—Blaise Pascal

If one accepts that God is a perfect being with perfect knowledge of a past and a future that have the same ontological status as the present, and if one further accepts that God is, directly or indirectly, the author of the Bible, then it is reasonable to assume that the holy scriptures are themselves perfect. For example, it would be impossible for God, when speaking through his prophets, to offer prophecies that fail to come to pass, and it would be impossible for God to contradict himself. For

Augustine, the Bible is *entirely* "edifying," and even its most insignifi-
cant-seeming passage "teaches faith, hope and love" (Preus, 1969, 13);
and for Aquinas (trans. 1947), "nothing false can ever underlie the
literal sense of Holy Writ" (I.1.10). Luther, too, strongly believed in the
perfect unity of the Bible: "Luther's approach to Scripture was never
atomistic. He treated the Bible as a homogeneous whole. For him it
was not simply a set of unrelated books, but a divine library, selected
by the Holy Spirit himself, in which no part was superfluous and all
parts were interlaced [. . .]. Luther appealed again and again to 'the
constant and unanimous judgement of Scripture'" (A. Wood, 1969, p.
149). There are no superfluities:

> The Holy Spirit was concerned not merely with the
> inspiration of the writers or of their message. He
> descended to details and was responsible for the
> words and even the letters. "All the words of God are
> weighed, counted, and measured," Luther declared.
> Every word of Scripture is precious since it comes
> from the mouth of God, is written down and pre-
> served for us and will be proclaimed until the end of
> the age. (A. Wood, 1969, p. 142)

Luther believed that the Bible—at least the original texts (the *Verbum*
of the God), not their copies (the *verbum* of humanity)[8]—contained
no textual corruptions or infelicities because the "God of truth could
not authenticate a book which contained even the slightest element
of falsehood" (A. Wood, 1969, p. 144). So confident is Luther in the
perfection of the Bible that he is willing to insist that, "unless all is
believed, nothing is believed" (A. Wood, 1969, p. 150); to deny Christ
at a single point is, for Luther, to deny him utterly (A. Wood, 1969,
p. 151).

Consequently, copying, correcting, and translating sacred texts is a
very sensitive issue. Although many different versions of the Christian
Bible have been published, Islamic orthodoxy has resisted all efforts—
scholarly or otherwise—to "correct" the oral Qur'an:

> The effort to protect the oral Qur'an from deforma-
> tion due to tampering with the written text only be-
> gins with the *scriptio defectiva* and the ambiguities
> that remain even after diacriticals were introduced
> (vowels, punctuation, cantillation marks): they in-

volved vigilance, as well, against perennial efforts to
"improve" the transcript, including "straightening"
the grammar, replacing words with better ones [. . .]
or making the text conform to reason. (Fischer and
Abedi, 1990, pp. 127–128).

As we shall see in the following section, the promotion and maintenance of people's confidence in the infallibility of scripture—despite
not only the tensions people have read within scripture as well as the
shocks of events that appear to defy its timeless prophecies—have required the immense, sustained institutional labor of ages and a host
of dazzling hermeneutic contortions; for, unlike most other texts, sacred writings suffer inordinately from the failure of even a single passage because they are expected to be, as Luther would have it, without
blemish.

Efforts to Interpret Scripture

For him [seventh-century Byzantine theologian Maximus
Confessor] the mystery of Christ is the unique object of the
spiritual sense of Scripture; it is not so much a case of understanding something of Christ through the Scriptures as
of understanding the Scriptures through Christ, and beyond
them the whole of the created realm. He will when required
have recourse to the literal sense, but at the other end of the
spectrum he maintains that "the logoi of all beings are contained by the Word of God, while It is not contained by any
being." For Maximus the language of Scripture rests on an
inverted apex, but opens out to infinity.

—Nicholas Madden

Signs may be ambiguous, but Luther in the Dictata has discovered that words by themselves are disturbingly unambiguous and clear. God threatens. God commands. God
promises. Once Luther discovers it, he can scarcely contain
himself.

—James Samuel Preus

Any form of mysticism that assumes God is the infallible, omniscient author of the natural world or of holy writings will quickly confront the problem of how to reconcile or at least rationalize away clashing interpretations of sacred signs, for the meaning of signs within the Book of Nature or the Holy Writ are clearly not self-evident given the history of fractious heretical movements and incessant theological disputations; readers come away from their encounters with nature and scripture with quite different and even contradictory beliefs about their meanings. The problem, of course, is why should this be so, if God has, as it were, inscribed meaning directly into physical objects or if sacred signs are themselves embodiments of meaning. Let us narrow the focus a bit to consider only sacred writing: Why is it possible to *misinterpret* what God has written, if God is Himself the foundation of and guarantor for meaning? In other words, if God is the ground of meaning, then how is it possible for readings that deviate from God's intentions to be *meaningful at all?* Why doesn't a sacred text in question appear to be *without sense* to *all* readers incapable of discerning its proper message, rather than *appearing* to convey a *different, even deceptive message?* From whence arises this other "message," a message without a sender?

A second problem that theologians of antiquity faced, especially those such as Augustine and Jerome who valued their training in classical rhetoric, was to justify why sacred writings, such as the Bible, seem littered with internal contradictions and vulgarities, unworthy of God even though they are composed by divinity or through divine inspiration (T. Miller, 1997, p. 129)? As Nietzsche (1886/1992a) once observed with his characteristic acerbity, "It was subtle of God to learn Greek when he wished to become an author—and not to learn it better" (p. 276). Although, as we shall see, theologians and philosophers have repeatedly attempted to resolve this vexing problem—were it not a vexing problem, there would be no need for repeated attempts to "save the phenomena"—their varied solutions do not offer a new understanding of meaning that rejects a text, sacred or otherwise, as a stable, timeless locus of meaning, but, on the contrary, serve only to explain away misinterpretations or provide rigorous procedures for securing that presumed meaning. Of course, it is hardly surprising, given the devotion of the faithful to the scriptures, that so much ingenuity and effort would be expended in defending them, rather than in revolutionizing the understanding of meaning. In what follows, I will

focus on Christianity and the interpretation of the Bible, but it should
be pointed out that the problem of reconciling apparent contradictions
and clarifying ambiguities within sacred writings has been practiced
by, among others, Stoics, Rabbinic Jews, and Muslims (Fearghail,
1995; Fischer and Abedi, 1990).

The most obvious strategy to pursue, if possible, is to exclude from
the canon of sacred writings those texts that deviate from dogma.
Consistency is preserved simply by excising whatever threatens that
consistency: The texts that people misinterpret were presumed to be
not authored by God in the first place. For example, the Old and New
Testaments of the (varied) modern (versions of the) Bible are shad-
owed by heretical or non-canonical texts, such as the Book of Mormon
or the collection of texts referred to as the Apocrypha. This strategy,
however, can be of only limited use, for it presumes that at a certain
point the books that remain will be universally acknowledged to be
internally consistent and coherent—i.e., that at some point, everyone
will agree that the cutting should stop. The Manichean heresy of the
early Church demonstrates that this agreement cannot be taken for
granted: The Manicheans, of which Augustine was once a member, rejected the entire Old Testament because they believed that "its crudity
and the patent 'immorality' of its God and its saints proved that it was
no revelation of the God and Father of Jesus Christ" (Preus, 1969, p.
10). The struggle between the orthodox Church and the Manicheans,
then, was not over *methodology,* for both *agreed* on what to do with
supposedly "spurious" texts, but over the fact that the Manicheans
wielded a razor *too sharp* for then-contemporary orthodoxy. The contemporary and by now long-standing stability of the Biblical canon
should not blind us to the contentious and protracted struggle over its
finalization.

A second limitation of this strategy is its agonistic logic, which
fragments what was once thought to be a united Christianity into an
"Us" who accepts or rejects certain books contrarily rejected or accepted by a "Them": To exclude a book from one's canon is also to exclude
the adherents of that book from one's religion, and one need only look
to the conflicts between Catholics and Protestants as examples of the
horrors that such a strategy can generate. Ultimately, such a strategy
is too blunt an instrument to be satisfactory; not only did it fail to explain why people misinterpreted or rejected the purportedly divinely
authored texts, but it also couldn't eliminate, despite repeated applica-

tions, the ambiguities, tensions, and even contradictions readers encountered within the scriptures that remained—flaws all-too-uncomfortably visible to even some of the most devoted, charitable readers (e.g., the human sacrifice of Jephthah's daughter in Judges 11:1–40).[9] Further, the flaws couldn't be ignored for long, so readers keenly aware of them had to choose between abandoning their religious convictions or finding some way of rehabilitating the texts to preserve their perfection.

The problems facing Biblical commentators who undertook such a rehabilitation project cannot be underestimated, for, as Corner (1990) puts it, the Bible is more a "library" than a single text: "the Christian Scriptures are not a single book but a collection of texts, written (if one includes the Old Testament) in different languages over the space of a millennium [. . .]. This recognition reminds the interpreter that the unity of the biblical message has to be established by criticism and cannot be presumed in advance" (p. 221). Of course, most of the exegetes of the scriptures made precisely this presumption, believing that the Bible is in reality unified and that, through careful reasoning, diligent scholarship, or inspired introspection (or a combination thereof), this *a priori* unity could be made manifest, just as Leibniz (1840/1968b) posited that a single line described by a mathematical formula could be drawn through any seemingly random scattering of points plotted onto a graph in the exact order in which they were plotted.

One of the most common approaches was to concede that, on the most superficial level, the scriptures indeed contained passages that seemed vulgar or inconsistent with dogma; however, the subsequent claim was made that, at a deeper or higher level of understanding, these passages are edifying and in perfect harmony with established doctrine. Thus, the classical, two-tiered distinction between the *letter* and the *spirit* of the text was born, with various commentators differing over how much they valued either side of the opposition. Philo, a Jewish exegete writing in the second century B.C., argued that the literal meanings of the scriptures were important, but less so than the spiritual sense (Fearghail, 1995, p. 47). Origen divided the Bible into its *soma* (body) and *psuchê* (soul), with the former "clearly inferior to the hidden, underlying truth" expressed by the latter (Fearghail, 1995, p. 56); he also believed that "there were many things in the Scriptures which could not possibly be literally interpreted" without appearing "incomprehensible" (G. Kennedy, 1980, p. 138).

Augustine (trans. 1997, II.15), however, defended the literal meaning of the Bible, arguing that ambiguous passages in the text contain no truths that are not elsewhere expressed plainly, and his three
steps for the interpretation of obscure passages begins with a careful
check of punctuation and articulation (III.3); only if the literal meaning could not in any reasonable way be made to reconcile with the
rule of faith—i.e., only if the questionable passage could not be made
to fit with dogma—should the interpreter attempt to devise a recon-
ciliatory, figurative reading (trans. 1997, III.3–4; cf. Preus, 1969, p.
13). But even what seems to be literal cannot be so blithely accepted,
for Clement of Alexandria (c. 200 A.D.) warned against complacency
when interpreting those sections in which "literal" readings appeared
to make perfect sense, for often they "require[d] more careful attention
than obscure ones" (G. Kennedy, 1980, p. 137).

In the twelfth century, Hugh of St. Victor defended the integrity
of the literal meaning of the Bible, observing that interpreters cannot
"despise the meaning of the letter, since it has been put there by the
Spirit himself to lead [readers] to spiritual things," and that without
the literal level, readers could not reach the spiritual level, which is
always "harmonious and clear" (Preus, 1969, pp. 29, 31). Yet Hugh
also allowed that sometimes literal readings of Biblical passages would
be insensible, or *incongrua*. To save the text, Hugh suggested that the
Bible cannot be read only literally or historically—i.e., read in chronological order—but must be read allegorically according to the order
of *cognitio* (i.e., understanding) (Preus, 1969, pp. 31–33). For Hugh,
one can no more understand the Bible by reading it linearly from first
word to last than the people living during the Old Testament era could
understand the spiritual or Christological meaning of the succession of
events that they experienced:

> the Old Testament people, who of necessity lived in
> temporal order, cannot have lived in an understand-
> ing of what God's intention was, since they were
> without benefit of him [Christ] who unlocks the
> meaning of their own history. In fact, their own un-
> derstanding was bound to be confused by the fact
> that although the words they heard were referring to
> things present or discernible to them [*res₁*], the words
> did not yet advise them that these present *res* were
> themselves signs of other, future things (that is, New

> Testament things, [*res$_{tl}$*]). And so they were unaware
> that their whole history was an allegory [. . .]. Only
> those few who were specially inspired, or who sur-
> vived until the actual appearance of Christ, could
> have detected the allegorical character of their own
> history, for knowledge of the nativity, preaching, pas-
> sion, resurrection, and ascension of Christ are abso-
> lute conditions for penetrating the mysteries of the
> ancient figures. (Preus, 1969, p. 33)

Understanding, or *cognitio,* can properly begin for human beings only
with the appearance of Christ, for only then does the Old Testament
become "edifying" (Preus, 1969, p. 31).

When one hidden level of the texts was considered insufficient to
unify them, exegetes found it necessary—and relatively easy—to add
on a few more dimensions; for if a text can have one hidden dimension, what could prevent it from having more than one? According
to George A. Kennedy (1980), Origen subdivided the Bible so that
it had three levels: (a) the *letter/literal meaning,* "addressed to those
who are still children in soul and do not yet recognize God as their
father" (p. 138); (b) the *soul/moral meaning,* which contains "a specific
but non-literal application to the audience addressed" (p. 138); and
(c) the *spiritual/theological meaning,* which expresses "essential truths
of Christianity" (p. 138). The eleventh-century commentator Guibert
posited four levels to scripture—(a) the *historical level* of actual events,
(b) the *allegorical level* in which one thing stands for another, (c) the
tropological level of moral instruction, and (d) the *anagogical level* of ce-
lestial topics and spiritual enlightenment (Murphy, 1974, p. 302)—as
did Aquinas (1225 or 1227–1274 A.D.), who found the *literal* level accompanied by the *allegorical,* concerned with faith, the *moral,* with
love, and the *anagogical,* with hope (McEvoy, 1995, p. 21). Aquinas
also made another distinction between the *sensus historicus,* set by the
intention of the human author, which "means just what it says," and
the *sensus litteralis,* set by the intention of the divine author, who com-
prehends "all the senses of Scripture—literal and spiritual, plain and
hidden, present and future" (Preus, 1969, pp. 52, 54).

Still, the positing of "hidden" meanings of the text required some
explanation for why, exactly, these meanings are visible to some readers and invisible to the rest. The solution that theologians and philosophers devised was this: If the scriptures are infallible, then the fal-

libility that results in the misunderstanding of them must lie within the interpreters. Blame the readers, not the texts: The assumption, of course, is that misinterpretation results from an inadequacy from the usual perfectibility of texts and interpreters—i.e., that if meanings diverge, someone or something must be blamed as defective so that the underlying premises about stable, fixed, *a priori* meaning may remain in place. Conflicting interpretations, then, result from reader-induced breaks into what has been metaphorically treated as an electrical "circuit" between reader and text (cf. Rosenblatt, 1978). We might think of this approach as the deficiency model of misinterpretation, in which misinterpretation invades—through mistakes, misapplications, misunderstandings—what would otherwise be a perfect system of meaning-transmission. That is, a misinterpretation—or, what amounts to the same thing, an interpretation that diverges from a predetermined norm—is, to use Derrida's (1967/1976, p. 256) phrase, a "catastrophe of disturbance" from outside of the system, non-explicable from the perspective of the system itself, which could presumably operate without misinterpretation at all.[10]

This deficiency-model solution has two variations. The first—and particularly insidious—method to preserve the integrity of a text at the expense of readers is to attribute immorality to readers incapable of discerning its truth: Only those who are themselves holy can be open to the holy message of the scriptures. This tenet lies at the heart of Gnostic movements, which believe the revelations of God are secretive, mysterious, reserved only for the elect few (Sullivan, 1999, p. 64). For example, Jacobus Faber Stapulensis, writing in the early sixteenth century, contends that even the literal sense of the Bible requires divine illumination to understand properly, and without that illumination, the "letter" of the text is "simply false," a "'*figmentum* and a *mendacium*'" (Preus, 1969, p. 139). To doubt the scripture, then, and make that doubt public, was to risk having oneself branded as *non-elect*.[11]

George A. Kennedy (1980) asserts that this weight placed upon the reader or listener is one of the defining features of what he identifies as *Judeo-Christian rhetoric,* key assumptions of which are that the truth of preaching "must be apprehended by the listener, not proved by the speaker" and that not all listeners have the "strength" to comprehend the messages of the scriptures (p. 127); to support his claim, Kennedy cites the parable of the sower, in which "some seed falls along the path, some on rocky ground, some among thorns, and some in good soil" (p.

127). And God may be not only the standard of meaning, but also the cause of understanding or misunderstanding, as in the Exodus story: Whether Moses will persuade Pharaoh to release the Israelites

> depends entirely on the extent to which God allows Pharaoh to listen [. . .]. Persuasion takes place when God is ready, and not through the verbal abilities or even the authority of Moses. Similarly, in Christian rhetoric God must act, through his grace, to move the hearts of an audience before individuals can receive the Word, and if he does pour out his grace, the truth of the message will be recognized because of its authority, and not through its logical argumentation. (G. Kennedy, 1980, pp. 122–123)

Augustine (trans. 1997) not only declared in *On Christian Teaching* that if a scriptural passage appears contradictory, the interpreter is at fault, but he also upheld his own text as a timeless locus of meaning: "I say to those who fail to understand what I write that it is not my fault that they do not understand" (Preface, 5). Augustine concedes that readers may be *misled* when reading scriptures, but not because the scriptures are *misleading* (I.86–88).

Such thinking lingers in a weakened form even into the twentieth century—for theologian Ernst Fuchs, a reader's difficulty with interpreting the Bible does not reflect *its* obscurity, but the *reader's* obscurity: "Now in the conventional orientation to the text, it is the text itself which requires interpretation. That is to say, the text, without the aid of exegetical help, remains opaque. But Fuchs proposes to turn this relationship around: what is opaque to him is not the text, but *our* situation. The text is obscure because our situation is obscure" (Funk, 1969, pp. 57–58). For Fuchs, the proper response for a reader of sacred writing is not to try to interpret the text, but to be himself or herself interpreted by it—to allow the text to interpret the present, rather than viewing the text as something from the past to be interpreted (Funk, 1969, p. 50). In a similar vein, Emerson (1844/1985d) believed that people who are unable to appreciate the symbolic meanings of nature suffered from an incapacity: "Since every thing in nature answers to a moral power, if any phenomenon remains brute and dark it is because the corresponding faculty in the observer is not yet active" (p. 267).

A second method for blaming readers for misunderstanding sacred texts presumes that most readers lack the necessary intelligence or training to understand the Bible. Philo felt that "literal interpretation is for those who are unable to see the underlying deeper meaning or bear the full truth," such as "those who lack wisdom, those impossible to instruct otherwise, the 'duller folk'" (Fearghail, 1995, p. 47). Augustine (trans. 1997) warns about the dangers of casual reading of the Bible and suggests that the ideal interpreter of the Bible must be learned (II.10, II.24–25). Luther (1513–1515/1982) admonished his students and readers, when encountering the Gospels, not to be like an "uneducated person [who] sees and grasps the letters only in a material sense, not as symbols of words" or a "barbarian [who] hears the voice and does not understand it" (p. 15). And Erasmus—Luther's contemporary and frequent adversary—advocated a return to the Biblical sources (*ad fontes*), reconstructing them by means of a scholarly erudition that "demands knowledge of the original languages and the grammatical and philological criticism of the text" (Aldridge, 1969, p. 59).

Erasmus's erudition, however, pales in comparison to Spinoza's (1670/1951b) criteria for interpretation—criteria so impossible to attain that one may doubt whether Spinoza actually thought interpretation could be achieved. Spinoza's formulation of the central axiom of his hermeneutic method seems simple enough: "The universal rule, then, in interpreting Scripture is to accept nothing as an authoritative Scriptural statement which we do not perceive very clearly when we examine it in the light of its history" (p. 101). By history, however, Spinoza means: (a) "the nature and properties of the language in which the books of the Bible were written, and in which their authors were accustomed to speak" (p. 101); (b) an "analysis of each book and arrangement of its contents under heads" that eventually provides a complete enumeration of "ambiguous," "obscure," or "mutually contradictory" passages requiring resolution (p. 101); and (c) a full and accurate description of

> the environment of all the prophetic books extant; that is, the life, the conduct, and the studies of the author of each book, who he was, what was the occasion, and the epoch of his writing, whom did he write for, and in what language. Further, it should inquire into the fate of each book: how it was first

received, into whose hands it fell, how many different versions there were of it, by whose advice was it
received into the Bible, and, lastly, how all the books
now universally accepted as sacred, were united into
a single whole. (p. 103)

It should be noted that Augustine (trans. 1997) offers a similarly
daunting list of criteria for interpretation:

> The student who fears God earnestly seeks his will
> in the holy scriptures. Holiness makes him gentle, so
> that he does not revel in controversy; a knowledge of
> languages protects him from uncertainty over unfa-
> miliar words of phrases, and a knowledge of certain
> essential things protects him from ignorance of the
> significance and detail of what is used by way of im-
> agery. Thus equipped, and with the assistance of reli-
> able texts derived from the manuscripts with careful
> attention to the need for emendation, he should now
> approach the task of analysing and resolving the am-
> biguities of the scriptures. (III.1–2)

Though differing in several respects, the mystical and the scholarly
approaches to Biblical interpretation both assume that, through some
kind of insight or methodology, at some higher level of abstraction the
Biblical texts can be fully harmonized. Further, both approaches parallel each other in solidifying the authority of "experts"—either cler-
ics, mystics, or scholars—who may properly interpret the scriptures
for those incapable of doing it properly themselves (cf. de Certeau,
1974/1984, pp. 171–172; Foucault, 1971/1972b, p. 216). Increasingly,
the authority to interpret the Bible resided with the Catholic Church,
the monopoly of which it held until the Reformation (Corner, 1990, p.
218).[12] In the fourth century, St. Athanasius, who was reverently called
the "Father of Orthodoxy" in his lifetime (Clifford, 1907/1999), believed that, while the scriptures were sufficient for the communication
of truth, they could and should be illuminated by the sacred writings
of the Church Fathers (Twomey, 1995, p. 85)—which, of course, requires knowledge of those sacred writings. By the beginning of the fifteenth century, theologian Jean Gerson attempted to solidify Church
authority still further with the curious *petitio principii* that Church
doctrines are based solely on the literal sense of the scriptures and *that*

literal sense is itself determined by the Church—thus invalidating the appeals of non-orthodox sects to their own "literal" readings of the Bible (Preus, 1969, pp. 79–80).

In addition to discrediting heretical interpretations, religious institutions must perpetually enforce authorized interpretations, not only by trying to control the reception of sacred texts by laypersons through the use of liturgy, homilies, sermons, commentaries, etc.—an the immense effort—but also by initiates. One of the most interesting procedures for securing (at least the appearance of) unanimity of belief— carried out by, for example, some Jews, Christians, and Muslims—is the requirement that scriptures can only be read aloud and discussed in the presence of other followers and/or a master. The Mishnah, a set of Jewish oral traditions stretching back possibly to the fifth century B.C. until its written compilation around 217 A.D. by Rabbi Judah ben Simeon, "stipulates that neither reading nor exposition could occur unless at least ten men were present" (Murphy, 1974, p. 272; cf. E. Segal, 2000). Similarly, Murphy (1974, p. 272) notes that in the early history of Christianity, oral recitation of Biblical passages was always accompanied by oral commentary on their significance. And Muslims, who believe that the Qur'an is primarily an oral "text" only secondarily transcribed into writing, must learn from masters who have already memorized it: "Still today, reciters of the Qur'an learn their recitation from oral masters, not from the written text; scribes write down the text from recitations, not from other texts; and students study with a teacher, never alone with a text. The oral remains authoritative for the written, not the other way around" (Fischer and Abedi, 1990, p. 127). Unlike Luther and other literalists (including such Puritan luminaries as Mather, Higginson, and Hubbard), who assume that the Bible is its own best interpreter (D. Olson, 1977, pp. 258–259; Roberts, 1998, p. 184), Muslims accept that the

> Qur'an is not self-explanatory—one cannot just read it and be guided. Nor is it a guide for everyone; it can mislead those who are not pious [. . .]. One needs guidance not to be misled. Such guidance comes in various dialogic forms: in the teacher-student, Ima[m]-follower, or student-student debating of dialectical argument-counterargument so as to clarify the basis for decision making. One may not study alone, with the text alone. (Fischer and Abedi, 1990, p. 133).

Ultimately, at least for Shi'ite Muslims, "the Imam is the standard of meaning" for the Qur'an, with further illumination provided by the *sunnah,* or, "the precedents of the Prophet and his companions," that Sunni Muslims alone rely upon to interpret the Qur'an (Fischer and Abedi, 1990, pp. 140, 141).

PANCHRONISM AND THE PRINCIPLE OF RATIONALISM

The sense of a proposition (or a thought) isn't anything spiritual; it's what is given as an answer to a request for an explanation of the sense. Or: one sense differs from another in the same way as the explanation of the one differs from the sense of the other. So also: the sense of one proposition differs from the sense of another in the same way as the one proposition differs from the other.

—Ludwig Wittgenstein

The sense of a proposition is not a soul.

—Ludwig Wittgenstein

To understand the (necessarily meaningful) design of nature is to understand the (necessarily) unchanging mind of God: Such was the dream not only of Augustine, Aquinas, and other theologians, but also of rationalist philosophers, such as Descartes (1637/1970a, 1641/1970b), Leibniz (1720/1968c, 1840/1968b), and Spinoza (1670/1951b, 1677/1951a), who attempted to find through introspection the timeless laws of rationality and logic that God himself must obey, for God Himself was a rational God.[13] Such accounts have great difficulty explaining, or even acknowledging, change—including changes of meaning—unless those changes are somehow already knowable *a priori* (i.e., the eventual change is already contained within the meaning itself). Time is irrelevant here; the divine or the ideal operates in eternity, which is the state *outside* of time (Arendt, 1958, p. 17–21). Of course, not treating time as a constitutive factor of meaning leads to certain embarrassments, such as Leibniz's (1840/1968b) acceptance of the premise that at any given moment an object has a fully determinate set of past, present, and future properties; on this view, the statement "Julius Caesar crossed the Rubicon" is an *a priori,* analytic truth (just as are all other true statements). This entails that if someone told young Julius that, several years hence, "You will cross the Rubicon," this, too, would be an *a priori*, analytic truth, even if Julius and the speaker himself were barred from knowing the truth of the statement. Every attribute of an object and every outcome of an event is predetermined; nothing is surprising—*except, perhaps, the fact that we are continually surprised by objects and events.*

This surprise (or randomness or indeterminacy) is not admitted to be a constitutive part of a fully meaningful physical universe; as Frege (1892/1984d) bluntly, almost matter-of-factly concedes: "Comprehensive knowledge of the thing meant would require us to be able to say immediately whether any given sense [description of a property or attribute] attaches to it. To such knowledge we never attain" (p. 143). It follows from this that meaning is never—or is only *exceptionally*—achieved. If I can "know" the meaning of "Julius Caesar" only by knowing all of his attributes, then I can never really know "the" meaning at all; I may only possess bits and pieces of that meaning that are not, in themselves, *sufficiently* meaningful. Perhaps that is why the study of logic feels most comfortable when discussing formalized statements like "If *p*, then *q*; *p*, therefore *q*." Here is a sentence—not a sentence, really, but a pseudo-sentence or Russell's (1919/1948) "propositional function"—that, deliberately evacuated of all other content, *appears* completely knowable, precisely because it means, from a logical point of view, so little.

An aside: My understanding of meaning consequentialism coheres with Frege that total knowledge of an object is impossible; but this is so not because the object has an infinite number of properties at any point in time, but because the Meaning of that object is comprised of its total set of consequences—consequences that propagate through time beyond the reckoning of any interpreter. There is, in fact, nothing else to know of an object other than its consequences (Peirce, 1878/1991b, p. 174). However, I would not say that a person who experiences only a few of these consequences is *lacking* in meaning, for we may speak of a lack only in opposition to an achievable wholeness: The Meaning of an object is comprised of—i.e., results from—its consequences and is not a standard against which those consequences are to be assessed as lacking or adequate. The Meaning does not govern the propagation of consequences, but *is* the propagation of those consequences. And to say that any given consequence is lacking the fullest expression of an object's Meaning would entail that there is ever a "fullest expression

of an object's Meaning"—i.e., that over and above the actual consequences of an object standards stands a super-consequence that subsumes all the others.

When time is mentioned in these rationalist accounts, it is only to
negate its relevance. For example, consider Frege's (1918–1919/1984a,
p. 370) speculations about whether a logical *thought* or proposition
(i.e., Frege's "sentence")—not to be mistaken with a person's actual
ideas or utterances—can change in truth value:

> Now is a thought changeable or is it timeless? The
> thought we express by the Pythagorean theorem is
> surely timeless, eternal, unvarying. But are there not
> thoughts which are true today but false in six months'
> time? The thought, for example, that the tree there is
> covered with green leaves, will surely be false in six
> months' time. No, for it is not the same thought at
> all. The words 'this tree is covered with green leaves'
> are not sufficient by themselves to constitute the ex-
> pression of thought, for the time of utterance is in-
> volved as well. Without the time-specification thus
> given we have not a complete thought, i.e. we have
> no thought at all. Only a sentence with the time-
> specification filled out, a sentence complete in every
> respect, expresses a thought. But this thought, if it
> is true, is true not only today or tomorrow but time-
> lessly. Thus the present tense in 'is true' does not refer
> to the speaker's present; it is, if the expression be per-
> mitted, a tense of timelessness. (p. 370)

It's commendable that Frege recognizes the importance of the context of utterance, but notice how the meaning and truth-value of the
thought is severed from the future, perfectly preserved from contami-
nation in a kind of semantic amber. If the sentence "is true" now, it
is true always; and the markers of tense are mere illusions of language
that logic, properly applied, dispels. For Frege (1918–1919/1984a), the
meaning and truth-value of thoughts *must* be preserved; in fact, time
is only important when considering the *utterance* of the thought, not
the thought itself: "The time-specification that may be contained in
the sentence belongs only to the expression of the thought [i.e., to the
utterance]; the truth, which we acknowledge by using the assertoric

sentence-form, is timeless" (p. 370). Frege admits that because of "the variability of language with time [. . .] the same words" may "take on another sense, express another thought," but this is an uninteresting phenomenon that "relates only the linguistic realm" and contributes nothing to the discussion of timeless thoughts (p. 370). It seems as if for Frege that natural languages are inferior vessels for the conveyance of timeless truths, so they must be reformed by the synthetic languages of logic, mathematics, or the hard sciences.[14] Change in meaning is a deformity to be corrected by the orthopedics of logic. What Frege cannot imagine is that there may not be a timeless form modeled on the paradigm of the Pythagorean Theorem beneath the "surface" of ordinary utterances that guarantees the continuity of meaning. And he cannot imagine (a) that continuity of meaning(s) may be an achievement that must be effected by perpetual maintenance—such as those of logicians repeatedly instructing their pupils about the "universal" laws of logic—liable to break down at any moment or (b) that there may be no continuity at all as meanings proliferate.

To understand why Frege argues as he does, one must recognize that the most basic division of logicians and mathematicians is that between those who believe these fields are branches of psychology (i.e., psychologism) and those who believe they are not descriptive studies of cognition, but normative accounts of how thought should operate (i.e., antipsychologism). In the history of logic, until the eighteenth century, logic was not thought to be concerned at all with actual human cognition (George, 1997, p. 214). For example, Augustine (trans. 1997), illustrating the linkage between mysticism and rationalism, claims that "the validity of syllogisms is not something instituted by humans, but observed and recorded by them, so that the subject may be taught and learnt. It is built into the permanent and divinely instituted system of things [. . .]. As for the study of number, *it is surely clear even to the dullest person* that it was not instituted by men, but rather investigated and discovered" (II.121–136, emphasis added).

Although Horkheimer and Adorno (1947/1988, p. 30) claim that Enlightenment rationality reduced cognition to logic, the important figures commonly associated with the Enlightenment, such as Condillac (1792/1982c), Hume (cf. George, 1997, p. 216), and Locke (1689/1987), resisting the dryness of Aristotelian scholasticism, actually attempted to "psychologize" logic. Such attempts, however, were not as influential as the work of antipsychologists like Leibniz

(1840/1968a), Kant (cf. George, 1997, p. 227), Frege (1897/1979a, 1894/1984e, 1906/1979b, 1918–1919/1984a), the early Husserl (1900–1901/1970b), C. I. Lewis (1929/1956), Russell (1919/1948), the early Wittgenstein (1922/1981), Carnap (1932/1959a, 1947/1988), Ayer (1946/1952), and Reichenbach (1947). For the antipsychologists, logic and mathematics are found, not invented; as Jourdain (1913/1956) puts it, using the familiar metaphor of archaeological excavation,

> Of this [the true nature of Mathematics] I will try to give some account, and show that, since mathematics is logical and not psychological in its nature, all those petty questions—sometimes amusing and often tedious—of history, persons, and nations are irrelevant to Mathematics in itself. Mathematics has required centuries of excavation, and the process of excavation is not, of course, and never will be, complete. But we see enough now of what has been excavated clearly to distinguish between it and the tools which have been used or are used for excavation. (p. 8)

Contemporary mathematician Gregory Chaitin prefers to think of mathematicians as field scientists collecting specimens, some more exotic than others: mathematics "is just a process of discovery like every other branch of science: it's an experimental field where mathematicians stumble upon facts in the same way that zoologists might come across a new species of primate" (Chown, 2001).

Wittgenstein's (1922/1981) work in the *Tractatus Logico-Philosophicus* offers possibly the most notable effort to theorize the rationalist dream of a logically perfect structure of timeless propositions. I will conclude this section with a brief consideration of Wittgenstein's vision of the *world* in the *Tractatus*—including a sketch of his so-called *picture theory of meaning* (or representation)—because it so clearly illuminates the influence of panchronic or block-time conceptions on rationalism and, consequently, marks a major point of convergence between rationalism and mysticism. In fact, in his introductory remarks to the *Tractatus,* Russell (1922/1981), who was Wittgenstein's teacher, admits having discomfort with some of his pupil's cryptic speculations about the limits of what can be said (e.g., that ethics cannot be discussed directly, but only shown by what is said); Russell believes that Wittgenstein makes far too strong an appeal to the "mystical" and the

"inexpressible" (p. 22). However, to work our way toward an understanding of Wittgenstein's concept of *world*, we must begin with his
picture theory of meaning, which is Wittgenstein's attempt to explain
why accurate representations of reality are possible—though we might
also think of it as Wittgenstein's effort to persuade readers that such
representations are possible.

In the case of a photographic image, the relationship between the
representation and the represented appears to be relatively simple. Suppose I take a snapshot of a book sitting on a table; beneath the table
rests a sleeping dog. Clearly, the photograph does not *fully* represent
the states of affairs represented; for example, it is a two-dimensional
image of three-dimensional objects, and it shows practically nothing
about the temperature or geographical location of the room, the odor
of the dog, the time of day when the picture was taken, etc., so we
might already wonder about the *loss* or *leakage*—ordinarily ignored as
irrelevant—of the representation. What the photograph does contain
are two-dimensional visual representations of three three-dimensional
objects: the book, the table, and the dog. But it shows more than just
those objects; it also shows that those objects are related to each other
spatially: the book is shown to be above the table and the dog, the
table is shown to be beneath the book and above the dog, and the dog
is shown to be below the book and the table. What the photograph
represents, then, is a combination of objects set in a determinate relationship, which Wittgenstein calls the "structure" of a "state of affairs"
or a "fact." For Wittgenstein, the photograph is able to represent a
state of affairs because the elements of the photograph (i.e., the representations of the book, table, and dog) share a form in common with
the represented state of affairs. That is, the objects represented in the
photograph are related to one another in a way that corresponds to the
way in which the actual objects are related to one another; and what
they share is a "logical form" (2.18).

However, there are limitations to what a representation represents;
it cannot, Wittgenstein says, *represent* its form *as* a representation, but
can only *display* that form. This is the *doctrine of showing* (4.121). The
problem is more acutely realized when speaking of propositions, which
are for Wittgenstein as much a logical picture of reality as is a photograph (2.1, 4.014). Consider the following proposition *P:* "The world
is spherical." How can we link the subject *s* of the sentence (the world)
to the predicate *p* (the attribute of being spherical). What joins *s* to *p?*

To say that the word *is* marks a relation R that holds between s and p, forming sRp, only sends us into an infinite regress, for we must then explain what links R individually to s and p, and so on. Wittgenstein would argue that the relationship R between s and p is not *stated* but rather is *shown* or *displayed* by the form of P; all that P can state explicitly about R is that R actually holds between s and p (3.1432, 4.012).

Wittgenstein argues that the correspondence between the represented objects and the actual objects is not arbitrary; there are rules that govern the *conversion* of a single logical form from one mode of representation to another (4.014, 4.0141). In the case of a photograph, those rules would involve the physical process of converting the waves of light reflecting off of three-dimensional objects into two-dimensional images on film. In fact, if one knew those rules of photographic representation completely, it would be possible to "retranslate" that two-dimensional image into a three-dimensional representation, such as a sculpture (of course, this assumes that one and only one physical arrangement would produce the photographic image). But Wittgenstein also argues that we can make much more radical, yet logic-governed translations of the visual representation, converting it into a linguistic representation that shares the same logical form (e.g., "The book was on the table; beneath the table slept a dog."). This assumes, of course, that all linguistic representations that express a proposition have a determinate, static, univocal meaning and that *representation* is narrowly conceived as expressing physical relationships between physical objects. Like Frege, Wittgenstein would argue that, properly speaking, propositions—and therefore only linguistic representations of propositions—are clear and determinate. A proposition, for Wittgenstein, has "one and only one complete analysis" of its meaning (3.25), and it "expresses what it expresses in a definite and clearly specifiable way: the proposition is articulate" (3.251). Incidentally, but not unimportantly, Wittgenstein describes other kinds of translations of a single logical form, such as that of a musical composition, which can be represented through the sounds of an orchestra, the grooves of a record (or, to make this more up-to-date, to the digital encoding of a compact disc), and the notations of a musical score. And he suggests that, if we knew the rules for doing so, we could map one kind of representation onto another; for example, we could reconstruct a musical score based on the grooves of a record (4.0141).

But let us return to our discussion of the photographic representation, one that purportedly depicts reality as it is (i.e., the photograph as an accurate or true representation). Wittgenstein suggests that we must also account for the possibility of representations that are inaccurate or false. Let's return to the example of the book, table, and dog. Suppose instead of taking a photograph, I decide to sketch the state of affairs described earlier. However, I do so poorly (even if we make a generous allowance for the obvious fact that a sketch cannot possibly be as mimetic as a photograph): In my drawing, the dog is on top of the table and the book is beneath the table. This seems to be a false picture, for the relationships shown to hold between the represented objects do not correspond to the relationships that hold between the actual objects. Clearly, Wittgenstein cannot defend the position that representations must be representations of actual states of affairs because, as in this case, on his terms representations may be false or inaccurate.

But if the sketch doesn't show what is actually the case, what does it show? What is it a picture *of?* Wittgenstein would hold that the sketch is still a *fact* (even if it is a false or "negative" fact), for the sketch shows that the elements of the picture are related to each other in a determinate way (i.e., that the sketch represents a determinate state of affairs), and that what makes the fact false is that *actual objects* are not related to each other in a way that corresponds to the way in which the *represented objects* are related to each other. But this is a highly questionable assumption, for there seems to be no physical laws governing the translation process of actual state of affairs to my sketched lines, despite attempts, such as Stampe's (1977), to devise a causal theory of linguistic representation. For example, how could we be certain about the spatial relations depicted, especially if I am uncertain about them myself? To determine how far the dog is from the table, we would need to know the actual size of the dog and table and then compare their relative sizes as they appear in the sketch. Is this information somehow coded into the structure of the representation?

According to Wittgenstein, we must make a distinction between (a) the determinate way in which the elements of a picture are arranged (what he calls the "structure" of the picture) and (b) the set of all possible arrangements (or "structures") of those elements (what he calls the "pictorial form" of the picture). The pictorial form is the link between representation and reality, for it is the *possibility* that the relations shown to hold between representations *correspond* to the relations that hold between actual objects. But if it is possible for representations to depict the world, argues Wittgenstein, they must share something in common with reality. As we have already discussed, that commonality is *logical form:* A representation can depict a state of affairs if it shares the same logical form as that state of affairs. But whereas in our earlier discussion of photographs, records, and musical scores, we seemed to limit a logical form to an actual state of affairs, we must now expand the term to cover any *possible* state of affairs. For Wittgenstein, just as a fact designates an actual *or* possible state of affairs, so too does a logical form. The key for Wittgenstein is that the set of all *actual* and *possible* states of affairs comprise the totality of reality or the *world.* For Wittgenstein, *reality* designates not only the actual *structure* of the world (i.e., the determinate totality of all objects and relations between objects), but also the logical *form* of the world (i.e., the totality of all possible structures of the world); thus, a possible world is part of the same *form* as the actual world, but does not share its *structure.* Logical form is a pivotal term for the Wittgenstein of the *Tractatus,* for it underlies his entire conception of representation and reality and it sets parameters on what is possible and impossible. This is complex argument that resists easy simplification: Briefly put, for Wittgenstein the *form of the world* is the set of all possible forms of states of affairs or facts (both positive and negative); the *forms of states of affairs* are themselves reducible to the set of all possible forms of objects; and the *form of an object* is the set of all possible relationships that object can have with all other objects.

These repeated references to "the possible" should not fool us into thinking that there is an essential indeterminacy or openness at work in the logical form of the world. Quite the contrary: The possible is that which always could have happened had the actual state of affairs of the world been different, and it is the limit for all future states of affairs. In short, the possible—the total set of all permissible states of affairs—is already set in advance, like the set of all legal arrangements of chess pieces on a chessboard. As Wittgenstein (1922/1981) declares in the opening of the *Tractatus:*

1.   The world is everything that is the case.

1.1   The world is the totality of facts, not of things.

1.11   The world is determined by the facts, and by these being *all* the facts.

1.12   For the totality of facts determines both what is the case, and also all that is not the case.

1.13   The facts in logical space are the world.

The actual world, then, simply occupies a changing configuration of points that may be mapped onto the logical form of the world: The actual world changes, but the logical form is *a priori*, timeless, a humanly-incomprehensible but finite totality of facts or propositions.[15] For Wittgenstein, these propositions are not manufactured by the activities of philosophers, but only made "clear" by them (4.112), and all inferences from one proposition to another is *a priori* as well (5.133), because whatever happens or can happen has already been anticipated by the logical form of the world. Thus, although logical arguments may be, like Spinoza's geometric substance, made manifest sequentially for human beings (cf. Burke, 1945, p. 29), there is in fact no *progression* of thoughts because logic requires no mind, but only logical relations, to bind the propositions of an argument together (George, 1997, p. 230).

I conclude by observing that for Wittgenstein, despite his mentor's concerns about his penchant for mystical obscurantism, God is not invoked as the ultimate foundation for logic: As Wittgenstein (1922/1981) cryptically says, "Logic must take care of itself" (5.473). Logic, with its apparently uncontestable truths, no longer requires a metaphysical crutch. But both rationalism and mysticism appeal to a timeless, eternal realm outside of ordinary sense experience. In place of a divinely ordered universe, with a spiritual realm shadowing—and a divine being directing—material existence, we now have a rationally ordered but essentially mindless universe, with a timeless logical world underlying—and timeless logical rules governing—the physical world of flux, which is only an illusion (6.3611). And, as we have seen, not only do these rules govern the actual world, but they also dictate what possible states of affairs could occur. In such a rationally ordered universe, just as in the divinely ordered cosmos, there are no surprises; as Wittgenstein (1922/1981) says, "In logic nothing is accidental; if a thing *can* occur in an atomic fact the possibility of that atomic fact must already be prejudged in the thing" (2.012, 2.0123). In sum: The panchronic, block-time worlds of mysticism and rationalism are *a priori*, pre-given, as are all of the meanings found within them.

PANCHRONISM IN RHETORIC AND COMPOSITION STUDIES

> A text stating what the whole world knows is false will state
> falsehood forever, so long as the text exists. Texts are inher-
> ently contumacious.
>
> —Walter J. Ong

Although the interpretation of sacred texts and the groups who offer
or impose interpretations are of interest to some researchers within
rhetoric and composition studies, that interest does not involve an
embrace of elements of semantic mysticism. Rather, researchers have
included them in (a) historical accounts of some element or elements of
hermeneutics (e.g., Conley, 1990; G. Kennedy, 1980; Murphy, 1974);
(b) theoretical critiques of the discursive practices of religious groups
(e.g., D. Olson, 1994; Roberts, 1998; Sullivan, 1999); (c) discussions,
occasionally critical, of how students with strongly-held religious beliefs interact with instructors and fellows students and resist secular
lessons (e.g., Berthoff, Daniell, Campbell, Swearingen, and Moffett,
1994; Bleich, 1990; Goodburn, 1998; Rand, 2001); and (d) descriptions of the teacher in religious terms, such as a missionary or preacher
(Tobin, 1993; cf. Banner and Cannon, 1997/1998, p. 8). No one working within contemporary rhetoric and composition studies, so far as
I am aware, is formulating a theory of meaning that places God as
its center, even if some figures in the field, such as Moffett (1968,
1994), find inspiration in theorists outside of the field, such as Buber
(1923/1966), in whose work emerges mystical or spiritual elements of
meaning apriorism.

However, if we widen the scope of our investigation to cover the
principle of panchronism, then we can find atemporal or block-time
theorizations of meaning actively at work within rhetoric and composition studies. For example, consider the emphasis on logic and logical
fallacies in the countless first-year composition handbooks assigned
year after year. Or consider the formalist fiction of intrinsic meaning
or information, which—in one influential manifestation derived in
part from work in cognitive science—conceives of the text as an objective conveyor of information, an "autonomous text" (D. Olson, 1977,
p. 268).[16] Other examples include: D'Angelo's (1975) claim that there
are "meaning-bearing words" (p. 13); Finn's (1995) definition of "entropy," borrowed from information theory (cf. Shannon, 1951), as the

"amount of information conveyed by a set of symbols" (p. 245); and Redish, Battison, and Gold's (1985) suggestions for "organizing, writing, and designing documents so that information is readily accessible to readers" (p. 131), as if that information could be directly encoded into the documents themselves, dictating how the text must be read and experienced—if it is to be properly understood—from the moment of its completion until, presumably, the end of time (cf. Dillon, 1981, p. 135; Hirsch, 1976, p. 87; Stratman, 2000, p. 557).

The least consistent account of intrinsic information I have encountered is Winterowd's (1976/1996), which attempts to merge reading theory with the rhetorical concepts of *logos, ethos,* and *pathos.* According to Winterowd, *logos* is analogous to "'pure' meaning, which includes information [. . .], logical consistency, and reference" (p. 157). The pages of the text, however, do not contain meaning, but only "information from which meaning can be derived"—information that is "arranged in a series of interrelated *cue systems:* graphophonic, syntactic, and semantic" (p. 157). But this is a circular argument that assumes—while explicitly denying—the meaningfulness of these cue systems, which cannot be objective properties of the text in the same way as are, to use Winterowd's example, the "black squiggles against a white background" (p. 157). The circularity is obvious in Winterowd's use of the term *semantic cues,* but the *graphophonic* and the *syntactic* are also placed within the domain of meaning, for how do we decide what a text feature "sounds like" unless we have already identified that feature as a grapheme or morpheme, or whether a word is noun unless we have interpreted the word as a noun as opposed to whatever else it could have meant? And later in the essay, Winterowd equates *logos* only to information, despite his earlier equation of it to pure meaning, thus constructing a schematic in which *logos* is the information on the page, *ethos* is the intentions of the writer as manifest in the text, and *pathos* is the use of the information of a text by a reader to construct meaning (p. 159).

The *property* of meaning we find here is quite peculiar: It is not, for example, mutable in ways that other properties of the text—such as its mass, radioactivity, or tensile strength—are. And it is certainly not a relational, contingent property—e.g., the meaning for Joe, the meaning for Anna, the meaning for Kyle. In fact, this property seems to belong not to the text at all, which, after all, can be utterly destroyed, but to what Tanselle (1989) would call the *work* that stands, like a Platonic form, behind all of its possible material instantiations.

Those who appeal to ghostly forms behind or beneath texts frequently conceive of them in terms of strings of *propositions* or *statements* into which texts are ultimately reducible. Although there are a number of ways in which propositions may be treated, they are commonly accepted as Frege or Wittgenstein conceived them—as semantic or logical structures expressing the content of a complete, atomic (often true or false) *thought* in subject-predicate form. Propositions, according to this view, are best thought of as semantic or logical types that are instantiated by linguistic (or non-linguistic) tokens; thus, the same proposition can be instantiated by multiple configurations of linguistic tokens in the same language, across languages, or even in non-linguistic sign systems (cf. Hirsch, 1976, pp. 72–73). We might also profitably compare propositions to Chomskyan deep structures that can be orderly transformed into many different surface structures with the same semantic content.

Propositions are relatively rare creatures in current research in rhetoric and composition studies, especially given our recent disciplinary focus on texts, contexts, and intertexts, not sentences per se. However, texts (and discourse generally) have been treated as "a sequence of propositions, each with a reference and predication" (Steinmann, 1982, p. 308; cf. D. Olson and Torrance, 1981, p. 246); further, the propositions are thought to be objective features of texts (Kintsch and Vipond, 1979; cf. Nystrand, 1986). For example, Bracewell (1999) argues that propositional analysis, which decomposes any given text or segment of speech into a series of propositions or semantic units, can provide "a database from which other more specific or more general units of analysis can be formed or derived according to the demands of the study" (pp. 87–88), thus providing, on Bracewell's account, a principled link between micro- and macro-level analyses of "situated literacy" (p. 77). And D. Olson (1977)—in whose work appears clear links between the principles of formalism and rationalism—argues that the apex of the written word is the "essayist technique," epitomized by the philosophical disputation of Locke, which attempts to make fully explicit and logically consistent its chains of propositions in order to make a text that is an "unambiguous or autonomous representation of meaning" (p. 258), one that does not rely upon "implicit premises or personal interpretations" (p. 268). To banish ambiguity, "a sentence was written to have only one meaning" (p. 268)—in short, the sentence would instantiate only one proposition or one complex propositional structure.

Propositions also emerge in discussions of synonymy; in fact, Hirsch (1976, p. 76) argues that synonymy can be possible only if there are propositions, which he equates to semantic content ("meaning"), because sentences can only be synonymous if they have the same meaning, a core meaning that does not change from context to context:

> Unless different sentences could carry the same meaning, we would always need to use the same sentence to convey the same proposition. But if we used the same sentence in a different context, it might, as every stylist knows, carry a different meaning, which is to say a different proposition [. . .].
>
> Shared knowledge requires shared and reexpressible propositions. But if different linguistic forms must express different meanings, they must always express different propositions. The only linguistic definition of a proposition so far proposed that is free from this embarrassment is the following: "A proposition is the meaning of a class of synonymous sentences." (p. 73)[17]

Hirsch's later work with Harrington (1981) on the *intrinsic communicative effectiveness* of prose depends upon whether two texts can be perfectly synonymous (i.e., semantically isomorphic) because they assume that a poorly written text will be processed by readers more slowly than its better written and synonymous counterpart; only by keeping content constant can the differences in reading time be attributed to properties of the text other than its content.

Assumptions about what kinds of structures, whether propositions or some other kind of formal entities, underlie texts have consequences for the analysis and interpretation of those texts; we frequently "find" what we expect to find, so we must always be wary of the limitations of analysis, especially the tendency of analysts to submerge differences into homogeneous concepts and to ignore tensions, whether deliberately or not, in the application of their favored frameworks or, as Burke (1965/1966a) might put it, "terministic screens" (p. 45). For example, consider van Wijk and Sanders's (1999) proposal for the "PISA technique." PISA is an acronym for Procedures for Incremental Structural Analysis, which is designed to "show how writing strategies can be reconstructed from a text" in an objective way (p. 51). The text is segmented according to certain syntactic criteria, and then the analysis is conducted incrementally, line by line, according to a list of *if-then* rules, with independent clauses "numbered according to their appearance in the text" and dependent clauses "marked with a, b, and so forth, added to the number of their host clause" (p. 52). To illustrate, here is part of van Wijk and Sanders's analysis of the text about Saint Nicholas written by a 12-year-old Dutch girl:

0	Saint Nicholas . . . .
1	Saint Nicholas is a man who comes by boat
1a	(such a thing that is on water)
1	to Holland with black peters,
2	a Black Peter is just like you
3	for he is black as well
4	and he also has a rod,
5	that are a lot of branches
6	Also he has a sack in which everything can be put
7a	for instance when children
7b	(that are small people)
7a	are naughty
7c	(that is not nice),
7	then they can be put in it
8	But now there are presents in it
9	Presents are: when for instance I give someone a banana
10	Black Peter walks with Saint Nicholas over the (houzes < houses,
11	(in them people do everything)
12	and then they throw something in the chimney
13	that is a thing from which comes smoke. (p. 53)

Van Wijk and Sanders note that the analysis is conducted without "a preceding global inspection of the text" (p. 54); but the fact that there is no preceding global inspection of the text is irrelevant to the results of the analysis. If van Wijk and Sanders assume the stability of word meanings in the text, then the meanings of the words in the earlier sections of the text would not change as a result of the later sections of the text having been read. That is, the order in which the text is read should not change the overall structure and meaning of the text. Thus, the sense of the model's real-time analysis leading to an openness to the temporality of discourse is also illusionary, for the assumption of a stable, spatialized text means that the analysis could only produce one predetermined result, *if the procedure is sound and soundly followed:* The text, and therefore the meanings it contains, is always already there, waiting for the PISA procedure to reveal the logic of its structures and processes. Only if the analytic procedures themselves were changed would the results of the analysis be different.

The product of such an analysis is the assignment "to a text a hierarchical and relational structure, that is, a fully connected tree with an interpretative label attached to each connection" (p. 54). Essentially, the analysis describes the content of the text and operations on that content—with the analysis *presuming* "a small and well-defined knowledge base about linguistic marking, discourse schemes, and word meanings" (p. 54). Thus, van Wijk and Sanders are not questioning what makes discourse amenable to linguistic markings or schemes or what makes words meaningful; their analysis can proceed, in fact, only by tacitly accepting a theory of discourse in which there are already markings, schemes, and meanings.

The application of the PISA procedure to a text written by the Dutch girl reveals that "the text has a consistent overall structure" that somehow, *despite that consistent overall structure,* "suffers from a digression [. . .], an interruption [. . .], and a number of loose ends" (p. 56). Perhaps it would be fairer to say that the PISA procedure has *manufactured* a consistent overall structure instead of *finding* one?[18] In fact, one of the virtues of this text structure, according to van Wijk and Sanders, is that "it can be used as a criterion for text evaluation and a guideline for text revision [. . .] [because] it identifies dangling segments, and it specifies how these can be moved to more appropriate positions" (p. 56). In other words, the PISA procedure, which is intended to *describe* the structure of a text, can be used to generate a *normative* structure to which the text should be made to conform if its consistent overall structure is, alas, not consistent enough.[19]

A further irony is that an analytic procedure designed to operate temporally to reveal the temporal processes of an author's thinking produces a spatialized document—Bourdieu's (1980/1990) *synoptic diagram*—that, on the page at least, is atemporal, fixed, fully connected, flattened. Such a document can only misrepresent the temporality of discourse. For example, to depict line 3 of a segmented text as connected to line 10 without acknowledging that the connection was made by the author only after the fact of—or, as a consequence of—the inscription of the word in line 10, distorts the nature of the connection. When the author wrote line 3, there was no connection at all, for line 10 did not yet exist, *not even as a possibility.* Nor was there a "chain" dangling from that word in line 3, groping for a partner sometime in the future; rather, we should say that line 10 later "grabbed" line 3. And the meaning of the connection is not to be found in the interval between line 3 and line 10, but in the consequences that unfold and continue to unfold after line 10. What seems like a connection always already there is actually a connection only just made, a connection always at risk of severance, between words that may in fact be both connected *and* severed as chains of consequences proliferate and fragment. Van Wijk and Sanders's PISA procedure converts the contrapuntal procession of discourses into a spatialized musical score, the temporal distension of the text and the propagating meanings of its propagating Meaning into an atemporal chart.

Summary

This explication of the principle of panchronism, though it engages work within analytic philosophy, biblical hermeneutics, composition studies, the natural sciences, phenomenology, rhetoric, and theology, is hardly exhaustive and, if patience allowed, could be indefinitely extended. That said, our investigation has positioned us to draw some tentative conclusions about some of the features of treatments of meaning and language in theories dating back to antiquity that subscribe—directly or indirectly—to models of time analogous to the eternity of classical and medieval theology and metaphysics and to the block time of contemporary physics that we discussed earlier in this chapter:

- Time has no constitutive or positive role to play in the production of meaning. In fact, there is no production of meaning at all, either in the sense that all future meanings are only waiting to be encountered, not produced, or in the sense that texts have static meanings that may be mapped onto an *a priori*, steady-state grid of logical propositions (or, more precisely, texts are meaningful only to the extent that they express propositions, which are themselves the units of meaning), the total set of which comprises the world of possibility and actuality. The future holds no surprises: Nothing, however unprecedented, is unanticipated.

- The mystical alternative to this logical view replaces God as the *a priori* foundation of the meaning of texts, even to the point of His composing texts and utterances and dictating the responses of the auditors.
- The flow of time, in fact, is illusory, a curious phenomenon produced by the limitations of human cognition. From an atemporal perspective, time has extension, like Diderot's tableau (cf. Barthes, 1973/1977c),20 but past and future depend only upon the one's placement within time, just as north and south depend only upon one's placement on the earth. The past has no ontological priority over the future: The future is as real as the present and past.
- In a sense, then, all utterances have already been uttered and all texts have already been written. The proleptic expression already "knows" whether it has its referent securely grasped, and the conversation one begins already has its ending, like a movie script or conversation analyst's transcript. The movement or progression of dialogue that we experience results only from our unfortunate ignorance of what we will say (or, better, have already said in the future)! As Derrida (1967/1978) puts it, for such a view there is only one Book, a book that "is distributed throughout all books" (p. 9).
- Meanings, then, are static because time does not move: The text has the meanings it has, even if they are experienced sequentially due to the limitations of perception, just as the desk I am sitting at has four legs, even if I can only see two of them at a time.

3 Panchronism and Consequentialism: The Labor of Meaning and the End of Interpretation

> If interpretation were the slow exposure of the meaning hidden in an origin, then only metaphysics could interpret the development of humanity. But if interpretation is the violent or surreptitious appropriation of a system of rules, which in itself has no essential meaning, in order to impose a new direction, to bend it to a new will, to force its participation in a different game, and to subject it to secondary rules, then the development of humanity is a series of interpretations.
>
> —Michel Foucault

> [T]he text finally disappeared under the interpretation
>
> —Friedrich Nietzsche

Our analysis in Chapter 2 focused—better, to the extent that it remains consequential for me, *focuses*—on multiple problems that attend panchronic manifestations of meaning apriorism in semantic mysticism and rationalism. In this chapter, I will challenge the notion that the commentators of sacred texts—or anyone generally—*interpret* texts that express panchronic meanings, and I will theorize, in terms of temporally distended *immediations, expropriations,* and *efforts,* what exactly these commentators—and readers generally—are doing if they are not interpreting texts. Two central questions that I have been attempting to think through are: How should one respond to the fact that people do not always agree about what a text "means" (i.e., that a text may have multiple, even incommensurable interpretations)? And what do "interpreters" in fact do when they "interpret" texts and utterances?

The response of theorists who subscribe to mystical or rationalist manifestations of meaning apriorism to the first question is clear: If one believes that sacred texts are secure and faithful vessels of meanings authored by a fully coherent and omniscient God, then, as we have seen, such diversity of response appears to be a defect, a lack, a failing on the part of readers whose flaws might include their being (a) too uneducated or unintelligent to perceive the literal sense of the text; (b) too unprepared in the disciplines of history, languages, philology, theology, and textual criticism that are prerequisites for a proper understanding of the text; (c) too unsophisticated or immoral to decipher its spirit behind its literal sense; and/or (d) too tied to the chronological order of its events, perhaps even living at a point in history when the meaning of the text is yet to be revealed. (In more modern guises, some of these problems can be reformulated as a reader's failure to know the correct code or language for deciphering the text; to place the text in its proper context or make accurate attributions of authorial intentions; and/or to belong to the proper interpretive community or activity system within which the text is made meaningful.) Or, if one believes that texts are a structured, determinate set of propositions or expressions of propositions taken from the totality of *a priori* propositions, then, once again, any response that "finds" in the text a different structured set of expressed propositions (or, worse still, a "something" not expressible in propositional form) must be rejected as a failure on the part of readers, for whatever reason, to perceive the actual structure of the text. Conflicting interpretations, as we have seen, result from reader-introduced breaks in the circuit between reader and text; and any interpretation contrary to the single authoritative reading of the text is a *misinterpretation* that must be corrected if possible, or punished if necessary.

It would be tempting, but equally wrong-headed from the perspective of meaning consequentialism I am developing, to reverse this deficiency model by shifting the inadequacy from *readers* to *texts*. For example, a theorist could argue that the Bible, because of its complex authorship and history of preservation, is plagued with self-contradictions, ambiguities, textual corruptions, etc., so that it is no surprise that readers with selective memories and strong ideological commitments will seize upon and promote certain favorable passages while ignoring or discrediting others. On this view, such problems are not endemic to texts per se, but only particular texts (i.e., that only if enough careful work had been expended on the Bible, it could have been made consistent). Or a theorist could argue that the Bible, as a text, is necessarily aporetic, incomplete, incapable of being self-consistent or of conveying fully determinate meanings.

One of the problems with these arguments is that they accept—the former explicitly, the latter implicitly—that the text is—or would be, *if meaning were possible*—the locus of meaning. For both, *the text itself* is ambiguous, self-contradictory, open-ended, indeterminate, aporetic. The text resists impositions of closure by readers because *it* is not closed or closeable; any reading of the text in which its meanings appear consistent is always already a *misreading* of the text (cf. S. Miller, 1989, p. 125), *a misreading that can be always exposed as a misreading by a more careful, nuanced reading of the text that unmasks its internal inconsistencies.* Thus, a deconstructive reader determined at all points to demonstrate that a sacred text is inconsistent would share many assumptions about the meaning of texts with a devout theologian determined to prove its infallibility.[1]

As I conceive of it, meaning consequentialism leads me (a) to reject any effort to fault readers *or* texts for the fact that texts propagate different consequences for different readers or for the same reader at different times, or in any way (b) to deny the meaningfulness of any of these consequences. For meaning consequentialism, divergent consequences of texts are not unnatural or unexpected problems in need of a solution: They do not represent a *catastrophe* from outside the normal operations of language and meaning. If the meanings of a text are its consequences, there is no *a priori* reason why those consequences must be consistent with each other, just as there is no *a priori* reason why those consequences, or at least some subset of consequences, could not be consistent with each other. Further, if my intuitions about meaning consequentialism are correct, then we should abandon the notion that any particular meaning/consequence of a text is to be privileged *a priori* over all others; an utterance or text has the consequences that it has, and those temporally dispersed consequences are the meanings that comprise its distended and open-ended Meaning. Thus, there are no *misinterpretations or misreadings* of a text because the text has no *a priori* standard against which to assess those *misinterpretations* or *misreadings*.

However, perhaps surprisingly, if we dispense with the notion of *misinterpretation*, then we must also dispense with the very idea of *interpretation* in the dual sense as (a) a mediating activity between a reader and a text that attempts to excavate, decipher, or translate the proper meaning of a text and (b) the result of that activity of excavation, decipherment, or translation (i.e., that the result of reading is an interpretation of the meaning of the text). These dual senses are used, for example, by David R. Olson (1994) when he claims that "interpretation is recovery, not invention" (p. 185), and by Rosenblatt (1978) when she argues that readers' interpretations must not be contradicted by elements in the text or projected onto the text. But an interpretation is not a *guess, theory,* or some other cognitive construct about, separate from, and held accountable to a recoverable meaning already contained within a text or an utterance; on the contrary, an interpretation—if the term be retained—is a newly propagated, *a posteriori* meaning of the text or utterance, a meaning that is experienced *immediately* because that experience, qua consequence of the text, *is* one of its meanings. That is why, for example, we do not experience a text, utterance, or other sign as an object first plus a meaning distinct or separable from the object, but as a meaningful object with which we are in consequential contact; take away that consequential contact, and you take away meaning. Similarly, we do not experience our emotions, beliefs, pains, etc., as representations of something else: The physical sensation of grief is not a representation of sadness, but is sadness apprehended immediately; a belief is not a representation of a conviction located elsewhere, but is that conviction. As Heidegger (1927/1962) would put it, our experience of objects being ready-to-hand in relation to our concerns is ontologically prior to our experience of objects-in-themselves separate from those concerns.

However, I would like to immediately *distance* this sense of *immediacy* from the way this phenomenological experience of meaning has been characterized in terms of *transparency,* as if readers or listeners "see through" utterances and texts to the meanings purportedly conveyed by them (e.g., Chafe, 1994, p. 65). This notion is particularly popular for those who subscribe to code- or convention-oriented theories of language, in which listeners and readers do not interpret utterances or texts that conform to these codes or conventions, but simply understand them through an automated process, with interpretation reserved for a conscious process of translating unfamiliar codes or conventions (e.g., Dummett, 1986; Hacking, 1986; Kemmerling, 1993; Luckmann, 1991; Searle, 1995). Consider Polanyi's (1958/1974) formulation of the concept:

> The most pregnant carriers of meaning are of course the words of a language, and it is interesting to recall that when we use words in speech or writing we are aware of them only in a subsidiary manner. This fact, which is usually described as the *transparency* of language, may be illustrated by a homely episode from my own experience. My correspondence arrives at my breakfast table in various languages, but my son understands only English. Having just finished reading a letter I may wish to pass it on to him, but must check myself and look again to see in what language it was written. I am vividly aware of the meaning conveyed by the letter, yet know nothing whatever of its words. I have attended to them closely but only for what they mean and not for what they are as objects. If my understanding of the text were halting, or its expressions or its spelling were faulty, its words would arrest my attention. They would become slightly opaque and prevent my thought from passing through them unhindered to the things they signify. (p. 57)

The conveyance metaphors are in full force: words are "pregnant carriers of meaning"; the meaning "conveyed by the letter"; "passing through [. . .] to the things they signify." *The Letter disappears when the Spirit is present.*

These conveyance metaphors may be in tension with other positions held by Polanyi, but they are not in tension with his claim that

> Communication is a form of address, calling someone's attention to its message and its speaker. Yet the possibility of communicating information to others is already foreshadowed in the mere descriptive powers of language. A small set of consistently used symbols which, owing to their peculiar manageability, enable to think about their subject matter more swiftly in terms of its symbolic representation, can

be used to carry information to other people if they
can use this representation as we do. This can happen
only if speakers and listeners have heard the terms
used in similar circumstances, and have derived from
these experiences the same relation between the symbols and the recurrent features (or functions) which
they represent [. . .]. I believe that even though people
may conceivably misunderstand any particular words
addressed to them, they can, as a rule, convey information to each other reliably enough by speech. (pp.
204–205)

Let me pause here to remind readers about my *use* of sources, which
might allay some concerns. For example, a reader might object, not
to my quotation from Polanyi (which is quite accurate), but that this
quotation (a) is taken out of its full context (i.e., the full context of
Polanyi's *Personal Knowledge* or even the fuller context of Polanyi's
entire set of published texts) and, so, is a misrepresentation of both
the quotation and some fully present entity called *Polanyi's thought*, or
(b) marks a curious lapse in Polanyi's argument that should, given the
totality of his philosophy, be charitably overlooked. But I do not think
that either objection is germane because the former depends upon an
intertextual view of meaning to which I do not subscribe, attributes
an impossible level of coherence of Polanyi's thought, and results in an
equally unreasonable standard for what comprises understanding even
small portions of it, and because the latter implies (a) that somewhere
apart from the fallible texts and utterances that comprise it subsists a
pure version of Polanyi's work, (b) that tensions in the formulation of
a theory, so long as they are *minor*, should go unremarked (perhaps
because we are so accustomed to such tensions that they seem *unre-
markable?*), and (c) most importantly, that I am using the quotation
as if it were a representative anecdote capturing the *essence* of Polanyi's
thought. In Chapter 1, I carefully explained not only the limitations I
see in the use of citations, but also that my finding meaning apriorism
manifesting itself in a particular theory does not entail that the theory
is relentlessly, or even largely, aprioristic; in fact, that meaning apriorism is made manifest in a theory that elsewhere resists it for me makes
that manifestation even more significant and worth exploring.

To return: How credible are the inferences Polanyi draws from this
"homely episode"? Is it accurate to say that he knew "nothing whatever

of its words," even in the very act of reading the text? It may be, for example, that Polanyi has *forgotten* his awareness of its words; as Dennett (1991) argues, our non-perception of an entity or an event may be simply the result of an immediate and total forgetting of a perception of that entity or event (i.e., there would be no phenomenological difference between an event that never occurred and an event that is immediately and totally forgotten); our *mind* does not record experiences with perfect fidelity, nor does its sense of the temporal relationships between experiences necessarily replicate the objective sequencing of those experiences.

More importantly, Polanyi neglects the fact that texts do not objectively contain *words,* but only inked shapes; rather than arguing that we look *past* words in order to find meanings (and trip up on words only when they are problematic), I posit that words becoming increasingly *visible* as they become increasingly meaningful or consequential (i.e., *imperceptible consequences* would be an oxymoron). What could be less visible or distinct than page after page of text with symbols that evoke little or no consequences within us—a text that we scan without any sense of comprehension, but with a growing sense of impatience or boredom; a text that may prompt us set it aside and never attempt to read it again; a text that is quickly and utterly forgotten; a text whose symbols could just as well be written in an invisible script? I suggest that our experience of transparency is an *illusion* that results in part, as in Poe's (1844/1987) "Purloined Letter," from the actual experience of the *obviousness* of the text and from the speed at which we are able to pass over—not pass through (the text has no *depth*)—particular signs because of our experience of their distinctive and obvious consequences. In short: It is not so much that I do not see the words, but rather that I see them so acutely that I need not look at them for long.

Texts, then, are experienced immediately, not in the sense that they are given in experience neutrally, objectively, passively, or even fully determinately—because experience is itself temporally distended and open to the propagation of further consequences—but in the sense that there is nothing called an *interpretation* which stands in between or joins together the reader, the text, and the meanings of a text. We do not have, in addition to readers, texts, and meanings of texts, interpretations of the meanings of texts; to add interpretations is just to add another theoretical concept that requires explanation. What we have, insofar as a text is consequential for a reader, are continuant *immediations,* not interstitial *interpretations.*

These immediations of the text cannot be *resisted,* in the sense that, for example, I cannot force myself to see something *in* the text that I do not see in the text, or, conversely, not to see something *in* the text that I actually see. This is, essentially, Wittgenstein's (1953/1968) challenge: "Make the following experiment: say 'It's cold here' and mean 'It's warm here.' Can you do it?—And what are you doing as you do it? And is there only one way of doing it?" (I.510; cf. pp. I.156–178). As I read a text, I have no sensation of imposing my will on the text or of rewriting the text, but rather feel imposed upon or guided by the text, as if I am written upon by or interpolated into the text—what Rommetveit (1974, pp. 84–85) describes as *imprisonment* within a text. Of course, we must be careful not to conclude that whatever shape the prison in which we find ourselves, aside from the physical characteristics of the text, is predetermined by the text itself—i.e., that all readers find themselves in the same prison, or would, if only their eyesight or intellect were sufficient to the task—but rather must think of it as a temporally distended *outcome* of the reading and its further consequences. (And to the extent that a text is made consequential only by and through its readers, we could reverse the proposition and claim that texts are imprisoned by their readers.)

Whatever I experience, I experience, perhaps aptly enough if we are to speak of imprisonment, with *conviction,* even if I am convinced only that the text has little meaning for me. But immediation, however much it induces conviction, has several important limitations. First, as a result of a consequential encounter with a text, I may be convinced to hold certain beliefs about that text, to talk about it in certain ways, to act upon it in certain ways, etc., without also believing that all other people should necessarily be held accountable to my own immediate experience of the text (such would be the position of a solipsist). I alone am accountable to that experience of the text to the extent that I should not deny what I experience, to myself or to others; but I should not hold others accountable *a priori* to that experience.

Second, we must recognize that immediations of entire texts, as opposed to segments of texts, are temporally distended, never fully present. A text, however brief, is never experienced in a single instant, but rather is experienced through a rolling, non-totalizable horizon of recollections, perceptions, and expectations whose Meanings may themselves proliferate. There is no "total reading" of a text (Derrida, 1967/1978, p. 24)[2]; nor, just as importantly, can there be a *total writing* of a text. For example, Eliot's (1919/1999a, p. 148) claim that we cannot "enjoy" particular literary works of Ben Jonson without having "saturate[d] ourselves in his work as a whole" must be rejected not only because there can be no saturation of the requisite kind by a reader, *but also because there was no such saturation for Jonson;* and, similarly, Eliot's (1929/1999b) suggestion that "every part of Dante is essential to the whole" must be rejected not only because no reader can possibly grasp the entirety of *The Divine Comedy,* but also because Dante couldn't either. (One could argue—though vacuously—that every part of *The Divine Comedy* is essential to the whole only in the sense that changing or deleting any part of it would change the whole, but Eliot is not limiting himself to such a bland claim.) As Hobsbaum (1970) puts it, "This is what I have called the concept of availability: just as all of his experience is not available even to the most gifted creative writer, so all of the writer's work is not available to even the most interested reader [or, I would add, even the most meticulous writer]" (p. 48).

At the same time, the *span of the now,* pace Augustine (trans. 1992), is not entirely without duration or infinitely divisible (otherwise, no segment of text, however brief, could be apprehended immediately); immediacy has a *duration,* calculated in humans to be about three seconds (Sebeok, 1991c, p. 134). It is possible, of course, to speculate that the *now* is a mental construct, a representation of time rather than time as its presents itself to us. As Dennett (1991) points out, the brain is responsible for coordinating asynchronous input from different areas of the body because of the differences in travel time for the electrical pulses to arrive. Thus, the temporal sequence in which signals arrive in the brain does not mirror the temporal representation constructed from those signals: The brain may represent event *A* taking place prior to event *B* even if the signal for event *B* arrived in the brain prior to the signal for event *A* (pp. 145–149). If this is so, then it is conceivable for the now to, in principle, extend beyond the 3-second limit—or G. Miller's (1956) "magical number seven, plus or minor two" for the processing of quanta of information (p. 81)—for organisms capable of constructing and sustaining without loss these temporal representations (e.g., a *now* that extends minutes, not seconds). *The modulus of the now need not be uniform for all conscious beings.*

The "vivid present," then, is not, pace Alfred Schutz (1962/1990), impossible to be "reflectively considered" (p. 173; cf. Peirce, 1868/1991c, p. 70), but our reflections must be *quick* (Chafe, 1994, p. 140; Skinner, 1957, p. 205) before events shift from the vivid present to the recollected past. I should caution that we must not confuse the phenomenological *vivid present* with the *present* of physical time (or of phenomenal time in general with physical time, though this not the place in which to trace the tensions between and within phenomenology and the physical sciences about the nature of time), for it is possible to measure units of time that are imperceptible to human beings; thus, the vivid present need not be continuous in the sense that it occurs during a span of the present that is itself indivisible.

Third, an immediation is the actual, concrete, synchronized contact with the concrete text or utterance through an act of reading or listening; an immediation does not endure beyond that contact, though it may be to some extent conserved with great effort (e.g., a text may be totally memorized, though even this memorial text is not the same text, but another text). Without periodic refreshment, the recall of the text or utterance itself changes, fragments, and refracts, like fatigued retinal cells unable to fix perpetually on an image (and even with that refreshment, or because of it, it may change) (cf. F. Smith, 1971, p. 97). Immediations propagate *mediations* as the initial consequences of the text propagate their own consequences, and so on (i.e., the Meaning of an immediation is not itself immutable, but dispersible). It is important to note, however, that this shift from immediacy to mediacy does not mark a point of *degradation* of the Meaning of the text—i.e., Nietzsche's text disappearing under the interpretation—but simply its extension and proliferation (and, in fact, the text can be consequential—hence meaningful—only to the extent that it is further mediated, for otherwise the text would require *its being continually read* for its continued consequentiality).

Fourth, immediations neither govern our responses—e.g., aversion, disagreement, joy, belief—to our experience of text's meaning nor govern our experiences of a text's meaning, but simply are our experiences of its meaning; but, at the same time, we cannot demarcate the affective from the semantic (cf. Worsham, 1998, p. 233), as so many theorists have attempted to do, separating the "literal" from the "emotional" (Ayer, 1946/1952, p. 35); the "sense" from the "idea" (Frege, 1892/1984d); the "denotative" from the "connotative"

(Mill, 1843/1949); the "designative" from the "emotional" (Carnap, 1947/1988, p. 6); the "meaning" from the "significance" (Hirsch, 1976, p. 2); the "semantic" from the "emotional" (Hirsch, 1977, p. 77); the "symbolic" from the "emotive" (Ogden and Richards, 1923/1946); and linguistic "consequences" from non-linguistic "effects" (R. Read and Guetti, 1999, p. 304).

Finally, we must qualify *immediation* so that it does not suggest pure constructivism, relativism, and solipsism—that the reader is the locus and arbiter of a text's meaning. What is needed, I think, is a conception of immediation that does not imply *ownership* of the experience by the experiencer (an implication I have already tried to avert by indicating the impossibility of resisting an immediation, even if one wishes). On the contrary, I think of immediation as an *expropriation,* in the double sense that I *disown* my reading of the text when encountering the text and the text *disowns* its Meaning in any given encounter. In short, reading is a process not of possessing the contents of texts, but of expropriating readers *and* texts: The reader *loses* himself or herself by opening up to the alien consequences of texts, but at the same time, the text *loses* its current Meaning in the process of propagating new consequences that belong to it—*in the sense that they are its consequences*—but over which it has no determinate control. Incidentally, we could also add a third sense of expropriation, that of the author from his or her text. As Derrida (1972/1988c) puts it, the text is set adrift, cut off from the consciousness of the author, marking an immediate discontinuity in the chain of signification (pp. 8–9); and for theorist Avital Ronell, writing is "a kind of *dis*possession, a mode of departing that's never quite sure where it's headed" (Davis, 2000, pp. 244–245).

Before continuing, let me note that my emphasis on expropriation is in direct contrast to Heidegger's (1959/1993b) speculations about language in terms of *propriation*—a complex notion difficult to explicate (and certainly one not reducible only to the assertion that we *belong to* or are *owned by* language), but one which encompasses such claims as

- Owning conducts what comes to presence and withdraws into absence [during speaking] in each case into its own. On the basis of owning, these things show themselves, each on its own terms, and linger, each in its own manner. Let us call the owning that conducts things in this way—the owning that bestirs the saying, the owning that points in any saying's showing—the propriating. (p. 414)

- The propriation that rules in the saying is something we can name only if we say: It—propriation—owns. When we say this, we are speaking in what is already our own spoken language. (p. 415)
- Propriation bestows on mortals residence in their essence, such that they can be the ones who speak. (p. 416)
- Propriation is the law, inasmuch as it gathers mortals in such a way that they own up to their own essence. (p. 416)
- Because the showing of the saying is an owning, our being able to hear the saying, our belonging to it, also depends on propriation. (p. 416)
- Propriation propriates human beings for itself, propriates them into usage. (p. 418)
- The essence of language does not submit to our circumspection, inasmuch as we—we who can say only by reiterating the saying—ourselves belong within the saying. (p. 423)
- For propriation—owning, holding, keeping to itself—is the relation of all relations. For this reason, our saying, as answering, constantly remains relational. (p. 425)
- Our relation to language is defined by the mode to which we belong to propriation, we who are needed and used by it. (p. 425)

From my perspective, our relation to meaning is not defined by a mode of belonging to meaning, but by the mode of being consequential, in the double sense that my actions, utterances, mental states, etc., produce consequences and, equally importantly, that my actions, utterances, mental states, etc. are themselves consequences. My actions, utterances, mental states, etc. do not belong to a hypostatized *consequentiality*, but simply are temporally distended and dispersed events that, because of their correlation to prior events, are, necessarily consequences (but not *necessary* consequences) of those events.

Now let us consider these two senses of *immediation as expropriation* in more detail. First, the irresistibility of immediations—as well as the fact that I may not like what I read—indicates that my reading of a text is not a product of my will imposed on a text, that I do not see only what I expected or wanted to see prior to my act of reading. The meaning that is produced does not belong to me, even if it is my experience that is the meaning, but to the text: I feel imprisoned by the text because what I experience is not my meaning, but a facet of *its* Meaning. Partly, this feeling results from the fact that a mediation of a text does not have the same phenomenological vividness as an immediation: Setting aside a text shuts down a potent, consequential contact with that text, so that it seems as if the text itself *contains that potency.* But, more importantly, there is an *otherness* about the text, a sense of the text's *infinitude,* like Levinas's (1961/1969) *face,* that resists totalization and solipsism; but it is not a hypothetical, abstract, shadowy, or vacuous *infinity* of *a priori* meanings whose depths that I will never live long enough to fathom, but rather a *plenum,* bounded but indefinitely extendable so long as its contingent consequences propagate, whose total set of actualities forever lies beyond the my reckoning.[3] I encounter the text knowing that it has been and perhaps will continue to be encountered by others; that is, I know that there have been and may be other readers, and only by acknowledging what Arendt (1958) refers to as the "presence of others" can I resist imprisoning myself with my own experience and accept the transience, contestability, and potential intersubjectivity of meaning, thought, and experience. And my recognizing other readers is not a "sharing" of ownership of the Meaning of the text with a kind of "joint-stock company" comprised of those readers, but questioning the very nature of the ownership of meaning (cf. Derrida, 1977/1988b).

Second, although I may speak of the Meaning of a text as the total set of consequences propagated by that text, and although the Meaning of a text is ontologically distinct from any of its particular consequences, and although texts are ontologically distinct from their readers, the Meaning of a text exists only *as* that text's consequences—consequences that are to be found anywhere but in the text (i.e., consequences are not *intrinsic* to the text, but *extrinsic*), consequences that are not fully determined by that text. The text does not *own* its consequences, but finds itself *responsible* for whatever consequences it propagates.[4] Every encounter with a reader disrupts the Meaning of a text by adding meanings to it, and such disruptions are not violations because the text can only have meaningfulness through consequential contacts with readers; but, at the same time, no reader controls the Meaning of a text either.

CONSEQUENTIALISM, MYSTICISM, AND
THE LABOR OF MEANING

The legitimate language no more contains within itself the power to ensure its own perpetuation in time than it has the power to define its extension in space. Only the process of continuous creation, which occurs through the unceasing struggles between the different authorities who compete within the field of specialized production for the monopolistic power to impose the legitimate mode of expression, can ensure the permanence of the legitimate language and of its value, that is, of the recognition accorded to it.

—Pierre Bourdieu

The synchronic law is general but not imperative. Doubtless it is imposed on individuals by the weight of collective usage [. . .] but here I do not have in mind an obligation on the part of speakers. I mean that *in language* no force guarantees the maintenance of a regularity when established on some point. Being a simple expression of an existing arrangement, the synchronic law reports a state of affairs; it is like a law that states that trees in a certain orchard are arranged in the shape of a quincunx. And the arrangement that the law defines is precarious precisely because it is not imperative [. . .]. It is childish to think that the word can be changed only up to a certain point, as if there were something about it that could preserve it.

—Ferdinand de Saussure

What light does this analysis of interpretation and expropriation cast on the panchronic hermeneutical approaches of the Christian, Jewish, and Muslim exegetes discussed earlier? If they are not interpreting, as they thought, meanings already and forever housed within sacred texts—because there are no interpretations of texts, but only meanings of texts propagated by expropriated immediations and mediations— what are they actually *doing?* From my perspective, these exegetes are attempting, insofar as they are faithful to their immediations and mediations of texts, to possess what can only be expropriated (i.e., the Meaning of the text) and to impose these immediations and mediations, *not on the texts,* which are meaningful only to the extent that they are immediated and mediated because these immediations and mediations comprise it Meaning, *but on other people.* Readers cannot impose meanings on texts, but may (and will likely) try to impose them on each other.

However much Luther might have believed in literal meanings that are painfully obvious to any reader of sense, his commentaries on the Biblical texts are not *reports* of their contents, but attempts to inaugurate a world in which readings that differ from his own—the heretical, the unorthodox—are excluded. Just as Aristotle constructed his defense of the principle of non-contradiction that is directed, "not to [a skeptical] opponent, but to a gallery of some sort that purports to show that the human community ought to accept the principle," (R. Price, 1996, p. 99), Luther does not so much try to persuade people who would dispute whether the Scriptures have a plain literal sense, as he tries to invoke a community of common sense and plain speaking—by writing in a way that takes for granted that community—in which the standard of literal meaning is already a given. "Become what you are" (Bourdieu, 1982/1991, p. 122): Join us as a reader of literal meanings that you, as a person of common sense, already are.

Such impositions, as I have already emphasized, are not alien to the workings of meaning and discourse, if one thinks of them in terms of *efforts* to control the consequences of texts and utterances. A consequential theory of meaning excludes neither the particular efforts of particular speakers and authors to produce particular consequences, nor their practical success in producing desired particular consequences; however, it would exclude drawing the conclusions (a) that the effort "contained" its consequences *a priori* (i.e., that the Meaning of the effort does not define what may be considered a proper consequence of that effort, but is comprised of the actual consequences of that effort); (b) that the effort determinately defined in advance the criteria of *practical success* or *desired particular consequences* (i.e., whether a text or utterance does what it is *supposed* to do may in fact be assessed by criteria imposed after the fact); and (c) that the Meaning of the effort or its particular consequences are ever definitively closed (i.e., what we understand that a Meaning may always, but not necessarily, change).

The continued effort, the sustained labor, the endless work of meaning: It is perhaps this point that is *least* counter-intuitive about meaning consequentialism, for it is a notion that winds its varied ways through the work of theorists of several orientations to language, meaning, and discourse, of which the following can only provide the barest sample:

- *Analytic Philosophy*: Kripke (1972/1996) argues that the continuity of reference for a term requires an effort on the part of the listener, who should, but need not, "intend when he learns [the term] to use it with the same reference as the man from whom he heard it" (p. 96); and for Searle (1995), institutional values must be continually affirmed or they will fail to produce their desired consequences (e.g., money has value not because it was assigned some value at a certain point in the past, but because we continue to accept and enact its value) (pp. 44–45).

- *Cultural Studies*: De Certeau, Giard, and Mayol (1994/1998) discuss the importance of "chatting" for the maintenance of the status quo (p. 19); Stuart Hall (1982) describes "the active labor of making things mean" (p. 64); Hartley (1987) argues that because "audiences" do not exist apart or prior to television, they need "constant hailing and guidance in how-to-be-an-audience" (p. 136); and Raymond Williams (1961) claims that meanings do not preserve themselves, but require "a continual re-creation of meaning, by the society as a whole and by every individual in it" (p. 31).

- *Dialogism*: As Bakhtin (1975/1981) puts it, "any concrete discourse [utterance] finds the object of which it was directed already as it were overlain with qualifications, open to dispute, charged with value" (p. 275); Rommetveit (1974) describes the "world" as "only temporarily and partially shared" (p. 24); and Vološinov (1929/1986) contends that the refraction of existence performed by linguistic signs results from "an intersecting of differently oriented social interests within one and the same sign community, i.e., by the class struggle" (p. 23).

- *Linguistics*: Roy Harris (1998) asserts that although people may make an effort to regulate meanings through language, language itself cannot guarantee the continuity of meanings over time (pp. 82, 88); Lentine and Shuy (1990) argue that the McDonald's corporation has not only expended great effort through advertising to create and promote a "McLanguage" for children and through legal avenues to preserve control over the phoneme "Mc," but it has also lost control over that

"McLanguage," which is often satirized or used in pejorative senses (pp. 352, 359–360); and Wardhaugh (1999) observes that the sixteenth to eighteenth centuries saw the formation of "academies" to "fix language"—Italy in 1582, France in 1635, Spain in 1713, and a proposed American academy in 1780 (pp. 73–81).

- *Literary Studies*: Lynn Bloom (1999) describes the importance of and the conditions in which literary essays are anthologized and re-anthologized; it is not enough that an essay has been published once, argues Bloom: "to survive [. . .] it must be reprinted time and again" (p. 401). And in his influential but contested account of oral cultures vs. literate cultures, Ong (1982) argues that, for oral cultures, knowledge must be continually repeated in order to be retained (pp. 23–24, 41).
- *Poststructuralism*: Barthes (1957/1982) writes of "the ceaseless making of the world" through ideology and myth (p. 145); and Foucault (1977b) argues that discursive practices require the support of institutions, practices, behaviors, pedagogies, that "impose and maintain them" (p. 200).
- *Pragmatism*: According to Dewey (1927/1985), community requires constant effort, and the "state" is a regulative mechanism—itself requiring maintenance—for behaviors that "may have extensive and enduring consequences which involve others beyond those directly engaged in them" (p. 27). These consequences must be "taken care of, looked out for," but not only by the individuals directly involved because "the essence of the consequences which call a public into being is the fact that they expand beyond those directly engaged in producing them" (p. 27).
- *Psychology*: In Skinner's (1957) behaviorist terms, "the learning process is a conspicuous effect of reinforcement, and practical problems of education make the rate of acquisition of verbal behavior important [. . .]. Reinforcement continues to be effective after behavior has been acquired. The availability of behavior, its probability of strength, depends upon whether reinforcements continue in effect and according to what schedules" (p. 204).
- *Rhetoric and Composition*: Bazerman (1988) describes the efforts made to enforce the regularity of genres (p. 23); Dyson (1997)

argues that children's fairy tales are constantly retold and that only those tales that are retold will endure (p. 276); and Susan Miller (1989) recounts the laborious efforts of ancient scribes and medieval monks to copy texts (pp. 54, 73).

- *Rhetoric and Speech Communication*: McGee (1975/1999a) asserts that social formations are rhetorical constructions—"they are conjured into objective reality, remain so long as the rhetoric which defined them has force, and in the end wilt away, becoming once again merely a collection of individuals" (p. 345); and Scott (1976) argues that whatever values a community made share is contingent upon their cooperative establishment and repeated renewal (p. 264).
- *Sociology*: Berger and Luckmann (1966/1967) contend the reality that people take for granted is always under pressure, requiring constant maintenance that is primarily conducted through localized conversations that make real and reaffirm the reality of what is discussed (and what is not discussed disappears) (pp. 24, 149–155).
- *Sociolinguistics*: Duranti (1997) emphasizes that social structures must be continually maintained through the use of language (p. 337); and for Schegloff (1996), the primordial scene of social life is conversation, which is how the social "gets done" (p. 54).

We must resist, as Spellmeyer (1993/1998) argues, presupposing "the existence of determining laws or codes that operate 'behind the backs' of those subject to them," instead investigating "why is it that people work so hard to impose their codes and systems on others" (p. 260). If meanings really comprised a steady-state, panchronic totality, then there would seem to be no good reason for all of this effort to preserve and propagate what should require neither *preservation,* because of its panchronism, nor *propagation,* because of its omnipresence.

The meaningfulness of the Bible, then, is not the intrinsic cause, but the exfoliated and expropriated outcome, of the long history of work expended upon it by theologians, scholars, commentators, priests, pastors, missionaries, redactors, scribes, lay readers, and what Murphy (1974) calls the "immense rhetorical output of the church" (p. 297). Without that sustained effort and without its continued labor of reception among those who adhere to them through the Christian liturgy, the Biblical texts would be inert:

> Through the proclamation of the Scripture the word
> of God is _received_ in faith by the participants as the
> living word of God; it is _assimilated_ in a variety of
> ways by them, made their own, translated into ac-
> tion, done; and it is actualized by preaching. And so
> it is _transmitted_. It is not enough, after all, simply to
> have the Bible [. . .]. Thus the history of salvation con-
> tinues, the divine plan is worked out, the mystery of
> Christ is accomplished, God's great deeds are some-
> how prolonged, when the Scriptures are proclaimed
> in the liturgical assembly. (McGoldrick, 1995, p. 31)

Rather than "transmitted," I would say, "propagated," but McGoldrick's
larger point is correct: That the Bible cannot guarantee its continuity
of Meaning and that its Meaning, whatever it might be, will not be
found in its pages, but in the temporally dispersed propagation of its
expropriated immediations.

CONCLUSION: THE END OF INTERPRETATION

> Must I understand an order before I can act on it?—Certainly,
> otherwise you wouldn't know what you had to do!—But isn't
> there in turn a jump from _knowing_ to doing?—
>
> The absent-minded man who at the order "Right turn!"
> turns left, and then, clutching his forehead, says "Oh! right
> turn" and does a right turn.—What has struck him? An in-
> terpretation?
>
> —Ludwig Wittgenstein

The moment that one recognizes (a) that the Meaning of a text is
not a blueprint for the construction of appropriate consequences determined for all time, but the temporally distended result of those
consequences; (b) that the Meaning of a text is not its prior "depths,"
but its subsequent dilation and exfoliation of consequences; (c) that
texts may be inert, but also catalytic; (d) that the apparent inertia of
texts and meanings is a product of effort, not momentum; (e) that the
act of reading is neither recovery of the Meaning, nor invention of
the Meaning, but an act of expropriated immediation that constitutes
through time, not all-at-once, a meaning or set of meanings of a text;

and (f) that immediations have no *a priori* privilege over mediations, but are as contestable as any other consequence of a text—*in that moment, one recognizes the end of panchronism and interpretation and the beginning of meaning consequentialism and expropriation.*

4 The Principle of Simultaneity: Absolute Time and the Spatialization of Society, Language, and Mind

As I discussed in Chapter 2, *eternity* or *block time* conceptualizes time *vertically*, as a container in which all times "exist," from an atemporal perspective, all-at-once. Our discussion now shifts to *absolute time*, which conceptualizes time *horizontally*, as a clearly demarcated linear succession of single-dimensional planes—called "achronal slices" (Ray, 1991, p. 212)—spanning the entire physical universe. In this chapter, I will discuss and critique absolute time and demonstrate how *a priori* conceptions of it, particularly those formulated in the principles of linguistic spatialism and linguistic holism, are made manifest in an interdisciplinary set of theories that conceive of *society, language, discourse communities, linguistic conventions, linguistic competence, culture, mind, idiolect,* and *intentions* as spatialized wholes.

ABSOLUTE OR NEWTONIAN TIME

> *Duration is but as it were the length of one streight Line,* extended *in infinitum,* not capable of Multiplicity, Variation, or Figure; but is one common measure of all Existence whatsoever, wherein all things whilst they exist, equally partake. For this present moment is common to all things, that are now in being, and equally comprehends that part of their Existence, as much as if they were all but one single Being; and we may truly say, they all exist in the same moment of Time.
>
> —John Locke

Although Aristotle is credited with recognizing the importance of time and motion and Galileo is credited with incorporating time into mathematics, it is Newton who most fully developed the notion of absolute time, which is, consequently, often referred to as Newtonian time (Davies, 1995, pp. 29–31). In his *Mathematical Principles of Natural Philosophy* (1729/1962), Newton argues that time is not intrinsically linked to motion, which would imply a relativity of time (i.e., objects moving at different speeds would have *different* times), but has its own essential property of *equable passage:* "Absolute, true, and mathematical time, of itself, and from its own nature, flows equably without relation to anything external, and by another name is called duration: relative, apparent, and common time, is sensible and external (whether accurate or unequable) measure of duration by the means of motion, which is commonly used instead of true time" (qtd. in Earman, 1989, p. 20). Objects exist in time and flow through time, but the existence and flow of time does not depend on the existence and flow of actual objects.

An absolute conception of time is connected to an absolute conception of space, which Newton defines thus: "Absolute space, in its own nature, without relation to anything external, remains always similar and immovable. Relative space is some movable dimension or measure of the absolute spaces; which our senses determine by its position to bodies; and which is commonly taken for immovable space" (qtd. in Earman, 1989, p. 20). Although absolute time and absolute space are conceptually related, what they refer to are independent features of the physical world; for Newton, because time is independent of space, "one could unambiguously measure the interval of time between two events [. . . and] this time would be the same whoever measured it, provided they used a good clock" (Hawking, 1988/1990, p. 18). At any particular moment of time—whatever may be the smallest unit of time that comprises the duration of the achronal slice (cf. Chapter 7)—we can imagine the totality of the universe in terms of a still picture, with every single object, despite its unique spatial position, sharing the same temporal position with all of the other objects found in the still picture. In short, the universe is a system, however incredibly vast in size, whose parts exist *simultaneously.* And, if one assumes, as did, for example, Aristotle (trans. 2001, II.7) and Descartes (1637/1970a, p. 108), that light propagates with infinite speed, then whatever one sees, however distant, shares the same *now* (cf. Novikov, 1998, p. 38).

However, with the advent of Einstein's (1916/1961) theories of special relativity (i.e., that the laws of science, such as the *finite* speed of light *in vacuo*, will be the same for all observers so long as they are in uniform motion) and general relativity (i.e., that the laws of science will be the same for all observers regardless of their motion), absolute time and absolute space had to be abandoned. Time and space, for Einstein, are not independent features of the physical universe, but "physical things, mutable, malleable, and subject to physical laws" (Davies, 1995, p. 16). According to Einstein (1922/1956), for the concept of time to have "physical significance [. . .] processes of some kind are required which enable relations to be established between different places" (p. 28), but whatever physical processes might be used to determine the simultaneity of events—such as the collection of light signals, the use of clocks, etc.—are subject to physical laws, not independent of them. Consequently, if "the gravitational field influences and even determines the metrical laws of the space-time continuum," then there can be no absolute standard of distance (p. 61); for if all bodies react to the curvature of space in the same way, there can be no ruler immune to the effects of the curvature that provides the absolute standard of distance.

In an ingenious thought experiment, Einstein (1916/1961) demonstrates how, because the speed of light is a physical constant for all observers, observers who do not share uniform motion will not share uniform time or space (see Figure 4.1).

Figure 4.1. Einstein's Thought Experiment

Einstein asks us to imagine an observer (standing at point M') on a train (T) traveling at a constant velocity v, and an observer (standing at point M) on an embankment (E) next to the train; consequently, in relation to the framework of the embankment, the embankment is stationary ($v = 0$) and the train is moving ($v > 0$). Assume that events A and B are lightning flashes along the embankment that, from the perspective of the observer at position M, are visible at the same moment and, consequently, are equidistant. The question Einstein asks is, given the fact that "every event which takes place along the [embankment] also takes place at a particular point of the train" (p. 29), will the two events *A* and *B*, "which are simultaneous *with reference to the railway embankment*," also be "simultaneous *relatively to the train?*" (pp. 29–30). Despite our intuitions about the seeming equality of the distances represented in the Euclidian diagram of Figure 4.1, Einstein argues that we must include the velocity of the observer at point M' into our considerations, for when events *A* and *B* occur, the observer at M' is moving toward *B* and away from *A*. This has an important result:

> Hence the observer will see the beam of light emit- ted from *B* earlier than he will see that emitted from *A*. Observers who take the railway train as their ref- erence-body must therefore come to the conclusion that the lightning flash *B* took place earlier than the lightning flash *A* [. . .]. Events which are simultane- ous with reference to the embankment are not simul- taneous with reference to the train, and *vice versa* (relativity of simultaneity). Every reference-body (co- ordinate system) has its own particular time; unless we are told the reference-body to which the statement of time refers, there is no meaning in a statement of the time of an event. (pp. 30–31)[1]

If the observers at *M* and M' do 'not share measurements of time, then they will not share measurements of distance either. This results from the fact that they must agree on the speed of light. For example, suppose the observer at M' sends a pulse of light from M' to a target at B', which corresponds to point *B* on the embankment; to measure the time it took to reach the target B', however, the observer at M' must wait for the light to be reflected back to him, and then divide the interval by 2. Notice, however, that the observer at M' is moving toward the light that is reflected back from the target at B', whereas the observer at *M* is not; thus, the light will be reflected back to the observer at M' sooner than it will for the observer at *M*. Thus, the observers will not agree on the time that it took for the pulse of light to strike the target at B'. But because the observers, whatever their motion, must agree on the speed of light, the fact that the observers disagree on the time it took the light to travel, from M' to B' and back to M' entails that they must disagree over the distance that the light traveled. For the observer at M, the intervals of distance between M' and B' will be longer, and, consequently, the interval of time between the sending and return of the pulse of light from M' to B' to M' will be longer, than they will be for the observer at M'.[2]

Thus, the counterintuitive upshot of Einstein's theories is that two presuppositions of classical mechanics must be rejected: (a) that "the time-interval (time) between two events is independent of the condition of motion of the body of reference" and (b) that "the space-interval (distance) between two points of a rigid body is independent of the condition of motion of the body of reference" (Einstein, 1916/1961, p. 34). Simultaneity is relative to reference-bodies because of the limiting factor of the speed of light, which prevents the propagation of instantaneous effects across distances (i.e., "action at a distance" requires time) (p. 71). In short, there is no universal *now*, no absolute simultaneity.

As I noted in Chapter 2, we must understand that Einstein's theory is a rejection of separately considered absolute space and absolute time, not a rejection of an absolute *space-time continuum*, which forms the *block time* universe. As Einstein (1922/1956) observes, "Just as it was consistent from the Newtonian standpoint to make both the statements, *tempus est absolutum, spatium est absolutum*, so from the standpoint of the special theory of relativity we must say, *continuum spatii et temporis est absolutum*" (p. 55).

MANIFESTATIONS OF THE PRINCIPLE OF SIMULTANEITY

Einstein's refutation of absolute time and absolute space renders untenable conceptions of meaning, language, discourse, mind, and time that depend upon notions of universal simultaneity (i.e., the principle of simultaneity). What is remarkable is not so much that theorists have conceptualized meaning, language, etc., in absolute terms, but rather that conceptualizing them in these terms continues to be propagated in contemporary theory. The purpose of this section is to illustrate and critique manifestations of principle of simultaneity in attempts to theorize concepts, such as *society, language, discourse communities,* and *linguistic conventions,* which fall under the domain of the principle of *linguistic spatialism,* and *idiolect, mind, intentions,* and *consciousness,* which fall under the rubric of the principle of *linguistic holism.*

Absolute Time and the Myth of Society

[For Leibniz] every compound is no more a single substance than is a pile of sand or a sack of wheat. We might as well say that the employees of the India Company formed a single substance. It is evident therefore that a compound is never a substance and in order to find the real substance we must attain unity or the indivisible.

—Paul Janet

Just as conceptions of meaning grounded in God reflect the temporality attributed to God, as we saw in Chapter 2, so also conceptions of meaning which locate meaning in the practices of vast collectives reflect the temporality attributed to *society*. Too often, especially for theorists who think of societies in terms of *structures, systems, machines,* or *organisms* (e.g., Berger and Luckmann, 1966/1967; Durkheim, 1895/1982; Humboldt, 1836/1988; Parsons, 1951), *society* is something that could be said to exist all-at-once without consideration of its spatial or temporal dimensions or the number of its members:

The idea of a sociological organism moving calendrically through homogeneous, empty time is a precise analogue of the idea of the nation, which also is conceived as a solid community moving steadily up (or down) history. An American will never meet, or even know, the names of more than a handful of his 240,000-odd [*sic*] fellow Americans. He has no idea of what they are up to at any one time. But he has complete confidence in their steady, anonymous, simultaneous activity. (B. Anderson, 1983/1996, p. 26)[3]

Anderson argues that this sense of "temporal coincidence," which is "measured by clock and calendar," succeeded medieval panchronism and that these innovations allowed the nation-state to develop because they allowed for greater control over and coordination of a multitude of people, converting them, however spatially separated, into *contemporaries.*

In addition to its simultaneity, *society* represents a synthesis of its members with properties unique to that synthesis; it exists and therefore should be studied independently of its particular members. Thus, for Durkheim (1895/1982), we may properly speak of laws governing "the mentality of the groups" and "collective thinking" (pp. 40, 42). Because "social facts" are "things, not concepts," they must be treated as independent entities that have essential properties that endure outside of the their "representations" by the individuals who comprise that society (pp. 60, 70): Society, then, has an objective existence that would retain its essential identity even if every single member that supposedly comprised it had conflicting beliefs about that society or even believed that they belonged to different societies.

For eighteenth-century philosophy Johann Gottfried von Herder (cf. Hassan, 2000, p. 39) and nineteenth-century philosopher Wilhelm von Humboldt (1836/1988, pp. 21, 39), nations have *Volksgeister, mentalities, spirits,* or *essences* distinguishable from those possessed by other nations. As Malkki (1994) argues, this kind of thinking endures in current tendencies to conceptualize a *global internationalism,* in which the world is populated by a "family" of nations, each with "its own distinctive spirit or genius, its own unique 'contribution' to make to humanity [. . .]. Each is unique and yet has a place within the scope of the whole [. . .] an overarching humankind" (p. 58). Thus, beyond nations, theorists may appeal to the "global community" (Delpit, 1988, p. 68), "humanity as a whole" (Moran, 1998, p. 209), the "whole of humanity" (Polayni, 1958/1974, p. 328), or even Brandom's (1994, p. 4) "one great Community" of language users.

Poststructuralist theorists have repeatedly critiqued conceptions of society as a totalized, closed system in favor of what Laclau calls the openness of "the social" (Worsham and Olson, 1999a, pp. 14, 18). For Foucault (1971/1977g), "this particular idea of the 'whole of society' derives from a utopian context [. . .]. 'The whole of society' is precisely that which should not be considered except as something to be destroyed. And then, we can only hope that it will never exist again" (pp. 232–233). Societies, nations, cities, and other large-scale collectivities are not *substantial,* but *imagined* (B. Anderson, 1983/1996): Such collectives are *ideas* (Fiske, 1989), *fantasies* (Bormann, 1972), *frames* (Brunsdon and Morley, 1978), *myths* (Barthes, 1957/1982; McGee, 1975/1999a), *rhetorical topoi* (Cintron, 1997), *empty signifiers* (Worsham and Olson, 1999b), or *interpretations* (R. Williams, 1961).

But, as McGee (1975/1999a) indicates, the notion that "social realities [. . .] are essentially fictional" (p. 352) is hardly peculiar to poststructuralist thought, appearing in Le Bon's (1895/1995) concept of the *popular mind* comprised of imagined commitments to others, Sorel's (1912/1999) notion of the *group fantasy* and *political myth*, and Ortega y Gassett's (1957) contention that *the people* is a linguistic construct. But such doubts extend back further than the late nineteenth century, particularly in the nominalism of Condillac (1746/1982c), Hobbes (1668/1994), Leibniz (1840/1968a), Locke (1689/1987), and Spinoza (1677/1951a). Leibniz especially uses the term "fiction":

> I hold, therefore, that a block of marble is no more a thoroughly single substance than would be the water in a pond with all the fish included, even when all the water and all the fish are frozen; or any more than a flock of sheep, even when the sheep were tied together so that they could only walk in step and so that one could not be touched without producing a cry from all. There is as much difference between a substance and such a being, as there is between a man and a community—say a people, an army, a society or college, which are moral beings, yet they have an imaginary something and depend upon the fiction of our minds. (p. 161)

Nominalism lingers on in twentieth-century analytic philosophy as well, particularly in the work of Kripke (1972/1996), Carnap, (1947/1988), Quine (1960), Russell (1940), and Ryle (1962).

Of course, for nominalists, the fact that general or universal terms "belong not to the real existence of Things; but *are the Inventions and Creatures of the Understanding*" (Locke, 1689/1987, III.iii.11) does not undermine their utility—and, conversely, their utility does not guarantee their agreement with reality. Carnap (1947/1988) rejects realist assumptions about the relationship between linguistic expressions and an objective reality. In his discussion of the "reality" of entities, Carnap makes a twofold distinction between "internal questions," which question the existence of entities within, to use Carnap's term, the "linguistic framework" used, and "external questions," which question "the existence *of the system of entities as a whole*" (p. 206). In the former case, for example, when we accept a linguistic framework that includes pens, we can ask, "Is that a real pen?" (as opposed to a pencil or a trick pen that squirts water). The question, Carnap says, is an empirical one, and to verify whether the entity is a pen we simply use the rules (implied or explicit) for verification built into the framework. The existence of pens is not at issue, only whether that particular object is a pen. Internal questions about reality are resolved if an entity is incorporated "into the system of things at a particular space-time position so that it fits together with the other things recognized as real, according to the rules of the framework" (p. 207).

On the other hand, external questions—which Carnap says only trouble philosophers (and, I would add, not only philosophers)—about the "reality" of the "real" cannot ever resolved. Why? Because "to be real in the scientific sense means to be an element of the system; hence this concept cannot be meaningfully applied to the system itself" (p. 207). What is debatable, however, is the utility of the linguistic framework; we have to decide "whether or not to accept and use the forms of expression in the framework in question" (p. 207). Such criteria informing our decision include "efficiency, fruitfulness, and simplicity," but, as Carnap observes,

> The thing language [i.e., a language that accepts objects as real] in the customary form works indeed with a high degree of efficiency for most purposes of everyday life. This is a matter of fact, based upon the content of our experiences. However, it would be wrong to describe this situation by saying: "The fact of the efficiency of the thing language is confirming evidence for the reality of the thing world"; we should say instead: "This fact makes it advisable to accept the thing language." (p. 208)

Usually, it is not a matter of conscious choice whether to accept the thing language, argues Carnap, "because we all have accepted the thing language early in our lives as a matter of course [during socialization]" (p. 207); but, crucially, we can deliberately restructure these frameworks if we so choose. And our decision does not commit us to metaphysical realism:

> To accept the thing world means nothing more than to accept a certain form of language, in other words, to accept rules for forming statements and for testing, accepting, or rejecting them. The acceptance of the thing language leads, on the basis of observations

made, also to the acceptance, belief, and assertion of certain statements. But the thesis of the reality of the thing world cannot be among these statements, because it cannot be formulated in the thing language or, it seems, in any other theoretical language. (p. 208)

That we are born into and tacitly accept linguistic frameworks, that these frameworks set their own rules for identification of entities and verification of truths, that these frameworks can be changed and be in conflict with other frameworks, and that we cannot impose questions of reality onto the frameworks themselves: These elements of Carnap's philosophy reach toward social constructionism and epistemic rhetoric. But they also assume that linguistic frameworks, like the artificial languages Carnap constructed, are entities that exist all-at-once and are capable of total description.

Likewise, Quine (1960) takes an operationalist view of theories, even scientific ones: Properties, numbers, and classes are to be admitted into our theories of the world because of "their efficacy in organizing and expediting the sciences" (p. 237). Physical objects, too, are just another concession, though one with more utility than that of abstract objects: "In a contest for systematic utility to science, the notion of physical object still leads the field. On this score alone, therefore, one might still put a premium on explanations that appeal to physical objects and not to abstract objects" (p. 238). Quine also undermines the distinction between reference and description because we can never get at *pure* objects apart from descriptions:

> One tends to imagine that when someone propounds a theory concerning some sort of objects, our understanding of what he is saying will have two phases: first we must understand what the objects are, and second we must understand what the theory says about them [. . .]. [Y]et much of our understanding of "what the objects are" awaits the second phase [. . .]. We do not learn first what to talk about and then what to say about it. (p. 16)

Thus, for Quine, theories should be treated as *useful myths,* ways of navigating the world and ridding our ontology of too many unrelated objects; but they only remain useful so long as we are not fooled into reifying our universals, what Ogden and Richards (1923/1946) would term the *hypostatic subterfuge* (p. 133).

Some theorists worry about the nominalist and poststructuralist erosions of large-scale social formations like *society* or *the public*. For example, Kaufer and Butler (1996) reject these conceptions of society, arguing that "despite the modern tendency to nominalize the abstraction of [the] public, rhetorical design relies on public being a realist abstraction" with a precision "not unlike the abstract but precise realities of geometry and physics" (p. 125). But to which "realities" of geometry and physics do Kaufer and Butler refer?—a timeless dimension of perfect spheres and frictionless surfaces, the ideas of which may be, as Descartes (1701/1970c) argued, clear and fully present before the mind in a single instant? Are publics as temporally flattened and precise as Kaufer and Butler appear to suggest? And we might also wonder how precise, exactly, are the measurements of contemporary physics; perhaps Kaufer and Butler are perhaps—inadvertently—thinking of physics prior to the development of quantum mechanics?

Kaufer and Butler do not claim that publics are *objective,* but they do assert that they are *real.* As a realist abstraction, the public "cannot be reduced to materialist particulars" (p. 128); it is "superimposed on a fluctuating and often indeterminate material reality," yet "cannot stray too far from material details" if appeals to the public are to be successful (p. 128). Their paradigm example is politicians from a representative democracy who must always in the end "respond to a public that is an abstraction of their own design" (p. 127), yet who must also "respond from the broader interests of the persons and organizations they represent, many of whom they barely know, if at all" (p. 126). The actual members of the public that is represented is a maelstrom of divergent opinions, so the representative, according to Kaufer and Butler, cannot simply *reflect* those opinions, which would lead to indecision, but must *construct* through her discourse a precise abstraction of the public, a "public model" (p. 130), that gives the representation, and presumably the audience for her discourse, "a decisive, not splintered target to aim at" because representatives are "expected and so must be able to talk and act decisively, even in the face of material uncertainty and the dissensus in the individuals who are thought to instantiate it" (p. 127).

I must confess that I fail to see little difference between Kaufer and Butler's position and the nominalist views they critique (i.e., their ideas seem to lead to similar consequences as those they critique); for Kaufer and Butler acknowledge that the *public* is not a substantial entity, but an instrumental construct that has *real effects*. The fact that the success of such constructions depends in part upon how well they factor in material constraints does not represent a significant departure from nominalisms—or at least those variants of nominalism, such as Locke's (1689/1987), Wittgenstein's (1922/1981), or Quine's (1960)— that allow for an objective reality independent of language or conceptual schemes, even if it is ultimately ineffable or indifferent to them.

Like Kaufer and Butler, Taylor (1991) decries the splintered and enervated conception of the social, particularly by postmodernist theorists, and he hopes to revive talk about "the whole of society":

> Fragmentation arises when people come to see themselves more and more atomistically, otherwise put, as less and less bound to their fellow citizens in common projects and allegiances. They may indeed feel linked in common projects with some others, but these come more to be partial groupings rather than the whole society: for instance, a local community, an ethnic minority, the adherents of some religion or ideology, the promoters of some special interest. (pp. 112–113)

But notice that *see* or *feel* implies (a) that the social emerges from an act of imagination, such as that proposed by Benedict Anderson, or of some kind of embodied, felt sense, such as that proposed by Bourdieu (1980/1990), Richard Miller (1996), and Worsham (1998), and (b) that the act of seeing or feeling themselves as members of a group is *constitutive* of their being a group capable of conjoint behavior; as Willima I. Thomas and Dorothy S. Thomas (1928) point out, beliefs have real effects, so people who act on beliefs about their membership in a society provide *society* with an efficacy that is no less real for its being fiduciary. And the fact that we are unable, as Spellmeyer (1993b) puts it, "to imagine and construct a society more consonant with out common interests" (p. 16) does not mean that society was ever something more substantial than those imaginings and constructions or that, during some golden age, consensus and heterogeneity were historical events. The "fragmentation of the social fabric," as de Certeau (1974/1984, p. xxiv) puts it, represents a failure of individuals to have a social imagination, not the failure of an abstract entity to maintain its integrity and coherence.

I conclude this section by noting de Certeau's commonplace metaphor for society as a *social fabric,* which would retain its simultaneity even if rent into various subsections; this feature of a spatialized society will reappear in our discussion of smaller social units, such as discourse or speech communities, meant to replace *society* that only end up producing smaller *societies.*

ABSOLUTE TIME AND THE MYTH OF "LANGUAGES"

[Noah] Webster wanted to give American English its own flavor. He wanted an American English that would be distinctively different from the British variety—"*A national language* is a brand of *national union*" he declared—but not so different that mutual intelligibility would be lost.

—Ronald Wardhaugh

For Men, being furnished with Words, by the common Language of their own Countries, can scarce avoid having some kind of *Ideas* of those things, whose Names, those they converse with, have occasion frequently to mention to them [. . .].

—John Locke

The correlative of a spatialized society is the *spatialized language* shared in common by all of the members of that society, a language that, as Saussure (1916/1959) puts it, is "almost like a dictionary of which identical copies have been distributed to each individual" (p. 19). Such a language has been called by various names: *common language* (e.g., Dummett, 1973/1996b, pp. 138–142; Gergen, 1994, p. 33; Jespersen, 1925, p. 38), *common tongue* (e.g., Abbott, 1990, p. 106), *national language* (e.g., Campbell, 1776/1988, p. 145; Humboldt, 1836/1988, p. 24), *"Standard" language* (e.g., Jespersen, 1925, p. 73; J. Lyons, 1995, p. 7; Moffett, 1968, p. 158; White, 1995, p. 31), *mother tongue* (e.g., Barthes, 1972/1977e, p. 182; Elbow, 1999b, p. 361; Halliday, 1978, p. 1; Alfred Schutz, 1962/1990, p. 326), *natural language* (e.g., Searle, 1995, p. 60; Suppes, 1976/1992a, p. 194), and the *established language* (Gusdorf, 1965, p. p. 62), though it may also appear in other guises, such as *social codes* (e.g., de Certeau et al., 1994/1998, p. 16), *grapholect* (e.g., Hirsch, 1977, p. 45; Ong, 1982, pp. 7–8), *ordinary usage* (e.g., Spinoza, 1670/1951b, 107; J. Austin, 1961/1979a, p. 68), etc. In principle, there is no reason why a language so conceived couldn't be shared by an almost infinite number of language-users almost infinitely separated in time and space, so long as each individual has access to—or has had *deposited* within his or her brain—the collective dictionary that language-users not only *use,* but feel *accountable to.*

The metaphor of the dictionary is not accidental, for the dictionary and its ancient precursors—grammars, such as the fourth-century A.D. *Ars Minor* of Donatus (trans. 1926), and rhetorics, such as Aristotle's (trans. 1991)—have been instrumental in the *construction* and *propagation* of the belief that languages form discrete, synchronic systems that run along political, social, cultural, national, racial, etc., lines. Some of the earliest English dictionaries were compiled and published in the first half of the sixteenth century (Wardhaugh, 1999, p. 78), with more systematic attempts to systematize languages in the eighteenth century (T. Miller, 1997, p. 1) and the nineteenth century—which has been called the "golden age" of lexicography, grammar, and philology, an age that coincided with the development of nationalism and nation-building (B. Anderson, 1983/1996, p. 71).[4] For Pattison (1982), this coincidence is not at all coincidental: "In many senses, every dictionary or handbook of grammar is a political document, dictating the permissible structures of reality" (p. 67).

Lexicographers (and linguists, rhetoricians, logicians, etc.) have struggled over whether their work is or should be *prescriptive* or *descriptive,* with the former approach—in the tradition of, for example, Samuel Johnson (1755) or E. D. Hirsch, Jr. (1977)—and the latter— in the tradition of George Campbell (1776/1988) or George Miller (1951, pp. 111–112)—gradually being superceded, at least overtly, by the latter; we might also think of Humboldt (1836/1988) as a kind of mediating figure between Johnson and Campbell in that he contends that grammarians "polish" language, resolving its "irregularities" but not adding anything to it (p. 150). The cases of Johnson and Campbell are especially instructive because they illuminate why Pattison's Whorfian argument is only near the mark: I suggest that, from my consequentialist point of view, dictionaries and grammars are *part* of efforts to imagine and enforce standardized languages, but the meanings of those imagined languages are not inscribed within dictionaries or even determined by them.

Johnson, for example, recognized the limits of dictionaries by understanding that he couldn't control or freeze the use of words, but could only offer a standard of *taste* that might gain adherence from readers who didn't already value the literary sources Johnson valued (Wardhaugh, 1999, pp. 80–81); his dictionary was less dictatorial than persuasive, an invitation rather than a command. Without sustained efforts to propagate and enforce its definitions, it would be reduced, as it in fact has been reduced, to a historical footnote; and even with those efforts, as educational institutions have repeatedly discovered, there is no guarantee of continuity of transmission. As Yarbrough (1999, p. 122) notes, the endless work of standardization can only mean that language resists being standardized. It should be noted that even some of Johnson's socially privileged readers rejected his dictionary as being itself "ungrammatical" (T. Miller, 1997, p. 156), leading me to wonder what assumptions of homogeneity underlie Pattison's model of "the political."

Whereas Johnson is a prescriptivist who recognizes that linguistic practices exceed prescriptions (at least his own!), Campbell (1776/1988) seems unaware that his self-avowed inductive/descriptive approach to language veers toward prescriptivism. On the one hand, Campbell ridicules prescriptivist grammarians:

> It is not the business of grammar, as some critics seem preposterously to imagine, to give law to the fashions which regulate our speech. On the contrary, from its conformity to these, and from that alone, it derives all its authority and value. For, what is the grammar of any language? It is no other than a collection of general observations methodically digested, and comprising all the modes previously and independent established, by which significations, derivations, and combinations of words are ascertained. (pp. 139–140)

The grammarian is only to "note, collect, and methodize" actual uses of language, not moralize about whether these "modes or fashions owe their existence, to imitation, to reflection, to affectation, or to caprice" (p. 140).

But whereas one hand giveth, the other taketh away, for Campbell's insistence on a language of "*general use*" (p. 141), a language used by "the people of a particular state or country" (p. 139), requires him, in the face of the "blunders" of the uneducated (or the children to whom he likens them)—who comprised at that time perhaps 99% of humankind!—to propose a distinction between "good use and bad use" (p. 142). For Campbell, the grammarian ought to consider only those uses of language that are *reputable* (i.e., the language used by *"celebrated authors"* [p. 145]), *national* (i.e., not provincial/dialectal or foreign), and *present* (i.e., relevant or current). Campbell justifies his criteria on the grounds that even the uneducated adhere to them, not because of the pressures of political or social hegemony, but because of "a natural propension of the human mind to believe that those are the best judges of the proper signs, and of the proper application of them, who understand best the things they represent," with the "great and rich" of course being those best judges (p. 143). Thus, in the course of only a few pages, Campbell moves from the position that grammar is a theoretical account answerable to actual usage to the position that even a usage that is "pretty uniform and extensive" may be "corrupt, and like counterfeit money, though common, not valued" (p. 142).[5]

What prompts this remarkable shift? I suggest that it results from Campbell's unquestioned acceptance of a common language. However, we should not draw the conclusion that, as regrettable as Campbell's error may be, a properly conducted descriptive study would avoid it. Any model of discourse that posits a *national language* or the like as the object of study has already shifted from description to prescription, for a *national language* is always already a normative ideal. One cannot say "I want to construct a grammar of the English language" or "I intend to study how English speakers [generally, in the US, in Oklahoma, in New York City, etc.] use the preposition 'with'" without having already committed oneself to a normative enterprise that reduces discourse to the use of a fully synchronic system of meanings.

Roy Harris (1998, p. 57), forcefully arguing for his integrationist approach to language, contends that students of language should be more interested in studying how grammars and dictionaries have been constructed and used, not in how grammars and dictionaries might be better developed; for Harris, the dictionary does not illuminate "Language," but rather serves as a privileged institutional tool to limit semantic indeterminacy, with the lexicographer proposing correlations between terms, not reporting on them (pp. 85–86). The grammarian is not, pace Quine (1953/1961b), a dispassionate cataloguer of linguistic forms and the "laws of their concatenation," and the lexicographer is not a neutral archivist of "mutually synonymous sequences for a given language or, perhaps, pair of languages" (pp. 48–49). On the contrary, both are implicated in and vested in the models they construct; as Harris puts it,

> to represent the activity of the lexicographer as a mere reporting of semantic facts is rather like portraying the banker and the stockbroker as mere go-betweens in financial transactions engineered by other parties. The reality is somewhat different. The banker and the stockbroker are themselves key figures in creating the market they administer. They are not somehow outside it, looking on as impartial observers. Nor, *mutatis mutandis,* is the lexicographer. (p. 88)

Nor, *mutatis mutandis,* is the philosopher, rhetorician, compositionist, anthropologist, psychologist. . . .

And educator. As Bourdieu (1982/1991) argues,

> the legitimate language is a semi-artificial language which has to be sustained by a permanent effort of correction, a task which falls both to institutions specially designed for this purpose and to individual speakers. Through its grammarians, who fix and codify legitimate usage, and its teachers who impose and inculcate it through innumerable acts of correction, the educational system tends, in this area and elsewhere, to produce the need for its own services and its own products, i.e. the labour and instruments of correction. The legitimate language owes its (relative) constancy in time (as in space) to the fact that it is continuously protected by a prolonged labour [. . .]. (pp. 60–61)

What I would dispute here is not Bourdieu's argument that educational institutions are implicated in the construction and propagation of *legitimate languages,* but his tendency to think of *the* legitimate language as a historical reality (i.e., a definite system with relative stability imposed across space and time), whereas I maintain that the legitimate language is an imagined construct whose reality depends upon people's beliefs and their actions as a result of those beliefs.

ABSOLUTE TIME AND DISCOURSE COMMUNITIES

Whether his [a speaker's] responses are typical of the verbal community of which he is a member—whether they show "normal" intraverbal responses—may also be of interest. The actual responses (the "content" of the behavior) may reveal collateral variables. Different subjects give different responses, presumably because of differences in their verbal history or in current conditions or circumstances.

—B. F. Skinner

If the notion of discourse communities is to be illuminating, it must not be used without attending to how such communities might be identified and defined and how communities shape the form and content of specific texts.

—Lester Faigley

Perhaps resulting from a desire for greater specificity or from a postmodern aversion to myths of the "whole of society," many theorists have tried to narrow the social dimension of language into what they presume are more manageable and concrete collectivities, variously called *discourse communities* (e.g., Berlin, 1988; Bizzell, 1979/1992c, 1992d; Bruffee, 1984/1996; Geisler, 1991/1996; Myers, 1990; J. Porter, 1986/1996), *speech communities* (e.g., Elbow, 1973, 1986; Halliday, 1978; Hymes, 1974; Moffett, 1968; Nystrand, 1982a, 1982b; R. Smith, 1992/1998), *verbal communities* (e.g., Skinner, 1957), *linguistic communities* (e.g., Bourdieu, 1982/1991; R. Harris, 1998), *interpretive communities* (e.g., Fish, 1980c; Mailloux, 1982), *textual communities* (e.g., D. Olson, 1994), or *inquiry communities* (e.g., Reither, 1985/1994).

However, as I will argue in this section, such collectivities simply replicate, albeit on a smaller scale and often despite theorists' efforts to avoid doing do, the same impulse to totalization, spatialization, and abstraction underlying the larger totalizations, spatializations, and ab-

stractions of *languages* (cf. Pratt, 1987, 1991); consequently, I agree
with Friend (1999) that the concept of discourse community (and its
next of kin) "has outlived its usefulness" (p. 663). To make my case, I
will critique six examples in which *discourse communities* and its companions either dissolve from concrete specificities into untenable abstractions or in which they are already abstractions.

O'Grady, Dobrovolsky, and Aronoff. In an introductory textbook
on linguistics, William O'Grady, Michael Dobrovolsky, and Mark
Aronoff (1993) define a *speech community* as follows:

> All sociolinguistic studies concern language in a
> social context, treating speakers as members of so-
> cial groups. The group isolated for study is called
> the *speech community*. Depending on the study, the
> speech community may have as few members as a
> family or as many members as China. The impor-
> tant characteristic is that the members of the speech
> community must, in some reasonable way, interact
> linguistically with other members of the community;
> they may share closely related language varieties, they
> may share attitudes toward linguistic norms, or they
> may be part of a single political entity. (p. 425)

There is a curious tension, to the point of a non sequitur, between the
"important characteristic" of speech communities, namely that their
members "must, in some reasonable way, interact linguistically with
other members of the community," and the authors' ease in accepting
speech community as a term encompassing units as small as a family or
as vast as the population of China (or even an *infinite* population). In
what "reasonable way" could a group comprised of one billion members be said to "interact linguistically" with each other? And notice
that what follows the semicolon is not a list of ways in which people
"interact linguistically," which could lead to the consequentialist position that community is a transient, temporally distended construct
that results from discursive interactions, but rather a list of *a priori*
conditions for membership in the community, such as shared or overlapping linguistic varieties (how do we determine empirically the extent of such sharing or overlapping without assuming that language is
something people possess in toto at a single instant of time?), shared
beliefs about linguistic norms (all of them? most? a few?—and how

do we reckon a person's total set of beliefs at a single instant?), or even membership in a political entity (a nation, state, city, neighborhood?).

Bloomfield. It is not only the authors of introductory textbooks, however, who jump to these hasty and inadequate conclusions. For example, in his authoritative study, succinctly titled *Language,* Bloomfield (1933/1961) begins his third chapter with the following definition of a *speech-community:* "A speech-community is a group of people who interact by means of speech (§ 2.5)" (p. 42). I include the "(§ 2.5)" because, if we visit that section, supposedly in concord with the definition just offered, we find that concordance is lacking: "A group of people who use the *same system of speech-signals* [italics added] is a *speech-community.* Obviously, the value of language depends upon people's using it in the same way. Every member of the social group must upon suitable occasion utter the proper speech-sounds and, when he hears another utter these speech-sounds, must make the proper response. He must speak intelligibly and understand what others say" (p. 29). It is not, then, that the extension of the term "speech-community" is delimited by whether people actually interact with each other through discourse, but by whether people share the same "system of speech-signals," such as, say Latin, Greek, Cantonese, English, etc.—in short, a *language*—that would allow for the potential to interact if suitable circumstances arose. Only if by "interaction" Bloomfield implies *potential interaction* could he, like O'Grady, Dobrovolsky, and Aronoff (1993), allow for speech-communities of, for all intents and purposes, unlimited size (cf. p. 43). Note also that Bloomfield is by no means reluctant to coagulate languages, such as Dutch and German, into a single speech-community if "there is no break between local speech-forms," and *even if* certain "extreme types" of either language are "mutually unintelligible" (p. 44).

Given his interest in abstract potentialities, Bloomfield's preference for talking about generalities such as "English speakers" despite—or perhaps because of—the problematic task of identifying particular English speakers is understandable:

> The difficulty or impossibility of determining in each case exactly what people belong to the same speech-community, is not accidental, but arises from the very nature of speech-communities. If we observed closely enough, we should find that no two persons—or, rather, no one person at different times, spoke exactly

alike [. . .]. There are great differences even among the
native members of such a relatively uniform group as
Middle Western American, and, as we have just seen,
even greater differences within a speech-community
(e.g. English) as a whole. (p. 45)

If no two people speak exactly alike and if no single person's "language"
endures with perfect continuity, what, then, does that imply about the
existence of a "system of speech-signals" that people share? Bloomfield
concedes there is "a very important" problem here, but does not resolve
it and, despite its great importance, even justifies *setting it aside:* "These
differences play a very important part in the history of languages; the
linguist is forced to consider them very carefully, even though in some
of his work he is forced provisionally to ignore them. When he does
this, he is merely employing the method of abstraction, a method essential to scientific investigation, but the results so obtained have to
be corrected before they can be used in most kinds of further work"
(p. 45). But there is nothing *mere*—or usually even *temporary* or *pro-
visional*—about these abstractions, which occlude crucial differences
that throw into doubt whether language as a spatialized system exists
at all, or whether it has any use as even an analytic construct.

For example, consider Bloomfield's curious contemplation of meaning in the ninth chapter of his book. He reminds of his definition of
"the *meaning* of a linguistic form as the situation in which the speaker
utters it and the response which it calls forth in the hearer" (p. 139);
situation is highly ambiguous, but Bloomfield argues that, "thanks to
the [happy] circumstance that every one of us learns to act indiffer-
ently as a speaker or a hearer," we may justifiably simplify the analysis
by "discuss[ing] and defin[ing] meanings in terms of a speaker's stimulus" (p. 139). But whatever simplicity this may bring to the analysis,
it remains infinitely complex: "In order to give a scientifically accurate
definition of meaning for every form of a language, we should have to
have a scientifically accurate knowledge of everything in the speakers'
world. The actual extent of human knowledge is very small compared
to this" (p. 139)—so small, in fact, that we cannot even *feel* its small-
ness, no more than I have a good *feel* for contrasting the actual number
of numbers I *know* from the infinite number of numbers. Perhaps it's
not so much that I have a rich concept of *the infinite* as that the claim
"for any whole number, x, there is a whole number, $x + 1$" makes sense
to me because no matter what number I treat as the variable, I will

always find an even larger number, seemingly "waiting there," so to speak.

Bloomfield acknowledges many other difficulties as well: (a) that scientific terms, like *sodium chloride,* and words closely aligned with those terms, such as *salt,* have more determinate meanings than most other words that people use, like *love* (p. 139); (b) that "even where we have some scientific classification (that is, universally recognized and accurate) classification, we often find that the meanings of a language do not agree with the classification (e.g., the German term for *bat* is *Fledermaus*) or with other languages (e.g., the continuum of the light spectrum is arbitrarily divided by terms for colors) (pp. 139–140); (c) that no situation is ever identical, so it would seem that no meaning could ever be identical, either (pp. 140–141); (d) that we do not possess the requisite knowledge for understanding "the state of the speaker's body," which "include, of course, the predisposition of his nervous system, which results from all of his experiences, linguistic and other, up to this very moment—not to speak of hereditary and pre-natal factors" (p. 141)—and this state will be as unique as the external circumstances in which a person speaks; (e) that people may refer to objects not in the immediate environment via *displaced speech,* so even if we could fully describe the external stimuli that impinge upon a speaker, we would still remain quite uncertain "as to the forms that a given speaker will utter (if he speaks at all) in a given situation (p. 142); (f) that utterances are modified by *vocal gestures* or *tones,* though these are "an inferior type of communication" (p. 147); (g) that people may deliberately distort their words (e.g., for comic effect or baby-talk) (p. 148); (h) that our *normal* or *central* meanings have variants that are *marginal* or *metaphoric* or *transferred* (p. 149); (i) that the dividing line between a "form as a single form with several meanings or as a set of homonyms" is often unclear (p. 150); (k) that speakers may mistake connotations—"personal deviations" in the use of words—for "explicit definitions of meaning" (p. 152); (l) that connotations include people's sense of the *propriety* and *impropriety* of terms (e.g., obscenity, euphemism, etc.) and, relatedly, their emotional *intensity* (pp. 155–156); (m) that languages may not only be infused with the vocabulary of other languages, but they may also, in relation to particular speech forms, "reflect our attitude toward foreign peoples" (p. 153).

However, despite all of these daunting considerations, Bloomfield remains confident about the prospects of a properly scientific study of language:

> Nevertheless, it is clear [is it so?] that we must [be-cause of a *logical necessity* or a *normative prescription?*] discriminate between *non-distinctive* features, such as the size, shape, color, and so on of any one particular apple [are these "non-distinctive features" really on a par with confounding factors (a)-(m)?], and the *dis-tinctive,* or *linguistic meaning* (the *semantic* features) which are common to all the situations that call forth the utterance of the linguistic form, such as the fea-tures which are common to all the objects of which English-speaking people use the word *apple.*
>
> Since our study ordinarily [as Bloomfield wishes it to be *ordinarily conducted*] concerns only the dis-tinctive features of form and meaning [a wonderful begging of the question: as our study is of only the distinctive features of form and meaning—and not an inquiry into whether there are such "distinctive features"—we will study only the distinctive fea-tures of form and meaning"!], I shall henceforth [as a judge might declare] usually omit the qualification *linguistic* or *distinctive* [thereby, *forgetting* the qual-ification], and speak simply [yes, what we speak of must be something that can be spoken about *simply*] of *forms* and *meanings,* ignoring [in a brazenly candid way] the existence of non-distinctive features. A form is often said [or will be, if Bloomfield persuades] to *express* its meaning. (p. 141)

Thus, as this passage transpires, we can witness what Bloomfield refers to the fundamental *presupposition of linguistics*—i.e., that "[i]n certain communities (speech-communities) some speech-utterances are alike as to form and meaning" (p. 144)—shift from being a non-founda-tional postulate or theoretical simplification to a foundational axiom from which implications—such as "that each linguistic form has a constant and specific meaning" (p. 145)—can be drawn. In other words, Bloomfield moves (a) from the claim that linguists must presuppose "the specific and stable character of language" *despite* the fact that "we have no way of defining most meanings and of demonstrating their constancy" (p. 144) in order to study language (b) to the claim that although this "basic assumption is true only within limits [. . .] its general truth is presupposed not only in linguistic study, but by all our actual use of language [not only *presupposed,* but surely also *confirmed;* for if it is not confirmed by any experience with language, why make the presupposition?]" (p. 145).

In a similar move, Bloomfield reduces the complexity introduced by the temporality of language-learning, which spurs on the diversity of speech within a speech-community:

> The most important differences of speech within a community are due to differences in *density of com-munication.* The infant learns to speak like the people round him, but we must not picture this learning as coming to any particular end: there is no hour or day when we can say that a person has finished learn-ing to speak, but, rather, to the end of his life, the speaker keeps on doing the very things which make up infantile language-learning [. . .]. Every speaker's language, except for personal factors which we must here ignore, is a composite result of what he has heard other people say. (p. 46)

But learning *what?* An unchanging system of speech-signals that no one single person possesses perfectly or identically? Where is this sys-tem to be found, then? And why must we exclude "personal factors," if it is not done to set aside threats to the presumed homogeneity of speech-communities? It doesn't help that Bloomfield's recognition of the temporality of language-use and language-learning challenges his earlier definition of native language and native speaker: "The child learns to speak like the persons round him. The first language a hu-man being learns to speak is his native language; he is a native speaker of this language" (p. 43). But what constitutes learning a language? What has one learned by learning a language? If it requires a full un-derstanding of an autonomous system of speech-signals, *then there are no native languages or native speakers.*

Problems of heterogeneity surface (where else, of course, but) else-where in Bloomfield's text, particularly in his discussion of *dialect*

geography, which is "the study of local differentiations in a speech-
area" (p. 321). The findings of such study are presented in distribution maps, which purportedly provide the "clearest and most compact
form of statement" aside from an impossible-to-achieve "complete and
organized description of a single local dialect" (p. 323); larger projects,
then, form *dialect atlases.* Bloomfield, perhaps because his illustrations
are drawn from the work of others, does not comment in detail on
the methodology for drawing the isoglosses that mark the boundaries
between various syllabic sounds, such as those for the words for *mouse*
and *house* in the Netherlands (p. 328). Who were the informants? How
were they selected? Who didn't (get) count(ed)? How were the data
quantified? Does the supposed data confirm the sharpness of the lines
drawn on the map? And over what *span of time* were the data collected?

Just to touch on a few of these factors: If the data are collected only
from *legal residents* (or only a subclass of those legal residents), then
the linguist maps not the syllabic sounds used in a given region, but
only the syllabic sounds used by privileged residents in that region—a
strategy that, moreover, appears to confirm the link between a nation-
state and its supposedly standardized language. For example, consider
Bailey, Jan Tillery, and Wikle's (1997) Survey of Oklahoma Dialects
(SOD) project. Although the researchers received completed surveys
from 632 respondents spread across four generations, all of them were
required to be not only "native Oklahomans," but also "life-long residents" of their particular square on the "grid" (see Figure 4.2); and
none of them could be under 20 years of age.

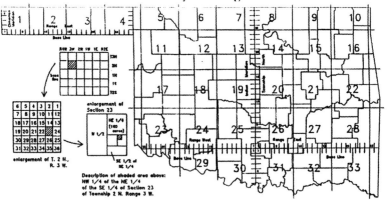

Figure 4.2. A Grid System for the Geographical Study of Dialects. From Bailey, Tillery, and Wikle (1997, p. 11); it is reproduced by permission of *Southern Journal of Linguistics* (formerly, *The SECOL Review*).

Bloomfield concedes that the isoglosses of phonetic, lexical, and grammatical features only "rarely coincide along their whole extent," which entails that *Every word has its own history*" (p. 328). Instead of revealing large-scale and clear-cut geographic divisions, dialect geography discovered fragmentation and differentiation: "It showed that almost every village had its own dialectal features, so that the whole area was covered by a network of isoglosses" (p. 340). Although the welter of overlapping isoglosses led some of his contemporaries to conclude that sharp classifications were impossible to make—"some students now despaired of all classification and announced that within a dialect area there are no real boundaries " (p. 341)—Bloomfield assures us that "it is easy to see, however, that, *without prejudice of any kind* [italics added], we must attribute more significance to some isoglosses than to others" (p. 341). But how are we supposed to judge which isoglosses deserve greater weight?

- The first criterion is *spatial dimension*: The "great isogloss shows a feature which has spread over a large domain [. . .]. The large division is, of course [italics added], more significant than small ones" (pp. 341–342).
- The second criterion is *clarity of demarcation*: The isogloss that "cuts boldly across a whole area, dividing it into two nearly equal parts, or even an isogloss which neatly marks off some block of the total area, is more significant than a petty line enclosing a localism of a few villages" (p. 341).
- The third criterion is *concordance of linguistic forms*: Preference must be given to "a set of isoglosses running close together in much [italics added] the same direction—a so-called bundle of isoglosses—evidences a larger historical process and offers a more suitable basis for classification than does a single isogloss that represents, perhaps, some unimportant feature" (p. 342). It should be noted that Saussure (1915/1959) also rejects the idea that dialect have "fixed well-defined zones" (p. 202), using this same criterion to define a dialect as "a sufficient accumulation of concordances" that need not be precisely bounded, but only nearly so (p. 203).
- The fourth criterion is *concordance of linguistic divisions to political divisions*: The results of dialect geography, argues Bloomfield,

demonstrate that "important lines of dialectal division run close [italics added] to political lines" (p. 343).

Armed with these supposedly objective criteria, which already admit to a degree of ambiguity (i.e., *much, close*), the linguist is free to ignore—because of their *unimportance*—highly localized and even idiosyncratic isoglosses as well as those isoglosses that do not mesh with the presumed stability of *political lines,* particularly the boundaries of nation-states. But by homogenizing the data in these ways, linguists are *constructing* dialects, not *finding* them.

Roy Harris (1998) has vigorously argued against what he calls *the dialect myth.* For Harris, dialects serve as a way for linguists who wish to reconcile their belief in language as a fixed code with the phenomenon of linguistic variation: "The function of the dialect myth in orthodox linguistics is to provide theoretical support for the idea that there can be linguistic unity in diversity. The dialect is thus identified as 'the system' constituting the immediate object of the linguist's description, and a language is construed (either synchronically or diachronically) as a set of dialects. It follows that a description of 'the language' is simply a description of its dialects" (p. 44). In short, orthodox linguists try to save the presumed systematicity of language in the face of differentiations by simply dividing up language into smaller and smaller subsystems until linguistic heterogeneity finally gives way to linguistic homogeneity. As Foucault (1969/1972a) suggests, researchers will go to great lengths to secure a coherence that is presumed *a priori* (p. 149) and to preserve with ad hoc devices, like the epicycles of Ptolemy, a system already made. To be fair, as Earman (1989) points out, "the need to add epicycles is not necessarily an indication of falsity, but the accumulation of enough epicycles may cause one to lose interest in the theory" (p. 153). For me, at least, such is the case here.

Saussure. Like Bloomfield, Saussure (1916/1959) attempts to reconcile his systemic view of language (*langue*) to the "diversity of languages" through space and through time (p. 191), but a diversity which can, through careful investigation, always be "observed and traced back to unity" (p. 197).[6] In fact, for Saussure, whereas space "cannot influence language" (which allows a single language to be spoken by an infinite number of speakers separated by infinite distance), time is the sole cause of linguistic instability: "At a particular moment and in a particular environment *u* became *ü*. Why did it change at that moment and in that place, and why did it become *ü* instead of *o?* That question we cannot answer. But *change itself* (leaving out the special direction it takes and its particular manifestations)—in short, the instability of language—stems from time alone" (pp. 198–199). Thus, whatever role time plays in language must be negative, an unsettling deviation from an already existing standard. Languages cannot be frozen into a state of "absolute immobility" (p. 199), but not because they are, for Saussure, essentially *mobile*.

Of course, Saussure assumes here an isolated group of speakers whose language changes without having come into contact with other languages (e.g., *ü* is privileged by a more dominant group). The paradigm example of such an isolated group is the population of a remote island: Take a subset of speakers of these "unilingual" islanders (who speak language *L*), transport them to a different and unpopulated island, then compare *L'* (the language of the colonists) at time *t*, *t* + 1, *t* + 2, ..., *t* + *n* with *L*. Saussure argues that various lexical, grammatical, and phonetic changes would creep inevitably into *L'*, but just as importantly, into *L* as well. Innovations occur not only through time, but somehow as a result of time, for both groups (pp. 197–198). Consequently, for Saussure, a single language does not evolve uniformly for all of its speakers, but fragments into various dialects that are, if broken into small enough units, homogeneous.

But Saussure's model of language evolution is quite problematic for several reasons. First, it assumes that it is possible to describe the structure of a language or dialect at any given moment without reference to actual utterances, texts, and responses to them. Langue is something that exists simultaneously, like a specimen on a microscope slide or, to use Saussure's preferred metaphor, the discrete configurations of pieces on a chessboard. Time is not integral to language or meaning, but appears as a perpetual threat to them. But we need to be clear: At no point is the stability of language itself really threatened, for one regime is merely replaced by another equally systematic regime. For Saussure, *language is never without systematicity*. The instability of language is rather more like the election of some new representatives to Congress or Parliament than a coup d'état.

Second, Saussure, like Bloomfield, appears to limit whose language counts as data to resident-citizens. To ask, "What language do they speak *here*?" already requires that one has constructed a notion of who counts as a resident *here* (and therefore whose language counts) and who is a visitor from an *elsewhere* with a different language.

Third, and perhaps most puzzling of all, Saussure's model of language change assumes either (a) that language has a uniform initial state or (b) that language may at some point achieve a uniform state. Notice how *casually* Saussure invites us to accept that a uniform language is not only a theoretical possibility, but a historical fact:

> Now take a unilingual country, i.e. one with a uniform language and a stable population, like Gaul around 450 A.D., when Latin was well established everywhere. What will happen?
>
> (1) Since there is no such thing as absolute immobility in speech [. . .] the language will no longer be the same after a certain length of time.
>
> (2) Evolution will not be uniform throughout the territory but will vary from zone to zone; no records indicate that any language has ever changed in the same way throughout its territory. (p. 199)

But if Saussure is correct (a) that a language cannot be absolutely immobile through time and (b) that the evolution of a language will always be fragmented and localized (i.e., L does not become L_1 simultaneously at $t + 1$ for all speakers of L at time t, but differentiates into $L_1, L_2, \ldots L_n$), then how did L ever become so uniform internally qua linguistic system and so uniformly widespread qua discursive practice in the first place? L's orderliness seems miraculous, on a par with the unlikeliest events permissible according to the probabilistic laws of thermodynamics (e.g., that all of the molecules of gas in a container gather in the left side rather than being evenly distributed). Indeed, it seems as if language could only be maximally uniform at its moment of (immaculate) conception. (There might be some truth to this, for the meaning of an utterance would be maximally uniform—or, better, it would be as uniform as it ever could be—in the moment of its being uttered. But this is not a route for which Saussure can serve as a guide.)

Finally, Saussure appears to accept as his paradigm of a community a set of people with a shared language, culture, etc., who never move away or even travel and who never welcome outsiders into their midst. Thus, in Saussure's conception of the linguistic world, a "traveler going from one end of the country to another would notice only small dialectal differences from one locality to the next" (p. 201); only if a traveler ventures far enough from the "center" of his or her linguistic universe would he or she "come to a language that [. . .] [he or she] would not be able to understand" (p. 201). As Horner (2001) points out, though individuals may travel far indeed and "develop fluency in the languages of a variety of these communities," models of language such as Saussure's assume "that these individuals with retain their fluency in and primary identification with the language of their 'home' community: people, too, have their place" (p. 743).

In contrast, Pratt (1987) argues that linguists, exercising a will to "unify social and linguistic worlds" (p. 52), have for too long conceptualized linguistic communities as isolated, discrete, and homogeneous collectivities, what she terms *linguistic utopias*. She asserts that language is best thought of in terms of contact between different groups—a *linguistics of contact*—rather than language used within a sealed community (p. 60). At times, that contact will have no other purpose but the disruption of communication; for example, Kristen Kennedy (1999) argues that cynic rhetoric constitutes a rhetoric of "noise" that rejects "community standards of decorum" in order to intrude upon "exclusionary speech communities" (p. 39), foregrounding "minority voices that get silenced under the monolith of majority 'conversation'" (p. 26).

Halliday. One of the targets of Pratt's critique is M. A. K. Halliday, particularly his *Explorations in the Functions of Language* (1973). For Halliday (1978), a speech community is

> an idealized construct [. . .] [that] combines three distinct concepts: those of social group, communication network, and linguistically homogeneous population. Each of these embodies some idea of norm [whose norms?]. A speech community, in this idealized sense, is a group of people who (1) are linked by some form of social organization, (2) talk to each other, and (3) all speak alike. (p. 154)

Despite acknowledging that no human group ever meets these criteria (and that in diverse settings the "classical model" breaks down entirely), Halliday claims that the members of isolated, rural communities or the quaint European villages of a bygone era may "approximate" them enough for the construct to work "reasonably well" (p. 154). But what does it mean for such a construct to work *reasonably well?* For what purpose? Does "working well" simply mean that the construct "finds" some system underlying most, but not all, of the limited linguistic data collected from a limited subset of the population of a community? Does the model work well if it finds the system that is presumed *a priori* to exist? Does it fail if it cannot systematize the data set?

We might also wonder about the notion of *isolation* that Halliday employs. Montgomery (2000) interrogates the concept of *isolation* in linguistics, claiming that "linguists need to move beyond a simplistic, static conception of 'isolation' that provides little insight into the culture of mountain and other peripheral communities and that all too often perpetuates stereotypes" (p. 44). He asserts that *isolation* as a theoretical construction is problematic in four ways:

- Isolation is frequently ill-defined or even undefined, even though there may be different kinds of isolation (e.g., physical, sociological, economic, etc.) (pp. 44–45).
- Researchers tend to focus on physical isolation of a community and attribute to it either an inflated causal role in producing other types of isolation or equate physical isolation with "infrequency of contact" with other communities (p. 45).
- The work of historians has demonstrated that some of the communities linguists have assumed to be isolated from outside contacts, such as those of Appalachia, were often hosts to visitors or travelers on the way to other destinations (pp. 46–47).
- Linguists tend to treat isolation as an "absolute condition" of communities, not a condition relative to the particular members that comprise the community (p. 47).

Of course, none of these arguments refute the fact that some communities, however few in number, would qualify as completely isolated, nor would Montgomery make that claim. Yet it seems startling to suggest that the paradigm (or "prototype" or "unmarked"; cf. Pratt, 1991, p. 50) speech community should be a community comprised only of adult, native, face-to-face, monolingual, monocultural speakers, "maximally homogeneous" (Pratt, 1991, p. 50)—a *type* of community that is so infrequently found that it must be *atypical.*

Fish. For Fish, the meaning of a text is not determined by its *content,* but is a construct of that text's readers that will vary from reader to reader, even from reading to reading. However, Fish (1980c) assures us that the meanings of texts are not, therefore, indeterminate or subjective:

> the reader is identified not as a free agent, making literature in any old way, but as a member of a community whose assumptions about literature determine the kind of attention he pays and thus the kind of literature "he" "makes" [. . .]. Thus the act of recognizing literature is not constrained by something in the text, nor does it issue from an independent and arbitrary will; rather, it proceeds from a collective decision as to what will count as literature, a decision that will be in force only so long as a community of readers or believers continues to abide by it. (p. 11)

Members of interpretive communities "share interpretive strategies not for reading (in the conventional sense) but for writing texts, for constituting their properties and assigning their intentions," and these strategies "exist prior to the act of reading and therefore determine the shape of what is read rather than, as is usually assumed, the other way around" (1976/1980f, p. 171). For Fish (1970/1980a), meanings are institutional and conventional, and only by "inhabiting them, or being inhabited by them" can these *a priori* meanings become *intelligible* (pp. 331–332). In fact, meaning cannot be indeterminate, for meaning *is* the structure of a determination: "the problem of meaning is only a problem if there is a point at which its determination has not been made, and I am saying that there is no such point" (1980d, p. 310).

Appealing to the standard of "competence," Fish (1970/1980e, pp. 44–45) argues that only shared competence will produce uniform readings among readers. Agreement on meaning is then prima facie evidence for readers belonging to the same community, and disagreement as prima facie evidence for readers belonging to different communities: Community is conceived as homogeneous. But where are these readers with shared competence? What if these readers agree on several readings, but disagree about several others? Surely Fish does not mean that each text has its own interpretive community or set of communities, or that readers within a community cannot disagree at all, but it is difficult to see how dissensus can be incorporated into Fish's model in a way that is not ad hoc, for the grounds of what counts as an allowable dissent would require *a priori* community sanction (i.e., dissensus would have to be folded into a wider sphere of consensus) (cf. Pratt, 1987). Barthes (1964/1977h) falls into this seductive trap of containing diversity within a wider system when he writes that the "system of meaning" must be extended, pace Saussure, to include the reception of signs and not only their emission; thus, language is not "merely the totality of utterances emitted," but "it is also the totality of utterances received: the language must include the 'surprises' of meaning" (p. 47).

To save his theory, Fish might respond that readers belong to multiple interpretive communities and, consequently, will not always apply the same set of interpretive criteria to a particular text; in this way, differences in interpretations are once more reducible to differences in community affiliation. This is a popular tactic to preserve language-, code-, convention-, or genre-based models of discourse in the face of linguistic diversity: The individual is unique only by virtue of occupying a unique point of convergence between competing *a priori* discourses or by belonging to multiple *a priori* communities (e.g., Barthes, 1964/1977h; Berlin, 1993; Halliday, 1978; J. Harris, 1989; Lyotard, 1979/1993). However, as Davidson (1974/1984c, 1993b) has argued, such models cannot explain without collapsing into an infinite regress how the individual selects which competing language, code, convention, or genre to apply, for that decision would of necessity be non-conventional or non-formulaic (i.e., to say that there is a convention for selecting conventions only adds another convention whose selection needs explanation).

Dasenbrock (1991/1993) contends that Fish's theory reduces reading to a futile exercise in which readers see only what they already expect to see; if reading is akin to looking in a mirror, asks Dasenbrock, then why read at all? According to Dasenbrock, reading marks an encounter with the otherness of a writer that can and likely will change the reader in the process. As Levinas (1961/1969) puts it,

> The relationship of language implies transcendence, radical separation, the strangeness of the interlocutors, the revelation of the other to me. In other words, language is spoken where community between the terms of the relationship is wanting, where the common plane is wanting or is yet to be constituted [. . .]. Discourse is thus the experience of something abso-

lutely foreign, a *pure* "knowledge" or "experience," a
traumatism of astonishment.
The absolutely foreign alone can instruct us. (p. 73)

In Fish's world of community-determined readings, there can be no
such astonishment and transformation in the confrontation with otherness, only unintelligibility and confusion; for language is conceivable
only where a community already exists, and this community must be
real, not constructed or imagined. For Fish, community is the precondition for communication, not something we transiently experience or
attribute as a result of successful communicative interaction with other
interlocutors (cf. Chapter 5).

  Bitzer. In his influential paper on "The Rhetorical Situation," Bitzer (1968) offers a comfortably familiar triadic model of (persuasive)
discourse comprised of an objective *exigence* (i.e., an urgent problem
that demands response), an objective *audience,* and the objective *constraints* both given by the rhetorical situation (e.g., an impending inva-
sion) and produced by a particular piece of discourse (e.g., the logical
argumentation of a speech). It is the middle term that I will explore
here. Bitzer carefully distinguishes a *rhetorical audience* from just any
"body of mere hearers or readers" (p. 8): "properly speaking, a rhetorical audience consists only of those persons who are capable of being
influenced by discourse and of being mediators of change" (p. 8). This
definition seems to limit a rhetorical audience to a concrete, finite actuality—not people who may or could hear a discourse, not even all
those who actually hear it, but only those *capable of being influenced.*
But how can it be determined who is capable of being influenced by
discourse, rather than, say, who was actually influenced by that discourse? *Capable* marks a *potentiality,* not an *actuality.* Is this capacity
a *property* a person possesses *prior* to hearing or reading a discourse
(e.g., before reading the Declaration of Independence, person X has
the property of capacity-to-be-influenced-by-the-Declaration-of-Inde-
pendence), or is it rather something someone *attributes* or *does not attribute* to a person a posteriori, contingent upon her actual response to
a discourse (e.g., "Martha wouldn't listen to a word I said. Her mind
was already made up."[7])? Bitzer, when he states that William Lloyd
Garrison couldn't know whether the people who heard his abolitionist
pleas comprised "a genuinely rhetorical audience" (p. 12), leans toward
the former possibility.

Even Bitzer's first sustained example of a rhetorical situation—the assassination of President Kennedy—appears ill-suited to support this definition of a rhetorical audience: "With the first reports of the assassination, there immediately developed a most urgent need for information; in response, reporters created hundreds of messages. Later as the situation altered, other exigences arose: the fantastic events in Dallas had to be explained; it was necessary to eulogize the dead President; the public needed to be assured that the transfer of government to new hands would be orderly" (p. 9). Who comprised the *public* that Bitzer mentions here? *All* and only *American* citizens? At what particular stretch of time (i.e., what is the modulus of the *public*)? And what *change* was the public being asked to *mediate?* To *inform, comfort,* or *reassure* the public is not to position "it" as a mediator of change, but as that which needs to be changed through the receipt of information, condolences, and reassurances.

Additionally, despite Bitzer's references to time (e.g., the maturity, decay, persistence, even perdurance of rhetorical situations; the continued relevance of certain pieces of discourse insofar as rhetorical situations endure; and the dissipation of rhetorical audiences) and to more concrete audiences (e.g., a judge and jury), Bitzer's rhetorical audience tends toward the temporally absolute abstraction of "the public" (pp. 7, 9) or "the nation" (p. 10). When President Roosevelt addressed the members of Congress after the attack on Pearl Harbor, who comprised his audience at time t, and how did that audience shift in membership at $t + 1$, $t + 2$, ..., $t + n$? And how is it possible for the diverse and shifting membership of that temporally distended, non-simultaneous audience to require of Roosevelt a singularly "fitting rhetorical response" that must be constructed at a singularly "propitious moment" (p. 13)?

ABSOLUTE TIME AND CONVENTIONALISM

If a spatialized *national language* is the correlative to a spatialized *society* or *nation,* then the correlatives of spatialized *discursive* or *interpretive communities* are spatialized *language games, genres, registers,* and other similar theoretical constructs, falling under the rubric of *conventionalism,* that conceive of discourse as the application of *a priori* linguistic and/or pragmatic rules. To demonstrate this claim, I propose examining, plank by plank, J. L. Austin's (1962) six-part schematic of the rules "necessary for the smooth or 'happy' functioning" of illocutionary acts (p. 14), found in the opening lecture of *How To Do Things with Words,* because it includes concepts that are important for any conventionalist account of language.

The first plank is the most crucial, almost the credo of conventionalism:

> (*A*.1) There must exist an accepted conventional procedure having a certain conventional effect, that procedure to include the uttering of certain words by certain persons in certain circumstances [. . .]. (p. 14)

Conventionalism begins with the assumption that the link between signs and meanings—or at least those that constitute "languages"[8]— is *inherently arbitrary:* The "must" of (*A*.1) is not *normative,* as "accepted" is normative, but *compulsory,* marking a non-arbitrary, *a priori* arbitrariness that can be stabilized only by *a priori* conventions shared by interlocutors. Sign *X* means *Y* only by virtue of the prior agreement of a community of speakers about how words qua tools should be *used,* not by any intrinsic link between *X* and *Y.* This decisive assumption is a feature not only of speech-act theory (e.g., J. Austin, 1950/1979e; Searle, 1965/1991; Strawson, 1950/1971), but also of the diverse work of theorists in analytic philosophy (e.g., Bridgman 1959/1966; Carnap, 1932/1959a, 1947/1988; Dummett, 1973/1996d; Grice, 1976/1991c; Wittgenstein, 1953/1968, I.7), classical and modern philosophy (e.g., Augustine, trans. 1997; Locke, 1689/1987), linguistics (e.g., Lois Bloom, 1994; Saussure, 1916/1959), poststructuralism (Foucault, 1969/1972a; Lyotard, 1979/1993), pragmatism (James, 1907/1981; Peirce, 1868/1991c), and rhetoric and composition studies (e.g., Couture, 1999; Hirsch, 1977; T. Johnson, 1999; Journet, 1999; C. Miller, 1984), ad infinitum.

At this point, I need to make two observations about social conventions. First, the agreement to these conventions may be tacit, not explicit, yet remain fully in force. For Whorf (1940/1956c),

> We cut nature up, organize it into concepts, and ascribe significances as we do, largely because we are parties to an agreement to organize it in this way— an agreement that holds throughout our speech community and is codified in the patterns of our language. The agreement is, of course, an implicit and unstated one, BUT ITS TERMS ARE ABSOLUTELY OBLIGATORY [so obligatory, it seems, that they

require an announcement in all capital letters]; we cannot talk at all except by subscribing to the organization and classification of data which the agreement decrees. (pp. 213–214)

However, as Davidson (1993b) argues convincingly, no such "implicit pact" can exist because entering into such a pact would require understanding each other prior forming that pact; if prior understanding is already achieved, asks Davidson, what would be the point of the pact?

My second observation is that theorists disagree about how many conventions a language has, ranging from Wittgenstein's (1953/1968) position that there are "countless different kinds of use of what we call 'symbols,' 'words,' 'sentences'" (I.23), to J. L. Austin's (1961/1979b) claim that "we should not despair too easily and talk, as people are apt to do, about the *infinite* uses of language. Philosophers will do this when they have listed as many, let us say, as seventeen; but even if there were something like ten thousand uses of language, surely we could list them all in time" (p. 234). It is not clear to me that Wittgenstein position is that such conventions are uncountable because they are infinite, but rather that they are, for pragmatic reasons, unable to be counted.

The second, third, and fourth planks,

(*A*.2) The particular persons and circumstances in a given case must be appropriate for the invocation of the particular procedure invoked.

(*B*.1) The procedure must be executed by all participants both correctly and

(*B*.2) completely. (p. 15)

merely reaffirm the criteria of the first, for we already know from (*A*.1) that a linguistic convention is a rule-governed procedure for producing certain effects when uttered by "certain persons in certain circumstances." It stands to reason, then, that only when properly conducted would the procedure work; and the proper conduct of a speech-act requires the use of an *a priori* procedure by individuals authorized by and circumstances determined by *a priori* criteria. In this way, conventionalism extends beyond regulating or even constituting the speech-act of the utterance itself to include regulating or even constituting the full context of its use. For some theorists, not only are utterances and texts constituted by conventions or genres, but so are writers, readers, speakers, and listeners: "The text, the writer, the context, and the critic, too, as a reader, are shaped by genre. That is the fuller power of genre" (Devitt, 2000, p. 703). Bawarshi (2000) offers a similar argument: "I hope to expose the extent to which genres are constitutive both of literary and nonliterary (con)texts as well as of literary and nonliterary writers and readers [. . .]. Genres [. . .] ultimately, are the rhetorical environments within which we recognize, enact, and consequently reproduce various situations, practices, relations, and identities (p. 336). The spatializing metaphor—*rhetorical environments*—is clearly an effort to concretize a highly abstract conception of genre as a *life-world* in which people and texts are made meaningful. But it is incoherent to claim that a genre is both constitutive of a context and *is* the context itself, as if genres constitute themselves. If, as Bawarshi claims, genres constitute "texts" (p. 335), "discourse" (p. 338), "social actions" (p. 335), and even social "institutions" (p. 347), what is left to constitute genres? Spellmeyer (1993a) has criticized this kind of social constructionist thinking: "If everything is a construct, nothing can be constructed; if individuals are created by communities, then who creates the communities themselves, and in response to what forces?" (p. 22). But Bawarshi goes one step further: social institutions are not even socially constructed, but *generically* structured.

The fifth plank involves one of the most contentious disputes *within* conventionalism (not a dispute about conventionalism itself): the role of intentionality in language use. According to Austin,

> (Γ.1) Where, as often, the procedure is designed for use by persons having certain thoughts or feelings, or for the inauguration of certain consequential conduct on the part of any participant, then a person participating in and so invoking the procedure must in fact have those thoughts or feelings, and the participants intend so to conduct themselves [. . .]. (p. 15)

But what prompts these "thoughts or feelings" in the first place, and who is the "I" who utters "I promise"? Do these thoughts and feelings well up from the interiority of the subject? Does the "I" signify an autonomous self constituted apart from language, something that always contributes meaning to an utterance in excess of its conventional meaning?

Derrida (1972/1988c) attacks this element of Austin's model—and, he claims, Western metaphysics in general—for its clinging to the authority of consciousness or the *interiority* of the subject:

> One of those essential elements [of Austin's total context of a speech act]—and not one among others—remains, classically, consciousness, the conscious presence of the intention of the speaking subject in the totality of his speech act [. . .]. The conscious presence of speakers or receivers participating in the accomplishment of a performative, their conscious and intentional presence in the totality of the operation, implies teleologically that no *residue* [*reste*] escapes the present totalization. No residue, either in the definition of the requisite conventions, or in the internal and linguistic context, or in the grammatical form, or in the semantic determination of the words employed; no irreducible polysemy, that is, no "dissemination" escaping the horizon of the unity of meaning. (p. 14)

For Derrida, signs are not suffused with the presence of the speaker or writer, but mark a discontinuity or separation of the sign from its absent utterer or writer (1972/1988c, p. 9), who may only cite an iterable formula that, even as it is altered from use to use, presupposes a "minimal remainder," encapsulating an unavoidable tension between identity and difference (1977/1988b, p. 53), rule and event (1988a, p. 119). Or, one might add, between *langue* and *parole*. Seen in this way, Derrida's iterability represents a tension that has been *widely observed.*[9] Conventionalism need not deny that such a tension exists, even as permanent part of the structure of signs, so Derrida's argument is not exactly a refutation of conventionalism.

Although Derrida is quite correct that Austin leaves little room for "irreducible polysemy"—and all the while we must keep in mind that, for Derrida (1988a, p. 148), polysemy is irreducible not because meanings are *indeterminate,* but because the choice between determinate meanings is ultimately *undecidable*—his larger criticism ultimately misses the mark because Austin's model does not embrace the autonomous interiority of the subject as the foundation of language; in fact, it rejects the notion that performatives depend upon completely "*self-*

conscious acts of utterance" (Winspur, 1989, pp. 170–171). Performative utterances cannot be primarily self-conscious or self-originating because performatives are, for Austin, social constructions governed by *a priori* "public rules" (Winspur, 1989, p. 169). True, individuals may choose or refuse to participate in particular performative actions, which is reflected in (Γ.1), but they do not create those performatives, which are prior to and independent of any individual *(A.1)*. Austin, then, does not advocate psychological, phenomenological, or mentalist accounts of language, but—like, e.g., Foucault (1987, pp. 10–11), Kent (1992, p. 62), Sellars (1956/1997, pp. 88, 90, 176), Skinner (1957, pp. 137, 140), Vološinov (1929/1986, p. 91), and Wittgenstein (1953/1968 I.335–337)—would rather posit that the intentionality of the speaking subject proceeds from, and does not precede, the intentionality of the language he or she uses. Austin (1962) in fact shies away from appeals to "inward and spiritual" acts, just as Vološinov (1929/1986) rejects a "plunge into inner being" (p. 11) and Foucault (1969/1972a, p. 122) rejects references to a Cartesian *cogito* that is free to say whatever it wishes to say.

The sixth plank,

(Γ.2) must actually so conduct themselves subsequently. (p. 15)

is, for me, the most intriguing of Austin's postulates, for it is only here that Austin moves beyond conventions agreed upon in the mythical past or the present moment of utterance to include the future: The felicity of a speech act cannot be determined at the moment of utterance, even if the intentions of the speaker or the listeners mesh with what we might call the "performative intentionality" of the invoked convention at the time of utterance. The gap between utterance and conduct may be small (e.g., a person says, "I bet you $5 that this coin lands on heads," flips the coin, and then pays up when tails shows), but it may also stretch across a significant span of time (e.g., a person says, "I promise to meet you at the restaurant next Tuesday" and then later breaks his engagement without notifying the other party). Until confirmed or disconfirmed by the subsequent action, questions about the felicity of the speech act are irresolvable; and however much one might intend to make a felicitous promise, which is a condition for the felicity of the promise, the felicity of the promise is not ensured by that intention, for other conditions apply as well.

Yet, in the end, the future has no bearing on the *meaning* of the utterance: Subsequent actions cannot change the meaning of the ut-

terance, which Austin isolates in the *locutionary* dimension of a performative speech act (i.e., the act of saying something with a certain
literal meaning), nor can they change the conventionally determined
illocutionary force associated with the performative (i.e., the act performed in saying something with a certain literal meaning). Subsequent actions, rather, are collected under the rubric of *perlocutionary
acts* (i.e., the act performed by saying something—the results of the
saying), and serve only to determine whether the intended act was
successfully carried out.[10] Austin is quite clear that the locutionary
and illocutionary acts must be separated from the consequences that
follow from them:

> We must avoid the idea [. . .] that the illocutionary
> act is a *consequence* of the locutionary act, and even
> the idea that what is imported by the nomencla-
> ture of illocutions is an *additional* reference to *some*
> of the consequences of the locutions, i.e. that to say
> 'he urged me to' is to say that he said certain words
> and in addition that his saying them had *or* perhaps
> was intended to have certain consequences (? an ef-
> fect upon me) [. . .]. The uttering of noises may be a
> consequence (physical) of the movement of the vocal
> organs, breath, &c.: but the uttering of a word is *not* a
> consequence of the uttering of a noise, whether physi-
> cal or otherwise. Nor is the uttering of words with a
> certain meaning a *consequence* of uttering the words,
> physical or otherwise. (pp. 113–114)

The separation is so clear for Austin that a judge familiar with the
language of which a particular performative forms a part could determine, on being told what was said, which "locutionary and illocutionary acts were performed" by that utterance without knowing any of
the perlocutionary acts that resulted from it (p. 121). This judgment
would not require any special discernment on the part of the judge
if, as Jerrold J. Katz (1977) argues, "information about illocutionary
force [is] embodied in the structure of a sentence" (p. xii). The sentence
wears its illocutionary force on its sleeve, as it were—a position that
assumes, of course, that the judgment of the judge is not itself a perlocutionary effect of the utterance.

Searle (1995) is even more dogmatic on this position—almost to the point of incomprehensibility. I do not make this comment lightly. Consider Searle's *extraordinary* claim that

> Whenever the function of X is to Y, then X is *supposed* to cause or otherwise result in Y. This normative component in functions cannot be reduced to causation alone, to what in fact happens as a result of X, because X can have the function of Y-ing even in cases where X fails to bring about Y all or even most of the time. Thus the function of safety valves is to prevent explosions, and this is true even for valves that are so badly made that they in fact fail to prevent explosions, i.e., they *malfunction*. (p. 19)

But Searle's analogy itself malfunctions severely, in a number of ways: (a) it reduces the relation of "happens as a result of" to causation; (b) it assumes that X has a single function, or at least that X could not possibly serve contradictory functions (e.g., the function of X [a pistol] is to protect myself from harm, but the function of X in the hands of an assailant who has wrested it from me is quite different); (c) it conflates, on Searle's terms if not my own, X as a particular token from X as a normative type (e.g., a particular safety value from the class of all safety valves), and (d) it treats a *normative linguistic type*—for Searle, a *word*—as an entity that could have *a function that it never succeeds in fulfilling* and still be said to have that function. But I do not think it is sensible to say that "X means Y, but X has never actually meant Y for anyone who has ever used X."

Let me conclude by observing in passing that the debate between the primacy of conventions or intentions—with, for example, J. L. Austin (1962), Searle (1969), and Sellars (1956/1997) on one side, and Davidson (1986b), Grice (1967/1991a), and Suppes (1986/1992b) on the other—is a debate over *where* meanings get fixed, not *whether* they get fixed; that is, it is a debate over which particular version of meaning apriorism should be suzerain. For meaning consequential, the attempt to locate meaning in either place is inaccurate.

The Idealized Speaker and Audience

I think that, in fundamental discussions of language, its social aspect should be ignored, and a man should always be supposed to be speaking to himself—or, what comes to the same thing, to a man whose language is precisely identical to his own.

—Bertrand Russell

If one accepts that a language (or dialect, language game, genre, convention, etc.) is a system fully present in any given moment and simultaneously shared by people whatever their location, then one must offer some explanation for why miscommunication occurs, not between people who know different languages—for if communication requires a shared language, dialect, etc., then there could be no miscommunication, only non-communication—but between people who ostensibly know the same language (or dialect, language game, convention, etc.). Just as we observed in Chapter 2, when conflicting interpretations threatened the presumed homogeneity of sacred texts, one of the solutions theorists have employed to contain—by ruling out as invalid or uninteresting—the unruly consequences of texts and utterances that threaten the orderliness of language, etc., is to find fault with the knowledge or application of that knowledge by actual speakers, writers, listeners, and readers who make mistakes when learning or applying a language. Those who adhere to this conception of language agree that a distinction must be drawn between the consequences that texts or utterances produce and the consequences that they should properly produce.

This, of course, is the classic distinction between *competence* and *performance* that is frequently associated with the work of Noam Chomsky. For Chomsky (1968/1972), like Saussure (1916/1959) before him, the true object of linguistics is the study of the system of language that is only imperfectly manifested in actual utterances and texts of actual speakers, writers, listeners, and readers: "To study a language, then, we must attempt to dissociate a variety of factors that interact with underlying competence to determine actual performance; the technical term 'competence' refers to the ability of the idealized speaker-hearer to associate sounds and meanings strictly in accordance with the rules of his language" (p. 116). However, it would seem to be more accurate to say that, for Chomsky, these *factors* do not *interact* so much as *distort* or *conceal* that presumed underlying competence; after all, shouldn't factors that interact with the system of competence be of interest for the study of that system? Yes, unless *all* such factors are akin to, for example, a cut on the lip or a lidocaine-numbed tongue that forces a speaker to lisp or slur her words.

However, Chomsky's (1957/1969, p. 13) criterion for determining the adequacy of a grammar constructed by a linguist (i.e., whether or not a "native speaker" adjudges the sentences generated by the grammar to be "acceptable") is in direct conflict with his performance-competence distinction. This incoherence goes further than a standard criticism of Chomsky's *native speaker* criterion—i.e., that the determination of the *native speaker* requires an arbitrary choice that privileges the language of a particular person as the standard for an entire community (e.g., R. Harris, 1998, p. 52), *which it does.* The problem is also that Chomsky requires, for the validation of a grammar, a *native speaker* whose judgment is infallible. As Jerry A. Fodor (1964/1971) points out, and as Chomsky himself concedes by making the competence-performance distinction, the *native speaker,* who is not merely an informant but also a judge, has fallible linguistic intuitions. How can a grammar ever be verified if its adequacy is assessed by how well it agrees with the intuitions of a person who is necessarily capable of committing performance errors?

Saussure (1916/1959) recognized that positioning a single, real individual as the final arbiter of a description of a language would lead to insuperable problems, so he avoided the problem by asserting that "language is not complete in any speaker; it exists perfectly only within a collectivity" (p. 14). However, although such a final arbiter cannot exist, it can be *imagined;* just as physics postulates frictionless surfaces, perfect spheres, and rigid bodies, so too structuralist linguistics postulates ideal speakers who have total knowledge of a language and who employ it with perfect competence. Thus, Chomsky (1968/1972) refers to "the idealized speaker-hearer" in the passage cited earlier (p. 116), but numerous theorists have espoused similar ideas about ideal speakers and ideal audiences. For example, Ryle (1946/1959) appeals to an ill-defined standard of *intelligent use:* "to talk about a given proposition is therefore to talk about what is expressed by any expression (of no matter what linguistic structure) having the same logical force as some given expression, as such expressions are or might be intelligently used by persons (no matter whom)" (p. 341). And, in an article about the rhetorical dimension of metaphor, Eubanks (1999) appeals to a similarly ill-defined normative standard of competence: "No metaphor can be uttered except by someone whose language is shaped by political, philosophical, economic, social, professional, and personal commitments. These commitments constrain what a competent utterer's metaphor can mean" (p. 194). Eubanks does not define "competent" here, nor does he explain how the meanings of a metaphor must be constrained by commitments, nor does he account for the incompetent utterer who can somehow manufacture metaphors without constraint.

The counterpart of the *ideal speaker* is the *ideal audience,* which both serves as the "hoped for" ideal of perfect communication, and, perhaps paradoxically, as an imagined entity exerting pressures on the speaking and composing processes. The former may be (a) a mirror image of the speaker, such as Eco's (1979, p. 7) *Model Reader* or Russell's (1940, p. 64) *hypothetical hearer,* who shares the latter's knowledge of a language or code; (b) a charitable, empathetic construct, such as Bakhtin's (1986/1996) *superaddressee* (p. 126), an ideal partner who fully understands, and wants to fully understand, the intended meaning of the speaker or writer (cf. Hirsch, 1967, p. 133); or, if not charitable or identical, at least (c) a standard of rationality or reasonableness, such as Bitzer's (1968) *scientific audience* (p. 8), Perelman's (1977/1982) *universal audience* (p. 14), Crosswhite's (1996) *ideal audience* (p. 163), or Fish's (1970/1980e) *informed reader* (p. 48). Examples of the latter—an imagined entity exerting pressures on the speaking and composing processes—would include Britton et al.'s (1975) *invisible audience* (pp. 58–59), Ede and Lunsford's (1984/1996) *audience* (p. 208), and James E. Porter's (1986/1996) *readers* (p. 228).

For some theorists, speakers and writers construct or "project" their audiences (Hirsch, 1977, p. 28)—i.e., their utterances and texts *set the conditions* that determine who may understand those utterances and texts and how they must be understood because the actual audience, the *audience addressed* (Ede and Lunsford, 1984/1996, p. 199), cannot be known.[11] For instance, Ong (1977) argues that a writer must "construct in his imagination, clearly or vaguely, an audience case in some sort of role" and, if his text is to communicate successfully, the "audience must correspondingly fictionalize itself" by playing "the role in which the author has cast" his readers, explicitly or implicitly (p. 12). Eco (1979) articulates a similar position: "To make his text communicative, the author has to assume that the ensemble of codes he relies upon is the same as that shared by his possible reader. The author has thus to foresee a model of the possible reader (hereafter Model

Reader) supposedly able to deal interpretatively with the expressions in the same way as the author deals generatively with them" (p. 7). According to Eco, the Model Reader can be conceptualized as "a textually established set of felicity conditions [. . .] to be met in order to have a macro-speech act (such as a text is) fully actualized" (p. 11); the text becomes a "syntactic-semantico-pragmatic device [. . .] [with a] foreseen interpretation" and a "system of nodes or joints [. . .] at which [. . .] the cooperation of the Model Reader is expected and solicited" (p. 11).[12]

But, as Ede and Lunsford (1984/1996, p. 204) suggest, writers cannot always expect readers who are cooperative and play the part. What are we to make of resistant, even conflicting readings of a text? For Ong or Eco, the answer could only be that such readings violate the conditions for the realization of the text's encoded meaning, representing not a different or alternative use of the text, but a *misuse* of the text that is somehow *meaningful despite its misuse.* Thus, Ong and Eco confront the same problems attending the unruly consequences of texts as the theological interpreters discussed in Chapter 2.

Researchers of a more empiricist bent than either Ong or Eco also confront, and I suggest are ultimately confounded by, these unruly consequences as well. For example, Steinmann (1982), in his quest for causal laws relating the content of a text to its effects on readers, separates *intended, actual,* and *ideal* readers in this way: "For a given discourse, the intended readers are the readers that the writer intends and expects to read it; the actual readers, the readers who, intended or not, actually read it; the ideal readers, the readers who—intended or not, actual or not—are such that, if they read it, they experience the illocutionary effect with maximum speed and also experience the intended perlocutionary effect" (p. 310). Steinmann is mainly interested in discovering what he terms *illocutionary effectiveness laws* and *perlocutionary effectiveness laws* that would not only describe a causal relationship between a text and the reader's understanding of its sense and force, but also between a text and all of its consequences. Steinmann asserts that these laws are *empirical,* not *normative:* One cannot choose to obey or to violate them (pp. 293–294). Thus, on Steinmann's account, laws could be formulated that describe not only the intrinsic capacity of a text to communicate a message, but also to cause further effects, such as persuading a reader. The ideal reader for Steinmann, then, is one whose reading is entirely determined by the supposed intrinsic property of texts to convey messages and create consequences. Steinmann concedes, with some consternation, that research has not yet uncovered these laws—with perlocutionary effectiveness laws being much more difficult to uncover because, as he admits, perlocutionary effects are much more variable than illocutionary effects—but he claims that all good writers must tacitly know these laws in order to be good writers (pp. 321–322). And good writing, for Steinmann, is reducible to readability/processing time: The more effective text is the text more speedily processed by readers (pp. 307–308), with the *ideal reader*—i.e., the reader who gets all and only the intrinsic information in the least time—serving as the final arbiter of the communicative effectiveness of the text.

Though they echo Steinmann's (and cognitive psychology's, for that matter; cf. Sperber and Wilson, 1986) concern about efficient cognitive processing of information, with the most *efficient* text being the *best* text, Hirsch and Harrington (1981) go one step further, claiming that the "court of last resort" for interpretation is the *common reader,* which is "no imaginary figure, but an empirically verifiable, cultural entity, required in all writing and assumed mutatis mutandis by all writers" (p. 197). Given their attempt to empirically measure "the quality of prose" (p. 189), Hirsch and Harrington cannot treat the common reader as a fiction, but rather as an empirical fact, as they acknowledge: "The possibility of a sound empirical measurement of communicative effectiveness, [*sic*] depends upon the existence of a personage long familiar to those involved in writing assessment in the literary sphere, namely *the common reader*" (p. 197). In the end, however, the common reader is a construct, an assumption of "*commonality* of knowledge, values and conventions, shared by all of these readers" in a particular demographic group that the writer intends to address (e.g., all of the readers of a particular journal in which an author publishes a paper) (p. 198).[13] To ensure this happy commonality, however, which is threatened by annoying "mismatches in shared knowledge [that are] due to random fluctuation in factual, linguistic, and cultural knowledge of the sample readers" (pp. 198–199) and that might disrupt the smooth transmission of meanings conveyed by the text, Hirsch and Harrington have to employ "screening of some sort" of their test subjects. In order to measure the *intrinsic communicative effectiveness* of a text (p. 189), Hirsch and Harrington must arbitrarily limit *readership,* and they must especially eliminate from consideration those unruly perlocutionary effects of a text, which are "too variable to be determined empirically for the heterogeneous audiences to which writing is normally directed" (p. 196), just as Beardsley and Wimsatt (1946/1954) famously discarded these effects as the result of the *affective fallacy*. Thus, despite the pretense to measure intrinsic communicative effectiveness as "derived from the actual effects of a piece of prose" (p. 189), Hirsch and Harrington consider only a few of the consequences of the text, ignoring those that seem to resist generalizations.

Of course, the standard of the competent speaker, the ideal reader, or the common reader can never be met, which reduces these concepts to empty formalisms that serve as pale, homogeneous substitutes for the messiness and disruptiveness of actual speakers and readers. Accounting for that messiness may be challenging for the empirical researcher, but that shouldn't prompt us to try to ignore it, as Hirsch and Harrington do, or to try to domesticate it, as Steinmann hopes one day will happen (i.e., that the unruliness of perlocutionary effects will be reduced to perlocutionary effectiveness laws).

It is possible to extend the notion of *audience* or *readers* as textual constructs to the notion of *author* as well—i.e., that the author is as much a structural feature of the text as is its audience. In short, the author is not a person, but a role occupied by a person. For example, Black (1970/1999) contends that any utterance or text is directed toward and structurally implies, in addition to the *second persona* (i.e., the ideal auditor or reader), the *first persona* of the textually implied author (cf. Nold, 1981, p. 71). In a response to Black's essay, Wander (1984/1999) adds to what seems to be a text already crowded with implications an even more ghostly *third persona,* which he defines as "audiences not addressed, unable to attend, and unable to respond to the 'text'" (p. 375). And Eco (1979) observes that the personal pronouns in texts do not indicate real people, either writer or reader, but are "textual strategies"; consequently, the authorial "I" of Wittgenstein's *Philosophical Investigations* (1953/1968) does not refer to the person who wrote the text but to *"a philosophical style"* (p. 11).[14] Such a conception is prevalent in poststructuralist approaches to language, in which the speaking or writing *subject* is constituted by language, rather than master of it (e.g., Barthes, 1968/1977b; Derrida, 1967/1978; Foucault, 1967/1977a; Lyotard, 1979/1993), so that it seems as if a writer or speaker is, as feminist literary theorist Avital Ronell believes, "merely taking dictation from language" (Davis, 2000, p. 246). *But what is the "language" that does the dictating?* A common language, a national language, a language game, etc. in which time plays no essential part, in which the language that dictates exists all-at-once, forever, imperishable?

ABSOLUTE TIME AND THE MYTH OF CULTURE

All of culture is implication in every instance of discourse.

—Michael Calvin McGee

Although a more detailed examination of this topic must wait for future work, I would like to note in passing the role of absolute time in the tendency to treat language as a bearer or mirror of cultural values, as if *culture*—in whole or in part—could be encoded directly the formal properties of the text, whether at the explicit level of surface features or the deep structural or functional level of *cryptotypes* (Whorf, 1956a; cf. Halliday, 1987, pp. 136–137). For example, according to Whorf (1956a), a *cryptotype* represents "a covert linguistic class [. . .] a submerged, subtle, and elusive meaning, corresponding to no actual word, yet shown by linguistic analysis to be functionally important in the grammar" (p. 70). To illustrate this claim, Whorf argues that in Hopi the use of the aspect and tense forms is often governed by cryptotypes: "They govern, for instance, the way of expressing the beginning of an action or state, the English 'begins to do' or 'begins to be' form. First, a different form (phenotype) is used, depending on whether the verb is active or inactive (either passive or static), and this is a cryptotypic distinction, for the formal apparatus of Hopi grammar does not set up any active-versus-inactive contrast" (p. 72). This phenomena has nothing to do with the intentions of speakers, but is simply part of the system that constitutes *the* Hopi language.

People who would undoubtedly reject the notion that texts and utterances have intrinsic meaning—and who would likely reject Marr's concept of *stadialism* (i.e., that languages can be matched with social classes) (cf. Newmeyer, 1986, pp. 115–116)—nevertheless treat as a commonplace notions that "language reflects culture" (Adler-Kassner, 1998, p. 212), that "signifying practices" are "immersed in ideology" (Berlin, 1993, p. 110); that "signs are the bearers of meaning that structure cultural practices" (Smagorinsky, 1997, p. 67), that "community beliefs and values are inscribed in patterns of discourse" (J. Segal, Paré, Brent, and Vipond, 1998, p. 74), and that the text "reproduces the structures and systems constituting the social environment" (D. Goodwin, 1999, p. 96).

An aside: Not only does any given text reflect current culture or the culture in existence at the time of composition, but it may also (will also?) reflect the accumulation of prior stages of that culture: Bazerman (1988), for example, contends that the genre of scientific reports "embodies the achievement of the three hundred years since the invention of the scientific journal necessitated the invention of the scientific article" (p. 59). I must defer interrogating this notion of accumulating meanings in detail until Chapter 6.

To continue: For a language to reflect, bear, inscribe, or reproduce culture—i.e., for every utterance and text to represent "a cultural position" (Comfort, 2000, p. 555)—a language must be something that not only can reflect, bear, inscribe, or reproduce meanings without (a legitimate) remainder, but also that *culture* itself is a fully-present totality, a temporally flattened monad, whose parts or whose entirety can be reflected, borne, inscribed, or reproduced. Notice, too, how utterances and texts become bearers of frozen meanings on this model, for presumably the utterance or text can only reflect—and must continue to reflect in perpetuity—those cultural meanings, and only those cultural meanings, that existed at the time of speaking or writing (e.g., John Milton's *Paradise Lost* reflects only the cultural milieu of seventeenth-century England, not ancient Babylon or twenty-first-century Argentina); consequently, Fish (1970/1980e) argues that the "critic has the responsibility of becoming not one but a number of informed readers, each of whom will be identified by the matrix of political, cultural, and literary determinants. The informed reader of Milton will not be the informed reader of Whitman, although the latter will *necessarily* comprehend the former" (p. 49; emphasis added)

ABSOLUTE TIME, COGNITIVE AND LINGUISTIC
HOLISM, AND INTENTIONALISM

The linguistic link between author and authority is neither accidental or insignificant—nothing in language ever is.

—John Fiske

I pointed out earlier that the concept of *discourse community* may be appealing because it appears to be so much more concrete than the concept of *society*. However, it is possible to doubt even whether discourse communities qua integrated systems exist without thereby abandoning the search for certain foundations for meaning and language, for one may appeal to the individual mind, or some smaller unit of which mind is concatenated, as a *totality*. The hope seems to be this: (a) that if there is no integrated collective mind, at least there is an integrated individual mind; (b) that if there is no integrated collective language or dialect, at least there is an integrated idiolect; and (c) that even if there is no integrated individual mind or idiolect, at least there is an integrated intentionality. In other words, the hope is that by subdividing long enough we will come to the atoms of meaning. In this section, then, I will critique holistic conceptions of mind, idiolect, and intentions.

Mind as totality. "I have the feeling," wrote Humboldt (1836/1988), "that everything engendered in the *mind,* as the outflow of a single *force,* constitutes a great *totality,* and that the detail, as if by the breath of that force, must bear marks of its connection with this whole" (p. 162). For Humboldt, then, mind is not simply the outcome of a passive *accumulation* of beliefs or thoughts prompted by sensations (as, say, empiricists like Locke, Hobbes, and Hume would have held), but a *structured, interrelated,* and *finite set* of beliefs or thoughts that forms what has been variously described as mental *models* (e.g., Chafe, 1994, p. 28; F. Smith, 1971, p. 28), *frameworks* (e.g., Halliday, 1975, p. 5), *networks* (e.g., Flower, 1988, p. 534; Polanyi, 1958/1974, p. 60), *webs* (e.g., Flower, 1994, p. 39; Quine, 1951/1961c, p. 42), *lattices* (e.g., Hardy, 1998, p. 19), *worlds* (e.g., Britton, 1970/1992, p. 32; Heidegger, 1927/1962, p. 120), *umwelten* (e.g., J. Uexküll, 1982, p. 29; T. Uexküll, 1982, p. 3), or *environments* (Lewontin, 1991, p. 109).[15] These concepts of mind include a durational element—i.e., that one's mind at any given moment represents the cumulative history of one's past experiences (cf. Britton, 1970/1992, p. 12; Flower, 1994, p. 77; Kress, 1997, p. 46; F. Smith, 1971, p. 28).—that will be better explored in Chapter 6; in this section, I will focus only some of the ways in which these models spatialize mind in terms of a large-scale cognitive system and/or a smaller-scale transcendental consciousness.

For Chafe (1994), "Every human being possesses a complex internal model of reality. Call it a worldview, call it a knowledge structure, this model is essential to the human way of coping with the world" (p. 27). This model, based as it is only on one's own experiences and inferences drawn from them, is idiosyncratic and centered around the "*self*" (p. 28); and, even though the model exists all-at-once, "only one small piece of that model can be *active* [in consciousness] at one time. At any given moment the mind can focus on no more than a small segment of everything it '*knows*'" (p. 28); Thus, *mind* is not limited by *consciousness:* One cannot "know" fully one's own mind, but only the contents of one's consciousness. Similarly, Hardy (1998) differentiates the *semantic lattice,* which is the "network organization of the whole mind-psyche" that "houses all of a person's knowledge, sensoriality, affectivity, and behavior patterns" (p. 19), from what she terms the *noo-field,* which is "the activated part of the lattice" (p. 20). Curiously, these models must postulate that the mind is essentially *unknowable:* One cannot ever know one's mind, only that aspect of its pre-given structure, otherwise shrouded in darkness, that consciousness, like a focused beam of light, illuminates. Such a model seems *intuitively* correct: Isn't it the case that I "know" a multitude of facts, hold a multitude of beliefs, remember a multitude of events? Obviously, these do not crowd my conscious awareness, which is limited to relevant aspects of my immediate environment, objects I feel may be missing or lacking, my current emotional state, dreams, etc. Surely there is more content in my mind than I can grasp at a single instant, something that *is* there, just outside the boundaries of my consciousness!

However, at least three objections to this characterization of mind can be raised. First, we might argue, following Condillac (1792/1982a), that ideas have no existence other than during their moments of instantiation:

> Like sensations, ideas are ways of being of the mind. They exist as long as they modify it. They no longer exist as soon as they cease modifying it. To look in the mind for those I am not thinking about is to look where they no longer are. To look in the body is to look where they never were. Where then are they? Nowhere. Would it not be absurd to ask where are the sounds of a harpsichord when the instrument has stopped resonating? (p. 377)

Equally absurd, suggests Condillac (1792/1982a), would be to ask "What happens to a body's roundness when it takes another form? Where is it preserved? And when the body becomes round again, where does the roundness come from?" (p. 377; cf. Skinner, 1957, p. 21). An unconscious idea—housed in an "unconscious intentionality" (Searle, 1995, p. 7; cf. Schildgen, 1993, p. 33)—would be a contradiction in terms: There are no unconscious thoughts (Peirce 1868/1991c, p. 79). But notice that Condillac immediately adds that, whereas ideas *cannot* be stored in the brain, the mechanical habits that lead to the reproduction of ideas *are* stored in the brain: "Although I do not know the mechanism of the brain, I can judge that its different parts have acquired the capacity to move on their own in the same way that the action of the senses moved them; that the habits of this organ are *stored* [italics added], and that every time it follows them, it regenerates the same ideas because the same movements recur in it" (p. 377). For an empiricist like Condillac, the number of habits a mind "stores" must form a finite set at any given moment because the mind can only recall from memory/habit only those ideas that it had earlier acquired from experience (cf. Locke, 1689/1987, I.iv.20); thus, the mind remains a *totality,* even if it is totality not of *knowledge structures,* but of *dispositions.*

Second, we might maintain that structural models of the mind are too rigid to represent actual operations of mind as it interacts with the flux of experience. For example, Linell (1982) claims that

> the assumption of large-scale integrated coherent knowledge structures is thoroughly unrealistic. It seems unlikely that we have ready-made models of all (or most) of the various parts of the world that we are acquainted with. Our knowledge of any universe of discourse has to be fragmentary and flexible, so that it can be used in many ways and for different purposes [. . .]. No static model of the world could satisfy the needs of such an active subject. (pp. 122–123)

Thus, although Linell would agree with Chafe and Hardy about the unifying stream of consciousness—that aspect of our knowledge which is attended to in any given moment—he contends that consciousness does not move like a beam of light across an already integrated totality, but rather jumps from "fragment to fragment" (p. 123). Whatever unity emerges from such a process of leaps is the transient *result* of the activity of a conscious agent reminiscent of the transcendental ego of phenomenology that binds past memories, present sensations, and future expectations together in a Husserlian *noetic moment,* the moment in which "consciousness constitutes the unity and identity in the multiplicity of its phases" (Peursen, 1972, p. 10).

This objection, however, suffers from its own embarrassments, for models of mind need not, and generally do not, configure the mind as a static totality given once-and-for-all. In fact, empiricist models must of necessity accept that the mind is only what it has acquired at some point in time—i.e., that the mind *learns.* Only Plato's (trans. 1956/1964b, trans. 1945/1964c) conception of mind, in which the mind can "learn" only what has in some sense been *remembered* (i.e., *mathesis* is defined in terms of *recollection*), would permit the kind of cognitive stasis that Linell criticizes. And the linguistic analogue of such Platonism would be any theory that embraces innate semantic ideas, such as Fodor's (1987) and Jackendoff's (1994). As Jackendoff puts it, "The full class of humanly possible concepts (or conceptual structures) is determined by the combinatorial principles of the conceptual well-formedness rules. That is, the conceptual well-formedness rules characterize the space of possible conceptual states—the resources available in the brain for forming concepts" (p. 130), and the child "learns" word meanings by "selecting [an *a priori*] conceptual structure for the word and linking it with a linguistic expression" (p. 133).

But the problem here is not, pace Linell, that these models conceive of mind as given *once-and-for-all,* but only that they conceive of it as given *all-at-once* (i.e., that at time *t* the totality of the mind's contents could be, at least in principle, fully described, because whatever happens after *t* has no bearing on the "content" of the "content" at *t*). Additionally, pace Linell, reducing the scope of the all-at-once to whatever exists for a unifying consciousness that transiently binds an otherwise fragmentary knowledge-base simply shortens the list of that totality instead of ultimately challenging the notion of a total description of mind; and to say that mind is a *totality of fragments,* however flexible, is not much of an improvement over claiming that mind is a totality of coherent knowledge structures. The pieces of a jigsaw puzzle, however chaotically they might be scrambled, still form a total set.

Third, it could be argued that mind cannot be limited only to cognitive processes that occur within the brain, but must include the role of environment and context—i.e., that mind is necessarily embodied, located within transient "material places" constituted and reconstituted by "cultural, historical, and ecological systems" (Fleckenstein, 1999, p. 281). The mind need not "store" a world representation in its memory, but may actually rely on the world to "store" memories that are *externalized* in books, computers, video tapes, etc. (Dennett, 1991, p. 220). From this perspective, the dualism between mind and body dissolves, tending either toward (a) a *materialism* in which thinking is a physical process or behavior influenced by the external world (e.g., Hoopes, 1991, p. 10; Dennett, 1991, p. 16; Skinner, 1957, pp. 14–15; M. Turner, 1994, pp. 97, 99), or (b) or a *co-geneticism* in which individual minds "construct their own environments out of bits and pieces of the physical and biological worlds" (p. 109), so that environments, though physical, are not neutral and must be defined in relation to particular entities (Lewontin, 1991, p. 109; J. Uexküll, 1982, p. 27).

In rhetoric and composition studies, the psychology of cognition and the neuro-physiology of the human brain meet most emphatically in the work of Oakley (1999), who argues that theorists must seek "a tighter fit between the structures of meaning and the structures of the brain" (p. 122) and who sees his research as an effort to "explore potential mappings between phenomenology and neurology in terms familiar to rhetoricians and cognitive scientists" (p. 122). While Oakley appears to frame his discussion in terms of mutual illumination, he admits his physicalist bias in the introduction to his essay: "The overall thrust of the article is this: Whatever theory of meaning scholars of verbal and written communication use should agree with present, hard-won insights into the behavioral and brain sciences" (p. 95). But this is far too strong a claim, for it assumes that these "hard-won insights" are beyond dispute and possible falsification, and it presumes that physicalism holds all of the trump cards on other possible ways to theorize meaning. *But this begs the question:* To claim that theories of meaning are bound to the findings of neuroscience is already dependent upon an implicit theory of meaning that locates it in the hardware and software of the human brain.

Although anti-dualist models are salutary in their resistance to Cartesian solipsism, they remain within an absolutist conception of time, for each posits that mind is *located* at a unique confluence of physical and social contexts: If only those contexts could be described without remainder at time t, so would the mind. Further, it would follow that the relationship between mind and world would be law-like, either (a) in the empiricist or materialist sense that physical laws regulate the chemical processes of the brain and the stimulation of sensory organs (and that mind is nothing other than the brain) or (b) in the phenomenological sense that *umwelten* are delimited by what the mind qua transcendental subjectivity may and does perceive. The mind/brain cannot respond to stimuli it has not yet received, but only to present stimuli; nor does the world extend beyond the "sensual perception [that] surrounds all living beings as if with bubbles that are sharply delineated but invisible to the outside observer, [. . .] [comprising] the bricks and mortar of reality" (T. Uexküll, 1982, p. 3). The fully contextualized mind, whether material or phenomenological, is an *absolute mind,* for claiming that the mind is in fact contextualized requires either that context fully exhausts mind or that mind exhausts context (cf. Derrida, 1972/1988c, p. 18). All three of objections I have discussed (and not the objections to the objections!), then, still conceptualize mind as a spatialized entity existing within a framework of absolute time. But what would a conception of mind that more adequately incorporates its temporality be like? That question I will defer until Chapter 5.

The idiolect. The linguistic analogue of the total mind is the *idiolect.* An idiolect may be conceptualized as a fragment of or deviation from a larger sociolect that constitutes the reality of language—in other words, *the individual has no language per se* (e.g., Saussure, 1916/1959, pp. 14, 113). Or it may be conceptualized as the peculiar, but still essentially complete, way in which an individual learns and uses a sociolect—in other words, the individual possesses a language, one that is idiosyncratically constructed yet answerable to the linguistic practices of the social groups of which he or she is a member (e.g., Quine, 1960, p. 8). However, it is far more commonly theorized as a totalized language system that an individual possesses, usurping the primacy of a sociolect that now becomes of only secondary importance (e.g., Grice, 1948/1991b; Donnellan, 1966). Thus, for Davidson (1973/1980c), language, described in psychological terms, is a "single, highly structured, and very complex disposition of the speaker [. . . to utter] any of a large number of sentences under specified conditions" (p. 255). But an idiolect, however complex or subject to modification, exists all-at-once, a point that becomes clearer when Davidson (1973/1980c) observes that, described in physical terms, language is "not a disposition, but an actual state, a mechanism" (pp. 255–256).

Roy Harris (1998) contends that the notion of the idiolect qua system "located inside the speaker's head is another way of reinstating the doctrine of the fixed code" that hopes to contain the observable diversity of linguistic phenomena, even for the people presumed to share the same dialect, within a postulated homogeneity (p. 49). *The idiolect, then, is a myth intended to demonstrate how linguistic diversity between interlocutors results from the linguistic homogeneity of individuals.* The crucial assumption, notes Harris, is that whereas individuals use language in ways that deviate from the idiolects of others, they cannot "depart from their own idiolects in practice" (p. 50), for if idiolects could be violated or modified from utterance to utterance, linguistic diversity would occur even at the level of the individual; but without the possibility of modification, communication between individuals seems unlikely, for it could occur only by a serendipitous matching of idiolects.

However, like Linell before him, Harris overgeneralizes. His criticisms work against particular targets, but theorists who advocate idiolectal conceptions of language need not accept Harris's characterization of the idiolect as a *fixed code.* For example, Suppes (1984/1992c) argues that languages are radically idiosyncratic, not only because each individual possesses his or her own (a) internal "dictionary," (b) procedures for constructing this dictionary, and (c) rules of usage (pp. 27–28), but also because (d) language use involves the continual creation of new rules: "Individual rules of grammar are created by speakers and listeners as required and are not a matter of something that is learned once for all at one's mother's knee. So the rules of grammar I use are ones that I generate often in new situations and very likely on many occasions forget, to be relearned and recreated as needed on new occasions" (p. 28). Consequently, asserts Suppes (1986/1992b), it is impossible to "characterize the speech of even a single speaker by a complete set of rules"; rather, language is comprised of "partial rules, just as there are partial rules of walking or chewing" that do not fully determine the properties of any particular action, and it is supplemented by ad hoc rules—therefore, *scarcely* rules at all—that are applicable only for single utterances (pp. 53–54). Similarly, Davidson (1976/1980a, p. 265) maintains that, even if cognition is determined by physical laws, those laws would be so specific to individuals at particular moments that the kind of generalizations sought by psychologists can never be successfully formulated. And Davidson (1986b) also, despite his dispositional account of language, allows for, and even argues for the primacy of, modifications of the idiolects of interlocutors to mesh better with each others' idiolects during communicative interactions—a conclusion that has found empirical support in the ways in which interlocutors verbally *accommodate* each other (cf. Coupland and Giles, 1988).

Intentions and speech plans. But I would argue, based on my understanding of meaning consequentialism, that Suppes's and Davidson's theories of language depend upon a logic of absolute time; for even as they appear to accept the liquidity, even incompleteness, of idiolects, they cannot resist postulating a speaker's *intentions* for saying an utterance as the *a priori* ground of the meaning of that utterance. In short, Suppes and Davidson reduce the size of the homogeneous object of study from the idiolect, which they do not accept is homogeneous, to a particular intention behind a particular utterance. For instance, Suppes and Crangle (1988/1992) assert that words do not have meanings apart from their contexts of use, but in contexts their meanings can be "fixed" precisely (p. 318) because they are precisely set by intentions that, even if they are not infinitely specific (e.g., a command to wash dishes does not *contain* an exact representation of the physical movements required to complete the particular task), "carry a bundle of ceteris paribus conditions that impose a variety of constraints on the specific procedures actually executed" (p. 319) (e.g., that one uses dishwashing liquid to wash dishes, that dishes are not clean if they have food residue on their surfaces, etc.). The meaning of an utterance, then, is frozen in place by the originating intention of the utterer, with its array of ceteris paribus conditions, and remains forever immune from whatever consequences result from the utterance—as does the meaning of the intention itself (p. 319).

Similarly, Davidson (1993a) maintains that "in the end the sole source of linguistic meaning is the intentional production of tokens of sentences" (p. 298), with intentions comprised of three types:

- the intention to produce a result that could be, in principle, achieved non-linguistically (e.g., I could threaten you by raising my fist as well as saying, "If you don't stop, I'll hit you");
- the intention to commit a particular kind of illocutionary act with a particular illocutionary force;

- the intention for the utterance to be interpreted as having a particular literal meaning.

For Davidson, a linguistic action will be "frustrated" if the "intended audience does not grasp the producer's intended semantic meaning and force" (p. 299); notice that Davidson does not claim that the action will be *meaningless,* though one wonders where the *content* of a misunderstood utterance comes from if meaning must be intentional. Of course, all of this presumes that the telos of linguistic action must be the communication of meanings and forces intended all-at-once at the time of utterance to an audience intended all-at-once at the time of utterance, with those intentions generating the standard by which the utterance must be interpreted. It also assumes, equally problematically, that the meaning and force of an utterance is fully and immediately transparent to its producer, for a speaker who does not know his or her own intentions cannot possibly use an utterance to convey them; thus, Davidson (1993c) is led to the extraordinary conclusion that "a person cannot generally misuse his own words, because it is that use which gives his words their meaning. What a speaker says can be misinterpreted by others, but it cannot be misinterpreted by the speaker" (p. 250). Finally, it assumes that the meaning of the utterance and the intentions that are expressed by it are immune from the consequences that the utterance generates: Like Austin (1962), Davidson assumes that the locutionary meaning and the illocutionary force of an utterance, over which the speaker may exercise total control, are separable from an utterance's inherently uncontrollable perlocutionary effects.

Such claims about the primacy of intentions run aground especially—but not only in relation to—when contrasted with the interactions of children with signs. For example, Dyson (1989), in her study of children's literacy, observes that one of her subjects, Ruben, would "study his pictures in order to discover their meaning" (p. 86); this process, in which children "develop [a posteriori] interpretations," especially "when pressed by an adult to account for their pictures," is called *romancing* (p. 86; cf. Golumb, 1974, pp. 4–9). A similar process, noted in psychological experiments, is called *confabulating:*

> there are circumstances in which people are just wrong about what they are doing and how they are doing it. It is not that they *lie* in the experimental situation, but that they confabulate; they fill in the gaps, guess, speculate, mistake theorizing for observ-

ing [. . .]. They tell us *what it is like* to solve the problem, make the decision, recognize the object. Because
they are sincere (apparently), we grant that that must
be what it is like to them, but then it follows that
what it is like to them is at best an uncertain guide to
what is going on in them. (Dennett, 1991, p. 94)

The lessons that I draw for meaning consequentialism from these examples are (a) that "intentions" can be supplied *a posteriori* and (b) that
the way people talk about their uses of language—especially when
that talk falls under the rubric of meaning apriorism—is not necessarily an accurate account of what they are doing when using language.

Unfortunately, I do not have time or space, even in a chapter and a
book of this length, to explore adequately even a partial list of *a priori*
intentionalist accounts of meaning—or, better, accounts of meaning
in which intentionalism at least plays a part. I can only point out that
intentionalism has advocates in dialogism (e.g., Bakhtin, 1975/1981,
1986/1996); literary theory (Bowers, 1959; Gibbs, 1999; Hirsch, 1967;
Tanselle, 1989); classical (e.g., Augustine, trans. 1997; Cicero, trans.
1970), modern (e.g., Campbell, 1776/1988), and contemporary rhetoric (e.g., Condit, 1989/1999); philosophy of language (e.g., Grice,
1948/1991b; Searle, 1969; Sidgwick, 1921; Stampe, 1975); philosophy
of mind (e.g., Dretske, 1981; Edelman, 1992; Fodor, 1987); rhetoric
and composition studies (e.g., Berthoff, 1999; Cooper, 1982; Kent,
1992; Murray, 1982/1996; Yarbrough, 1999); and semiotics (e.g.,
Kress, 1997). I want to emphasize once more that the question is not,
for me, whether there *are* intentions, but of their *transparency, deter-
minacy,* and *sufficiency* to fix the Meaning of utterances. For Suppes,
Davidson, and intentionalists generally, intentions, not utterances per
se, are of primary importance; but intentions are no surer grounds of
meaning than the conventions of literal meaning, for the Meaning of
an intention is not merely open to the consequences that result from it,
but is constituted by those consequences—consequences that would
include the utterance itself and the consequences propagated by that
utterance.

5 Simultaneity and Consequentialism: The Distensions and Discontinuities of Mind and Community

> No present thought (which is a mere feeling) has any meaning, any intellectual value; for this lies not in what is actually thought, but in what this thought may be connected with in representation by subsequent thoughts; so that the meaning of a thought is altogether something virtual.
>
> —C. S. Peirce

In the preceding chapter, my critique of the principle of simultaneity moved from the macro-scale of temporally flattened *societies* and *languages* to the micro-scale of temporally flattened *minds, idiolects,* and *intentions*. This final section will reverse course, moving from a sketch of a consequentialist account of mind to a consequentialist account of community, in an effort to explain how "the cognitive" and "the social" are meaningful without being foundational of Meaning. I will argue that mind and community are *distended, futural,* and *discontinuous* and that the meaningfulness of mind and community are not two different kinds of meaning, as if some meanings could be consequential and others not.

THE TEMPORAL DISTENSION OF MIND

> I am the self which I will be, in the mode of not being it.
>
> —Jean-Paul Sartre

How might we theorize, in a way that would extend the notion of meaning consequentialism, the temporal distension, as opposed to the simultaneity, of mind? This is a crucial question, especially if we are inclined to treat mind as a structure of meanings supervening on the brain or as the seat of a subject whose intentions determine the meaning of his or her utterances. If a consequentialist account of meaning leads us to reject both of these conceptions of mind, what positive account of mind could it offer in their place?

The first premise regarding mind from a consequentialist point of view is strongly poststructural in cast, but is also prompted by the observation that cognition cannot occur with infinite speed and so must occupy some discrete span of time (Dennett, 1991, p. 148):

(M1.0) Thoughts are *polythetic*, not *monothetic*.

For thoughts to be monothetic (i.e., graspable all-at-once), a consciousness capable of division into achronal slices without any duration whatsoever would be required because only such a consciousness would be capable of *grasping* the atemporal contents of those thoughts[1]; and, equally clearly, monothetic thoughts would require monothetic meanings. There is no single, essentially timeless "now" in which a thought may be grasped, but not merely because the finite speed of cognition foils the grasping of thoughts that would, in a perfect world, be atemporal, but also because the meanings of thoughts are constituted by the actual consequences of those thoughts (cf. Peirce, 1868/1991c, pp. 70–71; Gadamer, 1967/1977d, p. 25). As instructive as Peirce's (1868/1991c) observation is that "no present actual thought (which is a mere feeling) has any meaning, any intellectual value; for this lies not in what is actually thought, but in what this thought may be connected with in representation by subsequent thoughts; so that the meaning of a thought is altogether something virtual" (pp. 70–71), he also accepts the notion that there are absolute "states of mind" (p. 71) comprised of single *present* actual thoughts and that present thoughts must necessarily be non-reflective because the activity of reflection takes time. Thus, I suggest that a consequentialist account of meaning should reject models of mind which involve (a) ideas or thoughts that are fully present,[2] (b) spatialized *gestalten*,[3] and/or (c) the unity of a *transcendental ego*.[4]

If the meanings of thoughts (or concepts, beliefs, feelings, etc.) are constituted by their temporally dispersed consequences, then it follows that mind qua collection of thoughts can never be completely described because mind is necessarily incomplete. In other words,

(M2.0) Mind is, essentially, *futural.*

The notion of the *futural* emerges from Heidegger's phenomenological conceptualization of the temporality of *Dasein*—his term for any entity for whom asking questions about Being is one of its possible modes of Being (p. 27)—and, more generally, of Being itself, which can only be understood in terms of "temporality" (p. 20).

For Heidegger, Western thought has for too long neglected questions about Being, reducing ontology to what he terms *ontical* questions about the physical attributes of entities (p. 31). Instead of postulating the primacy of an objective space or time, Heidegger contends that space (qua *extension*) and time (qua *absolute time*) as objects of scientific investigation necessarily depend upon the *a priori temporality* of Dasein, from which emerges its *spatiality* as well. For Heidegger, the *spatiality* of Dasein, its "Being in space" (p. 134), is characterized by *de-severance* (i.e., "making the farness vanish—that is, making the remoteness of something disappear, bringing it close" [p. 139]) and *directionality* (i.e., a placing of "the particular 'whithers' to which something belongs or goes, or gets brought or fetched" [p. 143]). However, this spatiality itself is "grounded in [Dasein's] temporality" (p. 418) because (a) de-severance and directionality are grounded in Dasein's *involvements* (i.e., Dasein orders things into places); (b) Dasein's involvements cannot be understood separately and at a single instant, but only have meaningfulness considered in a totality, the *world,* that includes their temporality; and (c) involvements are grounded in *care,* which is necessarily temporal (and primarily futural) because it is Dasein's way of "Being towards the potentiality-for-Being" (i.e., an orientation toward Dasein's possibilities) (p. 236). Thus, space emerges from Dasein's spatiality, spatiality emerges from care, and care emerges from temporality. Consequently, for Heidegger, the phenomenology of Dasein necessarily precedes the ontology of the sciences because *"only as phenomenology, is ontology possible"* (p. 60): "The question of Being aims therefore at ascertaining the *a priori* conditions not only for the possibility of the sciences which examine entities as entities of such and such a type, and, in so doing, already operate with an understanding of Being, but also for the possibility of those ontologies themselves which are prior to the ontical sciences and which provide their foundations" (p. 31). The "objective" scientific investigation of entities in time is only one of the manifold modes of Being available to Dasein, who is primordially involved *with*, not residing apart *from*, a *world* whose structure is the totality of Dasein's involvements (p. 120).

But what, then, is the temporality of Dasein, if it is not an infinite succession of "nows"? For Heidegger, it is comprised of the three "*ecstases*," which are the "phenomena of the future, the character of having been, and the Present" (p. 377). "Temporality," he writes, "is essentially ecstatical" (p. 380); and these ecstases are not serial, but equiprimordial: "temporality does not first arise through a cumulative sequence of the ecstases" (p. 378). However, the future holds for Heidegger a special priority over the other two ecstases:

> In enumerating the ecstases, we have always mentioned the future first. We have done this to indicate that the future has *a priori*ty in the ecstatical unity of primordial and authentic temporality [. . .]. Primordial and authentic temporality temporalizes itself in terms of the authentic future and in such a way that in having been futurally, it first of all awakens the Present. *The primary phenomenon of primordial and authentic temporality is the future.* (p. 378)

The future is ontologically primary in that the past and present are oriented toward it and emerge from it: "the character of 'having been' arises from the future, and in such a way that the future which 'has been' (or better, which 'is in the process of having been') releases from itself the Present. This phenomenon has the unity of a future which makes present in the process of having been; we designate it as '*temporality*'" (p. 374).

Consequently, the temporality of Dasein—whose "*essence lies in its existence*" (i.e., its potentiality for Being—its "to be") (p. 67), and for whom the "*primary meaning of existentiality is the future*" (p. 376)—is essentially *futural:* "By the term 'futural,' we do not here have in view a 'now' which has *not yet* become actual and which sometime *will be* for the first time. We have in view the coming [. . .] in which Dasein, in its ownmost potentiality-for-Being, comes towards itself" (p. 373). This is a crucial point, for it allows Heidegger to avoid placing Dasein in a timeless, panchronic dimension. Dasein comes toward itself, then, not in the sense that its future "self" is already fully determined, but in the sense that Dasein's ownmost potentiality-for-Being is something that Dasein can in fact "come towards" (p. 372) through *anticipation*—i.e., a mode of Being in which Dasein is, in a sense, "constantly ahead of itself" (p. 386).[5] According to Heidegger,

> Anticipatory resoluteness, when taken formally and existentially, without our constantly designating its full structural content, is *Being towards* one's own-most, distinctive potentiality-for-Being. This sort of thing is possible only in that Dasein *can, indeed,* come towards itself in its ownmost possibility, and that it can put up with this possibility as a possibility in thus letting itself come towards itself—in other words, that it exists. This letting-itself-*come-towards-itself* in that distinctive possibility which it puts up with, is the primordial phenomenon of the *future as coming towards.* (p. 372)

Guided by the preceding analysis, I offer the following gloss of my second premise:

(μ2.0) Mind is, essentially, futural because mind, insofar as it is, is constituted by the propagating consequences of its potential to be otherwise.

This potentiality of mind, however, is not comprised of a determinate list of possibilities that wait patiently for their eventual realization or of possibilities that could have been realized even if they are never actually realized; nor is that potentiality to be considered some kind of a mysterious vitality that mind exerts. Rather, the potential for mind to be otherwise—*other-minded*—results from the fact that the Meanings of concepts, thoughts, beliefs, feelings, etc., cannot be *held* in mind because those Meanings are comprised of the propagating consequences of those concepts, thoughts, beliefs, feelings, etc. According to this consequentialist conception of mind, we shouldn't say that an utterance is *representational* (i.e., that it indicates the state of mind of the speaker at the time of utterance and subsequently preserves a record of the indicated state of mind) or, still less, *presentational* (i.e., that it manifests the state of mind of the speaker at the time of utterance and subsequently preserves a record of the revealed state of mind), but rather that it is *constitutional* (i.e., that the Meaning of the dispersed activities of mind is determined by the dispersed consequences of those activities).

Heidegger's phenomenology of time, however, cannot be fitted without resistance into a consequentialist conception of mind because of the *closure* of Dasein in death. Death—considered, as Heidegger would put it, "formally and existentially"—is Dasein's "ownmost potentiality-for-Being" because it is only in death that Dasein is *"fully* assigned to its ownmost potentiality-for-Being" (p. 294), in the double sense that (a) death undoes Dasein's relations to all other Dasein (i.e., it is the most *intimate* of Dasein's possibilities) and (b) death is "the possibility of the absolute impossibility of Dasein" (i.e., it is the possibility furthest removed from Dasein's actuality). Thus, Heidegger's paradox of Dasein and death: "This ownmost non-relational possibility [of death] is at the same time the uttermost one" (p. 294). Death is also unique in that it is Dasein's only possibility that cannot be "outstripped" (i.e., avoided) (p. 294): Death is always "impending" (p. 294).In death, Dasein achieves a *wholeness* or *totality* because there is nothing more *"still to be settled"* (p. 279),[6] but this wholeness represents more a *using up* than a *fulfillment:*

> as soon as Dasein 'exists' in such a way that absolutely nothing more is still outstanding in it, then it has already for this very reason become "no-longer-Being-there" [. . .]. Its Being is annihilated [. . .]. As long as Dasein *is* an entity, it has never reached its 'wholeness.' But if it gains such 'wholeness,' this gain becomes the utter loss of Being-in-the-world. In such a case, it can never be experienced again *as an entity.* (p. 280)

This wholeness or totality is bounded on the other *end* by the *beginning* at birth: "Only that entity [Dasein] which is 'between' birth and death presents the whole which we have been seeking" (p. 425). Dasein *"stretches along between* birth and death" (p. 425). Thus, Dasein, so long as it *is,* is not totalizable; and even when it achieves wholeness, Dasein's totality is unrepresentable by others because representation depends upon a Dasein's "possibilities of Being in Being-with-one-another in the world" (p. 283). (In a related way, for Levinas [1972/1987, p. 96] the Other resists representation because, revealed to the "I" through the "face," she is always breaking her form.)

The fact that Dasein cannot ever be experienced or known in its wholeness is not a problem that can be solved by epistemology, for the "reason for the impossibility of experiencing Dasein ontically as a whole which is [. . .], and therefore of determining its character onto-logically in its Being-a-whole, does not lie in any imperfection of our *cognitive powers*. The hindrance lies rather in the *Being* of this entity. That which cannot ever *be such as* any experience which pretends to get Dasein in its grasp would claim, eludes in principle any possibility of getting experienced at all" (p. 280). Notice how different this claim is from Frege's discussion of the total concept (cf. Chapter 2), which remains beyond our grasp precisely because of our limited cognitive powers.

However, I wish to complicate Heidegger's analysis, for I contend that there is no closure to mind, even in an individual's death, because

(M3.0) Mind is not reducible to consciousness, but is the Meaning of consciousness; it is not the *possession* of a Self but a perpetual *expropriation* of selfhood.

Death marks the necessarily terminus of a consciousness that will generate no additional thoughts, ideas, concepts, beliefs, utterances, etc., but not necessarily the terminus of the Meanings of its thoughts, ideas, etc., prior to death, some of which may continue propagating consequences in perpetuity. Here, I suggest, we can learn from Levinas (1972/1987):

> The future for which such an action acts must from the first be posited as indifferent to my death. A work which is different from play and from computations, is being-for-beyond-my-death [. . .]. To renounce being the contemporary of the triumph of one's work is to envisage this triumph in a *time without me,* to aim at this world below without me, to aim at a time beyond the horizon of my time, in an eschatology without hope for oneself, or in a liberation from my time.
>
> To be *for* a time that would be without me, *for* a time after my time, over and beyond the celebrated "being for death," is not an ordinary thought which

is extrapolating from my own duration; it is a passage
to the time of the other. (p. 92)

Even after an individual's death, the Meaning of that individual's
consciousness—its mind—remains futural (i.e., finite, but indefinite); and we may say with perfect accuracy that we do not *know our
own minds* (which are not really *ours* in the first place). Mind is extinguished—and utterly so, beyond the possibility of resurrection—only
when its last remaining thought, idea, concept, etc., has no potentiality for propagating consequences.

Unlike mind, consciousness is localizable *to* a particular individual; however, it is also non-localizable *within* that individual. Thus,
although we can say, in pointing at a person, that "he is a conscious
being," we cannot find within his body or, better, within his brain, a
single point at which consciousness *resides,* no pivot around which the
totality of the brain's cognitive processes are collected and synthesized.
Thus,

(M4.0) Consciousness is non-localizable within the brain.

This premise emerges from Dennett's (1991) "Multiple Drafts" theory of consciousness, which posits that there is no particular location
within the brain, no master control, where the information processed
throughout the brain is sent for inspection: "There is no single, definitive 'stream of consciousness,' because there is central Headquarters,
no Cartesian Theater where 'it all comes together' for the perusal of a
Central Meaner. Instead of such a single stream (however wide), there
are multiple channels in which specialist circuits try, in parallel pan-
demoniums, to do their various things, creating Multiple Drafts as
they go" (pp. 253–254). Rather, consciousness is a "multitrack process" that, on the scale of milliseconds, involves "additions, incorpo-
rations, emendations, and overwritings of content" (p. 135); and the
transient results of this "continual editing [. . .] yield, over the course
of time, something *rather like* a narrative stream or sequence" (p. 135),
but this "skein of contents is only rather like a narrative because of its
multiplicity; at any point in time there are multiple drafts of narrative
fragments at various stages of editing in various places in the brain"
(p. 135).

Thus, this *stream* cannot be defined apart from the manifold concurrent narratives or drafts used to describe segments of it, and "since
these narratives are under continual revision, there is no single narra-

tive that counts as the canonical version, the 'first edition' in which are laid down, for all time, the events that happened in the stream of consciousness of the subject, all deviations from which must be corruptions of the text" (p. 136). In a passage that deserves extended quotation, Dennett illustrates his Multiple Drafts theory of consciousness with an example drawn from publishing (or at least that section of the "publishing world" in which he finds himself!):

> In the world of publishing there is a traditional and usually quite hard-edged distinction between prepublication editing, and postpublication correction of "errata." In the academic world today, however, things have been speeded up by electronic communication. With the advent of word-processing and desktop publishing and electronic mail, it now often happens that several different drafts of an article are simultaneously in circulation, with the author readily making revisions in response to comments received by electronic mail. Fixing a moment of publication, and thus calling one of the drafts of an article the *canonical* text—the text of record, the one to cite in a bibliography—becomes a somewhat arbitrary matter. Often most of the intended readers, the readers whose reading of the text matters, read only an early draft; the "published" version is archival and inert. If it is important effects we are looking for, then, most if not all the important effects of writing a journal article are spread out over many drafts, not postponed until after publication. It used to be otherwise; it used to be that virtually all of an article's important effects happened *after* appearance in a journal and *because of* its making such an appearance. Now that various candidates for the "gate" of publication can be seen to be no longer functionally important, if we feel we need the distinction at all, we will have to decide arbitrarily what to count as publishing a text. There is no natural summit or turning point in the path from draft to archive.

Similarly—and this is the fundamental implication of the Multiple Drafts model—if one wants to
settle on some moment of processing in the brain as
the moment of consciousness, this has to be arbitrary.
One can always "draw a line" in the stream of processing in the brain, but there is no functional differences that could motivate declaring all stages and
revisions to be unconscious or preconscious adjustments, and all subsequent emendations to the content (as revealed by recollection) to be post-experien-
tial memory contaminations. The distinction lapses
in close quarters. (pp. 125–126)

We must be clear about the radical implications of Dennett's argument: Although he would agree with claims that the brain is the site of
parallel processing of information, he would reject the additional claim
that out of these concurrent activities of the brain emerges a peculiarly
privileged processing stream that serves, to use Polanyi's (1958/1974)
term, as our *focal awareness,* with the remainder clearly relegated to a
backgrounded, *subsidiary awareness* (p. 55). Rather, Dennett is arguing that *there is no single focus of awareness or stream of consciousness in
the first place.*

What we are aware of—including what we are aware of having
been aware of—is a continually (re)constructed, laminate; and this
multi-dimensional construction, if one attempts to survey it in segments spanning only milliseconds, becomes impossible to discern with
clarity and objectivity because

(M5.0) Consciousness is, essentially, indeterminate.

For example, not only are there concurrent narratives of experience
distributed throughout the brain, but these narratives need not agree
with each other upon the sequence of stimulations reaching the brain,
nor match the actual sequence of stimulations actually received by the
brain For example, as Dennett argues, a sequence of events in *objective
time,* "123456789," could be assembled into a different sequence in
experienced time, "abcgfdehfi" (p. 136). Which narrative gets used at a
particular moment to describe our awareness depends on the kinds of
probes or *stimulations* that prompt a person into describing his or her
experience. For example, to amplify on one of Dennett's (1991, p. 137)
examples, when you are driving a car, you may *lose* yourself in a con-

versation with a passenger for several minutes, recalling nothing about the drive itself (e.g., how many intersections you passed through, a person standing on a street corner, a billboard, etc.). You may even respond to a question like, "Did you see that billboard for the upcoming concert?" negatively. But this doesn't mean that, at the time you passed the billboard, you weren't aware of it (i.e., if asked, "Do you see that billboard for the upcoming concert?" you would probably have said "Yes" and, as a result of its being asked, the question would alter subsequent drafts of what had been part of one's consciousness). What has happened, in fact, is, as Dennett puts it, "better seen as a case of rolling consciousness with swift memory loss" (p. 137).

This indeterminacy, however, extends beyond the malleability of the contents of one's awareness to, at least at the scale of seconds and milliseconds, the structure of the *flow* of that awareness (i.e., the sequence of events that one is aware of). Dennett argues that we must distinguish between the timing of an objective sequence of events and the multiple ways in which the brain represents the timing of that sequence of events (p. 162). The brain does not simply respond passively to incoming signals, but must account for and respond accordingly to the fact that these signals are dispatched from sensory organs distributed at unequal distances from the brain and whose signals, therefore, do not arrive at the brain at precisely the same instant. The brain, then, may "proceed to control events 'under the assumption that A happened before B' whether or not the information that A has happened enters the relevant system of the brain and gets recognized as such before or after the information that B has happened" (p. 149). Our conscious experiences of perception and, equally importantly, our conscious recall of what those experiences were, then, are not independent of the brain's coordination of information; this effort of coordination takes time, so that our perceptions always lag slightly behind our sensory stimulations (Chafe, 1994, p. 32) and encompass a sequence of events that, on the level of milliseconds, *smear* together. Because of this smearing, it is impossible to say exactly when we become aware of some stimulation *if one's definition of exactitude requires one to list the sequence of events occurring objectively within the span of the smearing.* For example, to return to our driving example, if I am lost in conversation and suddenly slam on the brakes because I *notice* I am about to drive through a red light, it would be impossible to say exactly (as defined earlier) when the red light entered my awareness. Pragmatically, the lag cannot be a long one because too much delay would risk the survival of the organism. For example, a being whose conscious *sense* of immediacy comprised a one-hour span (i.e., a being having a consciousness capable of combining into a single representation the sensory input collected during a full hour), but who had therefore to wait one hour between conscious experiences, would be incapable of responding to a rock thrown at its head. Our delay, measured only in milliseconds, does not prevent our responding to the more mundane threats to our existence.

It would be wrong to think that the lagging of consciousness operates much like a *delayed broadcast feed*—i.e., that consciousness is a continuous awareness of a continuous stream of events momentarily delayed from entering consciousness. Rather, despite our awareness seeming to flow as a continuum,

(M6.0) Consciousness is *saccadic.*

and, relatedly,

(M7.0) Consciousness is, essentially, *discontinuous.*

The term *saccade* comes from the study of visual perception: A saccade is the "*jumpy, irregular, spasmodic, but surprisingly accurate leap*" (F. Smith, 1971, p. 99) of the eyes from one position to another. The important point is that during the leap from eye-fixation to eye-fixation, the eye is "practically blind," yet we are "never aware of these blank periods because continuity is provided by the brain" (p. 99). These fixations, of course, have a *duration*—i.e., they are not snapshots of a world laid out in absolute time. Saccades aren't the only empirical evidence of a discrete and discontinuous consciousness, for there are both spatial and temporal holes or gaps in consciousness, such as *blind spots* (see Figures 5.1, and 5.2),[7] *scotomata,*[8] *seizures,*[9] *comas,* etc. that cannot be experienced directly but only inferred from otherwise inexplicable features of or changes in the environment.

Dennett, playing on Edelman's (1989) observation that "one of the most striking features of consciousness is its continuity" (p. 119), concludes to the contrary that "one of the most striking features of consciousness is its *dis*continuity," despite our sense of its "*apparent continuity*" (p. 356). We must be careful to note that this "apparent continuity" is an *illusion of continuity* that is not itself *continuous* (i.e., there can be no *continuous* illusion of *continuity*), just as the apparent "filling in" of blind spots is a not a positive perception of

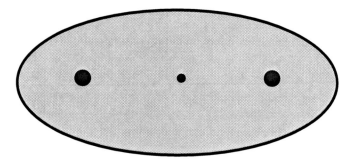

Figure 5.1. Blind spots and the apparent "filling in" of a colored field. Place the sheet of paper approximately 8 inches from your face; while focusing on the central dot, alternate closing your left and then right eye. As you close your left eye, the disk on the right should disappear, then reappear as you close your right eye just as the left disk disappears (you may have to make some adjustments in the positioning of the paper). Notice that there is no "hole" or vacancy in the perceptual field, which appears to be complete. This example is based upon Dennett (1991, p. 324).

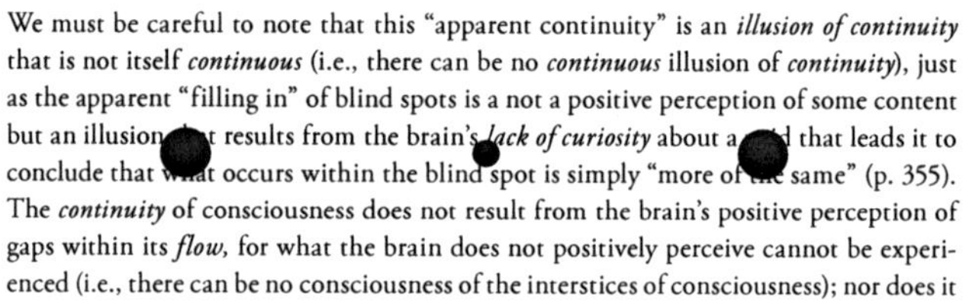

We must be careful to note that this "apparent continuity" is an *illusion of continuity* that is not itself *continuous* (i.e., there can be no *continuous* illusion of *continuity*), just as the apparent "filling in" of blind spots is a not a positive perception of some content but an illusion ●at results from the brain's *lack of curiosity* about a ●d that leads it to conclude that ●t occurs within the blind spot is simply "more o●e same" (p. 355). The *continuity* of consciousness does not result from the brain's positive perception of gaps within its *flow*, for what the brain does not positively perceive cannot be experienced (i.e., there can be no consciousness of the interstices of consciousness); nor does it

Figure 5.2. The apparent "filling in" of text.

some content but an illusion that results from the brain's *lack of curiosity* about a void that leads it to conclude that what occurs within the blind spot is simply "more of the same" (p. 355). The *continuity* of consciousness does not result from the brain's positive perception of gaps within its *flow*, for what the brain does not positively perceive cannot be experienced (i.e., there can be no consciousness of the interstices of consciousness); nor does it result from the brain's active filling in of these gaps, for the brain isn't curious enough about those gaps to bother filling them in. Rather, it results from the brain's inability to perceive gaps, its consequent disinterest in them, and its continual construction and editing of narratives about its conscious experiences (p. 356; cf. Minsky, 1985, and Neumann, 1990).

Dennett is especially critical of theorists who presume that gaps in perceptual fields are *filled in* with colors (i.e., pigments) supplied by the brain—what Dennett derisively refers to as *figment* (p. 346). On the contrary, argues Dennett, *filling in* is a phenomenon caused by the brain's neglect of these gaps. To illustrate this point, Dennett observes that, upon entering a large, empty room with wallpaper covered by small, identical, and high-resolution images of Marilyn Monroe, a person would immediately *see* the entirety of the room covered with small, identical, and high-resolution images of Marilyn Monroe, even though that person could not possibly have visually surveyed the entirety of the room with his foveal vision and, therefore, had to be relying on his parafoveal vision, which could not possibly have provided the acuity needed to distinguish roughly similar *Marilyn Monroe-shaped blobs* from identical images of Marilyn Monroe. How, then, does the person see the room as covered in identical images of Marilyn Monroe? Dennett argues that the brain doesn't take "one of its high-resolution foveal views of Marilyn and [reproduce] it, as if by photo-copying, across an internal mapping" of the room's wall (i.e., the brain doesn't generate a multitude of high-resolution images), for this would certainly involve a lot of needless effort. Rather, the brain, on the basis of identifying one or a few Marilyns, and "having received no information to the effect that the other blobs are not Marilyns [. . .] jumps to the conclusion that the rest are Marilyns, and labels the whole region 'more Marilyns's without any further rendering of Marilyn at all" (p. 355). Dennett observes that, from the standpoint of common-sense phenomenology, this isn't what seems to happen: It seems to the person "as if [he] were seeing hundreds of identical Marilyns," but these images of Marilyn Monroe are not "represented in [his] brain," but rather, his "brain just somehow represents *that* there are hundreds of identical Marilyns" (p. 355). For Dennett, *seeing* is a matter of judgments formed by the brain, not of representations constructed and viewed by something within it.

A second example Dennett provides to support this counterintuitive claim about perception and continuity involves experiments with eye-tracking equipment that is capable of not only detecting the *launch* of an eye-saccade but also of predicting, within milliseconds, its *destination*. What happens is this: The subject sits at a computer screen and, presented with several lines of text, begins reading. The tracker, upon detecting the start of a saccade, erases the destination word and

replaces it with a word of equal length. The subject, however, is oblivi-
ous to the changes to the text: The text, from beginning to end, appears to be the same, "as if the words were carved in marble" (p. 361).
But for an observer, whose saccades do not coincide with the subject's,
"the screen is aquiver with changes" (p. 361). The crucial point is that
the subject judges that the computer screen contains a stable text with
clearly defined print even though (a) he has not surveyed the entirety
of the screen with his foveal vision and so cannot have perceived with
clarity that all of the shapes were particular words and (b) there is no
stable text *there* to be read anyway. As Dennett observes:

> If your parafoveal vision can't discriminate the word
> at ground zero before you saccade to it, once you get
> there and identify it, there can't be any prior record
> or memory of it in your brain with which to compare
> it. The switch can't be noticed because the informa-
> tion logically required for such a noticing is simply
> not there. Of course it seems to you as you read this
> page [i.e., the page from Dennett's book], that all of
> the words on the line are in some sense present in
> your consciousness (in the background) even before
> you specifically attend to them, but this is an illusion.
> They are only virtually present. (p. 362)

Although I cannot put readers of this book through an eye-tracking
experiment, I can ask them to re-view Figure 5.2 and observe that,
as the black disks disappear, they *seem* to be replaced by additional
"text"—*text that is unreadable, of course, because there is nothing "there"
to be read.*

According to Derrida (1967/1976), it is precisely the gaps in consciousness that phenomenology cannot account for, that mark of limit
of the phenomenological method. Derrida describes these gaps in
terms of the *spacing* between words on the written page, which demonstrates how what was thought to be continuous—e.g., the flow of
discourse—is always already disrupted:

> *Spacing* (notice that this word speaks the articula-
> tion of space and time, the becoming-space of time
> and the becoming-time of space) is always the un-
> perceived, the nonpresent, and the nonconscious. *As
> such,* if one can still use that expression in a non-phe-

nomenological way; for here we pass the very limits of phenomenology. Arche-writing as spacing cannot occur *as such* within the phenomenological experience of a *presence.* It marks *the dead time* within the presence of the living present, within the general form of all presence [. . .]. As the phenomenology of the sign in general, a phenomenology of writing is impossible [. . .]. Constituting and dislocating it at the same time, writing is other than the subject, in whatever sense the latter is understood [. . .]. Spacing as writing is the becoming-absent and the becoming-unconscious of the subject. (pp. 68–69)

I will return to the notion of discontinuity and *dead time* in the development of a consequentialist theory of time in Chapter 7, even though I will ultimately disagree with Derrida's claim that the "living present" is always already ruptured: The living present need not be *durative* in order to have *brief durations.*

Now it is possible to gloss premises (M6.0) and (M7.0), from my consequentialist point of view(ing), as follows:

(μ6.0) Consciousness operates in *externally discrete* but *internally smeared* stretches of time—i.e., it is saccadic—between which it is, essentially, *non-existent;* and because temporality is intrinsic to consciousness, it cannot be accurately described in terms that subdivide these saccades of consciousness. The Meanings of the immediations and mediations that occur during these saccades of consciousness, as part of *mind,* extend beyond the moment of awareness to whatever consequences they propagate.

(μ7.0) Consciousness is a series of immediations and mediations disrupted by gaps during which no immediation or mediation occurs. Consciousness is not an inertial system flowing along a continuum, but, in terms Levinas (1961/1969, p. 284) uses to conceptualize time, something that is annihilated and (re)constructed, something that dies and is resurrected.[10]

Thus, we can now say (a) that the immediations and mediations that comprise our conscious experiences are *durable,* not *durational* and that consciousness itself is *discrete,* not *continual;* (b) that the *coherence* or *continuity* of consciousness is a *transient* and *non-continuous* illusion that results from the fact that discontinuities are routinely ignored by the brain and, therefore, are imperceptible to consciousness; and (c) that mind, as the Meaning of an always already temporally distended and discontinuous consciousness, is not the possession of the individual but something that may exist far apart from him or her (both temporally and spatially), insofar as the consequences of that consciousness (i.e., the consequences of particular beliefs, concepts, feelings, perceptions, etc.) continue to propagate.

Conclusion. The understanding of mind and consciousness is obviously quite important for the development of a proper philosophy of discourse, for discourse is generally discussed in terms of the meaningful language-use of conscious beings (and, even if it were not, we would still need to account for the language-use of conscious beings). What emerges from the preceding discussion, I suggest, is that the temporality and resulting indeterminacy of mind and consciousness preclude the possibility of an *a priori* idiolect (i.e., an idiosyncratic language that could be, at a single moment without duration, fully described in terms of a consistent and integrated system of grammatical rules and lexical items), for *there is no stable, single place where such a structured system could be housed.* Further, they preclude the possibility of *a priori* intentions (not *antecedent* intentions) that determine the meanings of utterances, for the meanings of those intentions, as part of a futural mind and a consciousness disrupted by discontinuities, are themselves constituted and propagated through time. *The openness of mind and consciousness necessitates the openness of the idiolect, and the openness of meaning necessitates the openness of mind and consciousness.*

COMMUNITY, COMMONALITY, AND CONGRUENCE

If we can share our signs, said Diderot, it is owing to their insufficiency. If God suddenly gave each individual a language that truly expressed its sentiments, we would no longer understand each other.

—Hans Aarsleff

A truly public language can never exist in any definitive form, but is perpetually under construction through our ongoing social life. Whereas no person speaks *the* public language, we each enter the public *dimension* of language whenever we

reaffirm the commonality of our worlds and the merit of exchanging our dissimilar ways of regarding them.

—Kurt Spellmeyer

Not: "without language we could not communicate with one
another"—but for sure: without language we cannot influence other people in such-and-such ways; cannot build roads
and machines, etc.

—Ludwig Wittgenstein

If the previous section offers the beginning of a consequentialist
theory of mind to replace *a priori* conceptions of "the mental," then
this section could be said to offer the beginnings of a consequentialist
theory of community to replace *a priori* conceptions of "the social."
However, at this early stage, I will present these claims more tenta-
tively, as assertions to be bulleted, not postulates to be numbered in
order to highlight glosses of them and to illuminate interconnections
between them.

The first premise ties together the discussion in Chapter 1 of community as a non-totalizable colloidal laminate whose distension requires and only results from continual effort:

> ↩ A community is inaugurated and propagated by
> transient acts of imagination which are conse-
> quential because—and only insofar as—people
> act upon and enforce them.

An imagined community is no less consequential for its being imagined, and therefore no less real; however, this reality is not given once-
and-for-all but is the temporally distended and discontinuous result of
transient acts of imagination that, as facets of mind and consciousness,
are themselves necessarily temporally distended and discontinuous. It
should be added, though, that just as mind extends spatially and temporally beyond a particular consciousness, so community extends spatially and temporally beyond a particular mind, so that even though
community is not durational, its durability, especially in relation to the
durability of consciousness, may make it *seem* so. We might say that
the *temporal viscosity* (Foucault, 1969/1972a, p. 175) or *individual time*
(Sharov, 1995/2001) of a community will differ from that of mind and
consciousness, and even that of other communities.

> ↩ If we are to think of meanings in terms of conse-
> quences, we must abandon the notion that one's

belonging to a community is determined by one's fulfillment of *a priori* criteria for membership; individuals do not gather into and fill spaces always already provided for. Communities do not subsist in some virtual realm prior to their inauguration, and they do not return to that realm to await a rebirth after they are extinguished.

ᴄᴏ A community is spatially and temporally bounded by the actual, not potential, propagation of these consequences.

Conceived in terms of a *layer* of a colloidal laminate, a community is a kind of relation that emerges from and is bounded by concrete interactions between individuals that produce *public* and *private* consequences.[11] This relation is not *global* (i.e., whether person A and B belong to community α has no bearing on whether they belong to community β unless α has, or comes to have, some consequential connection to β), *binary* (i.e., it is not logically contradictory for A and B concurrently to belong to the same community under one description and not belong to the same community under another description), *additive* (i.e., the fact that A and B belong to α does not mean that anyone who is connected with A in other communities of which B is not a member is necessarily is connected to B), *epiphenomenal* (i.e., A and B cannot belong to the same community without their membership in that community being consequential), or *subjective* (i.e., A and B may belong, or, better, be made to belong—through an effort of *annexation* made by other individuals—to the same community without their consent or even their awareness, and even after their deaths).

However, even though communities are not subjective, we must still account for the subjective experience or feeling of *belonging* to a community, *particularly of belonging to a community that extends beyond the range of one's consequential contact with others* (i.e., beyond the range of actual communities). First, I propose, following Kent (1993c), that

ᴄᴏ Our sense or feeling of belonging to the same community—i.e., commonality—as another person emerges from our sense of having successfully communicated with him or her, with communicative success defined in terms of an *a posteriori* congruence, rather than an *a priori* isomorphism.

That is, successful communication (in a sense to be defined later), even if it appears to confirm one's prior sense of commonality with another person, is constitutive of the subsequent experience of commonality: *Our communicative interactions aren't successful because we feel commonality, but we feel commonality because our communicative interactions are successful.* Consequently,

> ✎ A *community* is a consequence of successful communication, not its prerequisite.[12]

Of course, whether we engage in communicative interaction in the first place may be affected by our prior sense of commonality: I may decide not to say anything to a person whom I feel would be impossible to talk to. In this way, the lack of commonality becomes a kind of self-fulfilling prophecy, for it precludes the possibility of commonality being established. As Rommetveit (1974) writes, *"Intersubjectivity has thus to be taken for granted for granted in order to be achieved"* (p. 56).

Frequently, the experience of commonality is not tested by subsequent communicative interactions (e.g., I may feel *connected* to someone whom I have not seen or even talked to for ten years *precisely because I have not had any communicative interactions with him or her since*); it may not even be prompted by actual communicative interactions at all, but only indirectly imagined (e.g., in the aftermath of the World Trade Center attack, I may feel connected as a fellow American to a particular resident of New York I saw on television, or I may even feel connected in a very hazy way to all residents of New York, even if I do not know who they might be). Or it may even be the case that, in order to spare a prior sense of commonality from what Spellmeyer (1993a) refers to as "the ordeal of the present" (p. 19), we *avoid* communicative interaction with another person, so that one or both parties continue to believe that a prior commonality still holds—a belief that, paradoxically, ensures that that prior commonality still holds (e.g., it may be advantageous for me to appear as if a prior commonality with an interlocutor still holds, even if I do not still feel that commonality, so that my interlocutor still feels commonality with me).[13] In these ways,

> ✎ The sense of commonality involves *tolerating*, *reconciling*, or *neglecting* differences; our sense of community involves analogues of perceptual blind spots and scotomata.

In order to feel commonality with a person whom one has not had any dealings with for a long period of time or even a person whom has not ever dealt with, one must either *tolerate* the fact that commonality is not global, but discrete (i.e., by recognizing that commonality is a limited relation between otherwise different individuals), *reconcile* particular differences so that they are folded into a wider commonality (i.e., by accepting that community encompasses dissensus as well as consensus; cf. Trimbur, 1989), or *ignore* those differences entirely (i.e., by believing that commonality is a global relation, even if such a relation is actually impossible). That is, continuity of commonality depends upon a *filling in of the gaps between individuals,* so that (a) the only important differences between individuals are the differences that are noticed and acted upon and (b) the only differences that threaten community are those that are perceived to be, and as a result of this perception are, intolerable.[14] In other words, *the only differences that are meaningful are those that are consequential, and they are meaningful only to the extent that they are consequential.*

A lingering question, and the final one I will address in this section and chapter, is this: What is successful communication? How does one know that one has communicated successfully? Even the very notion of that one can communicate is quite problematic for my advocacy of meaning consequentialism because I want to resist treating discursive interactions as a transmission of meanings from sender to receiver. But whether we dispense with the term *communication,* we still need to answer questions about what interlocutors are doing when they engage in discourse and why they do it. I choose to preserve the term, but in a weakened sense, for *communication* can be read as a transient process through which interlocutors become meaningful to each other by *communing,* rather than as a process in which communal meanings are exchanged. Communication is not a *standard* by which the reception of utterances is judged, but a *way of being* in which interlocutors are receptive to utterances and their consequences; and we *judge* whether we are in fact communing by the responses, verbal and otherwise, of our interlocutors to what we say (Ayer, 1946/1952, p. 132).[15] Generally, we are satisfied that we have *communed* if the consequences of an utterance for us appear to be acceptably *congruent* with—not necessarily *identical* to—the consequences of that utterance for our interlocutors (i.e., that the consequences are *close enough*). The fact that people may believe they are exchanging identical meanings does not entail that they must be exchanging identical meanings, no more than a person's mistaking one twin for another entails that both twins must be the same person.

For Suppes (1973/1992a), logic-based conceptualizations of synonymy in terms of *isomorphism* or *identity* must be replaced by what he calls a *congruence theory of meaning* (p. 3): Sameness of meaning is not an absolute property of two sentences have when they express the same proposition, but a property two sentence's have when they are congruent *under some description.* Suppes contends that the concept of congruence, as developed in geometry, can serve as a useful analogy for understanding how it is possible for two sentences to appear to express the *same* meaning without expressing *identical* meanings. In geometry, congruence concerns the *similarity of figures,* so that in Euclidean geometry, for example, congruent figures have the same size and shape, but not necessarily the same orientation. Congruence can be strengthened to include, for example, sameness of orientation, but more importantly, argues Suppes, it can also be systematically weakened into, for example, an *affine* congruence in which only the number of lines of a figures must match, or a *topological* congruence in which one figure is a "homeomorphic image" of the other (i.e., a triangle is topologically congruent to a square because a square, if divided by a line running from opposite corners, will form two triangles). Congruence can even weaken to the point of highly abstract "one-one transformations" in which "cardinality is preserved but not much else," so that a single line is congruent to a single square (p. 5). Congruence, then, is not a single property, but a continuum of properties (Suppes, 1984/1992c, p. 25), so that what is congruent at some level under some description need not be congruent under all other possible levels and descriptions. For example, if A and B are X-congruent, but not Y-congruent, we can say without contradiction that A and B are both congruent and not congruent; it would only be contradictory to claim that A and B both are X-congruent and are not X-congruent.

Although our sense of congruence and commonality is consequential or *results-oriented* (e.g., I judge that my utterance of "Tom, please close the door" is successful if Tom gets up and closes the door as opposed to Tom staring blankly into the distance), the expectations that may prompt an utterance (i.e., the expectations for the result toward which the utterance is oriented) are *indeterminate* (e.g., I need not, and cannot, have in mind any particular way for Tom to close the door);

in fact, as Suppes and Crangle (1988/1992, p. 319) point out, trying to make such a complete determination, even for simple procedures, would be impossible because of the computational demands involved. These expectations are also *distended* (e.g., I may decide after the fact of utterance that particular ways of achieving this result are inappropriate, and I may change my mind, *well after any initial act of understanding,* about whether Tom has adequately fulfilled the request, so that his action no longer means to me what it had first meant). Furthermore, *the results themselves are indeterminate and distended as well:* In an important sense, we cannot know exactly how our interlocutors or readers are responding or will respond to our utterances and texts, not only because of the impossibility of observing the totality of those consequences (cf. Bridgman, 1959/1966, p. 16), but also, and primarily, because the Meanings of those responses are essentially futural.

CONCLUSION

I am also consoled by Francis Crick's adage that no theory should agree with all the data, because some of the data are sure to be wrong!

—Martin Rees

In Chapters 4 and 5, I have attempted to explode *a priori* conceptions of *language, community, idiolect,* and *mind* by demonstrating their suppression of and consequent inability to account for their temporality. I have argued that the distension and discontinuity characteristic of mind extends as well to the meanings that constitute *community* and to the experiences of *commonality* that comprise one's sense of belonging to a community; and I have offered some tentative premises for a consequentialist theory of mind and community. But the most important argument, I suggest, is that the essence of language, community, idiolect, and mind, insofar as they have essences, emerges from the necessarily *a posteriori* processes of Meaning, rather than determining *a priori* what those processes must be. *One does not first have a language, community, idiolect, or mind, and then have Meaning and meanings added onto them.* On the contrary, the potential for meaningfulness is a precondition for language, community, mind, and idiolect; and this potential for meaningfulness—i.e., what it means for something *to be* meaningful, not what particular things are meaningful and in what ways—is not determined by languages, communities, idiolects, or minds.

6 The Principle of Durativity: Duration, Evolution, Intertextuality, and the Problem of Surplus Meaning

> What we have here is merely an uninterrupted thrust of change—of a change always adhering to itself in a duration which extends indefinitely.
>
> —Henri Bergson

> What we have is a present which endures.
>
> Henri Bergson

Whereas *eternity* is conceptualized as a dimension outside of time or comprising all-time and *absolute time* is conceived as the flow of successive states of time for an objective reality, *duration* is the term generally used to label the psychological or phenomenological experience of time. For empiricist philosophers like Condillac (1754/1982b, 1792/1982a), Hobbes (1668/1994), Hume (1739–1740/1978), and Locke (1689/1987), an individual's inner sense of the passage of time is constituted by the idiosyncratic succession of his or her ideas, and the experience of duration exists only insofar as an individual has a succession of ideas: If there is no succession of ideas, there is no sense of the passage of time. Because these successions are idiosyncratic, no two individuals share the same sense of duration. This doesn't entail that each individual experiences the passage of time itself as accelerated or decelerated; for if time is the succession of ideas, it would be impossible to "align" single ideas in such a way as to "measure" and compare their "objective" temporal spans (Locke, 1689/1987, p. 190). Rather, an individual can only notice how different individuals appear, in relation to themselves, to "run" at faster, slower, or similar rates.

However, for my purposes, Bergson's (1946) phenomenology of time is of much greater interest because, for him, duration is not only an aspect of consciousness, but also an intrinsic feature of reality itself. In other words, the "pure, unadulterated inner continuity" of consciousness itself manifests what Bergson identifies as the *real* (p. 14); in fact, for Bergson, our sense of "our own person in its flowing through time, the self which endures" is an intuition of a duration that extends beyond consciousness (p. 162). It is not the "successive and distinct states" that philosophers and physicists have described (i.e., a spatialized time that is treated as series of fixed snapshots), but "the continuity of transition" of an unceasing change that is "indivisible" and "substantial" (p. 16). It is this indivisible change, not fragmented material states, that is paramount: *"There are changes, but there are underneath the change no things which change: change has no need of support. There are movements, but there is no inert or invariable object which moves: movement does not imply a mobile"* (p. 147). In other words, change and movement are not attributes added onto objects that would otherwise have a static existence. Bergson appeals to our intuitions about music for a proof: So long as we avoid spatializing a melody by conceiving of it in terms of a written score, all we apprehend is a movement or oscillation attached to nothing that moves or oscillates: "If we do not dwell on these spatial images, pure change remains, sufficient unto itself, in no way divided, in no way attached to a 'thing' which changes" (p. 148).

Change is a constant *breaking* of form, which is only "recorded movement" (p. 243), and the flow of time does not lead toward the "cold death" of entropy or entail the endless repetition of the same, but marks continual *creation* and *surprise:* Time is not entropic or predetermined, but "efficacious" (p. 26). And it is precisely this efficaciousness, says Bergson, that philosophers have been blind to, for they

> treat succession as a co-existence which has failed to
> be achieved, and duration as a non-eternity. That is
> why, in spite of all their efforts, they cannot succeed
> in conceiving the radically new and unforeseeable. I
> speak not only of those philosophers who believe in
> so rigorous a concatenation of phenomena and events
> that effects must be deduced from causes: such phi-
> losophers imagine that the future is given in the pres-
> ent, that it is theoretically visible in it, that to the

present it will add nothing new. But even those few
who have believed in free will, have reduced it to a
simple "choice" between two or more alternatives, as
if these alternatives were "possibles" outlined before-
hand [. . .]. They seem to have no idea whatever of an
act which might be entirely new (at least inwardly)
and which in no way would exist, not even in the
form of the purely possible, prior to its realization.
But this is the very nature of the free act. To perceive
it thus, as indeed we must do with any creation, novelty or unpredictable occurrence whatsoever, we have
to get back into pure duration. (pp. 18–19)

Duration is not an *unfurling*—i.e., "a rearrangement of the pre-existing"—but an *evolution* of something that "ceaselessly takes on forms
as new, as original, as unforeseeable as our states of consciousness"
(p. 21). In short, duration is a "creative evolution" in which "there is
a perpetual creation of possibility and not only of reality" (p. 21), so
that, for example, Beethoven's Fifth Symphony did not reside in some
abstract realm of possibility until its final actualization in 1808 (i.e.,
the composition was not a realization of something that always existed
as a possibility).

Not only do artworks, but truths themselves emerge in time; there
can be no timeless truths, but only truths that emerge at a specific time
and place:

Things and events happen at certain moments; the
judgment which determines the occurrence of the
thing or the event can only come after them; it therefore has a date. But this date at once fades away, in
virtue of the principle deep-rooted in our intellect,
that all truth is eternal. If the judgment is true now,
it seems to us it must always have been so [. . .]. To
every true affirmation we attribute thus a retroactive
effect; or rather, we impart to it a retrograde movement [. . .]. Our estimate of men and events is wholly
impregnated with a belief in the retrospective value
of true judgment, in a retrograde movement which
truth, once posited, would automatically make in
time. By the sole fact of being accomplished, reality

casts its shadow behind it into the indefinitely distant past: it thus seems to have been pre-existent to
its own realization, in the form of a possible. From
this results an error which vitiates our conception of
the past; from this arises our claim to anticipate the
future on every occasion. (p. 22)

For Bergson, duration can only be apprehended properly through
an intuition that eschews language, for language is an imposition of
intellectualized concepts that presume fixity and fragmentation onto
a reality that is actually a process of continuous creativity (pp. 18, 45);
concepts cannot fit exactly onto what they purport to describe (p. 167)
and only prevent their users' "direct contact with reality" (p. 29). That
is, we do not so much see objects as see our labels for them, substitut-
ing "the concept for the precept" (pp. 133, 138). Metaphysics requires,
therefore, "a break with [fixed] symbols" (p. 194): "If there exists a
means of possessing a reality absolutely, instead of knowing it relatively, of placing oneself within it instead of adopting points of view
toward it, of having the intuition of it instead of making the analysis of
it, in short, of grasping it over and above all expression, translation or
symbolical representation, metaphysics is that very means. *Metaphysics
is therefore the science which claims to dispense with symbols*" (p. 162).
The goal of metaphysics, then, is not the construction of a system of
a perfectible and ultimately timeless system of thoughts or a new and
better language that describes reality, but rather the "constant dilation
of our mind, the constantly renewed effort to go beyond our actual
ideas and perhaps our simple logic as well" (p. 196).

However, as much as Bergson enthuses about the surprises and
novelty of the future, he immediately yokes the unprecedented to a
past of perfect continuity, a past that "can preserve itself automatically" (p. 155), *a past that forgets nothing.*[1] Bergson refers to this notion
as the "integral conservation of the past" and even claims "empirical
verification" for it in Freudian psychoanalysis (p. 75): "your state tomorrow will include all the life you will have lived up to that moment,
with whatever that particular moment is to add to it" (p. 19).[2] In fact,
the distinction between past and present breaks down because, argues
Bergson, one cannot properly divide the continuity of duration in this
way: The past is not a present that once was and no longer exists (i.e.,
the past is not inexistent), but simply those elements of an enduring
but also cumulative present that a particular consciousness no longer

attends to. In fact, one's sense of "the present" is bounded only by that attention:

> My present, at this moment, is the sentence I am pronouncing. But it is so because I want to limit the field of my attention to my sentence. This attention is something that can be made longer or shorter, like the interval between the two points of a compass. For the moment, the points are just far enough apart to reach from the beginning to the end of my sentence; but if the fancy took me to spread them further my present would embrace, in addition to my last sentence, the one that preceded it: all I should have had to do is to adopt another punctuation. (p. 151)

A remarkable fancy, indeed, that can expand its present to cover a pair of sentences. But even this feat is a mere trifle for Bergson:

> Let us go further: an attention which could be extended indefinitely would embrace, along with the preceding sentence, all the anterior phrases of the lecture and the events which preceded the lecture, and as large a portion of what we call our past as desired [. . .]. The "present" occupies exactly as much space as this effort. As soon as this particular attention drops any part of what it held beneath its gaze, immediately that portion of the present thus dropped becomes ipso facto a part of the past. (pp. 151–152)

A "sufficiently powerful" attention would be able to encompass "the entire past history of the conscious person" (p. 152).

Bergson is so convinced of the self-sufficiency of the past that the interest of psychologists in memory is misplaced; in fact, memory requires no explanation at all, no appeal to a "special faculty" of the brain that stores "quantities of the past in order to pour it into the present" (p. 153). We have no more need the *faculty of memory* to preserve the past than we need a *faculty of gravity* to keep our bodies falling toward the center of the earth. What requires explanation, argues Bergson, is not the preservation of the past in memory, but its "apparent abolition" in forgetting (p. 153). "Apparent" is a key word here, because, on Bergson's account, there can be no actual abolition or obliteration of

the past (cf. Ratcliffe, 2000, p. 95). In a strong sense, we are inescapably our past, whether aware of it or not, because "any psychological
state, by the sole fact that it belongs to a person, reflects the whole of
personality. There is no feeling, no matter how simple, which does not
virtually contain the past and present of the being which experiences
it" (p. 170).

From a consequentialist point of view, Bergson's vision of duration
as the well-spring of unprecedented novelty has its attractions: (a) duration dispenses with a rigid determinism, for causes do not *contain*
their effects, and (b) possibilities do not subsist in a timeless dimension, but emerge through time. But despite these attractions, Bergson's
duration ultimately comprises an *a priori continuity* capable of digest-
ing any discontinuity[3]: The future may not be determined by the past
and present, but it is always already assimilatable into them; the process of change is not pre-given, but the history of that change is. And
the past has an intrinsic inertia, or, better, propulsion (i.e., Bergson's
élan vital) that requires no effort of preservation. The past endures
within and informs the present, and it is always in principle accessible
to the present. We might even think of duration as a kind of *eternity-
minus*—I am playing here on Burke's (1945) notion of an *agent-minus,*
which he describes in terms of an organism that can only react to external stimuli—in which only the past exists *in toto,* a past that grows
through time, with the correlative of an omniscient and panchronic
God being a holistic consciousness with a "sufficiently powerful" attention capable of surveying the entirety of its past.

These features of duration, then—i.e., the essential continuity of
time, the integral conservation of the past in the present, and the interconnection of all entities and events—comprise major features of
the principle of durativity; and in this chapter, I will trace how this
principle is made manifest in approaches to meaning that conceptualize (a) discourse in terms of *an unbreakable chain of communicative
interactions,* (b) language in terms of *evolution* (i.e., the principle of
evolution), (c) the concatenation of texts in terms of *intertextuality,* (d)
the mind in terms of *a continuous stream of consciousness,* and (e) the
multiplicity of meanings in terms of *polysemy.* It is only after I at least
partially illuminate the difficulties surrounding not only the principle
of durativity that I will be, in the next chapter, finally in a position to
offer the outlines of a positive sketch of some of the interconnections
between meaning and time that comprise meaning consequentialism.

DURATIVITY AND THE GREAT CHAIN OF DISCOURSE

Our capacity for saying keeps pace with the universality of reason. Hence every dialogue also has an inner infinity and no end. One breaks it off, either because it seems that enough has been said or because there is no more to say. But every such break has an intrinsic relation to the resumption of the dialogue.

—Hans-Georg Gadamer

Dialogue implies immediate unpremeditated utterance. It consists of replies, repartee; it is a chain of reactions.

—Lev Vygotsky

In this section, we will examine theories that attempt to explain the continuities of language, meaning, and discourse by appeal to intrinsic causal relations between a representation and what it represents and to intrinsic dialogic relations between a speaker/writer, utterance/text, and listener/reader; but I will argue that because these causal and dialogic relations are inviolable—*because continuity, however distorted, is never threatened*—these approaches manifest the aprioristic principle of durativity and cannot adequately account for the possibility of discontinuity.

The Continuity of Causation

One way that theorists have tried to explain the continuity of language, meaning, and discourse is by postulating their having causal powers to perpetuate themselves (of course, because causation itself requires a continuity between cause and effect, this is akin to saying that the continuity of language, meaning, and discourse arises from their having a special power to be continuous!). For example, consider the so-called *causal theory of reference* that has been advanced by Kripke (1972/1996) and Putnam (1975/1975b, 1978/1983b) to explain the problem of the "constancy of reference over time" (Mühlhölzer, 1993, p. 49). According to Putnam (1980/1983a), words endure through time due to an agreement among users of the same language: "The intention to preserve reference through a historical chain of uses and the intention to cooperate socially in fixing reference make it possible to use terms successfully to refer although no one definite description is associated with any term by all speakers who use that term" (p. 17).[4] Putnam's thesis, then, consists of two parts. First, people cooperate to preserve reference and form a "historical chain" that links the uses of words in an unbroken succession of transmissions extending back to the original reference; and second, no individual who uses a word understands its full extension, which is preserved only collectively, but individuals will likely understand enough of a word's "accepted meaning in the common language" to permit efficient communication (Dummett, 1986, p. 462).

The initial act of naming—both Putnam (1980/1983d, p. 72) and Kripke (1972/1996, p. 96) liken it to a *baptism*—establishes a *rigid designator,* the oral and/or written symbol which "refers to the thing as it were directly, without having to go through an identifying description" (Staten, 1989, p. 30); and, as the *"origin* of an object is essential to it" (Kripke, 1972/1996, p. 114), *so too the origin of a rigid designator is an essential element of any of its applications.* These rigid designators refer to specific objects or kinds or objects; Putnam (1980/1983d, p. 57) offers two examples: *Aristotle* refers to a particular Greek philosopher and *gold* refers to a kind of metal.[5] Described this way, rigid designators are comparable to proper names, which "function not as descriptions, but as pegs on which to hang descriptions" (Searle, 1969, p. 172). To use these rigid designators, people need not have read any of Aristotle's writing to know that the name *Aristotle* refers to a Greek philosopher, and they need not understand the chemical structure of gold in order to identify an object they think is composed of it. Instead, people use these words as they were taught to use them by their predecessors in the causal chain. *Non-rigid designators,* on the other hand, could apply to more than one object or kind of object, such as "the king of France" or "the breakfast muffin"; often, non-rigid designators are used in apposition to rigid designators, as in "Louis XIV, the king of France."

While Putnam's account goes far in explaining apparent continuity of reference and is intuitively appealing, his claim about the "cooperative" effort to preserve reference does not stand up to close scrutiny. Such a claim is warranted only if there is such an entity as *society* and, even if there is such an entity, that society operates (at least ideally) as a harmonious community,[6] an assumption often made in terms of the *social contract* (Stevens, 1987/1988), *consensus* (Habermas,

1973/1975), or *conventions* (D. Lewis, 1969).[7] Poststructuralists in particular have challenged this notion of collective goodwill, claiming that it is often used as a disguise for social control. For example, Foucault (1970/1977h) critiques "the tyranny of goodwill, the obligation to think 'in common' with others" (p. 181) in order to shield thought from disintegrating into a chaos of "pure difference" and "intensive irregularity" (p. 183); and he wonders what would happen "if we gave free rein to ill will" (p. 182). In place of universal consensus, Lyotard (1979/1993, p. 66) would substitute *paralogy,* the fragmented dissensus of localized language games.[8] For poststructuralists, reference cannot be grounded only on rational goodwill of individuals, but is always already an exercise of power (Berlin, 1993), whether through the indirect control of hegemony (Gramsci, 1948–1951/1971) or the direct control of ideological institutions (Althusser, 1970/1989). As a result, Putnam's social foundation for the continuity of reference already seems to be cracking.

Were this the entirety of the causal theory of reference, we would be hard pressed to understand what role causality plays in it, for, aside from the initial and unbreakable link between the rigid designator and its referent, the continuity of language appears to be largely the *product* of a continuous effort of enforcement. But Putnam also adds—as have philosophers such as Stampe (1977), Fodor (1984/1990), and Dretske (1981)—a much stronger link between a rigid designator and its referent, so that the objective properties of the referent delimit the permissible meanings of the referent because a representation of the referent is causally linked to what it represents; as Stampe (1977) puts it, *"representation* is an essentially causal phenomenon" (p. 42). (Note: Here we touch upon the *principle of empiricism.*) The paradigm example is that of a photographic image formed by an entirely mechanistic process of exposing film to light; but as Stampe (1977) proposes, linguistic representations can be treated analogously.[9] Fodor (1984/1990) concedes that causal theories of representation have difficulty accounting for the possibility of misrepresentation (i.e., if the relationship between a representation and the represented is causal, how can what is represented cause a *false* representation?); but he is so committed to a causal theory that he is willing to accept the counterintuitive claim that "there is no misrepresentation in normal circumstances" (p. 48), in which "normal circumstances" are defined teleologically or functionally. For example,

The teleology of the nervous system determines what must be the case if R represents $S;$ and it follows from the analysis that if R represents S and the situation is teleologically normal, S must be true. This is because what R represents is its truth condition, and its truth condition is whatever causes its tokening in teleologically normal situations. But this is entirely compatible with holding that what *makes* R true in teleologically normal situations is that its truth condition obtains; that R corresponds, that is to say, to the way that the world is. (p. 48)

In light of these other causal theories of reference, it appears that although Putnam (1975/1975b) acknowledges a social dimension to language and meaning, that social qua (curiously) economic dimension is primarily one of *using* and of *safeguarding a priori* meanings (of whatever sort):

Consider our community as a 'factory': in this 'factory' some people have the 'job' of *wearing gold wedding rings,* other people have the 'job' of *selling gold wedding rings,* still other people have the 'job' of *telling whether or not something is really gold* [. . .]. [E]veryone to whom gold is important for any reason has to acquire the word 'gold'; but he does not have to acquire the method of recognizing if something is or is not gold. He can rely on a special subclass of speakers. (pp. 227–228)

Putnam famously concludes that "cut the pie any way you like, 'meanings' just ain't in the *head!*" of an individual (p. 227). Instead, meanings are the essences—the contributions made to extension by "society" and (primarily) "the real world" (p. 245)—locked in rigid designators, which are only partially understood by any single individual.

A term, then, does not have a single meaning, but rather has "a finite sequence" or "vector" that includes at least four components: *syntactic markers, semantic markers,* any additional *stereotypical features,* and a *description of extension.* To provide an illustration of his model, Putnam (1975/1975b) speculates about the reference for "water": *syntactic markers* (e.g., mass noun, concrete), *semantic markers* (e.g., natural kind, liquid), *stereotype* (e.g., colorless, transparent, thirst-quenching, etc.), and *extension* (H_2O) (p. 269). However, Putnam also cautions that positing H_2O as the extension of *water* doesn't entail that the individual speaker or even society knows that water is H_2O but only "that (we say) the extension of the term 'water' as *they* (the speakers in question) use it is *in fact* H_2O" (p. 269). This notion of a meaning vector as a bounded set of permissible meanings is similar to theories of *meaning potentialities* that I critique later in this chapter.

The Continuity of Dialogue

Like Putnam, theorists identified with the formation and propagation of dialogism accept the essential continuity of meaning, language, and discourse. For example, Vološinov (1929/1986) argues that "this chain of ideological creativity and understanding, moving from sign to sign and then to a new sign, is perfectly consistent and continuous: from one link of a semiotic nature (hence, also of a material nature) we proceed uninterruptedly to another link of exactly the same nature. And nowhere is there a break in the chain, nowhere does the chain plunge into inner being, nonmaterial in nature and unembodied in signs" (p. 11). Similarly, Bakhtin (1986/1996) assumes that there is an "unbroken line of historical development" of discourse (p. 33), an essential *progressivity*[10]; each utterance is "a link in the chain of speech communication, and *it cannot be broken off from the preceding links* [italics added] that determine it both from within and without, giving rise within it to unmediated responsive reactions and dialogic reverberations" (p. 94). Utterances always respond to "prior utterances and therefore are *conditioned* [italics added] by those speech events" (Schryer, (1999, p. 82; cf. Heidegger, 1959/1993b, p. 418), so that every assertion is itself an answer to an already asked question (Meyer, 1995, p. 6; Sidgwick, 1921, p. 286), every inquiry an effort to resolve an always already prior doubt (Peirce, 1869/1991a, p. 150).

For Bakhtin (1986/1996, p. 5), words always already contain the words of others; they are deeply marked by past uses (Mecke, 1990, p. 201), uses that they are both a carrier and residue of (Morson and Emerson, 1990, p. 289). Words and the discourses they are located within have durative *memories* (Bartholomae, 1985/1996, p. 466; Freadman, 1998); as Faigley (1986/1994) puts it, "words carry with them the places where they have been" (p. 158). In a striking analogy to music, Bakhtin (1986/1996) compares these past voices to "*dialogic overtones*" that, though "half-concealed or completely concealed," echo through every utterance (pp. 92–93). No link is ever entirely forgotten, or stops resonating, for each link is part of the unbroken continuity of a "'great time' in which all utterances are linked to all others, both those from the primordial past and those in the farthest reach of the future" (Holquist, 1986/1996, p. xxi).

But notice that Bakhtin discusses *dialogic* utterances—whole units of spoken and written discourse—rather than *analytic* references, so that each link is a unique, active response to what has already been said *and* an active anticipation of what will be said next. Words are constantly re-used and re-evaluated: Language is *heteroglossic*, a site in which "words become dialogized, disputed, and reaccented in yet another way as they encounter another" (Morson and Emerson, 1990, p. 143). Thus, whereas Putnam and Kripke think of the causal theory of reference primarily in terms of preserving that reference or at least of uncovering latent properties of the referent, Bakhtin and other dialogic thinkers allow for the intrinsic possibility of tension and change—a "potential of other-languagedness" (Bakhtin, 1975/1981, p. 66)—through which speech genres may be *appropriated* (Brandt, 1998; de Certeau, 1974/1984), *parodied* (Bakhtin, 1975/1981, p. 364), *profaned* (Minter, Gere, and Keller-Cohen, 1995, p. 681), or otherwise *refracted* (Vološinov, 1929/1986, p. 9). Nevertheless, the choice of the metaphor of *refraction* is telling, for it suggests the *essential continuity* of discourse even in the face of its severest distortions: A refracted image, like the grotesques produced by fun-house mirrors, is still *an image of something* that itself exists independently of and therefore *survives* the refraction. That is, even the severest distortions, whatever the cause, are ultimately orderly (i.e., subsumable within an *a priori* system of order) because the process of distortion is itself governed by causal laws; but if that is the case, then the underlying conception of change cannot ultimately be one of unprecedented *transgressions* (Foucault, 1963/1977f, p. 35), but of rule-governed *transformations* or *derivations* (Chomsky, 1968/1972, pp. 31, 33). For example, if one holds that meaning is a necessarily social phenomenon constituted by social genres, then for social genres to change in meaning, the changes must themselves, to be meaningful, already be constituted by other genres: Social actions that change genres must already be generic, for social actions are constituted by genres (cf. Spellmeyer, 1993a, pp. 22–23).

Objections to Theories of Causal or Dialogic Continuity

Before discussing two other types of presumed continuity, those of mental associations and of interpretation, let us consider three possible objections to the two specific types we have just examined: (a) that language-in-use is not heteroglossic, but ahistorical; (b) that we should not conflate the repetition of a linguistic token from one link of discursive chain to the next as the repetition of a meaning or reference; and (c) that the continuity of meaning cannot be assured by prior social arrangements because there is no single, spatialized society in which those arrangements are made.

Objection 1. The first objection, emerging from the work of Eckford-Prossor and Clifford (1998), is phenomenological; they argue that whereas language conceived as an abstract system has a history and polysemic depth, from the perspective of the individual language user, language is without history:

> We believe that such natural histories and their related etymological projects, while enlightening to language *in abstraction,* conceive of language in a way different from that in which it is ordinarily *used.* This ordinary usage does not recover meanings from language, nor does it see language as a system or science of signs embedded in and thus reflecting history. It does not use language as a reflective tool, and it does not mine history from individual words. Instead, we assert that in everyday use, language has no history, be it diachronic or synchronic. Our point is not that language is ahistorical, but that when used it is atemporal. Language is both immediate and eternally enduring—in the moment of its use. The transparency projected by etymological arguments is precisely that, a projection of clarity onto a medium that is both unstable and opaque. (pp. 103–104)

Language is immediate not in the sense that "there is only one meaning available, the current one, but [in the sense] that the user has little to no notion of any alternative" (p. 105); and language is eternally-enduring in the sense that the language user, whose subjectivity depends upon language, does not have sufficient distance to notice changes to

that language.[11] Language appears static not because it is static (or because the social and physical world is static), but because the language-
using observer is herself "encase[d]," "enclose[d]," or "subject[ed]" by
the "forms and possibilities" of language (p. 106). For Eckford-Prossor
and Clifford, then, language does not mirror social reality, which is
in a constant state of flux, but actually serves to occlude that change
by "absorbing it rhetorically" (p. 102). Thus, rather than serving for
its users as a perfect index of social changes (i.e., by mirroring social
reality), language lags behind social reality, is out of synch with it, is
anachronistic (p. 102); and by *failing to change with the times,* it "engenders similarity and continuity of meaning" through time and "creates an illusion of history as linear development rather than of radical
epistemic upheaval" (p. 101).

     Eckford-Prossor and Clifford's argument about the "forgetfulness"
of language is very attractive for me as I think through meanings in
terms of consequences because—as I have argued and will continue to
argue in this chapter—I rejects the notion of hidden meanings, durative intertextuality, or linguistic evolution. But Eckford-Prossor and
Clifford are not relentless enough in pursuing possible ramifications of
their emphasis on language-in-use, and they end up manifesting several varieties of meaning apriorism, of which a few are (a) the principle
of durativity: Etymology "forces on language the rather human attributes of memory and duration" (p. 105)—which, of course, assumes
that memory as preservation of the past and consciousness as duration
are "human attributes"; (b) the principle of formalism: They accept the
bifurcation of language into langue and parole, noting that "although
language per se [as langue] may reflect social change, actual language
use obscures it" (p. 119); (c) the principle of linguistic holism: "It is of
the nature of language to bind us to a particular view of the world"
(pp. 124–125); and (d) the principle of stasis: Language is a "medium
of signification that *fixes* things in their meaning" and "can do little
else" (p. 124)

     Perhaps the strongest refutations of Eckford-Prossor and Clifford's
argument—strongest in the sense that they do not require accepting
the critique of meaning apriorism that meaning consequentialism offers—are that Eckford-Prossor and Clifford's argument, as much as
it appeals to the "ordinary" use of language, (a) cannot account for
extraordinary uses, such as theoretical discussions, that are somehow
able to pierce the illusions of language and unmask its workings—but

for me, language is meaningful because it is consequential: Meanings are not *largely* consequential, *frequently* consequential, *mostly* consequential, *usually* consequential, *generally* consequential, etc.—nor (b) can "ordinary use" itself be defined in a way that doesn't beg the question of what constitutes ordinariness. *In other words, whose use counts as "ordinary"?* (Cf. Chapter 4.)

It is not the case that only the "usages" of linguists or philosophers—whom Eckford-Prossor and Clifford would not accept as "ordinary"—distort, from their perspective, the proper understanding of language. Rather, groups of people whom Eckford-Prossor and Clifford might otherwise agree use language in ordinary ways do not use language as they suggest, either. For example, let us consider the discursive practices of a group of people whose uses of language Eckford-Prossor and Clifford might agree constitute *ordinary use:* The residents of Samoa whose discursive practices Duranti (1985, 1990) has studied. According to Duranti, for these Samoans, "meaning is jointly accomplished by speaker and audience. For this reason, a Samoan speaker does not reclaim the meaning of his words by saying 'I didn't mean it.' A person must usually deal with the circumstances created by his words as interpreted by others in a given context and cannot protect himself behind alleged original intentions" (p. 49).[12] Of course, we must all "deal" with the circumstances created by our words, even if our "dealing" involves denying responsibility for those consequences or at least blunting possible repercussions[13]; what distinguishes the Samoans whom Duranti (1990) studied is that they are held by others, and hold themselves, "responsible for the consequences of what [they] said, regardless of [their] putative original intentions. Samoan orators must thus be very careful about what they say. Although a speechmaker can gain in prestige and wealth from speaking on behalf of a powerful chief or from helping out in a difficult negotiation, he may also risk retaliation for having said what might be *later* defined as the wrong thing" (pp. 468–469). Thus, Duranti argues that for these Samoans, words "are not simply seen as representing some already defined world, but as shaping reality, as creating the world" (p. 468), a view shared by other groups living in the Pacific, such as the Ilongot (cf. Rosaldo, 1982; Verscheuren, 1983).

Objection 2. A second objection is that Putnam and other causal theorists conflate the continuity of the use of a word with the continuity of reference. For example, let us reconsider Putnam's example of the rigid designator *Aristotle*. Suppose I mention the name to a friend; although I'm thinking of a certain Greek philosopher, she mistakenly thinks I'm talking about Aristotle Onassis. Is reference being preserved in this linking of utterances, so that the next person my friend says "Aristotle" to will, or at least could in principle, detect within the word a trace of the Greek philosopher? Or has the chain been *disrupted*? Of course, the fact that my friend mistakes Aristotle for Aristotle Onassis depends upon her prior acquaintance with the rigid designator Aristotle Onassis, but that still doesn't invalidate the points that, in this particular instance, the causal chain has been broken and that, therefore, any causal chain is in principle breakable.

An aside: What is it that leads us to conclude that *Aristotle* and the *Aristotle* of Aristotle Onassis are instances of the same word? That is, of what is this sameness comprised that leads to such an identification, and what are the limitations of that identification; in other words, at what point do we distinguish a word with multiple meanings from a set of homonyms with single meanings? (We will consider the problem of polysemy later in this chapter.)

But now let us also consider a case in which meaning emerges from an "utterance" that itself replicates no prior rigid designators and continues no prior discourse, *an "utterance" that has no prior meaning.* Such cases can be found, I suggest, in Skinner's (1957) experiments with the response of subjects to a *verbal summator device:*

> [the verbal summator] consists of a phonograph or tape recorder which repeats a vague pattern of speech sounds at low intensity or against a noisy background as often as may be needed to evoke a response. The material sounds like fragments of natural speech heard through a wall [. . .]. Under satisfactory experimental conditions, a subject will generally hear something being said for each pattern, and most subjects require no more than ten or fifteen presentations of each stimulus. Hundreds of responses may be collected in a few hours. These bear very little formal relation to the echoic stimuli (different subjects seldom give the same response) and therefore permit certain inferences about other variables [that Skinner presumes determines the response] [. . .]. The subject remains unaware of the controlling sources and

is usually convinced that he is merely repeating what he hears, although possibly with some inaccuracy. (p. 260)

I find it a fascinating paradox that responses "bear very little formal relation to the echoic stimuli" despite the fact that what the listeners are given to respond to is a series of sound-forms. These sound-forms become meaningful (i.e., consequential) through responses that are, in fact, *responses to something that is not a prior utterance and so really aren't responses at all.* In the case of the verbal summator, then, words qua meaningful forms—*and is there any other kind of word?*—emerge as consequences from these particular sound-forms without having been originally put within them; but at the same time, these consequences do not belong to the listeners because they are not *put there* by the listeners.

Objection 3. A third objection is that causal and dialogic theories, insofar as they assume a language that is preserved not by individuals but by a larger, spatialized society, neglect the temporality meaning and discourse. For example, if utterances are unique events as opposed to simply the repetition of abstract sentences (i.e., that parole is more than simply langue repeatedly instantiated in material forms), then in what sense can we speak of collective chains? It would seem, even if one accepts the premises of causal or dialogic theories, that we would have countless chains running concurrently, with each chain, having gone through a unique sequence of development, therefore being informed by a unique "memory."[14] Wouldn't individuals have to discern which *chain* a particular word or utterance belonged to in order to understand it (cf. Ramberg, 1989, p. 25)? The chains would not be equivalents, of course, though they would most likely have some area of overlap; after all, each would have to diverge from an already existing chain, and all chains involving a particular rigid designator would ultimately be traceable back to a single source. But in what sense can we say that these chains are *concurrent* (i.e., that they evolve at the same rate), permitting their temporal and spatial unification in the "mind" of Society? Clearly, some chains would likely develop faster than others and be distributed in different areas. But, guided by my understanding of meaning consequentialism, I suggest that if we concede that there are countless chains of utterances being built by multiple networks of individuals in asynchronous stretches of time, we are no longer speaking of Society, at least not as something conceivable of as a whole.

DURATIVITY, LINGUISTIC EVOLUTIONISM, AND FORGETTING

For all its deflections and superficial applications where it did not fit, the Darwinian perspective was a fundamental one. Language has to be understood in a historico-evolutionary context, as part of evolutionary processes [. . .].

—M. A. K. Halliday

All things that we clasp and cherish,
Pass like dreams we may not keep.
Human hearts forget and perish,
Human eyes must fall asleep.

—Heinrich Heine

Implicit in the notion of diachronism advanced by Putnam and Bakhtin is *linguistic evolutionism,* which holds (a) that natural language—as a kind of *treasure-house* (Bakhtin, 1975/1981, p. 217; Alfred Schutz, 1962/1990, p. 14), *objective repository* (Berger and Luckmann, 1966/1967, p. 37), *reservoir* (Gadamer, 1967/1977d, p. 29), or *cultural baggage* (S. Hall, qtd. in J. Drew, 1998, p. 190)—*preserves* what has been called "the wisdom of the ages" (Gilmore, 1989/1992, p. 37; Hall, 1986, p. 20) or "the lore of our fathers" (Quine, 1956/1966, p. 125)[15]; (b) that knowledge *accumulates* through time, each generation adding onto the achievements of the past (e.g., Berger and Luckmann, 1966/1967, p. 41); consequently, (c) that language, both in its grammar and lexicon, *follows a continual path of improvement,* retaining what is valuable and useful while slowly, perhaps even deliberately,[16] discarding what is *insignificant, erroneous,* or *inefficient* (e.g., Spencer 1852/1933, pp. 12–17), and (d), in the most extreme form, that language, like an organism, contains its own internal principles of growth, maturation, and decay (e.g., Humboldt, 1836/1988, p. 143; Sapir, 1921/1949, p. 153).

   Aitcheson (1991, p. 212) traces this conception of language to the influence of Darwin in the mid-nineteenth century; and even if, as

Newmeyer (1986, pp. 24–25) suggests, Darwin's views of evolution had little resonance in the work of his contemporaries in comparative linguistics, they have been enormously influential in other theories of language and meaning.[17] Consider three prominent examples:

- J. L. Austin was a great advocate of linguistic evolutionism; he would study the history of words in minute detail in order to unearth the accumulated wisdom of the past.[18] For Austin (1966/1979d), words that survive through time survive because they are fitter than their rivals: "*in the very long run,* the forms of speech which survive will be the *fittest* (most efficient) forms of speech" (p. 281; cf. Austin, 1956–1957/1979c, pp. 181–182).

- Bakhtin (1986/1996) asserts that "there is not a single new phenomenon (phonetic, lexical, or grammatical) that can enter the system of language without having traversed the long and complicated path of generic-stylistic testing and modification" (p. 65).

- Sebeok (1991c), perhaps the more rigorous linguistic evolutionist, holds out the promise of perfect communication as language continues its slow development: "The adjustment of a species-specific mechanism for encoding language into speech [. . .] with a matching mechanism for decoding it [. . .] must have taken that long [several million years] to fine-tune, *a process which is far from complete* [italics added] (since humans [still] have great difficulty in understanding each other's spoken messages)" (p. 95).[19]

One possible objection to linguistic evolution emerges from the work of Descartes (1637/1970a, 1641/1970b), Francis Bacon (1605/1900b), and Condillac (1792/1982a): That our reverence for the knowledge of the past is misplaced because our "inheritance" is largely comprised of falsehoods. There has been little "advancement," as Bacon would put it, in human knowledge, but mostly an accumulation of errors:

> Because, in childhood, we get our thoughts from others, we adopt all their prejudices. When we reach an age where we believe we think for ourselves, we still continue thinking second hand, because we thinking according to the prejudices they have bequeathed us. Under these conditions, the more progress the mind seems to make, the further afield is strays, and errors

pile up from generation to generation. (Condillac,
1792/1982a, p. 386)

And because these errors are so "closely intertwined [. . .] [that they]
mutually defend each other" (Condillac, 1792/1982a, p. 387), the
only solution is essentially to renounce all prior knowledge and to
begin anew the acquisition of knowledge based upon a surer epistemological method. However, in addition to the question of whether
this renouncement is at all possible (cf. Peirce, 1868/1991c, p. 55), it
is important to note that this objection, whether in its rationalist or
empiricist guise, presumes the continuity of tradition, even if it is a
continuity that is a *devolution,* not an *evolution,* an accumulation of
foolishness, not of wisdom.

   A more compelling set of objections emerges from Cohen's (1962)
refutation of Austin's attempt to excavate the wisdom buried within
ordinary language:

> [Austin] seems to assume, at least in his Presidential
> Address, that all reasonable men would agree in con-
> demning these features [superstition, error, fantasy]
> when detected, and that ordinary language lacks the
> intermingled mass of lumber—customs once gener-
> ally agreed to be used but now more controversial
> [. . .]. He also apparently assumed ordinary language
> to preserve in unimpaired vitality all the gains ever
> achieved in the course of its development. He did not
> express any fear that some laziness, carelessness or in-
> tellectual short-sightedness may lose a people parts
> of its cultural inheritance. He implicitly rejected the
> view, maintained by J. S. Mill, that in the long his-
> tory of human language word-uses sometimes slow-
> ly deteriorate and experience is as often lost as pre-
> served. (p. 78)

Although I would distance myself from Cohen's nostalgic claim that
language may "deteriorate"—languages (or, better, discourses) do
not improve or deteriorate, but only change (cf. Aitcheson, 1991, pp.
210–221)—Cohen raises a number of points that are consonant with
meaning consequentialism: (a) that language is not a coherent, homogeneous system, (b) that language is a site of struggle or controversy,
(c) that language does not have some inner vitality (i.e., it does not

preserve itself), and (d) that language, or at least parts of it, may not simply change, but disappear entirely.

It is this last point, about *loss* or *forgetting*, that I will pursue here. Such loss or forgetting may result from the failure of utterances and texts, for whatever reason, to generate further consequences; if we grant that this occurs, then the accumulating march of progress of linguistic evolution must be replaced by a recognition of, as Tanselle (1989) puts it, "the fragility of the thread by which verbal statements hang on to perpetual life. Those statements depend either on human memory (and a cultural climate in which they get repeated) or else, if written down, on the survival of documents" (p. 42). Thus, instead of an easy expectancy about the continuity of a cultural heritage, Tanselle suggests, because "each document is a product of so many contingencies, and its survival the result of so many more, that we must always marvel at what we have, while as students of the past we continue to lament what we have lost" (p. 43). Thus, for Tanselle, the successful transmission of texts (verbal or written) through time is largely the exception to the rule; so much more is lost than is retained, and what survives does not do so by virtue of its inherent superiority or vitality, but by the accidents of chance and the determined and sustained efforts of individuals and groups to preserve it.

I would suggest that, especially after the poststructuralist critique of what Foucault (1969/1972a) calls "total history" (p. 9), there has been a growing recognition (a) that the past does not preserve itself or even provide an adequate index of the events that comprised it[20]; (b) that terms like *tradition, influence, development*, and *evolution* often untenably presume the continuity of meanings that they purport to explain (Foucault, 1969/1972a, pp. 21–22; cf. S. Miller, 1991, p. 36); (c) that utterances, texts, and meanings may disappear beyond the possibility of recovery[21]; (d) that signs might become *mute* (Derrida, 1967/1978, p. 166) or *unreadable* (Read, 1981, p. 108), their meanings *detached* (Winsor, 1994, p. 247), *uncoupled* (S. Hall, 1982, p. 78), *estranged* (Worsham, 1998, pp. 213–214), or even *dead* (Sartre, 1948/1965b, p. 327); and (e) that despite the centrality of efforts, both individual (e.g., diaries, scrapbooks, etc.) and collective (e.g., libraries, museums, etc.), to preserve and "stockpile the past in plain view" (Baudrillard, 1983, p. 19), the durability of the monuments we construct more closely resemble that of Shelley's (1817/2002) Ozymandius than Yeats's (1928/1988b) artifacts of "unageing intellect" (8), not a reality of but a dream of "a permanence that will outlast nature" (Malinowitz, 1999, p. 71). Occasionally, that recognition is accompanied by a fear that history is being forgotten (cf. Kinneavy, 1986/1996, p. 220; Bowers, 1959, p. 150), that our writing and reading of texts have become, through a paucity of preparation and erudition, superficial (J. Williams, 2000, p. 28; T. Miller, 1997, p. 35; Yarbrough, 1999, p. 134)

Admittedly, this argument for irretrievability cannot conclusively settle the matter, but, then again, neither can any argument for retrievability, though for a different reason: We cannot know whether any meanings, utterances, or texts have been irretrievably lost, *for this determination would itself constitute some kind of retrieval;* and we cannot infer from the fact that some meanings, utterances, or texts are, or at least seem to be, retrievable (e.g., a copy of a text long thought destroyed is unearthed) that all must be so. Our decision about whether to accept continuity or the possibility of discontinuity, then, must ultimately be based on our assessment of either claim's *probability.* Given what we know, is it likely that meanings are always recoverable, that utterances are never forgotten, that texts are never destroyed, that links in the great chain of discourse are never broken, or is it likelier that the apparent continuity of meaning and discourse is itself contingent and partial, the result of efforts whose success can never be guaranteed in advance? From the perspective of meaning apriorism, continuity is presumed and forgetting is inexplicable; from the perspective of meaning consequentialism (as I now think of it), continuity is never taken-for-granted, even when the propagation of meanings appears to be continuous. The point is not whether meanings may be *propagated*—and thereby seem *preserved*—but whether that continuity actually constitutes a *preservation* and whether meanings are always preserved; if not, our theory of meaning must be able to explain in a principled way how it is possible for meanings to become extinct and of what that extinction consists.

DURATIVITY AND INTERTEXTUALITY

Should a view, along these lines, of a modulated biosphere prevail, it would in effect mean that all message generators/sources and destinations/interpreters could be regarded as participants in one gigantic semiosic web; and, if so, this would at the very least affect the style of future semiotic discourse.

—Thomas A. Sebeok

To try to inventory up all the contexts of language and of the positions in which interlocutors can find themselves would be a demented undertaking. Each word-meaning is at the confluence of innumerable semantic rivers.

—Emmanuel Levinas

In its weakened form, *intertextuality* (i.e., the premise that any given utterance or text is linked to and interanimated by other utterances and/or texts) is an indubitable quality of the utterances and texts we encounter and produce.[22] Our professional role as researchers confronts us with the anteriority of the already said and, especially, the already written, but even in our daily affairs we always find ourselves responding to utterances and texts that, if not prompted by our own utterances or texts, are always a response to someone else's utterances or texts. Intertextuality of this sort, in which connections between utterances and texts are concrete but not necessarily continuous in terms of transmitting meanings and in which any text or utterance could be, or at least could have been, "reduced to a point within another text" (Myers, 1996, p. 12), is perfectly consonant with meaning consequentialism.

However, intertextuality is often strengthened to the point "other utterances and/or texts" in specific times and locations become "all other utterances and texts" spread throughout all time and all locations. In this guise, intertextuality is an extension of a durativity that intertwines the manifold threads of discourse into a single rope:

> Not infrequently, and perhaps ever and always, texts refer to other texts and in fact rely on them for their meaning. All texts are interdependent: We understand a text only insofar as we understand its precursors.
>
> This is the principle we know as intertextuality, the principle that all writing and speech—indeed, all signs—arise from a single network [. . .]. Intertext

is Text—a great seamless textual fabric. (J. Porter,
1986/1996, p. 225)[23]

The utterance or text is always already a *tissue* (Barthes, 1968/1977b,
p. 146), *weave,* or *quotation* of prior signs that are themselves always
already iterations (Barthes, 1971/1977d, pp. 159, 160); thus, each utterance or text is itself composed of the fragments of other utterances
and texts and is itself a "structured fragment" that will be sutured into
subsequent utterances and texts (McGee, 1990/1999b, p. 70).

Even if the chain of iterations is ultimately untraceable (Barthes,
1971/1977d, pp. 159–160) and even if the intertext itself is continuously changing,[24] the meaning of an utterance or text is, in Leibnizian
fashion, still constituted by its complex relationship to all other prior
utterances and texts at any given moment of time, so that no utterance
or text can be properly understood apart from this relationship.[25] And,
conversely, no prior text can be properly understood without including a consideration of subsequent utterances and texts that form the
intertext at the time of interpretation. For example, Eliot (1919/1999c)
famously argues that

> No poet, no artist of any art, has his complete mean-
> ing alone. His significance, his appreciation is the ap-
> preciation of his relation to the dead poets and artists.
> You cannot value him alone; you must set him, for
> contrast and comparison, among the dead. I mean
> this as a principle of æsthetic, not merely historical,
> criticism. The necessity that he shall conform, that
> he shall cohere, is not one-sided; what happens when
> a new work of art is created is something that hap-
> pens simultaneously to all the works of art which
> preceded it. The existing monuments form an ideal
> order among themselves, which is modified by the
> introduction of the new (the really new) work of art
> among them. The existing order is complete before
> the new work arrived; for order to persist after the su-
> pervention of novelty, the *whole* existing order must
> be, if ever so slightly, altered; and so the relations,
> propositions, and values of each work of art toward
> the whole are readjusted. (p. 15)

Every new work affects and is affected by the "whole existing order," without any loss or rupture, with novelty always folded into continuity.

However, by drawing such a high standard for *understanding*, understanding becomes *impossible* (for no single individual can conceptualize the intertext); and by grounding the meaning of an utterance or text as the position of that utterance or text within the intertext, meaning becomes *impossible* as well. For example, consider Cherwitz and Darwin's (1995) claim that "[e]very theory is what it is by virtue of its relation to all competing theories [. . .]. Theorists cannot account fully for their particular philosophies of meaning without observing the connections between their own and other (related) theories; all theories are at some level relationally intertwined (p. 27). Notice how easily Cherwitz and Darwin slip from a weaker, yet still objectionable, form of intertextuality (i.e., that theories of meaning are what they are because of the web of their relations with a limited set of competing theories) to the much stronger claim that a theory is what is because of its relationship with all other theories. The progression moves from "competing theories" to a parenthetical "(related) theories" to "all theories." But, as critics of holistic or differentialist views of meaning have frequently pointed out,[26] the assumption that the meaning of a word, utterance, text, etc., is determined by its placement within a total system of other words, utterances, texts and/or by its difference from those other words, utterances, texts, etc., can only result in "a theory of meaning of unmanageable complexity" (Dummett, 1975/1996b, p. 140), for "to understand the word x is to understand infinitely many things" (Stampe, 1968, p. 153). Or, perhaps better put, it would require that *one already understand the infinity of relationships in which* x *is already bound.*

Despite the fact that the meaning of utterances and texts is determined by their location within the intertext and that no language-user can conceptualize the intertext, *language-users still find utterances and texts meaningful.* Yet how is this possible? From where do these non-intertextual meanings arise? A few possible—though not equally forceful—arguments for saving the strong version of intertextuality suggest themselves:

> ✑ There are no non-intertextual meanings: The intertext has some kind of mysterious power of preserving itself without loss or discontinuity that

234   Kevin J. Porter

allows it to operate "behind the backs" of language users, who perpetuate it without any kind
of awareness at all (or, with what amounts to the
same thing, an awareness that, itself comprised of
a process of signification, is itself structured by the
intertext) (e.g., H. Bloom, 1973).

But this argument is circular because it presumes the continuity it purports to explain (i.e., an already continuous intertext always already
has the power to extend its continuity). It is also unsatisfactory because
it leaves no space for agency, creativity, or surprise.

         ✑ There are no non-intertextual meanings: Even though
          language-users cannot situate an utterance or text in
          relation to the intertext, they nevertheless manage to
          guess, based on textual and contextual clues or perhaps
          some kind of *intuition* or *preestablished harmony,* what
          its intertextual meaning is.[27]

Yet how exactly a person could make successful guesses of this kind,
based upon only a paucity of clues—at least, a paucity in comparison
to the intertextual manifold—is unfathomable.

         ✑ There *appear* to be non-intertextual meanings, but ac-
          tually these non-intertextual meanings are not mean-
          ings at all, but only *pseudo-meanings.*

Not only does this option recreate the problems associated with presumptions of *defective* meanings critiqued in Chapter 2 (including
where *defective* meanings come from), but it also would *appear to* imply that we are all surrounded by utterances and texts with intertextu-
ally determinate meanings that, nevertheless, can only *appear to* be
meaningful to us because we cannot know the intertext and therefore
cannot know the actual meanings.

    Both intertextuality and meaning consequentialism accept the
chaining of utterances and texts, but, by being based upon different
premises about how those chains operate, draw very different conclusions about meaning, language, and discourse. From the perspective of
intertextuality, no one can know the meaning of an utterance or text
because no one can fully comprehend the fully determinate position of
that utterance or text in relation to all other utterances and text; from
the perspective of meaning consequentialism, no one can know the
Meaning of an utterance or text (though they can know one or more

of its meanings), not only because the consequences of utterances and texts are non-simultaneous and dispersed, but also because any effort to determine a Meaning necessarily adds to that Meanings. From the perspective of intertextuality, every utterance and text is a monad that contains all other utterances and texts; from the perspective of meaning consequentialism, the Meaning of an utterance or text is the totality of its consequences, none of which contain or reflect that totality.

DURATIVITY AND MIND

A critic might at this point suggest, "Well, suppose I agree with you that there are no such holistic, continuous, intersubjective systems as 'languages' or the 'intertext.' But it seems to me that one can abandon the requirement that systems be intersubjective without abandoning entirely the notion of systematicity and continuity. Surely at the level of the individual mind we will find, if not closure, at least a necessary persistence of consciousness and an accumulation of experience?" But, as I argued in Chapter 4 about the effort to save the systematicity of language by narrowing its scope from national languages, to dialects, and finally to idiolects, what such a critic is suggesting is that, if only we keep cutting long enough (i.e., if we trim away intersubjective language or the intertext and consider only the individual mind), we will find that kernel of durativity which has so far eluded us.

This section continues the argument of Chapter 4 that critiqued conceptions of mind as a spatialized totality by examining how, through the principle of durativity, that spatialized totality is extended through time on both the micro- and macro-levels. At the micro-level of the present, theorists have argued that the stream of consciousness is a necessarily continuous stream. For example, Peirce (1868/1991c) conceptualizes semiosis as a train of associated thoughts—i.e., one thought suggesting and also being interpreted by the next—without a caboose: "If, after any thought, the current of ideas flows on freely, it follows the law of association. In that case, each former thought suggests something to the thought which follows it, i.e. is the sign of something to this latter" (p. 67). Our train of thoughts may be interrupted, but that interruption takes place through time, so that no thought dissolves "abruptly and instantaneously" (p. 68); and, further, that dissolution need not be so much an *annihilation* as a *backgrounding*, for "in addition to the principal element of thought at any moment, there are a hundred things in our mind to which but a small fraction of attention or consciousness is conceded" (p. 67). Only in death is the stream of consciousness ever truly broken (p. 68).

But this argument can be extended much more broadly: It is not merely that any given moment in the stream of consciousness is linked to and conditioned by its *immediate predecessor,* but that the present moment of consciousness is linked to and conditioned by *all of its predecessors.* That is, one's present consciousness is informed by the total history of one's consciousness[28]; our mind changes through time, but that change is always *supercession,* not *loss* (cf. Vygotsky, 1962/1986, pp. 202–203). For example, Alfred Schutz (1962/1990) contends that "Man finds himself at any moment of his life in a biographically determined situation [. . .]. To say that this definition of the situation is biographically determined is to say that it has its history; it is the sedimentation of all man's previous experiences, organized in the habitual possessions of his stock of knowledge at hand, and as such his unique possession, given to him and to him alone" (p. 9). In psychological terms, our experiences accumulate within and are encapsulated by a "world representation" (Britton, 1970/1992, p. 15) or "model of the world" (F. Smith, 1971, p. 28) that not only determines how we view the world and what we expect from it, but also that is subject to revision based on further experiences which, however extraordinary, are then subsumed into our world representation. As Britton (1970/1992) puts it, *"Every encounter with the actual is an experimental committal of all I have learned from experience"* (p. 15).

That the world representation is *idiosyncratic* does not make it any less aprioristic or determinative. In fact, the notion of unique world representations can be used, as we saw earlier with the fragmentation of languages into dialects and idiolects, to preserve apriorism in the face of undeniable diversity, even discontinuity. For example, consider Kress's (1997) explanation of the variability of readers' responses to texts: "The principles are the same, for all readers: the readings differ. Not, as one kind of current common sense has it, because we're all individuals and can read anything we want into anything, but rather because we are all individuals with distinct life-histories, which give us different means to bring to our readings" (p. 46). Reading, for Kress, is not "anarchic, willful or terribly unpredictable" (p. 46).[29] In other words, the propagation of meaning through texts, however varied, is always, in principle, *predictably varied,* determined by the prior history of whoever writes or encounters those texts.[30]

One need not appeal to phenomenological notions of *duration, ego,* or *apperception* or to a mentalist vocabulary of *representations* and *models,* however, in order to presume the perfect conservation of past experience in the present. For example, although a behaviorist like Skinner would reject such notions as obscurantist, he would also argue that our present actions, speech acts included, are informed by our total history of stimulations and conditioned responses to them (p. 143).[31] But as Dennett (1978, pp. 67–69) points out, the problem with this theory—and, *mutatis mutandis,* with all theories that make presumptions about the integral conservation of the past—is not simply (a) that Skinner offers no convincing proof for generalizing from simple experiments with pigeons to complex human activities, (b) that his theory cannot possibly be empirically confirmed (i.e., how can we determine what constitutes an individual's total history of stimulations and conditioned responses, and how can we be sure that that total history informs present actions?),[32] or even (c) that it is viciously circular (i.e., Skinner can always postulate the required prior history necessary to "explain" current actions), but the fact (d) that its fully determined or conditioned present cannot allow for unprecedented actions, unprecedented meanings, or actions in the face of unprecedented circumstances.

DURATIVITY, SIMULTANEITY, AND THE
MULTIPLICITY OF MEANING

We come back to the same problem, our sole and continuing concern: the origin of a spoken discourse does not exhaust that discourse; once set off, it is beset by a thousand adventures, its origin becomes blurred, all its effects are not in its causes. It is this *excess* which here concerns us.

—Roland Barthes

In this final section, we will explore the interrelated problems of *polysemy* (i.e., the apparent property of a sign to "contain" multiple meanings) and *surplus meaning* (i.e., the apparent inexhaustibility of the meaning of a particular utterance or text), alternatively described in manifold ways as:

- *depth: bottomlessness* (e.g., Bakhtin, 1986/1996, p. 127); *depths* (e.g., Bakhtin, 1986/1996, p. 7; Gadamer (1960/1977b, p. 226);

pregnancy (Dretske, 1981, p. 73); *richness* (e.g., Bergmann, 1982/1991, p. 485; Ricoeur, 1969/1974, p. 94); *thickness* (e.g., Barthes, 1971/1977a, p. 168), etc.

• *accrual:* accrual (e.g., Crosswhite, 1996, p. 138); *accumulation* (e.g., Ricoeur, 1969/1974, p. 70; G. Turner, 1990, pp. 18–19); *acquisition* (e.g., Peirce, 1868/1991c, pp. 83–84); *growth* (e.g., Bakhtin, 1975/1981, pp. 421–422); *synthesis* (Nietzsche, 1887/1992b, p. 516), etc.

• *polysemy:* connotations (e.g., Cherwitz and Darwin, 1995, p. 22; Elbow, 1999a, p. 146; Polanyi, 1958/1974, p. 112; *heterogeneity* (e.g., Pratt, 1991, p. 37); *heteroglossia* (e.g., Bakhtin, 1975/1981, p. 67); *manifold* (e.g., Emerson, 1844/1985d, p. 260); *multiplicity* (e.g., Flower, 1994, p. 44; Perelman, 1977/1982, p. xiii; Vološinov, 1929/1986, p. 101); *overtones* (e.g., Bakhtin, 1986/1996, p. 92); *plenitude* (e.g., Holquist, 1975/1981, p. xx); *plurality* (e.g., Barthes, 1971/1977d, p. 159); *polysemy* (e.g., Barthes, 1964/1977h, p. 39; Ricoeur (1969/1974, p. 68; G. Turner, 1990, p. 36); *polyvalence* (e.g., Condit, 1989/1999, p. 498; Spellmeyer, 1993b, p. 79); *promiscuity* (e.g., Spinoza, 1670/1951b, p. 109); *stereophony* (e.g., Barthes, 1971/1977d, p. 160), etc.

• *latency:* concealed meanings (e.g., Bakhtin, 1986/1996, p. 93); hidden meanings (e.g., Burke, 1950/1969, p. 111); *implications* or *ramifications* (e.g., Carnap, 1932–1933/1959b, p. 166; Polanyi, 1958/1974, p. 95; Derrida, 1967/1978, p. 25; Pattison, 1982, p. 9); *latent meanings* (e.g., Derrida, 1967/1978, p. 32; Papoulis, 1993, p. 137); *repressed meanings* (e.g., Davis, 2000, p. 249), etc.

• *excess:* deferral or dissemination (e.g., Barthes, 1971/1977d, pp. 158–159, 1971/1977i, pp. 126–127, 1971/1977a, pp. 167–168; Derrida, 1967/1978, p. 25, 1972/1981, p. 7); *excess* (e.g., Ashcroft, 1994, p. 33; Barthes, 1971/1977k, p. 206; Cain, 1999, p. 93; Fiske, 1989, pp. 5–6; Gadamer, 1964/1977a, p. 102); *inexhaustibility* (e.g., Bakhtin, 1975/1981, pp. 345–346; Barthes, 1972/1977e, p. 184; Ross, 1994, p. 94; Schwebke and Medway, 2001, p. 378); *magic* (e.g., Burke, 1945, p. 65); *surplus* (e.g., Ashcroft, 1994, p. 39; Levinas, 1961/1969, p. 74; Maranhão, 1990, p. 12; Minter, Gere, and Keller-Cohen, 1995, p. 673; Ross, 1994, p. 95; N. Welch, 1998, p. 384); *unintended mean-*

ings (e.g., Carnap, 1947/1988, p. 240; Condillac, 1746/1982c, p. 152; Daniel, 1994, p. 27; Dretske, 1981, p. 221; Elbow, 1973, p. 132, 1999a, pp. 146, 166; Putnam, 1975a, p. 278; Russell, 1940, p. 72; Ryle, 1946/1959, p. 331), etc.

• *potentiality: possibility* (e.g., Bakhtin, 1986/1996, pp. 6, 82; Bridgman, 1959/1966, p. 19; Dretske, 1981, pp. 174–175; Jackendoff, 1994, p. 131); *potential* (e.g., Bakhtin, 1975/1981, p. 356; Fiske, 1989, p. 43; Halliday, 1975, p. 4, 1978, pp. 1–2, 1987, p. 138; Heath, 1983, p. 81; Knoblauch and Brannon, 1984, pp. 87–88; Marková, 1992, p. 51; G. Miller, 1951, p. 112; Ricoeur, 1969/1974, p. 71; Rommetveit, 1974, p. 72; Sartre, 1948/1965a, pp. 226–227; Vološinov, 1929/1986, p. 101), etc.[33]

A text, utterance, word, sign, carries its full history with it (i.e., *depth*)—a history that accumulates without forgetting (i.e., *accrual*) and may even result in a manifold of (not necessarily coherent) meanings (i.e., *polysemy*)—and contains a wealth of only partially discernible implications (i.e., *latency*) and only partially controllable meanings (i.e., *excess*) that can only be partially realized in any particular use or interpretation of the text, utterance, word, or sign (i.e., *potentiality*). I have already treated questions of *depth, accrual,* and *latency* in this chapter, so I propose to critique in more detail manifestations only of *polysemy, potentiality,* and *excess,* focusing especially on the work of Ricoeur, Halliday, and Barthes.

An aside: Notice here how the principle of durativity blends with the principle of simultaneity, in that an utterance, text, word, or sign carries, at any given moment, the entirety of its accumulated history and that each additional meaning or interpretation is instantaneously added and shared by all other meanings or interpretations that follow, whether or not they are concretely connected to the particular addition. This blending should not be surprising or considered out of place, given my acknowledgment in Chapter 1 that these principles of meaning apriorism are blurred, not discrete.

Ricoeur. One of Ricoeur's (1969/1974) central projects is the reconciliation of the division of *semiology* from *semantics* (p. 93), *structure* from *function* (p. 95), *system* from *execution* (p. 69)—in other words, Saussure's division of *langue* from *parole.* To effect this reconciliation, Ricoeur argues that we must properly conceptualize the unit that has a reality within both the perspective of language-as-system and language as-event and that that unit is the *word:* "the word is, as it were, a trader between the system and the act, between the structure and the event. On the one hand, it relates to structure, as a differential, but it is then only a semantic potentiality; on the other hand, it relates to the act and to the event in the fact that its semantic actuality is contemporaneous with the ephemeral actuality of the utterance" (p. 92). The word, then, is "the pivot of semantics" around which and through which occur "exchanges between the structure and the event" (p. 93). Unlike an utterance (Ricoeur's "sentence"), a word is not an actualization of a meaning, but an always already ordered polysemic potential out of which a particular meaning or subset of meanings is actualized; but, also unlike an utterance, a word has a durability that "survives the transitory instance of discourse and holds itself available for new uses" (p. 92)—new uses that it always "returns to the system" (p. 93). Ricoeur's elaborates on this process:

> By virtue of the cumulative process which I was speaking of, the word tends to be charged with new use-values, but the projection of this cumulative process into the system of signs implies that the new meaning finds its place within the system. The expansion—and, if the case obtains, the surcharge—is arrested by the mutual limitation of signs within the system. In this sense we can speak of a limiting action of the field, opposed to the tendency to expansion, which results from the cumulative process of the word. Thus is explained what one could call a regulated polysemy, which is the law of our language. Words have more than one meaning, but they do not have an infinity of meanings. (p. 93)

But from the perspective of meaning consequentialism, there are no words outside of utterances or texts, and so "words" qua units of an autonomous system have no "cumulative process" of acquiring meanings. What is cumulative—or, better, *aggregative*—about the Meaning of a word *in use* is its propagating consequences, but none of these consequences "contain" or "preserve" the aggregated Meaning.

For Ricoeur, the word is a "structure, which, in itself, it outside of time" that also has, by virtue of its eventfulness, a "tradition," history, or past (p. 95). The word is also the level at which the multiplicity of

meaning occurs both at any given instant (i.e., in a framework of simultaneity) and diachronically (i.e., in a framework of durativity):
The synchronic definition: in a given state of language, the same word
has several meanings; strictly speaking, polysemy is a synchronic concept. In diachrony, multiple meaning is called a change of meaning, a
transfer of meaning. Of course, the two approaches must be combined
in order to take a global view of the problem of polysemy at the lexical level; for in polysemy, changes of meaning are considered in their
synchronic dimension, that is to say, the old and the new are contemporaneous in the same system. (p. 68)

Polysemy is multifaceted, then, extending horizontally and vertically, and it is "not itself a pathological phenomenon [. . .] [but] part
of the constitution and the functioning of *all* language" (pp. 71–72).
All words are polysemic, and we might think of the context of utterance and the utterance itself—except, Ricoeur suggests, in literary
language, which "celebrates" polysemy (p. 94)—as a means of impov-
erishing this polysemy (p. 94).

But, crucially, despite all efforts of impoverishment, polysemy cannot be evacuated entirely, *except in the most artificial or technical languages* (p. 71):

> When I speak, I realize only a part of the potential
> signified; the rest is erased by the total signification
> of the sentence, which operates as the unit of speak-
> ing. But the rest of the semantic possibilities are not
> canceled; they float around the words as possibilities
> not completely eliminated. The context thus plays the
> role of filter [. . .]. It is in this way that we make uni-
> vocal statements with multivocal words by means of
> this sorting or screening action of the context. It hap-
> pens, however, that a sentence is constructed so that
> it does not succeed in reducing the potential meaning
> to a monosemic usage but maintains or even creates a
> rivalry among several ranges of meaning. (p. 71)

Thus, the semantic possibilities of a word always surround, however
imperceptibly, every use of that word like an aura. The word-qua-
event can only momentarily subtract from the plenitude of the aura of
the word-qua-structure or permanently add to that plenitude. In other
words, the word-qua-event must *forget* the plenitude of meanings, and

even the word-qua-structure does not retain the same set of meanings in perpetuity as particular meanings are forgotten; but what is *unforgettable,* both for the word-qua-event and the word-qua-structure, is *the total history of the word itself.*[34]

Halliday. Like Ricoeur, Halliday attempts a reconciliation of parole and langue, but it is an attempt that, I suggest, immediately misfires as langue resumes its privilege. For example, notice how Halliday compromises his promising claim, at least according to my way of thinking, that language is comprised of utterances, not sentences, and veers toward a transmission model of linguistic communication as the conveyance of *a priori* meanings: "Language does not consist of sentences; it consists of text, or discourse—the *exchange of meanings* [italics added] in interpersonal contexts of one kind or another" (1978, p. 2). But perhaps Halliday would rather say that "language does not *only* consist of sentences," for he repeatedly describes language in terms of a semiotic system that, even if it does not determine the particular choices that a speaker or writer makes, determines *a priori the total set of meaningful elements from which the speaker or writer may choose when constructing texts that fulfill certain functions* (i.e., text is the concatenated result of choices from a systemic set of options, with each choice constraining further choices; cf. 1975, pp. 15–16): "the learning of language will be interpreted as the learning of a system of meanings. A child who is learning his first language is learning how to mean; in this perspective, the linguistic system is to be seen as a semantic potential. It is a range of possible meanings; together with the means whereby these meanings are realized, or expressed" (1975, p. 8). It is through discourse that sentences—and the linguistic system itself—is actualized or realized (1978, p. 135), but these realizations themselves can be made sense of—i.e., made meaningful—only by relating them to the potentiality that they actualize and by relating that particular potentiality to the total set of options available to the speaker or writer.

The key term Halliday uses is *meaning potential,* which he describes in ways that sometimes resemble an idiolect:

> If there is anything which the child can be said to be acquiring, it is a range of potential, which we could refer to has his 'meaning potential.' This consists in the mastery of a small number of elementary functions of language [i.e., *instrumental, regulatory, interactional, personal, heuristic, imaginative, informative*],

and of a range of choices in meaning within each one. (1978, p. 19)

And, elsewhere:

> The child is learning to be and to do, to act and interact in meaningful ways. He is learning a system of meaningful behaviour; in other words, he is learning a semiotic system [. . .]. So the content of an utterance is the meaning that is has with respect to a given function, to one or other of the things that the child is making language do for him. It is a semiotic act which is interpretable by reference to the total range of semiotic options, the total meaning potential that the child has accessible to him at that moment. (1975, p. 15)

The functionality of language is a crucial concept for Halliday: "Language is as it is because of the functions it has evolved to serve in people's lives" (1978, p. 4), and language itself is a "functional potential" (1975, p. 5). But I would argue that whatever functionality language has cannot simply be the result of the human need to have certain functions fulfilled (i.e., that satisfying human needs is the intrinsic telos of language), but rather that functionality depends upon the fact that language is consequential: *Consequentiality* (i.e., the potential of signs to produce consequences) precedes *functionality* (i.e., the desire for certain signs to produce certain consequences), and in some ways may, and likely will, frustrate it.

Moving beyond the child's "total meaning potential," Halliday also refers to language more expansively in terms of a sociolect that is, at least in principle, fully accessible to any language-user:

> A child learning language is at the same time learning other things through language—building up a picture of reality that is around him and inside him. In this process, which is also a social process, the construal of reality is inseparable from the construal of the semantic system in which the reality is encoded. In this sense, language is shared meaning potential, at once both a part of experience and an intersubjective interpretation of experience. (1978, pp. 1–2)

Meaning is "in the last analysis interpreted in sociological terms"
(1975, p. 5), so that, at any given moment, the possible meanings expressible by an idiolect is bounded (i.e., a "total meaning potential");
and the range of possible idiolects is, at any given moment, bounded
by the sociolects from which they are pieced together. What the individual speaker says is properly interpreted only in light of what she
or he could have said, but chose not to (1978, pp. 28, 40, 137); what
could have been said is delimited by an *a priori* "total set of options
that constitute what can be meant" (1978, p. 109); and what can be
meant is delimited *a priori* by what that sociolect can be used to do
within the constraints of cultural "situation types" (1975, p. 130). This
is not to say that the meaning of an utterance or text need be *singular*
(i.e., that an utterance or text must select only a single option out of
the total set of options); in fact, for Halliday, an important distinction
between "child language" and "adult language" is the ability of the
latter to be "plurifunctional" (i.e., the ability to use language to do
and mean many things in a single utterance) (1975, pp. 30, 42, 48).
It only means, rather, that whatever polysemy an utterance or text
has is always already, as Ricoeur puts it (1969/1974, p. 93), a *regulated
polysemy.*

An aside: I must admit that I do not find Halliday to be very consistent in his handling of meaning potential. Rather, he oscillates between conceiving of language as an idiolect and a sociolect. For example, consider his claim that "What the speaker can say, i.e., the
lexicogrammatical system as a whole, operates as the realization of the
semantic system, which is what the speaker *can mean*" (1978, p. 39).
But *the* lexicogrammatical system as a *whole* is not something that a
speaker possesses, so the lexicographical grammatical system cannot
be "what the speaker can say" but rather a larger totality out of which
the speaker has only partial familiarity. And elsewhere, Halliday conflates, within the span of a few sentences, meaning potential as "what
can be meant—the potential of the semantic system" from meaning
potential as "the meanings that make up his [the child as individual]
semantic system at that time" (1975, p. 124).

To resume: Given Halliday's theory of the sociolect, how are we to
account for miscommunication between individuals assumed to share
the same sociolect? How is it possible for individuals who share the
same sociolects to misunderstand each other? For Halliday, miscommunication of this sort does not call into question whether individuals

in fact share a language (i.e., a questioning of the distribution of and access to a language system), but can be explained in terms of different judgments about what elements of that system are relevant in a given context: "All children have access to the meaning potential of the system; but they may differ, because social groups differ, in their interpretation of what the situation demands" (p. 27). In other words, we all have access to the same dictionary even if we do not (a) use that dictionary in the same way or (b) even agree that there is a certain way that that dictionary should be used.

A reader at this point might object: Doesn't Halliday also discuss language and meaning as dynamic, open-ended, even indeterminate—a resource that not only "transmits" the "social semiotic," but also through use "transforms" it (1975, p. 60). Doesn't Halliday argue that the "normal condition of the semantic system is one of change" (1978, p. 78)? And my response would be: Yes. But I would add two crucial qualifications. First, even if these particular premises advocated by Halliday are opposed to meaning apriorism—which I will argue they do not—they cannot preclude any manifestation of meaning apriorism in Halliday's work: *I make no claim that Halliday's views on language and meaning that manifest meaning apriorism are without contradiction or incoherence.*

And second—and more importantly—I would argue, following Roy Harris (1998), that variety and transformation are not inimical to *a priori* conceptions of language, so long as variety and transformation are orderly, systematic, evolutionary, and/or developmental processes (i.e., processes governed by, accounted for, or fully assimilable into, an *a priori* system). That is, so long as *changes to the system are always explicable from within the a priori constraints of system.* For example, consider Halliday's (1978) contention that

> The components of the sociolinguistic universe themselves provide the sources and conditions of disorder and of change. These may be seen in the text, in the situation, and in the semantic system, as well as in the dynamics of cultural transmission and social learning. All the lines of determination are *ipso facto* also lines of tension, not only through indeterminacy in the transmission but also through feedback. The meaning of the text, for example, is fed back into the situation, and becomes part of it, changing it in the

process; it is also fed back, through the register, into the semantic system, which it likewise affects and modifies. The code, the form in which we conceptualize the injection of the social structure into the semantic process, is itself a two-way relation, embodying feedback from the semantic configurations of social interaction into the role relationships of the family and other social groups. (p. 126)

Thus, there appear to be two ways in which the "sociolinguistic universe" undergoes modification: (a) the inherent corruptibility of a transmitted meaning (i.e., *disorder, noise, entropy,* etc.)[35], and (b) the accumulation of utterances and texts (*change, accrual, evolution*), which, by adding to an existing situation, necessarily change that situation, and, by adding to the totality of utterances and texts, necessarily shift the probabilities of occurrence of elements within the semantic system. Because it is in constant flux, the sociolinguistic universe has, as Halliday (1978) describes physical reality itself, "periodicity without recurrence" (p. 139), but a periodic non-recurrence that is nevertheless, like Bergson's duration, *continuous.* Each utterance and text, then, not only actualizes a meaning potential, but also transforms the system itself; the system is realized through usage, but usage subsequently alters the semiotic system by shifting, however imperceptibly, the probability of occurrence of the elements within that semiotic system. That is, the semiotic system is a "system of meanings [. . .] [that] is constituted out of innumerable acts of meaning which shape and determine the system" (1975, p. 121). But one cannot conclude that these "innumerable acts of meaning" form a system without having already accepted a systematic method for ruling out of further consideration innumerable other acts of meaning; in other words, a semiotic system does not include, nor is it modified by, just any utterance or text—unless that semiotic system, as I discussed in my critique of intertextuality, extends throughout the entire universe.

This apparently open-ended, probabilistic, and *a posteriori* position, I suggest, actually marks a subtle return to meaning apriorism, manifesting the principles of simultaneity and durativity. For example, consider Halliday's (1987) curious comparison of the probability of weather patterns to probability of linguistic patterns:

Now, just as, when I listen to the weather report every morning, and I hear something like 'last night's minimum was six degrees, that's three degrees below average,' I know that that instance has itself become part of, and so altered, the probability of the minimum temperature for that particular night in the year—so every instance of a primary tense in English discourse alters the relative probabilities of the terms that make up the primary tense system. Of course, to make these probabilities meaningful as a descriptive measure we have to sharpen the focus, by setting conditions: we are not usually interested in the average temperature at all times anywhere on the surface of the globe (though this is a relevant concept for certain purposes), but rather in the probable daily minimum on Sydney Harbour at the time of the winter solstice. (p. 139)

Halliday's formulation has a number of problems: (a) it assumes the existence of an already spatialized English language whose patterns are subject to constant modification by English speakers engaging in "English discourse," so that whatever variety might lead us to conclude that, in fact, these speakers do not share the same language is folded into a wider systematicity that includes variation; (b) it assumes that the calculation of global probabilities for a generalized *Everyenglishspeaker* might be a "relevant concept for certain purposes"; (c) it conceives of language as a system governed throughout by a Boolean or associationist logic, so that each use of a linguistic term, *equally weighted*, changes the probability of that event's occurring throughout the entire system in equal measure, with all English speakers knowing, whether explicitly or not, the "inherent probability" of a particular occurrence of a lexical term or grammatical feature at any given time (e.g., my writing "doggie doggie doggie doggie doggie doggie" has just now shifted the entire probability for all English speakers of the appearance of "doggie" rather than "dog" throughout the whole of English discourse, but my writing "dog dog dog dog dog dog" has just now equitably restored that prior probability)[36]; (d) it confuses the *descriptive* calculation of averages from the predictive *calculation* of probabilities (e.g., if I flip a fair coin 100 times and heads appears 56 times, I can say that heads appeared an average of 56% of the time, but not that the probability of the coin landing on heads or tails has changed so that the next flip of the coin is 12% more likely to be heads); (e) further, weather forecasters do not rely solely on "minimum averages" of temperatures from an abstract day from the calendar year to make predictions about the temperature of a particular day, otherwise meteorology would be little different from accounting; (f) a purely *a posteriori* probabilistic model cannot account for the probability of the initial use of a term, nor for the fact that, after only a single use, that usage would be 100% likely; and (g) it is difficult to conceive how such a probabilistic system would not lead toward uniformity, rather than diversity (e.g., probable usages should tend only to grow increasingly more probable, until the probability of deviation became statistically insignificant).

Barthes. Unlike Ricoeur (1969/1974, pp. 74–75) and Eco (1979, p. 24), for whom semantics or semiology involves in part a search for the description of the stable "semic nucleus" of signs, Barthes (1971/1977a) argues that the goal of semiology is *disruptive:* "the problem is not to reveal the (latent) meaning of an utterance, of a trait, of a narrative, but to fissure the very representation of meaning, is not to change or purify the symbols but to challenge the symbolic itself" (p. 167). Semiology aims at "less the analysis of the sign than its dislocation" (p. 166); and a semiologically informed analysis of a text would not explain "*from where* the text comes (historical criticism), nor even *how* it is made (structural analysis), but how it is unmade, how it explodes, disseminates—by what coded paths it *goes off*" (1971/1977i, pp. 126–127).

However, Barthes is not consistent, for semiology at times seems to serve as

- a description of how all signs necessarily operate: e.g., that whatever stability of meaning we perceive in a text is "imaginary" (1971/1977d, p. 157), that discourse is always "punctured" by its audience (1971/1977k, p. 195), and that "the origin of a spoken discourse does not exhaust that discourse" (1971/1977k, p. 206);

- a description of how the operations of signs have changed at a certain historical junctures: e.g., that whether reading is an active performance or a passive reception, a "consumption" or a "collaboration," is historically and culturally variable (1970/1977f, p. 149; 1971/1977d, p. 163); or

- a description of how a certain subset of signs operate: e.g., that only certain films have an "obtuse meaning" which goes beyond the obvious meanings of its always already coded images (1970/1977j, p. 65), that only certain voices possess a "grain" that goes "beyond (or before) the meaning of the words, their form [. . .], and even the style of their execution" (1972/1977e, p. 182), that the determinate, regulated meaning of speech is fundamentally different from the indeterminate, transgressive meaning of writing (1971/1977k, p. 191), and that one must actively resist the impulse to reduce the polysemy of Text to the monosemy of a Work (1971/1977i, p. 141), disorienting the "Law" of signification by "floating" (1971/1977c, p. 215).

This tension is particularly manifest through Barthes's varied attempts to define what he calls *signifiance,* an excess of meaning beyond the code-governed "informational level" of communication and code-governed "symbolic level" of signification that "seems to open the field of meaning totally, that is infinitely [..]. out into the infinity of language" (1970/1977j, pp. 52, 55).[37] Curiously, despite being referred to as the "third meaning" beyond information and signification, *signifiance* is also somehow a rejection of meaning or, rather, of "the tyranny of meaning" (1972/1977e, p. 185):

> Finally, the obtuse meaning can be seen as an *accent,* the very form of an emergence, of a fold (a crease even) marking the heavy layer of informations and significations [. . .] a sort of gash rased of meaning (of desire for meaning) [. . .]. This accent [. . .] is not directed towards meaning [. . .] [and] does not even indicate an *elsewhere* of meaning (another content, added to the obvious meaning); it outplays meaning—subverts not the content but the whole practice of meaning. (1970/1977j, p. 62)

Signifiance is not part of the semiotic system (which, for Barthes, must be always already coded), but something—e.g., an *emotion* (including *pleasure* [*jouissance*] or *trauma*), an *evaluation,* an *accentuation,* a *grain,* a *physicality* or *materiality*—that stands outside of the system and resists the closure that the system attempts to, and frequently succeeds in, imposing (1961/1977g, p. 30; 1970/1977j, pp. 59–60; 1972/1977e, p. 182). In other words, signifiance, a "new—rare—practice affirmed against a majority practice (that of signification)" (1970/1977j, p. 62), is not intrinsic to discourse, which can operate at the informational and symbolic levels without it,[38] nor does it even, when present, obscure these other levels.[39]

As much as I find (much of) Barthes's work attractive—especially its notion of the text as an "explosion" of meanings and the "play" of signifiers—I find it to be highly problematic in several ways, not the least of which is its equivocations of *semiology, signifiance,* and even *meaning* itself. First, I do not find Barthes's theories about language to be explanatory, for by rejecting all positive talk of origins, Barthes cannot account for the first sign (cf. Chapter 1). It may very well be that language "calls into question all origins" because these origins are "lost" (1968/1977b, pp. 146–147) or even that these origins do not contain all the consequences that they propagate, but that doesn't entail that the signs and meanings that comprise language are without origin (i.e., without a first occurrence).

Perhaps sensing an undesired implication of his strong conception of intertextuality, Barthes (1971/1977d) assures us that

> The intertextual in which every text is held, it itself being the text-between of another text, is not to be confused with some origin of the text: to try to find the 'sources,' the 'influences' of a work, is to fall in with the myth of filiation [which Barthes (1971/1977d) elsewhere defines as "a determination of the work by the world, a consecution of works amongst themselves, a conformity of the work to the author" (p. 160)]; the citations which go to make up a text are anonymous, untraceable, and yet already read: they are quotations without inverted commas. (p. 160)

But I fail to see how saying that the always "already read" citations that comprise a text are "anonymous" and "untraceable" frees us entirely from the myth of filiation, for one cannot cite or quote a passage from a text that hasn't been written. In fact, other comments from Barthes actually lead to the opposite conclusion—that texts, "'woven' in familiar codes" (1971/1977i, p. 126), are necessarily comprised of filiations. For example, Barthes (1968/1977b) argues that the novelty of the writer—though he prefers the term *scriptor*—is simply his or her (possibly) unique concatenations of words selected from a pre-given lexicon:

> The text is a tissue of quotations drawn from the in-
> numerable centres of culture [. . .]. [T]he writer can
> only imitate a gesture that is always anterior, never
> original. His only power is to mix writings, to coun-
> ter the ones with the others [. . .]. Did he wish to *ex-
> press himself,* he ought at least to know that the inner
> 'thing' he thinks to 'translate' is itself only a ready-
> formed dictionary, its words only explainable through
> other words, and so on indefinitely [. . .]. Succeeding
> the author, the scriptor no longer bears within him
> passions, humours, feelings, impressions, but rather
> this immense dictionary from which he draws a writ-
> ing that can know no halt: life never does more than
> imitate the book, and the book itself is only a tissue
> of signs, an imitation that is lost, infinitely deferred.
> (pp. 147–148)

Consequently, not only does language not have any origins, but it also has no creativity beyond the novel concatenation and juxtaposition of anterior signs that comprise the "ready-formed dictionary" from which the postmodernist (or perhaps even pre-modernist) "scriptor"— not the modernist Author—selects elements when composing a text (1968/1977b, p. 146); thus, Barthes's conception of language remains principally code-oriented and intertextual, manifesting both *simulta- neity* and *durativity*.

And second, Barthes's poststructuralist notion that signification is infinitely deferred—i.e., that signs lead only to other signs, ad infini- tum, never reaching what Derrida (1967/1978) calls the "transcenden- tal signified" (p. 280)—implies that meaning is indefinitely deferred, never achieved; whereas, as I think of it, meaning is not deferred or incomplete or "postponed" (Spivak, 1976, p. lxv), but temporally dis- tended and dispersed (i.e., we do not need to experience the Meaning of an utterance or text for that utterance or text to be meaningful, so that we do not need to "chase" a Meaning that must inevitably elude us). The Meaning of an utterance may always be unfinished, in the sense that more meanings could be added to it, but that doesn't imply that the Meaning is incomplete or has a lack. As Wittgenstein

(1953/1968) writes, "Do not say: 'There isn't a "last" definition.' That is just as if you chose to say: 'There isn't a last house in this road; one can always build an additional one'" (I.29). *There is no "infinity of language," if one thinks of language in terms of actual utterances and texts, and there is no infinity of meaning either.*

7 Meaning and Time

No facts are to me sacred; none are profane; I simply experiment, an endless seeker with no Past at my back.

—Ralph Waldo Emerson

The sun is new each day.

—Hêracleitus

In his discussion of the philosophy of Emmanuel Levinas, Mecke (1990) argues that we must make a distinction between a "general principle of *temporality* and the different specific forms of *time* it produces" (p. 205). Although the latter are amenable to positive definition of some sort (e.g., the time of narration, the time of dialogue, the time of physics, etc.), the former eludes it:

> The necessity of a negative definition of time by nonpresence stems from the ontological status of time itself, because it resists a metaphysics of presence that is firmly anchored in Western culture and language. The only positive statement that can be made about time is that it "temporalizes," that it engenders its own forms in contact with Western metaphysical presuppositions and reduces them to substance and essence [. . .]. Thus the impossibility of a positive definition of time on the ontological level is intrinsic to temporality. (p. 160)

Mecke's argument is full of curious and problematic assertions—e.g., that time comes into "contact with Western metaphysical presuppositions," that there is such a thing as a "Western culture and language" to which "a metaphysics of presence [. . .] is firmly anchored"—but the larger point, I think, is simply wrong: *It is not impossible to provide a positive definition of time qua temporality, even if it is exceedingly difficult to do so.*

Meaning consequentialism is a positive account of meaning that requires a positive account of time, for *meaning is not hampered by time, but constituted within it.* I suggest that, now that some of the limitations of the conceptions of time I have grouped under the principles of panchronism, simultaneity, and durativity have been exposed, we are finally in a position not only to pursue an alternative yet still positive account of time, but also to understand why such an account needs to be pursued in the first place. This section, then, is a speculative sketch of a positive account of the properties of time that explores and ties together some of the interconnections between that account and the premises of meaning consequentialism. I also suggest that, pace Mecke (1990), we can use Levinas's intricate philosophy to help construct a positive account of time in terms of *fecundity.*

THE ASYMMETRY OF TIME AND MEANING

For a consequentialist point of view (i.e., one in which time plays an essential role) to be valid, time must itself play an *essential role* in whatever comprises the reality in which users of language and signs generally find themselves: Time cannot be superfluous, parasitic, or illusory. This claim is a rejection of the ways time is treated by those theories that manifest the principle of panchronism in terms of eternity or block time; but this rejection must be warranted not by a desire for a time that is not illusory, but by the properties that time actually has. The first proposition I will offer about the essential role that time plays is

(T1.0) Time is asymmetrical.

which can be glossed as

(τ1.0) Time introduces asymmetries between past and present that prevent the reversibility of events: Time has a direction.

(T1.0) emerges from work on chaos theory (e.g., Prigogine and Stengers 1979/1984; 1996/1997), and it resists the principle of panchronism because the asymmetries introduced through time necessarily preclude their being the predetermined, essentially *a priori* future of eternity or block time.[1] According to Prigogine and Stengers (1996/1997), physical laws governing the interactions of objects are stochastic, not deterministic, so that the present is not always already "pregnant" with the future: "we are now able to include probabilities in the formulation of the basic laws of physics. Once this is done, Newtonian determinism fails; the future is no longer determined by the present, and the symmetry between past and future is broken" (pp. 5–6).

The importance of the asymmetry of time for my attempt to think through meaning in terms of consequences is that it warrants a fundamental distinction between an antecedent and its consequent:

(C1.0) An antecedent X necessarily precedes its consequent Y.

which we can gloss as

(χ1.0) The relation between X and Y is non-commutative: Under no true description can X be subsequent to Y.

Because of (T1.0), (C1.0) does not express a tautology: Time has a direction, so describing the temporal relation between objects and events in terms of *precession* and *succession* is not an arbitrary choice. *The material utterance or text necessarily precedes the events that comprise its various immediations and mediations.*

However, (C1.0) is an insufficient criterion for distinguishing consequences of an antecedent from events occurring after X that are otherwise unrelated to X. So we require

(C1.1) Y is a consequent of X if and only if Y is subsequent to X, Y could not have occurred had X not occurred, and Y might not have occurred even though Y occurred.

(C1.1) stipulates a relationship between X and Y that is *non-arbitrary*— i.e., the relationship between X and Y isn't just any possible correlation that is or could be drawn between X and Y. An encounter with an utterance or text cannot occur unless there is an utterance or text already there to be encountered (e.g., I cannot read *Moby Dick* if someone has not already written it). But (C1.1) also precludes that relationship being causal, not only in the sense that *the text does not determine how it is read,* but also in the sense that, given the same set of initial conditions, *a reader would not necessarily perform the same reading.* The asymmetry of time also allows us to support another distinction, made in Chapter 3, between immediate and mediate consequences of utterances and texts:

(C1.2) Y is an immediate consequence of X if and only if no other event Z intervenes between X and Y; otherwise, Y is a mediated consequence of X.

THE APERIODICITY OF TIME AND MEANING

The events that occur through time are not only arranged in a particular sequence, but they are also non-repeatable:

(T2.0) Time is aperiodic.

(τ2.0)   Events are unique particulars that behave aperiodically—that is, events are never repeated, rendering impossible "any prediction of a future state in a given system" (Donahue, 1997/2002).

Without (T2.0), (T1.0) would not rule out a cyclical or palingenetic universe, such as those imagined by the Stoics or the Mayans (Whitrow, 1972/1975, pp. 12–13, 17), in which events A_1, B_1, C_1, ..., Z_1 loop around again to A_2, B_2, C_2, ..., Z_2 and repeat themselves exactly, ad infinitum; A_2 is not A_1 (i.e., the earlier time is not lived through again), but it is identical to A_1 in every way other than its location within the endless cycles of time. But with (T2.0), there can be no "rolling back the clock," no return to an earlier state, no repetition of the same. As Donahue (1997/2002) observes, aperiodicity is not only a feature of very complex interactions between multiple objects, but even of interactions that can be described in very simple terms: "History is indeed aperiodic since broad patterns in the rise and fall of civilizations may be sketched; however, no events ever repeat exactly. What is so incredible about chaos theory is that unstable aperiodic behavior can be found in mathematically simple systems. These very simple mathematical systems display behavior so complex and unpredictable that it is acceptable to merit their descriptions as random."

I suggest that (T2.0) provides support for claims about the primacy of parole:

(C2.0) Discourse is aperiodic.

(χ2.0)   Discourse is comprised of utterances and texts that are unique particulars.

Bakhtin and Vološinov are key figures here.[2] For both theorists, the "concrete reality of language" is manifested through discursive interactions, not "*stable system[s] of normatively identical forms*" that are abstracted from these interactions (Vološinov, 1929/1986, p. 98); and situated utterances and texts, not abstract sentences, are the "real units that make up the stream of language-speech" (Vološinov, 1929/1986, p. 96; cf. Bakhtin, 1986/1996, p. 71). Because they are necessarily situated, utterances are unique particulars:

> language and speech communication (as a dialogic exchange of utterances) can never be identical. Two or more sentences can be absolute identical (when they are superimposed on one another, like two geometrical figures, they *coincide* [italics added]); moreover, we must allow that any sentence, even a complex one, in the unlimited speech flow can be repeated an unlimited number of times in completely identical form. But as an utterance (or part of an utterance) no one sentence, even if it has only one word, can ever be repeated: it is always a new utterance (even if it is a quotation). (Bakhtin, 1986/1996, p. 108; cf. Vološinov, 1929/1986, pp. 99–100)[3]

However, I do not think that Bakhtin's formulation goes far enough because it still accepts a fundamental distinction between parole and langue, with the latter irreproducible and the former not. Notice that Bakhtin describes sentences in terms of "geometrical figures." I suggest that this is a poor choice because a sentence, unlike a triangle, is not a purely formal unit devoid of significance.[4] A triangle Δ does not represent itself as being a triangle or represent the notion of triangularity, but *is a triangle,* and determining whether two triangles Δ Δ are identical—or at least indiscernibly congruent—is a simple matter of superimposing one form on the other.[5] But are these sentences,

(1) Tom is sick. (Tom Smith isn't feeling well.)

(2) Tom is sick. (Tom Jones is disturbingly weird.)

identical? Perhaps, if one is willing to consider graphonyms as the same word with any number of acceptable meanings. Similarly, one could argue that the *bear* of (3) and (4) is the same word, too, with multiple meanings:

(3) I can't bear this waiting any longer.

(4) I saw that black bear standing in the river.

But at what point is one willing to abandon, in a principled way, the identity of particular "words"? Is graphonymy enough, as in (5) and (6)?

(5) Jerry is a barber.

(6) The students in French class were tested on the verb "barber" today.

Graphonymy apart from homonymy?

(7) Robert is sick.

(8) Robert ist malade.

Homonymy apart from graphonymy?

(9) Empedocles leaped.

(10) Empedokles liebt.[6]

Homonymy apart from graphonymy and even shared syntactic form?

(11) I saw that black bear standing in the river.

(12) The cupboard is bare, and I'm starving.

Surely, *bear* and *bare* aren't the same words, but on what grounds could one make this distinction if one accepts that the *bear* of (3) and the *bear* of (4) are the same words? Because they are *written differently*, even though they are homonyms? Would *bear* and *bare* be identical words, then, if "English" were only a spoken "language"?

Bakhtin's geometric argument breaks down entirely if one—not Bakhtin—thinks of *forms* in terms of *logical forms* or *propositions* underlying utterances, so that

(1a) Tom ist krank.

(1b) Tom est malade.

both express the same proposition as that which underlies (1). But, I suggest, the postulation of the underlying and undetectable self-same proposition is an effort to rescue a presumed formalist conception of language from the failure of (1), (1a), and (1b) to be *formally* congruent. I suggest that any effort to enforce the distinction between an abstract sentence and its manifestation in an utterance, between a decontextualized word and its contextualized use, between a formal type and its concrete tokens is either (a) untenable because it provides clear boundaries that can nevertheless be shown to be violated or (b) vacuous because it provides no principled way of demarcating a word from other words (i.e., why does the polysemy of *bear* stop at the point where the polysemy of *bare* begins?). I do not presume to have solved the type-token problem, but I will say that the consequentialist premise of the aperiodicity of discourse is not a denial of the iteration of verbal and written forms; rather, it is a radical questioning of what comprises iteration that would look at how *sameness* is not *something that utterances possess a priori* and completely, but *something that emerges as a limited consequence of those utterances* (i.e., something that need not be shared by all consequences of those utterances).

THE INDETERMINACY OF TIME AND MEANING

No matter how much we know, none of us knows the future. None of us can be sure about the consequences tomorrow of actions taken today, nor even can we ascertain to everyone's satisfaction the relationship between past events and the present.

—Kurt Spellmeyer

For the consequentialist account of meaning that I am developing, it is not enough for time to be asymmetrical and aperiodic, for it is still possible to fold directionality and non-repeatability into an *a priori* conception of time. For example, one could hold that the future has in a sense already happened even if (a) the events that are distributed through block time must occur in a certain succession and (b) no single event, though fully determined, is ever repeated.[7] But, as I have mentioned before, the uncertainty of the future is not simply *epistemological*, but *ontological*.[8] Time has an essential role to play in physical reality and is not an arbitrary way of segmenting a four-dimensional space-time that stretches from the *beginning* of the universe to its *end*. Thus, we may say that

(T3.0) The future is indeterminate because it does not *exist*.

(T3.1) Nothing lies beyond the *event horizon* of the present.

which I gloss as follows:

(τ3.0)   The future is not an *a priori* reality that is made *present*, an *a priori* dimension into which the present expands, or an *a priori* plenitude from which the present chooses particular elements, but a name for the infinity of nothingness that lies beyond the limit of the present. The expansion of the present is analogous to the expansion of the universe: There is *nothing* beyond the universe *into which* it expands.

(τ3.1)   The event horizon marks the boundary of the eventfulness of the present.

I will explicate the notion of *the infinity of nothingness* below; what I will pursue in the remainder of this section is the concept of the *event horizon* and the larger connection of (T3.0) to meaning consequential-ism. As used in contemporary physics, the term *event horizon* refers to the region surrounding a black hole at which even light signals have insufficient velocity to escape the gravitational pull of the black hole. According to Hawking (1988/1990), "The event horizon, the bound-ary of the region of space-time from which it is not possible to escape, acts rather like a one-way membrane around the black hole: objects, such as unwary astronauts, can fall through the event horizon into the black hole, but nothing can ever get out of the black hole through the event horizon" (p. 89). Consequently, "no signal that could bring information about events inside the black hole can cross the horizon and reach [an] observer" (Novikov, 1998, p. 98). Obviously, in this sense, the boundary between present and future is not an event hori-zon because the future is not an already existing entity with which it is physically impossible to communicate; but, despite this, I find the term itself quite suggestive for understanding the movement of time in several ways: (a) the *inescapability* of the event horizon is analogous to the inescapability of the present (i.e., one always finds oneself in a present); (b) the *irreversibility* of the event horizon is analogous to the asymmetry of time (i.e., one is always *falling through* the event horizon of the present into the future, not the past); and (c) the *uncertainty* of events *beyond* the event horizon is analogous to the uncertainty of events *beyond* the present (i.e., uncertainty is ontological, not only epistemological).

The indeterminacy of time is crucial for a consequential account of meaning because it entails that meaning itself has an essential in-determinacy.

(C3.0) The consequences of an utterance or text are not predetermined.

(C3.1) The boundary between an utterance or text and its immediate and mediate consequences—and, by extension, between an immediate or mediate consequence of an utterance or text and the immediate and mediate consequences of that immediate or mediate consequence, ad infinitum—is the *event horizon of meaning.*

No matter how much speakers or writers labor over the composition of utterances or texts, no matter how much they try to secure agreements on the meaning of terms, and no matter how rigidly they adhere to what they believe are already secured agreements on meanings, *the consequences of utterances and texts are always unforeseeable, even if one makes accurate predictions about some of those consequences* (i.e., the fact that I guess accurately does not entail that my guess constituted certain knowledge of the future). Speakers and writers cannot *see* past the event horizon of meaning and know the consequences of their utterances and texts because there is nothing beyond the event horizon to be seen or known: One cannot know what occurs after the event horizon because *there is nothing beyond the event horizon that has occurred.* (Note that this essential unknowability differs from the kind that results from the impossibility of speakers and writers, especially in regard to utterances and texts that propagate on a large scale, to track the proliferating chains of consequences, some of which might extend well past their death.)

THE GRANULARITY OF TIME AND MEANING

In Chapter 2, I argued that immediations and mediations of utterances and texts are not durational, but nevertheless have a duration—a claim that depends upon not only how one conceives of time, but also how one conceives of the relationship between time and consciousness. I argue that

(M2.1) Time is intrinsic to consciousness.

(μ2.1) Immediations and mediations of utterances and texts are necessarily temporally distended and, consequently, cannot be adequately understood apart from time.

An immediation or mediation is not a *state* that can be properly described in terms of a single frame culled from a series of essentially timeless instants that capture the total, simultaneous state of one's consciousness because time is not a succession of an infinite number of timeless instant.

Zeno's famous paradoxes exposed—and depended upon—the absurdity of the infinite divisibility of time (cf. Ray, 1991, pp. 5–23); but some contemporary thinkers still conceive of time in precisely this way. For example, Foucault (1970/1977h), following Deleuze (1968/1994, 1969/1990), argues that time is not an infinite "succession of present instances that derive from a continuous flux and that, as a result of their plenitude, allow us to perceive the thickness of the past and the outline of a future in which they in turn become the past" (pp. 193–194). Rather, time is the infinite recurrence of a present that "recurs as singular difference" (p. 194)—a present that is always already infinitely divided into past and future and, consequently, not a present at all:

> It is the straight line of the future that repeatedly cuts the smallest width of the present, that indefinitely recuts it starting from itself. We can trace this schism to its limits, but we will never find the indivisible atom that ultimately serves as the minutely present unity of time (time is always more supple than thought). On both sides of the wound, we invariably find that the schism has already happened (and that it had already taken place, and that it had already happened that it had already taken place) and that it will happen again (and in the future, it will happen again): it is less a cut than a constant fibrillation. What repeats itself is time; and the present—split by this arrow of the future that carries it forward by always causing its swerving on both sides—endlessly recurs. (p. 194)

Although I agree with Foucault that time is not a continuous duration (i.e., "continuous flux"), I do not agree with him that time must, then, necessarily be without any distension whatsoever; in other words, I do not agree that one must chose either between a time of *infinite plenitude* (i.e., the *thickness* of the principle of durativity or the principle of panchronism) or a time of *infinite impoverishment* (i.e., the *thinness* of the principle of simultaneity).

Foucault's key mistake, I suggest, is to assume that "time is always more supple than thought" (p. 194). This is certainly true in the sense that, whatever the span of the primary unit of time might be—referred to as a *chronon*[9]—it will certainly be of shorter duration than the temporally distended processes of cognition. But it is false in the sense that mathematical constructs, such as *an infinite series,* may be *more supple than space and time:*

> In the mathematical domain, we may readily imagine a series closed at one end and open at the other or a length divisible continuously ad infinitum; but in the physical world lengths are measured by rulers and other such instruments—and we always read off a discrete finite amount, a rational number for any distance we measure [. . .]. [W]e do use mathematics in our physical theories with a tremendous degree of success. But even an enthusiastic acknowledgement of the utility of mathematics should not carry with it the presumption that because it works it must *strictly* apply to the physical world. (Ray, 1991, p. 21)

Thus, I would argue, pace Foucault, that

(T4.0) Time is not infinitely divisible, but *granular.*

(τ4.0) Objects and events do not occupy timeless *instants,* but are necessarily distended through time.

(T4.1) The fundamental *granule* of time is the *chronon.*

Quantum mechanics, in fact, assumes that at their most fundamental levels, space and time are not continuous, but have "quantum properties" of discreteness (Novikov, 1998, p. 137), an assumption which abrogates the paradoxes of continuity and infinite divisibility.

What I am referring to as the granularity of time has some relation to, but also crucial differences from, concepts of *temporal granularity* (hereafter, *granularity*) developed in philosophy of time and in computer science. Dyreson, Evans, Lin, and Snodgrass (2000) define *granularity* as "the unit of measure for a temporal datum" (p. 568), so that there is no single "granularity" for time, but an infinite number of possible granularities: "Many different granularities exist and no granularity is inherently 'better' than another" (p. 568). For example, a granule may comprise a second, an hour, a day, a week, a business week, etc., but none of these spans represent an ideal "segmentation of the time-line" (p. 569).[10] Within a particular granularity, the granules are "nonoverlapping and totally ordered," but they need not be contiguous either internally or externally (p. 570). These granules can form aggregates of "coarser granularity" or can be subdivided into aggregates of "finer granularity" (p. 571), but the latter process must stop at the point where a "bottom granularity" (Bettini, Dyreson, Evans, Snodgrass, and Wang, 1998, p. 412) or "minimal cell" (B. Smith and Brogaard, 2000/2002) is reached. The "top granularity" or the "maximal cell" would comprise the longest possible span of time, which would be, in block time, the life-span of the universe.

I suggest that these approaches to time help illuminate notions of *discreteness* (i.e., that time does not "overlap" itself), *contiguity* (i.e., that discrete spans of time *may be* adjacent to each other in such a way that no event occurs between them), and *aggregation* (i.e., that contiguous spans of time may, for certain purposes and under certain descriptions, be treated as a single, larger unit of time) that have direct bearing on the relationship between time and meaning. The granularity of time provides a warrant for such consequentialist claims as

(C4.0) There is no timeless instant in which a purely abstract, formalized language can subsist.

(M6.1) Consciousness is durable, not durational.

(μ6.1) Consciousness is a series of discrete and not necessarily contiguous saccades; it is not a *continuous stream* of sensations experienced by, memories recollected by, or fantasies constructed by a subject. Consciousness is always timely.

However, these conceptions of temporal granularity are also hindered by serious problems that require rectification, not the least of which is a tendency for some theorists to treat the granularity of time as a *purely theoretical construct* imposed by fiat upon a time that is itself continuous. For example, Dyreson et al. (2000) refer to granularity as a conventional unit of *measurement* that arbitrarily segments an otherwise continuous time line, and Smith and Brogaard (2000/2002) contend that the "boundaries [of granules, whether temporal or spatial] are then not physical discontinuities in the underlying domain of objects, but are rather the products of our acts of demarcation" (p. 2). Without their being a real boundary of some sort, the postulation of a "minimal cell" for time, such as Smith and Brogaard's (2000/2002, p. 3), is necessarily ad hoc, a convenient way of avoiding the problem of the "infinite complexity" of granules; and it also contradicts the presumption that one may always construct if needed "a new granularity, finer than all existing bottom granularities" (Dyreson et al., 2000, p. 575).

THE RELATIVITY OF TIME AND MEANING

A second difficulty with conceptions of granularity involves the tendency to include discontinuous granules into a wider framework of absolute time that *smoothes out* the discontinuities not only *within* a given granularity (i.e., discontinuities are predictable, even predetermined), but also *between* granularities (i.e., that at some finer level of analysis, seemingly incommensurate granularities are commensurable because the boundaries of these finer granules of which they are comprised are congruent). Suppose, for example, that the granules of a granularity, J, are comprised of business days (Monday through Friday, excluding holidays)—J_0, J_1, J_2, etc.—and that the granules of K are comprised of business days and holidays. The granularities of J and K are not identical because J would have gaps that do not appear in K, but *the boundaries of their granules would be simultaneous;* and K itself would contain gaps when compared to a granularity L *without gaps* that is comprised of all days. But the time of J and K cannot be separated from the location of the events that comprise those series—that is, the timing of the events within J and K cannot be compared to an absolute, universal standard of time that L somehow tracks, but only in relation to each other from the perspective of an observer (cf. Chapter 4). *The business day* J_0 *does not measure a span of time that is shared contemporaneously throughout a universe that exists simultaneously.*

Thus, we must include in our model of time, in addition to asymmetry, indeterminacy, and granularity, the premise that

(T5.0) Time is relative.

Without (T5.0), our prior premises about time could still fit within the framework of the principle of simultaneity. I would light to highlight two important implications of the relativity of time. The first is, as I have already indicated,

(τ5.0) There is no universal *now*, only localized *nows:* Granules of
time are finite not only in their duration, but also in their
spatial extension.[11]

Time is not a dimension that spans the entire universe in a single instant. And second,

(τ5.1) Time is not something that unfolds at the same rate for
each object and event. Each object has an "individual time"
(Sharov, 1995/2001) that passes with a unique "viscosity"
(Foucault, 1969/1972a, p. 175)[12]; and each set of interacting objects has its own "specific time not reducible to any
individual time" (Sharov, 1995/2001).

Even the chronon cannot provide a greatest common factor for all
individual times because the chronon is itself, though indivisible, *malleable*[13]; just as there can be no rigid bodies to provide a universal
standard of distance, there can be no rigid time spans to provide a
universal standard of duration (cf., Chapter 4).

I suggest that (T5.0) provides support for a consequentialist rejection of manifestations of the principle of simultaneity:

(C5.0) There is no single, unbounded *now* in which a spatialized
language can be found.

(χ5.0) There cannot be synchronic descriptions of a language because there is nothing synchronic to describe.

(C5.1) The consequences of utterances and texts, and their propagation, are not governed by a single standard of time.

(χ5.1) Consequences are not necessarily of equal duration (i.e.,
a consequence is not measured by a standard number of
chronons), and particular strands of consequences need not
propagate with the same granularity.

Nothing about (C5.0) or (C5.1) prevents language from being theorized or even used *as if it were synchronic,* but theorizing about or using
language in this as-if way does not, pace Yarbrough (1999, p. 10), *make
language synchronic,* no more than postulating epicycles makes the apparent retrograde motion of the planets a reality.

THE DISCONTINUITY OF TIME

My aim was to analyse this history, in the discontinuity that no teleology would reduce in advance; to map it in a dispersion that no pre-established horizon would embrace; to allow it to be deployed in an anonymity on which no transcendental constitution would impose the form of the subject; to open it up to a temporality that would not promise the return of any dawn.

—Michel Foucault

Although the model of time that I have been developing so far allows for the possibility of the aggregation of granules, aggregation is not the continuity of, say, the principles of panchronism or durativity, for (a) the continuation of an aggregate is never assured *a priori* because the aggregate does not *collect* granules from a future that is always already there (i.e., aggregation is not like the adjoining of already existing boxcars to an already existing train)—*the indeterminacy of time;* (b) the antecedent elements of the aggregate do not determine what the next element of the aggregate must be—*the indeterminacy of time;* (c) the aggregate is not an extension of itself (i.e., the train does not lengthen because the boxcars enlarge themselves), but an accumulation of non-repetitive otherness—*the aperiodicity of time;* (d) whatever continuation there is from granule to granule does not erase the boundary between granules (i.e., even maximally contiguous granules do not lose their discreteness)—*the granularity of time;* and (e) there is no total aggregation occupied by all objects and events in the universe—*the relativity of time.*

In order for time to be formable into aggregates, it must already be comprised of smaller granules. Our consideration of time, then, cannot stop only at what *occurs during the granules,* but must consider the importance of the fact that granules are *necessarily bounded.* Time is not infinitely divisible, but it is divided:

(T6.0) Time is discontinuous; it is a rupturing, a cleavage. Cf. Sartre (1943/1956), who describes *nihilation* as a "cleavage between the immediate psychic past and the present" (p. 27).

(τ6.0) The granules of time do not merge into one another seamlessly.

(τ6.01) The past cannot preserve itself across this rupture of its own accord (i.e., the past has no inertia).

(T6.1) The rupture of time—the passing of the present into the past, the creation of the future into the present—is *traumatic.*

(τ6.1) The experience of time is, as Levinas (1961/1969) describes the experience of discourse, "the experience of something absolutely foreign, a traumatism of astonishment" (p. 73).

(τ6.11) The trauma of time does not result only from our sense of an encounter with a future that is alien, but also from our sense of alienation from a past that has departed.

According to Foucault (1971/1977g), the "shock of daily occurrences" is blunted by an array of purportedly panchronic categories, such as "truth, man, culture, writing, etc.," that "function to exclude the radical break introduced by events" (p. 220). That is, efforts are made to make what is radically new about the future seem to be just more of the same—e.g., that "I" remain and will remain who "I" already was, that utterances are merely concrete concatenations of the same words and sentences, that the meaning of an utterance is and will always be what it was, etc. But I would argue also that there are efforts made as well to blunt our shock *that the past is no longer with us.* For example, categories are not only a tool for establishing expectations that future events must fit into, but also a tool for establishing expectations that the past acted in an orderly way, that the events of the past did not so much form *a posteriori* categories—even those that occurred prior to the explicit formation of the categories—but always already fitted into *a priori* ones.

In what ways do (T6.0) and (T6.1) harmonize with premises of meaning consequentialism? First, I suggest that they illuminate why the Meaning of an utterance or text (i.e., the totality of its consequences) must be treated as a propagating aggregate of meanings, not a seamless whole:

(C6.0) The Meaning of an utterance or text is the temporally distended aggregation of its propagating consequences.

(χ6.0) The Meaning of an utterance is formed through time by its consequences and is not contained by any single one of those consequences; but there is no single *instant* in which the Meaning of an utterance *exists* because the propagating consequences of an utterance do not share a single instant of time.

Second, I suggest that (T6.0) and (T6.1) provide the necessary break between events to preclude the determination of the future by the past:

(C6.1) The Meanings of the past do not linger into the present because of their own vitality (cf. Chapter 2).

(χ6.1) The Meaning of an utterance or text does not have an intrinsic inertia.

And, third, it provides the necessary break to preclude the *a priori* preservation of an antecedent in its consequent(s):

(C6.2) The fact that *Y* is a consequent of *X* does not entail that *Y* preserves *X*, that *X* contains *Y*, or even that *X* becomes *Y*.

(χ6. 2) The antecedent Meaning of an utterance or text is not an *a priori* constraint on the subsequent consequences of that utterance or text; it does not provide a self-same criterion that distinguishes proper consequences from improper consequences.

The Fecundity of Time

The one thing which we seek with insatiable desire is to forget ourselves, to be surprised out of our propriety, to lose our sempiternal memory and to do something without knowing how or why; in short to draw a new circle [. . .]. The way of life is wonderful; it is by abandonment.

—Ralph Waldo Emerson

The passage from chaos to cosmos must be ceaselessly repeated.

—Georges Gusdorf

The trauma of time—the timeless interval that separates even maximally contiguous granules of time[14]—cannot be conceived only in terms of a *negation* or *nihilation* of a past, for it also marks the point at which not only a past can be at least partially continued, but also at which a future may be *created out of nothingness.*

(T7.0) Time is fecund

(τ7.0) The discontinuity of time allows for the possibility of an "absolute youth" that is unprecedented.

The notion of creation from nothingness is not unprecedented in the empirical sciences,[15] but my conception of the fecundity of time emerges from my reading of Levinas's (1961/1969) philosophy of time developed in *Totality and Infinity.*

According to Levinas, "Time is the non-definitiveness of the definitive, an ever recommencing alterity of the accomplished—the 'ever' of this recommencement [. . .]. There must be a rupture of continuity, and continuation across this rupture" (pp. 283–284). This definition of time differs from Bergson's duration, in which the new—however unprecedented—emerges from, is burdened by, and folds back into the old because the old and new are *continuous:*

> If time does not make moments of mathematical time, indifferent to one another, succeed one another, it does not accomplish Bergson's continuous duration either [. . .] [in which] time adds something new, something absolutely new. [For] the newness of springtimes that flower in the instant (which, in good logic, is like the prior one) is already heavy with all the springtimes lived through. The profound work of time delivers from this past, in a subject that breaks with his father [. . .]. The work of time goes beyond the suspension of the definitive which the continuity of duration makes possible. (pp. 283–284)

In a crucial way, this definition also resists Heidegger's (1927/1962) conception of primordial time as essentially *finite* (i.e., marked by the boundaries of the birth and death of Dasein):

> It is not the finitude of being that constitutes the essence of time, as Heidegger thinks, but its infinity.

The death sentence does not approach as an end of being, but as an unknown, which as such suspends power. The constitution of the interval that liberates being from the limitation of fate calls for death. The nothingness of the interval—a dead time—is the production of infinity. Resurrection constitutes the principal event of time. There is therefore no continuity in being. Time is discontinuous; one instant does not come out of another without interruption, by an ecstasy. In continuation the instant meets its death and resuscitates; death and resurrection constitute time. (pp. 283–284)[16]

For Levinas, then, time is essentially discontinuous, a rupture of totality (i.e., an infinity) in which even continuation marks a point of necessary disjunction (i.e., death and resurrection).

But how is *continuation*—not *continuity*—reconcilable to the premise of discontinuity in (T7.0)? A continuation marks the point of aggregation between two granules *across which* something continues but might have not continued (i.e., a continuation is contingent, a posteriori), whereas a *continuity* or *continuum* would require not simply that something necessarily continues from granule to granule, but rather that there are no essential boundaries between granules (i.e., there are no discrete granules at all). According to Levinas, we can make this reconciliation if we think of continuation as something made possible by *fecundity*:

true temporality, that in which the definitive is not definitive, presupposes the possibility not of grasping again all that one might have been, but of no longer regretting the lost occasions before the infinity of the future. It is not a questions of complacency in some romanticism of the possibles, but of escaping the crushing responsibility that veers into fate, of resuming the adventure of existence so as to be to the infinite [. . .]. Without multiplicity and discontinuity—*without fecundity* [italics added]—the I would remain a subject in which every adventure would revert into the adventure of a fate. *A being capable of an-*

other fate than its own is a fecund being [italics added].
(p. 282)

A fecund being is capable of another fate because, considered onto-logically, fecundity does not take the form of a transformational re-lationship (e.g., that between a seed and the oak that develops from it), but of a transcendent relationship that Levinas likens to *paternity:* "In paternity, where the I, across the definitiveness of an inevitable death, prolongs itself in the other, time triumphs over old age and fate by its discontinuity. Paternity—*the way of being other while being one-self* [italics added]—has nothing to do with a transformation in time which could not surmount the identity of what traverses it, nor with some metempsychosis in which the I can know only an avatar, and not be another I. This discontinuity must be emphasized" (p. 282).

A fecund being is a "transcendent" being in the sense that it "can not be encompassed" (Levinas, 1961/1969, p. 293) or totalized be-cause it does not simply extend a prior totality, but marks a point of *creation:*

> To affirm origin from nothing by creation is to con-test the prior community of all thing [*sic*] within eternity, from which philosophical thought, guided by ontology, makes things arise as from a common matrix. The absolute gap of separation which tran-scendence implies could not be better expressed than by the term creation, in which the kinship of beings among themselves is affirmed, but at the same time their radical heterogeneity also, their reciprocal exte-riority coming from nothingness. (p. 293)

Considered ontologically, the father who dies continues on through the son, *even though the son is not the same as the father, but an Other.* Thus, there is an essential gap between father and son, an interval or "dead time that separates the father from the son" (p. 284) and that allows for an "absolute youth" which is still a "recommencement" (p. 282). If we think of time as "the recurrence of difference"—i.e., that "differ-ence recurs"—then a recommencement or a return is "freed from the curvature of the circle" (Foucault, 1970/1977h, pp. 193–194).

But, pace Levinas, I would argue that fecundity is not reducible to paternity, which always already marks a successful continuation; if it were, fecundity would be an *a priori* principle of continuity. In fact, for Levinas, the relation to the past cannot be wholly severed; the past cannot be *forgotten,* but only *pardoned.* The "recommencement of the instant, this triumph of the time of fecundity over the becoming of the mortal and aging being, is a pardon, the very work of time" (p. 282):

> Pardon refers to the instant elapsed; it permits the subject who had committed himself in a past instant to be as though that instant had not past on, to be as though he had not committed himself. Active in a stronger sense than forgetting, which does not concern the reality of the event forgotten, pardon acts upon the past, somehow repeats the event, purifying it. But in addition, forgetting nullifies the relations with the past, whereas pardon conserves the past in a purified present. The pardoned being is not an innocent being. (p. 283)

Without the pardon—without an ability to absolve ourselves, or for others to absolve us, of our past actions while still acknowledging that they occurred—"our capacity to act would, as it were, be confined to one single deed from which we could never recover; we would remain victims of its consequences forever" (Arendt, 1958, p. 237).

As Arendt (1958) points out, the act of forgiveness is creative because it breaks the cycle of transgression and vengeance:

> In contrast to revenge, which is the natural, automatic reaction to transgression and which because of the irreversibility of the action process can be expected and even calculated, the act of forgiving can never be predicted; it is the only reaction that acts in an unexpected way and thus retains, though being a reaction, something of the original character of an action. Forgiving, in other words, is the only reaction which does not merely re-act but acts anew and unexpectedly, unconditioned by the act which provoked it and therefore freeing from its consequences both the one who forgives and the one who is forgiven. (p. 241)

However, I find a number of problems with this formulation. First, in keeping with Levinas's religious terminology, *death need not be followed by resurrection,* nor, alluding to the epigraph from Foucault that begins this chapter, *night by dawn* (e.g., past moments may be forgotten, meanings do not always arrive at Bakhtin's postulated homecoming, correlations between objects that once interacted within a system may break down).

(C7.0) The Meaning of an utterance or text is fecund not because its consequences extend far into the past, but only insofar as its consequences continue to propagate into the future.

(χ7.0) The fecundity of the text is not a measure of the depths of an *a priori interiority*, but of the dispersion of an *a posteriori exteriority.*

(χ7.01) The antecedent fecundity of an utterance does not guarantee continued fecundity: Utterances and texts that have been consequential may cease being consequential.

Second, a pardon is relational, not absolute: I may pardon myself *for myself,* but I cannot pardon myself *for others* (e.g., I may deny responsibility for certain consequences of my utterances and texts, and I may not even feel responsibility for them, but that doesn't entail that others will not hold me responsible for them) (Arendt, 1958, p. 237). Similarly, the fact that I forget an utterance or text utterly does not entail that that utterance or text is utterly forgotten (i.e., has ceased being consequential).

(C7.1) The consequences of an utterance or text for its speaker or writer have no special privilege over the consequences of that utterance or text for other people.

(χ7.1) Speakers and writers are not, *a priori*, the final adjudicators of what their utterances and texts mean, even if their utterances and texts are consequential only for themselves or even if listeners and readers accede to the results of any adjudication.

And third, we must allow for, however rare it might be, a *birth without paternity,* a dawn without a prior night, "order out of chaos" (Prigogine and Stengers, 1979/1984), an unconditioned action, an unprecedented consequence, the creation of a token without an antecedent type—a *first meaning.*

(C7.2) The moment when a non-consequential antecedent entity or event becomes consequential is the moment of *first meaning*.

(χ7.2) This first meaning is not only the moment of *baptism* in which an antecedent but otherwise non-consequential entity in a chain of discourse becomes consequential in that chain of discourse (Kripke, 1972/1996, p. 96; Putnam, 1980/1983d, p. 72), but it also the marks moments in which that entity becomes variously consequential as those consequences propagate into various other chains.

(χ7.21) An antecedent entity that becomes consequential in multiple chains of discourse will have multiple first meanings. The first meaning is not a moment that necessarily occurs only once for an antecedent.

(χ7.22) *Non-consequential* and *consequential* are not absolute terms, just as *meaning* and *non-meaning* are not absolute terms. An entity may be consequential in certain ways for certain entities, but differently consequential or even non-consequential for other entities. The principle of contradiction does not hold: It may be equally true to say of the same entity that it is both consequential and non-consequential.

CONCLUSION

I cannot conclude this chapter here with a pat declaration about *why time is fecund* (or aperiodic, or discontinuous, etc.) or *why consequences may emerge that are not caused*. These questions require much more inquiry to discern not only *whether they can be answered*, but *whether they must be answered*. For it may very well emerge from further inquiry that the fecundity of time and meaning cannot be further decomposed (i.e., explained in terms of other underlying concepts), but must be treated as primitive terms. This need not be cause for despair or for further mystification—we need not try to simplify the data in order to construct a fully ordered system (e.g., Saussure, 1916/1959), and we need not try to assign *causes* for fecundity, such as the Stoics' special faculty of *phantasia* (Flory, 1996, p. 158), that are only themselves black boxes masquerading as explanations. On the contrary, we might end up with nothing else left to say, learning the truth of Wittgenstein's (1922/1981) conclusion in the *Tractatus Logico-Philosophicus* that "Not *how* the world is, is the mystical, but that it *is*" (6.44), and that in the face of the "inexpressible," the "right method of philosophy" would be to say nothing at all: "Whereof one cannot speak, thereof one must be silent" (7).

And so, for now (or at least until the next chapter), silence.

8 Severity, Charity, and the Consequences of Student Writing: Toward a Consequentialist Pedagogy

Of all signs there is none more certain or worthy than that of the fruits produced, for the fruits and effects are the sureties and vouchers, as it were, for the truth of philosophy.

—Francis Bacon

So far, all of the chapters of this book have been focused on the construction of a consequentialist philosophy of discourse that could eventually *travel,* to use Said's term (1983, p. 226), far outside of rhetoric and composition studies. In fact, little has been written so far that could be said to be *especially* concerned with the problems investigated by researchers and educators in our discipline; after all, meaning consequentialism does not limit itself, for example, to the study of written texts or the development of writing pedagogy. From my own perspective, the questions raised by trying to think through meaning in terms of consequences, even in its early stages of development, should be of sufficient theoretical interest to engage researchers in our field—although, of course, it is not for me to decide whether my view is correct. But I also recognize that some compositionists expect theory at some point to be translated into pedagogical practices—and I agree with them. If meaning consequentialism is a viable account of meaning and discourse, then it must be able to help us understand how meaning and discourse operate or fail to operate in our classrooms. The task of this final chapter, then, is to shift from building a general account of meaning and discourse to speculating about how that theory can illuminate—and be illuminated and changed by—problems encountered within our composition classrooms. I wouldn't say that this chapter *applies* meaning consequentialism, whereas the previous chapters *build* it; for this chapter is not the unfolding of pedagogical implications already housed within meaning consequentialism, but an inauguration of those implications.

The problems that I have been most concerned with in my role as a researcher-educator revolve around the harm that results from the practice of authoritarian, rigid teaching methods that comprise what I have, in "A Pedagogy of Charity: Donald Davidson and the Student-Negotiated Composition Classroom" (2001), termed *pedagogies of severity*. Like some of my colleagues in the field, I worry about (a) the ethics of the imbalance of power between teachers and students (e.g., Bizzell, 1991; Elbow, 1986; Lamb, 1991); (b) the ways in which these austere pedagogies, whether inadvertently or deliberately, disrupt dialogue between teachers and students and impoverish the means by which students engage their own texts and the texts of peers (e.g., Newkirk, 1984a, 1984b; Nystrand, Gamoran, Kachur, and Prendergast, 1997); and (c) the seemingly ceaseless repetition of sterile, unmotivated writing assignments (e.g., Britton, 1970/1992; Britton et al., 1975; Lindemann, 1995; Ohmann, 1976/1996; Cheryl Reed, 1996). But, more immediately, I worry about how I can help the students who enter my composition classroom already marked by these pedagogies, and I worry about the extent to which my own classroom praxis resists or conforms to pedagogies of severity. In short, I am deeply concerned about the consequences of the pedagogies that my colleagues and I practice.

This concern about the consequences of pedagogies practiced in composition classrooms is hardly peculiar to me. Researchers in rhetoric and composition studies—especially those who have essays and books published!—tend to be quite reflective about the consequences of writing pedagogies, whether their own or others'. We wonder (and argue) about, among other issues, the validity of writing assessment methods (e.g., R. Johnson, Penny, and Gordon, 2001; Hayes, Hatch, and Silk, 2000; Herrington and Moran, 2001; White, 1995); the nature of learning and how best to foster it in classrooms (e.g., Carter, 1990; Freire, 1971; Knoblauch and Brannon, 1984; Nystrand, Gamoran, Kachur, and Prendergast, 1997); the relations between pedagogy and ideology (e.g., Berlin, 1988; Lynch and Jukuri, 1998; R. Miller, 1998; Worsham, 1998); the implications of electronic technologies for writing instruction (e.g., Anson, 1999; Selfe, 1999; Selfe and Selfe,

1994); the inclusiveness of classrooms populated by diverse students (Fishman and McCarthy, 2001; Silva, Leki, and Carson, 1997; Valdés, 1992); and the responsibility of writing instructors to the institutions that support them (and students who expect them) to teach a standardized English grapholect (e.g., Corbett, 1981; Delpit, 1986, 1988; Elbow, 1986; Carol Reed, 1981; J. Smith, 1997). Some of us have even wondered (and argued) about whether writing can be, or should be, taught at all (Berthoff, 1978; Elbow, 1973; Kent, 1993c; Roemer, Schultz, and Durst, 1999; Yarbrough, 1999). In short, one of the major problems confronting our field is finding an answer to a question posed by Chenowith and her colleagues (1999): "Are our courses working?" (p. 29)—but "working" in a sense larger than mere efficiency. Of course, we want to know whether our courses accomplish the goals we set for them, but we also want to know whether we have set and acted upon the proper goals for ourselves and our students and whether these goals or our methods for achieving them are more harmful than beneficial. Should we be doing what we are doing? If not, why were we doing it in the first place?

In this chapter, I will examine, this time through the lens of meaning consequentialism, some of the consequences of pedagogies of severity—for some of the students whom I have been fortunate enough to teach and for myself—because these pedagogies can be resisted only if they are properly understood. But to assume that these pedagogies can be understood apart from the consequences they propagate is akin to assuming that we can understand what a text means without knowing any of its consequences. In fact, pedagogies of severity become meaningful through and only through the consequences that they propagate, not only as they are made manifest and propagate through the writing and reading of books and essays, but also as they are made manifest and propagate through actions performed inside and outside of our classrooms. If we take meaning consequentialism seriously, we must accept that in an important sense the Meanings of pedagogies, as with any thing else, are determined by the consequences they propagate, not by the *intentions* or *desires*, however reasonable or equitable, that motivate their designers and practitioners. And we must accept, as educators, (a) that the Meanings of our verbal interactions, written comments, writing assignments, and other utterances that we construct in our roles as teachers are not for us (alone) to determine and (b) that the value of those interactions, comments, assignments is not for us (alone) to determine or assess; of course, a necessary corollary is that our students (and colleagues, and administrators, and parents, etc.) that the meanings and values of classroom interactions, either.

To make my case against and construct an alternative to pedagogies of severity, I will (a) briefly summarize the arguments and findings from my published essay on severity and charity; (b) argue that pedagogies of severity violate the principle of charity, which requires interpreters to assume other interlocutors are rational beings with mostly true and coherent beliefs, *but only as part of a larger effort to limit the consequences of texts and utterances,* particularly those of students, in order to enforce their aprioristic conception of meaning and language[1]; (c) examine manifestations of severity beyond the violations of charity, particularly in terms of their oscillation between formalism and intentionalism; (d) analyze my own complicity with pedagogies of severity in my conduct of the course; (e) discuss and critique pedagogical strategies, such as service learning, that attempt make student writing more consequential; (f) assert that my earlier effort to theorize a pedagogy of charity represents a promising, but ultimately limited, start toward the development of a much more constructive pedagogy informed by meaning consequentialism; and (g) sketch a consequentialist pedagogy that incorporates a pedagogy of charity as a tactic to be used until the intentionalist view of meaning it depends upon can be undermined.

A reader may ask why I wish to revisit my earlier work. I do so for a number of reasons:

- In that essay, I emphasized that pedagogies of severity, by conceptualizing students as irrational, incoherent, and error-prone, violate a precondition for interpretation, the principle of charity, thereby leading to breakdowns in communication between teachers and students. But describing *how* these pedagogies of severity violate charity is not an explanation for *why* they do so.

- I am no longer convinced that charitable pedagogy is, without modification and subsequent incorporation into a pedagogy informed by a thinking through of meaning in terms of consequences, sufficient to serve as a viable alternative to pedagogies of severity because the principle of charity depends upon causal and intentionalist versions of meaning apriorism.

- Upon reconsideration of my essay through the lens of meaning consequentialism, I now find that, despite my best efforts, I frequently remained complicit with pedagogies of severity, not only in my conduct in the classroom, but the ways in which I constructed the essay itself.

As I hope should be evident by now, my rereading of this antecedent work will not (a) unearth hidden meanings that slept within the text until now; (b) influence or alter in a single instant the meanings of whatever strands of consequences that my text has already generated; (c) impose by fiat a new, *authorized* meaning of my text that disqualifies any meanings not in conformity to it (i.e., attempt to regain control over the meanings of my text); or (d) ignore whatever resistances I find evoked within me in order to harmonize my earlier advocacy of a pedagogy of charity with my current advocacy of meaning consequentialism (i.e., to gloss over whatever manifestations of meaning apriorism may have informed my earlier construction of a pedagogy of charity to show that, after all, I am quite *consistent*). What I am doing through the performance of this rereading, I suggest, is not retracting what I have said, but *adding* new meanings to the Meaning of that text (i.e., reopening a text that was never closed in the first place, despite its privileged status as a publication).

UNDERSTANDING (THE CONSEQUENCES OF) PEDAGOGIES OF SEVERITY

In my essay, "A Pedagogy of Charity: Donald Davidson and the Student-Negotiated Composition Classroom," whose earliest draft was written in the Spring 1998 semester (nearly two years before I started to work on my dissertation, which was an early draft of the text you are now reading), I discuss the verbal and written responses of my first-year composition students to an anonymous essay—actually written by me—which I asked them to grade as if they were an composition instructor, keeping in mind the kind of comments about their own writing that they found the most or least useful. I was surprised to find that students not only easily adopted the negativism and sarcasm of the stereotypical English teacher in their written comments, but they also enjoyed tearing apart the paper—admittedly, without the "author" present—in a class discussion that was probably the liveliest of the semester. Given some measure of authority over a text, the students did not hesitate to exercise that authority in ways that they had resented when applied to their own texts. Perhaps my surprise reflected my own naïveté, for, as White (1995) has observed, "[i]mproving the bad sentences that other people write is *good fun* and not very difficult, even for students who have a hard time producing good sentences of their own" (p. 16, emphasis added). Good fun, indeed, until it is time for one's own sentence to be scrutinized.

My first attempt to understand what had happened in my classroom during the grading assignment episode led me to focus on the ways that pedagogies of severity violate Davidson's interpretive *principle of charity*. Davidson (1970/1980d; 1973/1984d; 1974/1984a; 1974/1984c; 1976/1980b) argues that the principle of charity, which requires us to accept other people as rational beings with mostly true and coherent beliefs, must be observed if we wish to interpret utterances of interlocutors and (hopefully) communicate with them.[2] In other words, we must optimize our agreements with other interlocutors by accepting that they have reasons for their action—including speech acts—and that there are *veridical* (i.e., causal) relations between these actions and the state of affairs in the world that can, in principle if not in fact, hold between us and the world as well. If we assume uncharitably that interlocutors are non-rational (i.e., that they do not act for reasons), then we could not even guess at the meaning of their utterances because "*any* interpretation would be *equally* likely" (K. Porter, 1998, p. 434).

We must keep carefully in mind the difference between *optimal* agreement and *total* agreement. Charity does not require that a listener accept as true every single belief of a speaker, but it does presume that false beliefs can be reconciled only against a background of widespread agreement. For example, if I disagree with a student's claim that Abraham Lincoln was the twentieth President of the United States, I need not dismiss the student as an irrational being, for the claim itself assumes much that I would accept as true: that Lincoln was a President, that there is an office of the Presidency, that there is a United States government, etc. The disagreement does not reflect a disjunction between incommensurable world views. For Davidson, charity forces us to assume that there are links between what a person believes, what a person does, and what the world is, even if it at the same time does not justify these beliefs or guarantee that any particular utterance is true (Davidson, 1986a); charity can only assure us that a rational being's beliefs are immune from global error, the holding of mostly mistaken beliefs (Davidson, 1970/1980d). In Davidsonian terms, it would be impossible for a rational being to be mistaken most of the time because rationality requires coherence, and it would be very unlikely for the total set of a person's beliefs, if most of them are false, to form an internally coherent set.

Stimulated by Davidson's work, I argued that "the impoverished kinds of discursive options available to my students" and a wider pattern of miscommunications or failures to continue communication in classrooms resulted from the uncharitable ways in which certain pedagogical practices treat students as *error-prone, incoherent,* and *irrational,* and thus in need of constant *surveillance* to discover students' erroneous beliefs or lack of skills, constant *evaluation* that "encourages" students to avoid committing mistakes by punishing them, and constant *guidance* toward pre-determined destinations because students are incapable of initiating any worthwhile inquiry on their own. Worse still, by treating students uncharitably, teachers encourage students to treat teachers uncharitably as well, perpetuating the cycle by inhibiting any kind of transformative dialogue that might break it. I *remain convinced* that pedagogies of severity are uncharitable pedagogies that tend to strain the ability of students to make sense of teachers or educational institutions, and conversely, the ability of teachers and educational institutions to understand, rather than label, students. However, I am *no longer convinced* that the analysis goes far enough toward understanding the reasons motivating these violations of charity in the first place, the other consequences of severity besides violations of charity, or the substantive difficulties surrounding the principle of charity itself.

From where, then, arise these motivations to severity? Is the practice of severity a result of teachers' roles as the sifters and sorters of the workers needed for the machinery of capitalism (cf. Berlin, 1987, 1988; Douglas, 1976/1996; Ohmann, 1976/1996)? Is it the result of personal or institutional prejudices against members of non-privileged races, genders, or social classes (cf. Bernstein, 1971–1975; Hoover and Politzer, 1981; Prendergast, 1998; Smitherman, 1999; Villanueva, 1999)? Even if, as I argued in Chapter 4, my notions about meaning consequentialism put into question aprioristic conceptions of *culture* or *society,* teachers and educational institutions *act* upon discriminatory beliefs about races, classes, and genders; but it is equally clear to me that we cannot use those prejudices to explain all manifestations of severity because not only have forms of severity antedated the rise of capitalism, but they also have been practiced even on students who are identified as members of the most privileged social groups (cf. Murphy, 1990; K. Welch, 1990).

I suggest, then, that although prejudices may exacerbate the excesses of severity, the problem has much deeper roots in the links between meaning apriorism, epistemology, and pedagogy (i.e., links between meaning, knowledge, and teaching). For example, if meaning is conceptualized in rationalist and formalist terms of logical propositions encoded objectively within linguistic tokens, which entails that whatever linguistic tokens *cannot* be read as encoding a logical proposition *cannot* be read as meaningful, and if knowledge is conceptualized as the possession and application of true propositions, then pedagogy becomes a matter of teacher-experts who possess knowledge in certain subjects using utterances and texts with static meanings to convey that knowledge to student-novices who do not have it; the relationship of learning is one-way: Experts do not learn from novices. To prove that they are learning the material, students must repeatedly respond to teacher prompts with verbal and written responses that convey the desired information (whether *propositions* or some vaguer notion of *content*). However, because students may not possess these propositions at all, extract them properly from texts or utterances, or apply them correctly, they often cannot encode them clearly into their utterances and texts, which therefore contain, unlike those of experts, errors and ambiguities. In fact, student utterances and texts (and, consequently, the thought-processes that they are assumed to encode) do not enjoy the presumption of correctness and clarity, but must be first closely scrutinized with an eye or ear toward finding mistakes, falsehoods, and obscurities (i.e., teachers do not read to learn from their students, but to discover what their students have or have not learned); and compared to the exemplary texts of experts, student-authored texts are defective containers of meaning that, in some extreme case, may be so flawed as to convey *no meaning at all,* leading to the conclusion that the students who write these defective texts cannot think at all or can think only defectively or inferiorly. In this way, a pedagogy informed by meaning apriorism can lead to a missionary vision of education in which teaching becomes a matter of introducing pre-existing knowledge to the unenlightened and the dull-witted; writing becomes a matter of encoding this pre-existing knowledge; reading becomes a matter of decoding it; learning becomes a matter of memorizing it; and intelligence becomes a matter of appropriately displaying it. And anything that "shorts" this educational "circuit"—like students who misread or miswrite texts—is treated as a problem in need of a solution. An aside: Nothing in this paragraph will be particularly new to researchers and practitioners in rhetoric and composition familiar with, say, Freire's (1971) deservedly famous critique of the "banking" model of education; but, I suggest, it is important to note that one may arrive at the same destination as Freire without sharing the same point of departure, particularly his investment in Marxism.

But what harm justifies the intensity of the responses to these problems? Why do pedagogies of severity hold such great contempt for the *misreading* and *miswriting* of texts? Why do they labor so hard to eradicate or at least punish them? If misreading and miswriting are simply mistakes that students commit (and some students more than others), then the punishments of severity seem to be, well, more severe than is warranted by the offenses. However, I suggest that the stakes involved are much higher than might seem at first glance: If *properly understood* rather than *resisted* or *dismissed,* students' "misreadings" and "miswritings" would be seen not merely as breaking the transmission of stable meanings channeled through the educational circuit, but as casting doubt on the very existence of that circuit and, by doing so, revealing the truth about pedagogies of severity: *That they do not neutrally transmit neutral, a priori, static meanings, but purposefully and selectively work to sustain a limited range of consequences of certain texts and utterances at the expense of not only of other, unprivileged texts and utterances, but also the very texts and utterances that are privileged.*

Conceptualized in these consequentialist terms, the severity of the response to students' "misreadings" and "miswritings" becomes *understandable,* though hardly *excusable,* because these unruly events threaten the integrity of the semantic and epistemological assumptions of the pedagogical model itself; they also threaten, by implication, the integrity of those dispersed systems—or, better, colloidal laminates (cf. Chapter 1)—outside of educational institutions that also rely on those assumptions. Every moment in the classroom is fraught with danger for that pedagogical model: At any moment, the "transmission" of meanings portrayed as stable and univocal can be unmasked as unstable and fragmentary, even discontinuous, for every assigned reading risks proliferating the consequences of texts, every writing assignment risks exposing the limitations of the assignment (or, better, the lack of limitations, despite the teacher's efforts to disambiguate assignment instruction), and every student response risks altering or challenging the Meaning of the question. Thus, it could be argued that the intolerance of pedagogies of severity results from their fragility—a fragility that is, paradoxically, borne of their rigid conceptions of meaning, knowledge, and pedagogy. As Deleuze conjectures, "If the protests of children were heard in kindergarten, if their questions were attended to, it would be enough to explode our entire educational system. There is no denying that our social system *is totally without tolerance;* this accounts for its extreme fragility in all its aspects and also its need for a global form of repression" (qtd. in Foucault, 1972/1977c, p. 209).

Thinking along these lines has led me to conclude that pedagogies of severity do more than violate the principle of charity; on the contrary, the violation of charity is simply a result of their more general—and frequently successful—*effort to enforce rigid limits on the propagation of consequences of utterances and texts* by promoting a narrow range of meanings of privileged utterances and texts, such as

- teachers' evaluations and grades (e.g., the teacher is an expert whose evaluations carry more weight than students' evaluations of their own work)
- expert, canonical, or exemplary texts (e.g., the teacher selects which texts to read and how those texts are to be acceptably interpreted)

while at the same time striving to diminish the consequentiality of

- student engagement with texts, whether their own, other students,' or published authors'
- the verbal interactions of students with their teachers and with other students

which, at any moment, could overthrow the belief that the privileged set of rigid meanings comprises the *only* set of Meanings for these utterances and texts.

(RE)READING THE SCENE: THE PRACTICE OF SEVERITY BEYOND CHARITY

In this section, I will examine in detail some of the ways in which severity, apart from its violations of the principle of charity, stifled the propagation of consequences, both in my classroom and in my writing of the original essay by promoting and enforcing an "exemplary text" that acts as an *a priori* standard by which all possible responses are to be measured, limiting not only what responses are *acceptable,* but also what answers are *acceptably unacceptable.*

An exemplary text is an actual or idealized text that sets the standards of efficiency by which other texts attempting to perform the same task are judged. In the case of writing assignments, an exemplary text would be either an actual text that the teacher asks students to emulate because it successfully met the demands of the assignment (e.g., a teacher who distributes to her class an "A" paper written by a student she taught in the previous semester), or an idealized template of features that the teacher expects the students' texts to contain (e.g., a teacher who gives full credit to students' short-answers about the causes of the Civil War if and only if they list the four major ones mentioned in class). The exemplary text, then, represents an attempt to impose an *a priori* limitation on what constitutes an acceptable response to a writing assignment—i.e., an attempt to insulate the Meaning of the writing assignment from whatever consequences it generates that deviate from its predetermined outcome by labeling those texts as "defective" and punishing them accordingly. In short, it is a tool for disciplining the potentially destabilizing consequences that any writing assignment generates; and writing assignments which rely upon exemplary texts do not so much ask questions, for the answer is already "known," as demand repetition or imitation of what is presumed to be the already known.

It now seems to me that my antecedent discussion of the grading assignment is haunted by the ghost of the exemplary text, a ghost that I thought I could exorcise by distributing a text that was not represented as or even intended to be a model for the students to copy. But clearly not, for immediately after I observe that the sample was "not meant to be an exemplary text to be copied," I add that my goal was "to see if the students could discern in what ways the text did not fulfill the assignment" (2001, p. 577). The text that I distributed, then, was not, as I conceptualized it, an exemplary text, but its alter-ego, the *flawed* text. A flawed text implies an exemplary text because it is only against a standard of correctness that determinations of error can be made; and, in a sense, the flawed text *is* exemplary in that it exemplifies *what not to do.* What I was asking students to do, then, was use their understanding—so that I could *assess* their understanding—of the implied exemplary text of the writing assignment to identify the elements of the flawed text that did not adhere to the predetermined criteria. What I did not expect or encourage students to do was challenge those predetermined criteria, either in their responses to the sample paper or in their own subsequent drafts of personal narratives.

And, for the most part, the students did not disappoint those expectations: They did not challenge the predetermined criteria in the sense of *rejecting* them, even if they had difficulty at times in determining what they might be or in applying them. Confronted by a text that appeared to resist the requirements of the assignment, the students labored to enforce those requirements, as they understood them, on the text itself—e.g., by altering or, to use Collins's (1999, p. 555) phrase, "talking over" the text with scribbles, overwrites, leading questions, etc. But the students also, through their discussion, labored to enforce those requirements *on each other* by "poisoning the well," so to speak: The public excoriation of the sample paper served as a warning that papers judged to be similar would be similarly treated.

The issues surrounding exemplary texts become even more complicated when including in our thinking the notion that the Meaning of any text is its consequences. This entails, of course, that the stability of the Meanings of writing assignments and their accompanying exemplary texts, whether actual or abstract, results from, and does not cause, the replication of their consequences. And whatever stability of meaning there *is* is always partial and transitory, for no one can comprehend or control all of the consequences of his or her utterances and texts, even for himself or herself (e.g., we cannot rule out the possibility of instances in which the Meaning of a writing assignment and its accompanying exemplary text change as a result of a teacher's reading a student-authored text).

That stability may also be entirely *illusory*, the result of adding meanings to a term without a conscious acknowledgment of the fact that the Meaning of the term has been changed (i.e., the change of Meaning has been "forgotten"). Let us consider how this might happen. Wittgenstein (1953/1968) offers the following puzzle: "Someone says to me: 'Shew the children a game.' I teach them gaming with dice, and the other says, 'I didn't mean that sort of game.' Must the exclusion of the game with dice have come before his mind when he gave me the order?" (I.70). It is impossible to believe that the speaker had mentally catalogued all of the games he knows and carefully separated the acceptable ones from the unacceptable ones; and we might read his response to Wittgenstein's choice of game as simply, "Now that you've made your selection, I find that I don't like it." Or consider how a question like, "What do you believe should be done about the budget surplus?" could prompt the *generation* of those beliefs, rather than a *report* about them. And if I ask, "Do you believe that George W. Bush can wear boots?" and you say, "Yes, of course," does that entail that you had that belief already stored away in your head, even though you would have given the same reply to the same question if asked yesterday, or three weeks ago, or two years ago?

For Wittgenstein, his thought experiment illuminates the fuzziness of concepts or meanings (i.e., that where we usually expect certainty, we may find only ambiguity). However, my consequentialist reading differs from Wittgenstein's (already an indication that even its author cannot control its total set of consequences). I argue that the thought experiment illustrates how the Meaning of an utterance is propagated and extended. Whether the exclusion of dice-games was "in" the original utterance (or even whether the original utterance was "fuzzy") is a moot question, superseded by the subsequent action of the other speaker; the speaker has not "unearthed" a meaning hidden within the utterance, but, by rejecting consequences it initially evoked (i.e., the teaching of the dice-game) or by coming to believe something new about his earlier statement, has imposed one from without.[3] The Meaning of the utterance, of course, isn't determinately settled by this subsequent action, for suppose we rewrite the scenario as follows:

> Someone says to me: "Shew the children a game." I teach them gaming with dice, and the other says, "I didn't mean that sort of game." So I say: "Well, if you didn't want me to teach them gaming with dice, why didn't you say so in the first place? I did exactly what you told me." And the other replies, "Yes, you're right."

The second response, "Yes, you're right," does not return the Meaning of the utterance to its original value (which would require that the intervening consequences had never occurred), but it clearly marks a distancing of the other speaker from one of the consequences of his utterance. *Yet we cannot annul the consequences of our utterances, even if we may try to (and be allowed to) divorce ourselves from some of them!*

The point I am leading to is this: Just as Wittgenstein's interlocutor appears to believe (mistakenly) that he had an *a priori*, determinate list of appropriate and inappropriate games at the time of his initial utterance, so too teachers may believe (mistakenly) that the Meanings of their writing assignments and complementary exemplary texts, actual or ideal, exist independently of and entirely prior to their subsequent efforts to hold students "accountable" to them. For example, a teacher may *decide* to reject a student's use of internet sources for a term paper even if she had never before considered whether to allow them ("I didn't mean by 'This paper should include at least 3 sources' that sort of a source."). Without that subsequent effort, the Meanings of writing assignments are likely to propagate into a diverse and dispersing set of consequences (e.g., the Meaning of "sources" changes); and each of these consequences, *however much it contradicts other consequences,* is a meaning of the particular writing assignment.

For example, let us consider the following admittedly outlandish scenario: In response to a writing assignment, students turn in a variety of papers, some not even in the form of recognizable essays (e.g., one student hands in a photocopy of five pages of the phone book). Each student believes that he or she has fulfilled the terms of the assignment. And each paper, including the photocopied one, receives the grade of A+. What would happen to our conception of the Meaning of the writing assignment if the event constructed by this scenario actually occurred? What would happen to it if any possible written response from a student would be assigned an A+? Most likely, if we had read the writing assignment, we would doubt the *sanity* or integrity of the teacher before we would doubt the *stability* of the Meaning that appears to be encoded in the writing assignment.

But now suppose that we are observers in the classroom, watching the teacher return an entire set of A+ papers to his students. Such a remarkable success rate piques our interest. Suppose we do not have access to the text of the writing assignment, but we manage to collect the entire corpus of papers. What could we *infer* about the Meaning of the writing assignment based on a study of these "exemplary texts"? Perhaps we might *construct* a writing assignment with a question that appears quite different from that posed by the writing assignment. Perhaps we would infer nothing at all about the writing assignment because we are unable to manufacture some underlying commonality that suggests the texts were all *answers* to the *same* question. Or, just perhaps, *we might conclude that the students were not responding to the same question at all, but were in fact each given a different assignment* (i.e., an assignment with a meaning that differs from those of the other assignments) that they individually excelled at completing.

Without access to the *a priori* standard of the writing assignment, we seem to be forced to rely upon inferences or conjectures about what the Meaning of the assignment might be based only on the consequences of the teacher's responses to the students' texts. Had the teacher *responded* differently (and not had the teacher written a different assignment in the first place, for remember that we have no access to that assignment sheet), our estimations of the Meaning of the assignment, including whether there was in fact more than one assignment, would likely be different, too. But we never have access to an *a priori* standard of meaning that preserves itself in perpetuity, whether or not we have physical access to a text, for there is no such standard available; and if that is the case, then we cannot make inferences or conjectures about that standard, even if we believe we are doing so, for there is nothing to infer or conjecture about. Rather, these inferences or conjectures about what the Meaning of an utterance or text might be are actually determinations or, better, inaugurations of some of the actual meanings, however ephemeral, that comprise the temporally distended Meaning of the utterance or text.

The conclusions that I have drawn so far from this scenario do not entail that the teacher didn't have any expectations whatsoever, when writing the assignment sheet, about what kinds of consequences he hoped it would produce in his students. Nor do they entail that the text of the writing assignment was not already consequential for the teacher prior to his distributing copies of it to the class. In this sense, and in only this sense, can the text of the writing assignment be said to have "prior" or, better, antecedent meanings. Nor do they entail that these antecedent meanings must necessarily be challenged by subsequent consequences of the text. What they do entail, however, is that these antecedent meanings, even if they mark the actual limit of the text's consequences (i.e., its Meaning), cannot prevent *a priori* that limit from being transgressed: There is nothing *within* the text with the power to prevent the proliferation of consequences that differ from those consequences intended prior to the completion of the utterance or those generated after it.

My claim that there are actual limits to the consequences of the text is close to Foucault's (1969/1972a) complex notion of the "historical *a priori*," which I quote at length:

> [W]hat I mean by the term is an *a priori* that is not a condition of validity for judgements, but a condition of reality for statements. It is not a question of rediscovering what might legitimize an assertion, but of freeing the conditions of emergence of statements, the laws of their coexistence with others, the specific form of their mode of being, the principles according to which they survive, become transformed, and disappear. An *a priori* not of truths that might never be said, or really given to experience; but the *a priori* of a history that is given, since it is that of things actually said [. . .]. It has to take account of the fact that discourse has not only a meaning or a truth, but a history, and a specific history that does not refer back to the laws of an alien development [. . .]. Moreover, this *a priori* does not elude historicity: it does not constitute, above events, and in an unmoving heaven, an atemporal structure; it is defined as the group of rules that characterize a discursive practice: but these rules are not imposed from the outside on the elements that they relate together; they are caught up in the very things that they connect; and if they are not modified with the least of them, they modify them, and are transformed with them into certain decisive thresholds. The *a priori* of positivities is not only the system of a temporal dispersion; it is itself a transformable group.
>
> Opposed to formal *a prioris* whose jurisdiction extends without contingence, there is a purely empirical figure; but on the other hand, since it makes it possible to grasp discourses in the law of their actual development, it must be able to take account of the fact that such a discourse, at a given moment, may accept or put into operation, or, on the contrary, exclude, forget, or ignore this or that formal structure [. . .].

Nothing, therefore, would be more pleasant, or more inexact, than to conceive of this historical *a priori* as a formal *a priori* that is also endowed with a history: a great, unmoving, empty figure that irrupted one day on the surface of time, that exercised over men's thought a tyranny that none could escape, and which then suddenly disappeared in a totally unexpected, totally unprecedented eclipse. (pp. 127–128)

This is an intricate and compelling argument, though I find Foucault's decision to cling to the term "*a priori*," rather than devise a new one, unnecessary and potentially confusing. More importantly, although I agree with Foucault that we may speak of a history of things actually said—or, from my perspective, a history of actual consequences of utterances or texts—this history is not closed to the future, nor is each specific consequence a carrier of that history. How can one, then, recover this history, when there is no single "now" from which that entire history could be surveyed and when even the attempt to recover that history must necessarily rewrite it and thereby alter it?

Equally troubling, for me, is Foucault's search for the "rules that characterize" discursive practices or for the "laws of their development," because meaning consequentialism rejects "discursive practices" for its implicit simultaneity. As Kent (1999) explains, one can always find some explanation for the occurrence of events after the fact (i.e., one can always manufacture coherence for events after they occur); and we may even call that explanation a *law*. But the question is whether this law in fact governed those events and determined that those events, and only those events, had to occur. Thinking of meaning in terms of consequences leads me to conclude that there are no laws that govern the actual propagation of consequences, but only the efforts of individuals and collectives to impose limits on that propagation; in other words, there are no laws of development for the Meaning of an utterance, but only the purposeful *and* random accretion of dispersed consequences.

I suggest that this analysis clarifies my claims about the fragility of pedagogies of severity, a fragility which results from the fact that pedagogies of severity rely on an ultimately untenable model of meaning that at every moment (i.e., with each question, each test, each assignment that demands *response*) threatens to be exposed for the myth it is. No wonder, then, that so often practitioners of pedagogies of severity use techniques—e.g., multiple-choice tests, scripted teacher-student exchanges (e.g., the "dialogues" read through in language courses), or "educational" software with canned tutorials (e.g., the grammar software distributed for use by minority students that Selfe and Selfe [1994] critique)—in an effort to rig the answers in advance and make errors easy to identify, quantify, and justify. There is little risk to the belief that our meanings represent the Meanings of the questions we ask and the answers we expect if our interlocutors can only respond, even *erroneously,* in the ways we wish them to. Multiple-choice tests, then, are analogous to interrogations in which the inquisitor demands and will accept only a "yes" or "no" answer, ignoring all others responses as out of order. Writing "f" on a test that provides only five choices or leaving the circles blank on the test sheet counts as an "error" as surely as scribbling in the letter that corresponds to an erroneous answer or darkening the wrong circle. No wonder, then, that, insofar as educational institutions that promote pedagogies of severity are concerned, students' papers are reducible to grades that replace and forget the papers they purport to represent.

When handing out copies of the writing assignment, I wasn't distributing documents *containing,* objectively or potentially, all the possible consequences they would evoke in my students, even if that was what I thought I was doing; rather, by disseminating copies of the text in a situation in which its consequences would propagate, I was putting at risk my belief that *my* conception of the writing assignment (i.e., the consequences that it evokes in *me*) represented, and would always represent, its full Meaning. If the students read the text differently, I would either have to abandon my belief and open myself to the reality that the students' readings are alternative, but not defective, meanings of the writing assignment (i.e., that they are meaningful readings of the writing assignment that in fact contribute meanings to the Meaning of it); or, in order to preserve my belief, I would have to find ways to rationalize away the students' readings as "misreadings" and "errors" and then enforce my vision of the Meaning through subsequent actions that punish students for their "faults" (i.e., publicly deprivilege those alternative meanings) and subject them to a discipline that, hopefully, reshapes their interpretations of the writing assignment into likeness of my own exemplary text.

Resisting the Practices of Severity

Anyone who teaches argument must at times feel uncomfortable with what goes on in the class. How often are the student arguments successful in getting someone seriously to reconsider a position? In my experience students spend a great deal of time trying to make their case persuasive to either some universal or fictional audience, and hence they engage in an abstract exercise that they see as merely academic. If anything governs this work, it is the attention to the requirements of a particular form [. . .]. The result is a well-formed essay that, I suspect, has little if any *impact* [italics added] on anybody. I suspect further that the students at some level sense this.

—James L. Kastely

If we wish to replace pedagogies of severity, we must be careful to do so for the right reasons or else risk perpetuating severity in a different form. For example, concerns about traditional writing pedagogies have led some researchers and practitioners to characterize formulaic academic writing assignments and traditional, teacher-oriented assessment as distortions of *normal* discourse. Applebee (1981), for instance, charges that to position teachers as the sole readers of students' work is "to create writing situations with atypical audiences" that "destroy the normal intention to communicate" (p. 5); without such intentions, students' writing is an exercise in "pointlessness" more focused on recitation than communication (p. 52; cf. Shelton, 1994, pp. 8–9). For some critics, traditional academic writing assignments and assessment *subvert* language use to the point where teachers form not simply an "atypical audience" (after all, many specialized audiences could be labeled as "atypical," and what exactly would be a "typical" audience?), but an *unreal* audience, as opposed to "a real audience" (Shaughnessy, 1977, p. 39), whose unreality in part stems from its penchant for commandeering the texts it reads (cf. Adler-Kassner, 1998). "Real" audiences reside and "real" writing tasks occur outside of classrooms in the "real world" (e.g., Dorman and Dorman, 1997; Heilker, 1997; Kixmiller, 2004; Mansfield, 1996; Rudinow and Barry, 1999; Stevenson, 1985; Trimmer, 1999), and only such tasks can foster "real" investment on the part of students.[4] Without such "real" investment in "real" projects, students' writing may be grammatically correct, but lifeless—e.g., Coles's (1978) "themewriting," Macrorie's (1970) "Engfish," Petraglia's (1995) "inauthentic writing," Tamor and Bond's (1983) "pseudotransactional writing," and White's (1995) "McPaper."

As much as we may dislike the impoverished, even damaging consequences that tend to result from pedagogies of severity, it is not accurate to say that these practices violate the normal workings of discourse. *The effort to limit the propagation of consequences is not unnatural: It does not distort meaning, language, or discourse, forcing them to do things that they would not otherwise be capable of doing.* Such an effort does not represent a *catastrophe* from outside of meaning, language, or discourse that thwarts their otherwise smooth operation (cf. Derrida, 1967/1976). Nor is it something peculiar to academia or academic writing: Efforts are made to restrict, privilege, or disallow certain consequences of texts in the "real world," too. Academia isn't the only setting in which meaning apriorism shapes the ways in which people conceive of texts and utterances as conveyances of meanings. For example, much of the writing done in settings outside of academia (e.g., memos, business reports, contracts, tax returns) are disciplined to limit the range of acceptable consequences *and* acceptably unacceptable consequences, with people held accountable to privileged meanings of these documents; and writing outside of academia may be written in fact for only a single evaluator who is as unsympathetic, unreasonable, and uncharitable as even the strictest teacher. The teacher is but one coercer among many; and our students must cope, as must we all, with the pressures placed upon us by literate practices we do not create, with audiences we do not willingly choose, and with consequences our texts and utterances generate we do not intend.

For pedagogies of severity to be unnatural, they would have to violate something more than our *goals* for writing classes, our *beliefs* about what constitutes a valuable writing assignment, and our *conceptions* of proper teacher-student and student-student relations; and they would have to violate something more than even the principle of charity. To be *unnatural*, they would have to *violate the premises of meaning consequentialism itself*, which would require that they not simply render certain utterances and texts inconsequential—for this fits comfortably within thinking of meaning in terms of consequences—but *produce* utterances and texts whose Meanings are not consequences of them and whose Meanings are immune to the consequences propagated by them. Meaning consequentialism does not *require* that all utterances and text be consequential, nor does it even *describe* at what point an inconsequential text becomes a consequential text; it only *asserts* that, if a text is to be meaningful, it cannot be *non-consequential:* It must propagate consequences of some sort, for those consequences are its meanings. As a result, *we cannot reject pedagogies of severity on the grounds that they violate meaning consequentialism, for they do not violate its premises.* Rather, we should reject pedagogies of severity because *we as educators*—and not some abstract entity called *meaning consequentialism*—find that the specific consequences of specific pedagogical practices harm our students; and we—and not meaning consequentialism—decide what constitutes *harm.* Simply put, there is nothing *in* the workings of discourse to prevent pedagogies of severity from being practiced, just as nothing *in* the workings of discourse sustains them. Meaning consequentialism is not something that *proscribes* pedagogies of severity or *condemns* meaning apriorism; rather, it provides us with *a way of understanding* why a person who wishes to enact a pedagogy of severity, who wants to wield absolute control over the consequences of his or her utterances, or who believes that meanings are fully determinate must be prepared to (a) work very hard (b) for an indefinite period of time (c) without an assurance of success (with success measured by whether students learn only what they are supposed to learn, whether our utterances produce consequences we did not intend or want, or whether everyone who hears an utterance is in agreement about what it "means").

It is crucial to note that our concerns about particular forms of coercion should not lead us to (or spring from) a dream of *a time without constraint* when meanings propagate limitlessly—as if the *absence of constraint* were the highest possible good; as if meanings in themselves *want* to propagate and will do so unless thwarted by people with sinister motivations; as if thinking of meanings in terms of consequences requires one to adopt as an ethical stance the position that all consequences must be allowed to propagate. Our utterances *are* consequential, and, because they are consequential, we have good reason to be concerned about them. How could we not? Who would dispute that our utterances have consequences? However, what would be disputed are beliefs about, for example, (a) the identity of specific consequences of specific utterances (b) the desirability or morality of those consequences that are mutually recognized, or (c) the extent to which people should be held accountable for the consequences of what they say.

I suggest that the proposals offered and enacted by some of the very researchers and practitioners who want to infuse "real world writing assignments" and assessment into otherwise "unreal world" classrooms can help us move toward a more fruitful way of characterizing and re- solving the problems with traditional writing assignments and assess- ment than asserting a mythical separation of academia from a world outside of it (cf. Ackerman and Oates, 1996; Trimbur, 2000b) or as- serting a division between "unnatural" and "natural" discourse, ever could. For example, a frequently advocated assignment is letter-writ- ing, in which the finished letter is mailed to someone other than the instructor, whether it be to an editor of a newspaper, a business, a pro- fessional, or a consumer (e.g., Ellis, 1999; D. Hall and Nelson, 1987; Martin, 1983; Stoddard, 1985). Other common assignments include writing proposals or technical reports that are subsequently submitted to businesses or other public organizations (e.g., Burnett, 1996; Cheryl Reed, 1996), or writing texts for distribution to members of local com- munities or for publication in a variety of forums, including electronic media (e.g., Beidler and Mackes, 1986; Janangelo, 1998; Parks and Goldblatt, 2000; Aaron Schutz and Gere, 1998). In some cases, edu- cators argue that students, as well as their texts, must be physically removed from classrooms and thrust into public or civic activities (e.g., Chaput, 2000; Selfe and Selfe, 1996); as a result, we find an increas- ing interest in service-learning that combines classroom activities with community service or professional internships (e.g., N. Bacon, 1997; Hilosky, Moore, and Reynolds, 1999; Huckin, 1997; Minter, Gere, and Keller-Cohen, 1995; Peck, Flower, and Higgins, 1995; Savage, 1997). Rather than saying that what unites these alternative pedagogi- cal practices is the attempt to make student writing "real," I suggest that we can conceptualize these practices instead as efforts to extend the *consequences* of student-authored texts by finding audiences for them comprised of, or at least including people other than, teachers[5]; but notice that to say we want to *extend* the consequences of student- authored texts is already to accept that traditional student-authored texts produce *some* consequences, even if only a few.

We must be careful, however, that our proposals for alternative pedagogies do not enact the same aprioristic premises about meaning, language, and discourse that underlie pedagogies of severity; importing "real world" writing assignments into the classroom or exporting students and their writing from it without also challenging these aprioristic premises can only end up perpetuating the kind of thinking that limits the propagation of consequences of texts and utterances, especially those of students, in the first place. Let us consider four examples of how this might happen: (a) Kaufer and Carley's (1994) proposal to set student texts in competition with each other, with a text's grade determined by how well that text monopolizes the class's attention; (b) Shelton's (1994) conception of technical writing as the smooth transfer of clear information, whereas academic writing relies on obfuscating jargon; (c) Aaron Schutz and Gere's (1998) warning that service-learning courses with a tutoring component can reinforce, rather than question, transmission models of education by placing students in the role of expert; and (d) Herzberg's (2000) effort to encourage students to "imagine" how to "translate" their researched, academic arguments on particular issues into more suitable forms for public dissemination and consumption.

First, Kaufer and Carley (1994) argue that classrooms do not adequately simulate what they call the "reach" of written documents, "the number of people whose mental model an individual can affect with a signatured communication" (p. 25). In the "real world," writers must compete for the attention of readers, and their rewards for writing, especially for professional writers, are "commensurate with their reach" (p. 38); but in the classroom,

> [s]tudents, on the other hand, must subsidize their readers (teachers), and the reach of their work is almost never measured as a dependent variable. Their texts are seldom put in a competitive situation where they have to compete for readers based on principles of relative similarity with the reading audience. In sum, classrooms are seldom organized to simulate, even in the weakest respects, the distance characteristics of written and print communication in the real world. (p. 38)

To rectify this situation, Kaufer and Carley suggest simulating this "free market" of texts, which can be done

> by having a teacher grade a student's text on the voluntary circulation it achieves in competition with

other texts. In addition, if reading is taught [. . .].
Lessons in multiplicity can help students understand
why writing and reading are competitive activities (as
copies of a few excellent student texts can potentially
hog all the cognitive reading resources of the remaining members of the class). Nominating excellent student texts to become models for future classrooms
provides students with an excellent lesson in durability. (p. 38)

Though it may be a novel twist to let students in essence "vote"
through their reading preferences for the grades that papers will receive, the result—a grading scale that ensures some papers must receive poor marks—is hardly innovative. And one wonders whether
this lesson is even needed, or merely reaffirms students, as do many of
the lessons performed by pedagogies of severity, of what they already
know: That "exemplary texts"—or "models," as Kaufer and Carley
call them—can be privileged only at a cost paid by those texts that are
not exemplary. And it should be noted (again) that this privileging of
exemplary texts requires continued effort: "excellent students texts" do
not "potentially hog all the cognitive reading resources of the remaining members of the class" because of some vitality they possess, but
must be made to do so by classroom practices that encourage this to
happen by working to make it happen (e.g., by requiring students to
read these texts or by ensuring that there is time only for students to
read the "best" texts).

Second, Shelton (1994), in his manual for technical writers, argues that, whereas academic writing demands the demonstration of
learning in order to impress teachers, writing in the "real workplace"
requires the smooth "transfer of information and ideas" from authors
presumed to know what they are doing by their audience (pp. 8–9).
Shelton does acknowledge the importance of readers in determining
whether a text is successful: "Readers dictate the success of any piece of
writing. It doesn't matter how well you understand the subject matter
if your readers miss the message. If they don't understand, your writing has failed. Think first of your audience. Evaluate their needs as
well as their ability to understand technical content" (p. 4). However,
we should note that "success," for Shelton, is measured by the conveyance of content: If the text is unable to deposit the content it carries,
it is, like a ship that is unable to deliver its cargo intact, a failure.

The readers do not affect the meaning of the document, but may only block its transmission.

Third, Schutz and Gere (1998) advocate service learning because "it brings into classroom discourses and activities in the world outside the academy, mediating the relationships between the discourses and needs of the academy and those of actual community contexts" (p. 147). However, they caution that service learning courses that involve students as tutors in local communities may devolve, if the students' classroom work lacks a critical dimension, into situations in which the students see themselves as the "saviors" of their tutees (p. 133) by bringing knowledge to unenlightened, even "alien" communities (p. 134). Rather than overturning the expert-novice distinction of pedagogies of severity, these courses simply "promote" students to the status of experts, the possessors of "an expert knowledge of literacy that cannot be entirely transformed and contextualized through the tutor-tutee relationship" (p. 134). As Schutz and Gere point out, tutors are not immune from change based on their tutoring experiences, but such moments are rare: "Although there are moments of promise, tutees like David never become equal participants in the relationship, as the child never possesses a store of knowledge or discursive skills that can be placed on the same level as that of any tutor—in a sense, this inequality is central to the very definition of 'tutor'" (pp. 134–135). Of course, teachers who practice pedagogies of severity aren't immune to change based on their own experiences, either, but that's not at issue: The point is that such moments only cast in doubt the aprioristic transmission model to which missionary-style service learning projects subscribe.

And fourth, Herzberg (2000) describes a course that he teaches in which he encourages students to think about how to bridge the gap between academic discourse and public discourse; it is a course that asks the question, "How could you—or someone who held your position on the issue you have studied and who was motivated to do so—bring your arguments effectively before the public?" (p. 395).[6] Agreeing with Wells's (1996) assessment of formulaic writing assignments, "such as an essay on gun control, or a letter to a nonexistent editor" (p. 328), Herzberg encouraged his students to think about the following questions: "What is going to happen to your work when you are finished? Will it go anywhere other than my desk? Can we imagine ways of going public?" (p. 399). Herzberg was pleased by the students' efforts, which included proposals for letters to specific editors of actual newspapers or news magazines, fliers for local distribution, internet postings, even a benefit rock concert. I suggest, however, that by only "imagining" the discourse "going public," Herzberg converts what could be an assignment that propagates the consequences of student texts beyond the classroom into an assignment that *only imagines it does;* after all, is there much difference between the consequentiality of a text written for a nonexistent editor that is read only by the teacher and of a text written for an actual editor that is only read by the teacher? Herzberg is not unaware of such an objection, for immediately after conceding that merely a handful of these proposals were ever carried out, he states that "only a few of the efforts had the feel, to me, of a fake exercise. When I raised that possibility with students, however, they told me that I was the only one worried about it" (p. 401). (Of course, would students admit to their instructor that, in fact, their writing was unmotivated, fake, formulaic?) Perhaps more importantly, Herzberg says nothing about the consequences of those few texts that were sent out, as if the course ended at the point where the texts were "finished" enough to be disseminated. Did the texts do what their authors hoped? Did the Meanings of their texts surpass their efforts to control them? Without extending its scope beyond the point of "imagining" consequences beyond the classroom to the point of generating consequences beyond it, Herzberg's course, I suggest, risks perpetuating the faulty notion that what happens after a text is written has no bearing on what that text Means—a notion that will not be challenged if nothing happens after a text is written. *Simply imagining that something could happen is insufficient.*

I suggest that these few examples illustrate that it isn't enough to extend particular, privileged consequences of student utterances and texts—whether in the form of advice to tutees, letters to the editor, community newsletters, local fliers, or technical reports—while at the same time fostering and validating misconceptions about the meanings and Meanings of utterances and texts that work in tandem with efforts to suppress non-privileged consequences. In short, leaving the classroom need not be a challenge to the premises about the consequentiality or inconsequentiality of students' utterances and texts that underlie pedagogies of severity.

On the other hand, we do not necessarily need to leave the classroom or import "real world" assignments into the classroom in order to resist pedagogies of severity and their manifestations of meaning apriorism. I will argue that we can begin to undermine both severity and meaning apriorism through a *consequentialist pedagogy* that encourages suppleness in interpretation not only by readers and listeners (students *and* teachers), but also by writers and speakers (again, students *and* teachers). This flexibility, I suggest, tends to extend the consequences of texts and utterances by promoting continued dialogue about them. Such a pedagogy would resist notions of texts as "static" or "closed" (a) by fostering situations in which students and teachers are "surprised by response," (b) by enacting the open-endedness of texts through revisions based on those responses, and (c) by revealing to students and teachers how what they thought was the Meaning of a text may change—or, better, be shown to be only one of the meanings of the Meaning of the text—*without a single physical change being made to the text itself.*

Toward a Consequentialist Pedagogy

My original diagnosis of the problem with pedagogies of severity (i.e., that they violate the principle of charity) led me to an obvious solution: Practice a pedagogy that observes the principle of charity (i.e., practice a pedagogy that encourages teachers and students to act on the assumption that everyone in the classroom is a rational being with mostly true and coherent beliefs). I hoped that the practice of charity would promote flexibility in interpretation by delaying, if not ultimately preventing, the determination that text features were "mistakes"; such a determination, by rationalizing the reader's confusion away as a result of a flawed text, often marks the end of engagement with a text and its author (i.e., "I don't need to puzzle over this any more—it's just a mistake"); a reader who hastily labels text elements as "errors" (or texts themselves as "defective") is a reader unwilling to be changed by what he or she reads, a reader who is trying to inoculate himself or herself from propagating the consequences of texts. A charitable pedagogy, then, is valuable to the extent that it encourages interlocutors, writers, and readers to keep open the lines of communication that could conceivably transform all of the parties involved.

However, as it is currently formulated, a pedagogy of charity provides an insufficient alternative to pedagogies of severity, in two ways: (a) without modification, the principle of charity is incompatible with meaning consequentialism; and (b) without modification, a pedagogy of charity cannot address the wider suppression of the consequences of utterances and texts practiced by pedagogies of severity. What I propose to do in this final section, then, is sketch a consequentialist pedagogy that, in a principled way, preserves the dialogic productivity of a pedagogy of charity without clinging to aprioristic conceptions of meaning, language, and discourse that tend to undermine such productivity.

Reconfiguring the Principle of Charity

For Davidson, the principle of charity is, *a priori*, a precondition for *interpretation,* not only of linguistic signs, but also of the actions of rational agents generally. By *rational,* Davidson (1976/1980a) means only that rational agents act for reasons (i.e., that person *x* says *y* because he believes *z*), not that these reasons are necessarily justified or even well-conceived (i.e., person *x* may say, "Don't sail past the Canary Islands" because he believes that the world is flat and comes to end just beyond sight of the Canary Islands). For Davidson, reasons, whether justified or not, have causal efficacy: The reason why a rational agent performs an action is the cause of that action, and that reason, in effect, supplies and determines the "meaning" of the action, distinguishing it from other actions that, outwardly at least, may be indistinguishable (i.e., the action is meaningful because it is done for a reason, and the particular meaning it has is fully determined by that reason). For example, a person's act of running may be interpreted as "running because he's late for the bus" (if I see him heading in the direction of a bus stop where a bus is getting ready to leave) or as "running because he wants to stay in shape" (because of the kind of clothes he is wearing), but which act it *is* depends upon what that person believes it to be or intends it to be.

What is important to note is how Davidson, despite his efforts to weaken the principle of charity to a presumption of and not guarantor for reasons that themselves may not be justified, conceives of successful interpretation (i.e., communication) as an uncovering of the actual causal/rational/intentional relations between a person's beliefs about the world, a person's actions in the world, and the actual state of affairs of the world because those relations determine the meaning of an action or utterance.[7] Charity may be a weak foundation for interpretation, but only in the *epistemological* sense that it precludes our ever knowing for sure that we are dealing with a rational agent or that our interpretations are accurate, not in the *semantic* sense that it precludes a causal or intentional determination of meaning. As Davidson configures it, charity does not resist semantic foundations, but depends upon them, because Davidsonian interpretation not only requires the presumption that a person has a reason for doing x or saying y (i.e., interpretation requires that one *treat* an interlocutor as a rational agent who has intentions that motivate and determine the characterization of his actions), but it also requires, if it is to be successful (and validates, if it is successful) that the interpreter decipher(ed) the *actual* reason for that person's doing x or saying y (i.e., successful interpretation requires that one actually be interacting with a rational agent whose intentions determine the meanings of his actions). In other words, the requirement of charity that interlocutors presume each other to be rational beings who have and act upon mostly true and coherent beliefs can only be a requirement if successful interpretation in fact depends upon whether interlocutors *are* rational beings who have and act upon mostly true and coherent beliefs. In short, despite Davidson's interest in the reception or interpretation of utterances rather than in their production, his conception of the speaker as final arbiter of meaning fits comfortably within manifestations of meaning apriorism that ground and freeze meaning in a speaker's or writer's intentions.

Equally troubling is Davidson's claim that the principle of charity governs the interpretation of utterances and actions (i.e., that to begin the process of interpretation, one must charitably assume that potential interlocutors are rational beings with mostly true and coherent beliefs). Davidson's philosophy, then, does not offer a general account of interpretation, but a more limited account of the interpretation of the linguistic signs and actions of rational agents. Thus, charity cannot govern—and Davidson's account cannot explain—the interpretation (i.e., the propagation of meanings) of utterances, actions, and/or other signs produced by (a) a "divinity" who is assumed to have beliefs that are totally true and coherent, (b) beings assumed to be non-rational agents (e.g., the "uncivilized," the mentally infirm, infants, animals)[8]; (c) a non-agentive reality (e.g., footprints, tree rings, light wavelengths, etc.). In other words, there are instances of interpretation in which charity is *superseded* because one's interlocutor is presumed infallible, *violated* because one's interlocutor is presumed to be non-rational, or *irrelevant* because one has no interlocutor at all.

Davidson might well respond, "So what? I never suggested that my theory would explain these instances." And that would be correct. But I would argue that Davidson, if he wishes to contrast interpretation that is governed by charity from interpretation that is not governed by it, has formed an opposition so strong that it is difficult to conceptualize what might be the commonalities that unite them under the rubric of *interpretation*. Similarly for *meaning*: Some meanings are set by intentions, some not, but what would suggest to us that the same term, *meaning*, would be applicable to both?[9] But suppose we grant that, in fact, interpretation can be divided up into charitable and noncharitable types. I would then argue that since charity does not extend to all cases of interpretation, it is a misnomer to call it an *interpretive* principle; rather, it would be applicable only to a subset of interpretation—in Davidson's case, a subset that conceives of its telos in terms of *communication* between rational agents (i.e., the correct decipherment of an utterance's or action's meaning as set by intention). The principle of charity, then, would not be an *interpretive* principle, but a *communicative* principle; and violating charity would not, then, lead to breakdowns of interpretation, which could proceed without it, but to breakdowns in communication between interlocutors.

But is charity, even limited in this way, a viable concept? Does it account even for that subset of interpretation it claims to govern (i.e., the utterances and actions of rational agents)? I contend that it cannot because, as I indicated earlier, charity rests on the false assumption that meanings—or at least some subset of meanings—are in fact determined by intentions. That is, if charity is conceptualized as governing the interpretation of utterances and actions whose meanings are determined by the intentions of actors, *then there is nothing for it to govern*. It is not a king without a kingdom, but a king who *never* had a kingdom. What Davidson fails to see, I suggest, is that the principle of charity will *appear* to be a principle governing the interpretation of language (or non-linguistic signs that express propositional content) only if one accepts and acts upon an *a priori* intentionalist theory of meaning and a temporally flattened, holistic conception of mind (i.e., one in which at any given moment a person has a quantifiable, if not specifiable, number of beliefs that form a coherent "web"). Take away those presumptions, and charity loses its anchorage.

Davidson's mistake, however, also points to a way of salvaging the principle of charity, at least temporarily and in a weakened form. Rather than conceptualizing charity as a *transcendental* principle for interpretation (i.e., something that is imposed onto interpretation from the "outside"), I suggest that charity is best conceived as a *normative* principle for discourse that emerges from certain beliefs that certain people hold about "interpretation" and meaning. People may act upon the principle of charity in consequential ways, including ways that hold other interlocutors accountable to it, without charity as they conceive it actually governing those interactions, in the same way that people may act upon, and hold other people accountable to, a host of false beliefs without the success of their actions being attributable to those false beliefs—that is, I may believe I am "interpreting" a text even if I am actually encountering it through an immediated expropriation. In other words, we might think of the principle of charity as marking the *limit of the willingness* of a person who thinks of himself or herself along the lines of a *Davidsonian interpreter* to engage with the utterances and actions of others, not the *limit of interpretation* itself. We might also think of it as an *expectation* that such a Davidsonian interpreter has for the proper reception of his or her own utterances and text—an expectation that, if disappointed by an interlocutor unwilling to treat him or her as a rational agent with mostly true and coherent beliefs, might result in the Davidsonian interpreter's unwillingness to engage in further dialogue with that person. Consequently, someone who or something that fails to play the game that a Davidsonian interpreter assumes *must* be played—becomes impossible—in a normative, not transcendental sense—to understand and speak to.

Charity and a Consequentialist Pedagogy

What role, if any, would this normative principle of charity play in a consequentialist pedagogy? An important, but ultimately reduced, role: It no longer serves, as I originally thought, as *the linchpin for an alternative pedagogy to severity,* but rather as *a tool whose usefulness may diminish through time,* in a way similar to Wittgenstein's view of his philosophy as a ladder that, once climbed, will have served its purpose and should be discarded. Charity cannot be abandoned entirely because, as I have argued, pedagogies of severity do violate the (now normative) principle of charity, *but only for those students for whom charity is an important consideration:* Charity can be violated only when it is at issue (i.e., severity as the limiting of consequences of student texts could operate even for people who have no investment in charity).

I suggest that our classrooms are populated, though not exclusively, by students who conceive of themselves as beings who act on beliefs that generally fit together and accurately represent the actual state of affairs of the world and who assume that their intentions determine the meanings of their utterances and texts, and that these students will frequently find the practices of severity uncomfortable. These students will resent characterizations of their work that differ from their understandings of it, and will resent overwrites, corrections, or other alterations to texts that change what they perceive as the meanings they put there in the first place; and they will resent other features of severity that put into question their status as rational beings, promoting the cessation of dialogue between students, teachers, and school administrators.

If our immediate concern is to ameliorate the most corrosive effects of severity caused by its violations of charity (i.e., the discouragement of dialogue and the disregard for what students say and write), then the fastest way to bring relief to our students would be to practice a consequentialist pedagogy that, at least at first, embraces the observance of charity and exposes for students the ways in which severity (a) impoverishes dialogue and the interpretation of utterances and texts and (b) limits the propagation of the consequences of students' work. It would be counterproductive, I suggest, to practice a consequentialist pedagogy that immediately puts into questions both the formalist conception of meaning underlying severity and the intentionalist conception underlying charity, because it would risk alienating students who find either—or both conceptions (i.e., that texts contain the meanings put in them by their authors)—intuitively obvious. *Thus, the practice of charity in a consequentialist pedagogy is a tool used to keep open the possibility of dialogue when interacting with students who accept and act upon the principle of charity;* for until—if at all—students agree that the intentionalist view of meaning and the holistic conception of mind have been discredited, the observation of charity would be necessary to promote continuing dialogues between teachers and students and among students. And it is only through such a continuing dialogue that charity could itself eventually be put in question and perhaps discarded; for a pedagogy that alienates students is a pedagogy that will be hard pressed to persuade students.

However, given the limitations of composition courses (both in terms of time and of their ability to persuade students to abandon

deeply held beliefs), and given the entrenchment of intentionalist conceptions of meaning, it may very well be that charity, even in its weakened form, can never be entirely discarded (and it should be noted that
a consequentialist pedagogy would not discount intentions entirely,
but only their privileged role as the final arbiter of what an utterance
or text means). Still, I would suggest that even my original formulation
of a pedagogy of charity, with its fostering of dialogue and respect for
students' work, would at least be preferable to the practice of severity,
even if such a pedagogy ends up perpetuating aprioristic conceptions
of meaning. Why? Because by encouraging the discussion of, rather
than dismissal of, students' work, such a pedagogy would, even if inadvertently, encourage the proliferation of consequences of students'
texts and utterances about those texts, and each of these consequences
has the potential to shock or surprise the intentionalist conception of
meaning that charity supports. In other words, the very practice of a
pedagogy of charity, like the practice of severity, always puts at risk the
very conception of meaning it believes (falsely) that is forced upon it,
when in fact it assumes, acts upon, and enforces that conception.

Practicing a Consequentialist Pedagogy

The goals of a consequentialist pedagogy, as I conceive of it, are three-
fold: (a) to encourage the propagation of consequences of texts and
utterances, particularly those of students; (b) to promote flexibility
in interpretation and in response to others' interpretations not only
by readers and listeners (teachers and students), but also by writers
and speakers (teachers and students); and (c) to explicate, illustrate,
advocate, *and make contestable* premises of meaning consequentialism.
These three goals must work in tandem if they are to work at all:
Without (b) and (c), (a) could easily collapse into situations in which
students' texts are simply added to the total set of exemplary texts or in
which students assume they are in full control of their meanings; without (a) and (b), the explicit discussion—and interrogation—of meaning consequentialism would risk appearing to be arid, even dogmatic
speculation that lacks a connection to the practices of and purposes
behind pedagogy. It is important to note that these goals can never
be definitively achieved, in that they require continued work to sustain them: A consequentialist pedagogy has no more inertia than do
pedagogies of severity. The consequences of students' texts and utterances will only proliferate if teachers and students work to proliferate

them, and meaning consequentialism can only be made contestable if teachers are willing to allow it to be contested (i.e., teachers must be flexible enough to recognize that the Meaning of meaning consequentialism is open-ended). From the perspective of a consequentialist pedagogy, the chief value of such propagation is in its potential to expose through the surprises of response the limitations of aprioristic conceptions of meaning; after all, one cannot be surprised by response if one does not ask for, expect, or receive any responses.

How, then, might a consequentialist pedagogy be enacted? Given the complexity of the issues it addresses, and the limits on what can be accomplished in a single semester, the shape of such a pedagogy would, obviously, depend upon the particular interests and goals of the instructor and her students. In what follows, I describe in some detail three directions that the practice of consequentialist pedagogy might assume: service learning, "movies of the mind" peer responses, personal narratives.

Service Learning. Service learning is a powerful tool for encouraging the proliferation of consequences for students' writing because it situates students and their texts in wider forums than the classroom. However, as I indicated earlier, it can easily lead to a situation in which students assume the roles of expert-teachers with predetermined meanings to transmit to their tutees. To avoid this problem, Aaron Schutz and Gere (1998) argue that service learning should incorporate what they call a "'public' model" (p. 144) that produces "structures that allow those who are 'served' to become more active members of a public space where the differences participants bring with them become productive and crucial contributions to the development of the common project" (p. 144). For example, Schutz and Gere recommend projects that "focus on the needs of the students' campus community [which] may make it more difficult for students to treat the "others" they meet there—often their own peers—as less than equal participants" (p. 144). Done well, they argue, service learning places "those in positions of privilege and power in the university [. . .] in the positions of 'learners,' as they request and negotiate entrée into communities, often disenfranchised communities, within and beyond their own" (p. 146).

But even this is not enough, if the collaborations that service learning fosters culminate in written projects whose meanings are conceived in *a priori* terms (e.g., that a proposal "contains" an argument, albeit one constructed by multiple authors). From the perspective of a consequentialist pedagogy, the chief value of service learning is realized by an accompanying critical examination of the consequences generated by the collaborative interactions, verbal and written, between students and their peers outside the classroom leading up to the "completion" of the project (e.g., a proposal to be submitted to the student government association or a local library), and, of equal if not more importance, the consequences that result from the project itself. For example, a consequentialist pedagogy would pursue such questions as:

- Was the letter written to the editor of a local newspaper actually sent? Was it published? Did others read and respond to it? Did the letter produce the desired consequences? Did its Meaning fragment? If so, in what ways?
- Were the fliers that the group planned to distribute actually distributed, and where? Were some of the fliers "overwritten" or buried and forgotten under later postings?
- In what ways did the Meaning of the project change through time, not only in its development, but through its dissemination? Which meanings were propagated, which abandoned or "forgotten," and why? What work was required—or attempted—to keep the meanings of the project from proliferating out of control?

By including this critical component to a service-learning course, the "success" or "failure" of the course need not be predicated on the success or failure of the particular students' projects, for even those that produce limited consequences (e.g., a proposal that is rejected or even returned unread, fliers that are mutilated) serve as (i.e., are consequential as) useful examples for understanding the consequential nature of meaning.

Movies of the Mind. Elbow's (1973, 1986) notion of "movies of the mind" as a method of responding to texts, suitably modified, could be a useful pedagogical strategy that encourages the propagation of consequences of texts and makes them manifest. This method, developed by Elbow (1973) for his "teacherless" writing class, is an attempt to help writers understand what their "words make happen in readers" (p. 76). It works as follows:

> Everyone reads everyone else's writing. Everyone tries
> to give each writer a sense of how his words were ex-

perienced. The goal is for the writer to come as close
as possible to being able to see and experience his own
words *through* seven or more people. That's all.

> To improve your writing you don't need advice
> about what changes to make; you don't need theories
> of what is good and bad writing. You need movies of
> people's minds while they read your words. (p. 77)

The responses that readers offer, according to Elbow, are not answers
to "a timeless, theoretical question about the objective qualities of
those words on that page [. . .] [but] a time-bound, subjective but
factual question: what happened in you when you read the words this
time" (p. 85). Although Elbow conceives of the response occurring at
the end of the reading (or listening, in cases where the author reads her
text aloud), it could also be performed "on-line," so to speak, as the
reader reads the text.

However, Elbow's technique, despite its salutary interest in the
consequences of texts as they made manifest through readers, remains
locked within an aprioristic conception of meaning that mixes formalism, constructivism, and social constructivism by postulating that
texts do not "contain" meanings but only "a set of directions" (p. 152)
for readers to build meanings "in the head" that may be similar to
those in the writer's head, with the "correct reading of a text" determined by the interpretation "which the speech community builds into
those words" (p. 156) or "*could build in* without violating its rules" (p.
157). It is unclear to me how postulating a text's containing a "set of
directions" for meaning is any different from postulating its containing a meaning in the first place. To conceive of the text as a set of
directions is already to conceive of it as having certain meanings that
provide the desired destination for any interpretation of it. Thus, as
much as he values the responses of actual readers, Elbow argues that
they "never see accurately enough, experience fully enough. There are
always things in the words you cannot get" (p. 100) because speech
communities, not individual readers, determine the meanings of the
text—that is, there are only certain "movies permitted by the speech
community's rules" (p. 157). In other words, over and above the actual
readers that a text may encounter, who may or may not conform to the
movie-script prepared in advance for them, there is an *idealized reader*
who represents the "speech community" with perfect fidelity and who

always knows which "movies" are "permitted by the speech community's rules." As a result, writers are advised to listen to these responses and "take it in, but not be paralyzed or made helpless by it" (p. 104), *even if the total set of actual readers are unanimous in their interpretations of the text* (pp. 104–105), because those readers do not comprise the full membership of the speech community.

Elbow is correct that readers never experience the full Meaning of a text, but not because there are "things in the words" that lay hidden from readers; rather, it is because the text has produced different consequences in different readers, including the author, *none of whom ever experiences the full Meaning of the text*. In addition, there is no "community" that determines the meanings that comprise the Meaning of a text, but only a temporally distended colloidal laminate comprised of networked individuals for whom that text is consequential, a laminate that did not exist—either actually, virtually, or potentially—prior to the text, but was inaugurated by it; bringing the text into consequential contact with other readers does not insert the text into a pre-existing discourse community, but rather extends the laminated communities of the text. Thus, there is no "higher court of appeal" for meaning that the writer may legitimately call upon above and beyond the actual consequences that his text propagates, whether for himself or for his readers. How the writer reacts to those responses, of course, is for her to decide: Does she believe in the myth of the idealized reader or the notion that texts contain a set of instructions? Does she try to persuade readers to experience his text differently? Does she ignore her immediate audience and seek the evaluations of other readers, whose readings might be similar to her own?

Thus, rather than a vehicle for "improving" writing, a consequentialist pedagogy would use the "movies of the mind" technique to interrogate the relationships between text and response, writers and readers, meanings and "interpretations"; and it would promote the "movies of the mind" technique as a vehicle for propagating the consequences of student-authored texts and for making some of their consequences transiently manifest without privileging those consequences as determinations of a text's full Meaning, but only as some of its actual meanings.

Personal Narratives. Even that old chestnut, the personal narrative, can be usefully incorporated into a consequentialist pedagogy if done to subvert, not to reinforce, expressivist conceptions of personal writing (e.g., Elbow, 1973; Macrorie, 1970; Murray, 1982/1996, 1991/1994; Stewart, 1972). Personal narratives should not be treated as documents through which authors' subjectivities or self-concepts (cf., W. Harris, 1996; Harvey, 1994; Shaw, 1997), the social construction of those subjectivities or self-concepts (cf., Bartholomae, 1995; R. Miller, 1996; Zawacki, 1998), or even the tension between the two (cf., Hindman, 2001) are made present, but instead must be treated as documents through which subjectivities or self-concepts may be transiently inaugurated by writers and made contestable by readers (Spellmeyer, 1993b). A consequentialist pedagogy would expose the artifice and selectivity—and the limits of that artifice and selectivity—behind personal writing that portrays itself as "reporting" personal experiences with perfect fidelity rather than as propagating meanings of those experiences (or even of "experiences" that never occurred) (Hindman, 2001; Herrington, 2001; Schilb, 1999); and it would reject the privileged position of the writer to determine the meanings of those experiences (Brandt, 2001; Herrington, 2001; Spigelman, 2001). Once a writer exposes her text, even an autobiographical text, to readers, the Meanings of that text extends beyond her control; each consequence, however, unintended or even impossible from the perspective of the writer, is a member of the Meaning of that text.

For some readers, this claim will be questioned precisely because it questions our sense of—or our experience of being—a fundamental and (fundamentally) private self. But suppose, following Sellars (1956/1997) and Rorty (1979), that our sense of "first-person privilege"—i.e., our sense that an individual is in a "specially privileged position" to describe his or her mental states—is a product of social interactions, not natural necessity (Kim 1996/1998, pp. 16–17). As Rorty (1979) puts it, we should "think of incorrigible knowledge simply as a matter of social practice—of the absence of a normal rejoinder in normal conversation to a certain knowledge-claim" (p. 96). That is, such claims (e.g., "my toe hurts") are incorrigible not *because they are indisputable,* but *because we don't bother to dispute them.* As Wittgenstein (1969/1972) puts it, "Suppose it were forbidden to say 'I know' and only allowed to say 'I believe I know'?" (366). A consequentialist pedagogy would not deny the writer his or her immediations or mediations of the text because those immediations and mediations form part of its Meaning, or even deny that writers will or may struggle to control what their texts mean (cf. Dasenbrock, 2001, p. 103; Dyson,

1992); however, it would make explicit that those particular meanings do not comprise the whole Meaning.

Thus, from the perspective of a consequentialist pedagogy, the purpose in requiring personal-narrative writing would not be to teach students how to smoothly and faithfully encode personal experiences into texts, but to undermine, through the shocks of response, the conception that writers are in control of the Meanings of their texts—*or even of their experiences*—without denying that writers may try to and even expect to evoke particular consequences in their readers. The writer is deposed as locus of meaning, but not in order to be replaced by the reader (cf. Barthes, 1968/1977b).

9 (In)Conclusion: An Envoi

> Our priority throughout what follows will be the attitudes
> and values, the beliefs and suppositions that give rise to
> method, that cause teachers to prefer doing things one way
> rather than another. In short, we will be talking about the
> philosophical context of instruction. We want to encourage
> writing teachers to become philosophers in their classrooms.
> [. . . But] who has time or inclination to become a philoso-
> pher?
>
> —C. H. Knoblauch and Lil Brannon

Who, indeed?

Like Knoblauch and Brannon, I write in the hope that my words
will propagate and resonate within the future work of the researchers
in rhetoric and composition studies. I write in the hope that my words
will eventually wander into the path of researchers and educators who
are already interested in many of the philosophical questions that I
have investigated or who might be persuaded to pursue them further
in their own work. I write with the recognition that, in a crucial sense,
the consequences that this book engenders form as much a part of
meaning consequentialism as my own contributions to it. And I write,
knowing full well that if meaning consequentialism is a viable account
of the operations of meaning, my text may be utterly forgotten, its
Meaning utterly extinguished, if others within the field or outside of it
do not read it or remember it. As Foucault (1969/1972a) writes of his
own work on an archaeology of knowledge,

> Last, it may turn out that archaeology is the name
> given to a part of our contemporary theoretical con-
> juncture. Whether this conjuncture is giving rise to
> an individualizable discipline, whose initial charac-

teristics and overall limits are being outlined here, or
whether it is giving rise to a set of problems whose
coherence does not mean that it will not be taken up
later elsewhere, in a different way, at a higher level, or
using different methods, I am in no position at the
moment to decide. And, to tell you the truth, it is
probably not up to me to decide. I accept that my discourse may disappear with the figure that has borne
it so far. (p. 208)

The dispatch has been sent: How will it be read, if at all, by others?
And how will I read it, if at all, in future days? I can conclude with
only one certainty—that the Meaning of this book is not for me to
decide, or even to know, for no one can see beyond the event horizon
of Meaning.

Appendix: Premises about Time, Discourse, and Mind

T1.0   Time is asymmetrical.

τ1.0   Time introduces asymmetries between past and present that prevent the reversibility of events: Time has a direction.

T2.0   Time is aperiodic.

τ2.0   Events are unique particulars that behave aperiodically—that is, events are never repeated, rendering impossible "any prediction of a future state in a given system" (Donahue, 1997/2002).

T3.0   The future is indeterminate because it does not *exist*.

τ3.0   The future is not an *a priori* reality that is made *present*, an *a priori* dimension into which the present expands, or an *a priori* plenitude from which the present chooses particular elements, but a name for the infinity of nothingness that lies beyond the limit of the present. The expansion of the present is analogous to the expansion of the universe: There is *nothing* beyond the universe *into which* it expands.

T3.1   Nothing lies beyond the *event horizon* of the present.

τ3.1   The event horizon marks the boundary of the eventfulness of the present.

T4.0   Time is not infinitely divisible, but *granular.*

τ4.0   Objects and events do not occupy timeless *instants,* but are necessarily distended through time.

T4.1   The fundamental *granule* of time is the *chronon.*

T5.0   Time is relative.

τ5.0   There is no universal *now*, only localized *nows:* Granules of
        time are finite not only in their duration, but also in their
        spatial extension.

τ5.1   Time is not something that unfolds at the same rate for
        each object and event. Each object has an "individual time"
        (Sharov, 1995/2001) that passes with a unique "viscosity"
        (Foucault, 1969/1972a, p. 175); and each set of interacting
        objects has its own "specific time not reducible to any indi-
        vidual time" (Sharov, 1995/2001).

T6.0   Time is discontinuous; it is a rupturing, a cleavage. Cf.
        Sartre (1943/1956), who describes *nihilation* as a "cleavage
        between the immediate psychic past and the present" (p.
        27).

τ6.0   The granules of time do not merge into one another seam-
        lessly.

τ6.01   The past cannot preserve itself across this rupture of its own
        accord (i.e., the past has no inertia).

T6.1   The rupture of time—the passing of the present into the
        past, the creation of the future into the present—is *trau-
        matic.*

τ6.1   The experience of time is, as Levinas (1961/1969) describes
        the experience of discourse, "the experience of something
        absolutely foreign, a traumatism of astonishment" (p. 73).

τ6.11   The trauma of time does not result only from our sense of
        an encounter with a future that is alien, but also from our
        sense of alienation from a past that has departed.

T7.0   Time is fecund.

τ7.0   The discontinuity of time allows for the possibility of an
        "absolute youth" that is unprecedented.

PREMISES FOR A CONSEQUENTIALIST PHILOSOPHY OF DISCOURSE

C1.0   An antecedent X necessarily precedes its consequent Y.

χ1.0   The relation between X and Y is non-commutative: Under no true description can X be subsequent to Y.

C1.1 Y is a consequence of X if and only if Y is subsequent to X, Y could not have occurred had X not occurred, and Y might not have occurred even though Y occurred.

C1.2 Y is an immediate consequence of X if and only if no other event Z intervenes between X and Y; otherwise, Y is a mediated consequence of X.

C2.0   Discourse is aperiodic.

χ2.0   Discourse is comprised of utterances and texts that are unique particulars.

C3.0   The consequences of an utterance or text are not predetermined.

C3.1   The boundary between an utterance or text and its immediate and mediate consequences—and, by extension, between an immediate or mediate consequence of an utterance or text and the immediate and mediate consequences of that immediate or mediate consequence, ad infinitum—is the *event horizon of meaning*.

C4.0   There is no timeless instant in which a purely abstract, formalized language can subsist.

C5.0   There is no single, unbounded *now* in which a spatialized language can be found.

χ5.0   There cannot be synchronic descriptions of a language because there is nothing synchronic to describe.

C5.1   The consequences of utterances and texts, and their propagation, are not governed by a single standard of time.

χ5.1   Consequences are not necessarily of equal duration (i.e., a consequence is not measured by a standard number of chronons), and particular strands of consequences need not propagate with the same granularity.

C6.0   The Meaning of an utterance or text is the temporally distended aggregation of its propagating consequences.

χ6.0   The Meaning of an utterance is formed through time by its consequences and is not contained by any single one of those consequences; but there is no single *instant* in which the Meaning of an utterance *exists* because the propagating consequences of an utterance do not share a single instant of time.

C6.1   The Meanings of the past do not linger into the present because of their own vitality (cf. Chapter 2).

χ6.1   The Meaning of an utterance or text does not have an intrinsic inertia.

C6.2   The fact that Y is a consequent of X does not entail that Y preserves X, that X contains Y, or even that X becomes Y.

χ6.2   The antecedent Meaning of an utterance or text is not an *a priori* constraint on the subsequent consequences of that utterance or text; it does not provide a self-same criterion that distinguishes proper consequences from improper consequences.

C7.0   The Meaning of an utterance or text is fecund not because its consequences extend far into the past, but only insofar as its consequences continue to propagate into the future.

χ7.0   The fecundity of the text is not a measure of the depths of an *a priori interiority*, but of the dispersion of an *a posteriori exteriority*.

χ7.01   The antecedent fecundity of an utterance does not guarantee continued fecundity: Utterances and texts that have been consequential may cease being consequential.

C7.1 The consequences of an utterance or text for its speaker or writer have no special privilege over the consequences of that utterance or text for other people.

χ7.1 Speakers and writers are not, *a priori*, the final adjudicators of what their utterances and texts mean, even if their utterances and texts are consequential only for themselves or even if listeners and readers accede to the results of any adjudication.

C7.2 The moment when a non-consequential antecedent entity or event becomes consequential is the moment of *first meaning*.

χ7.2 This first meaning is not only the moment of *baptism* in which an antecedent but otherwise non-consequential entity in a chain of discourse becomes consequential in that chain of discourse (Kripke, 1972/1996, p. 96; Putnam, 1980/1983d, p. 72), but it also the marks moments in which that entity becomes variously consequential as those consequences propagate into various other chains.

χ7.21 An antecedent entity that becomes consequential in multiple chains of discourse will have multiple first meanings. The first meaning is not a moment that necessarily occurs only once for an antecedent.

χ7.22 *Non-consequential* and *consequential* are not absolute terms, just as *meaning* and *non-meaning* are not absolute terms. An entity may be consequential in certain ways for certain entities, but differently consequential or even non-consequential for other entities. The principle of contradiction does not hold: It may be equally true to say of the same entity that it is both consequential and non-consequential.

PREMISES FOR A CONSEQUENTIALIST PHILOSOPHY OF MIND

M1.0 Thoughts are *polythetic*, not *monothetic*.

M2.0 Mind is, essentially, *futural*.

μ2.0   Mind is, essentially, futural because mind, insofar as it is, is constituted by the propagating consequences of its potential to be otherwise.

M2.1   Time is intrinsic to consciousness.

μ2.1   Immediations and mediations of utterances and texts are necessarily temporally distended and, consequently, cannot be adequately understood apart from time.

M3.0   Mind is not reducible to consciousness, but is the Meaning of consciousness; it is not the possession of a Self but a perpetual expropriation of selfhood.

M4.0   Consciousness is non-localizable within the brain.

M5.0   Consciousness is, essentially, indeterminate.

M6.0   Consciousness is *saccadic.*

μ6.0   Consciousness operates in *externally discrete* but *internally smeared* stretches of time—i.e., it is saccadic—between which it is, essentially, *non-existent;* and because temporality is intrinsic to consciousness, it cannot be accurately described in terms that subdivide these saccades of consciousness. The Meanings of the immediations and mediations that occur during these saccades of consciousness, as part of *mind,* extend beyond the moment of awareness to whatever consequences they propagate.

M6.1   Consciousness is durable, not durational.

μ6.1   Consciousness is a series of discrete and not necessarily contiguous saccades; it is not a *continuous stream* of sensations experienced by, memories recollected by, or fantasies constructed by a subject. Consciousness is always *timely.*

M7.0   Consciousness is, essentially, *discontinuous.*

μ7.0   Consciousness is a series of immediations and mediations disrupted by gaps during which no immediation or mediation occurs. Consciousness is not an inertial system flowing along a continuum, but, in terms Levinas (1961/1969, p.

284) uses to conceptualize time, something that is annihilated and (re)constructed, something that dies and is resurrected.

PRINCIPLES FOR A CONSEQUENTIALIST PHILOSOPHY

We can simplify these premises about time, discourse, and mind into the following set of principles related to the notion of *consequences*.

P1   Asymmetry

P2   Aperiodicity

P3   Indeterminacy

P4   Granularity

P5   Relativity

P6   Discontinuity

P7   Fecundity

About the Author

Kevin J. Porter (PhD, Wisconsin) is Assistant Professor of English at the University of Texas at Arlington, where he teaches courses in rhet-

Notes

Chapter 1

[1] Of course, these importations often serve as valuable introductions for members of our field of ideas at work in other disciplines, thus widening the available perspectives on meaning and language. They become problematic, however, when these new perspectives are (a) absorbed without critique (importations are only as good as what is imported), (b) treated in isolation from alternative intellectual movements, and (c) framed in such a way that our field appears to be merely a site for applying theoretical approaches to meaning and language rather than as a equal contributor to the understanding of them. The derivativeness of much of the research within rhetoric and composition studies may account in part for the fact that so little of our theoretical work is exported to other disciplines. That is, our field is comprised primarily of borrowers, not lenders, when it comes to the theorization of meaning and language. We can do better than that.

My point is not that theorists within rhetoric and composition studies shouldn't read or cite work produced outside of our field (far from it!)—or even that we have the ability to determine whether our work will be read by others outside of our field—but only that the purpose of that reading and citing should be to join, shape, and even inaugurate wider conversations, not to provide summaries of privileged texts for the consumption of people within our field.

[2] For example: Nora Bacon (2000), who writes without any elaboration that students "had come to class eager to undertake meaty, meaningful writing tasks" (p. 595) and that "a sentence's meaning is shaped by the circumstances in which it is uttered" (p. 599); similarly, Branch (1998): "There exists, in other words, a negotiated relationship in which the meaning of literacy is one of the issues at stake" (p. 212); Collins (1999) quotes M. Fulkerson (1994, p. vii) with approval and without explanation to the effect that "feminism 'cannot account for the systems of meaning and power that produce that [women's] experience'" (p. 547); Elbow (1999b): "If a student really wants feedback on surface features on early drafts, I'll give it,

but only if this doesn't deflect attention from thinking, organization, and clarity of meaning" (p. 368); Giroux (2000): "it [pedagogy] encompasses every relationship that young people imagine to be theirs in the world, where social agency is both enabled and constrained across multiple sites and where meanings enter the realm of power and function as public discourses" (p. 11); hooks (1999/2000): "I had been taught in the segregated institutions of my childhood church and school that writing and performing should deepen the meaning of words, should illuminate, transfix, and transform" (p. 2); Jarratt and Reynolds (1994): "*êthea*, a plural noun meaning 'haunts' or, more colloquially, 'hang outs'" (p. 48); S. Lyons (2000): "While the meanings of sovereignty have shifted and continue to shift over time, the concept has nonetheless carried with it a sense of locatable and recognizable power" (p. 450); Mathieu (1999): "Like the needs explored here, meaningful alternatives cannot be desired by people until they are articulated" (p.124); Moss (1992/1996): "Will the ethnographer make assumptions about what certain behaviors signify or how meaning is established in this community based on pervious knowledge or on actual data collected?" (p. 393); Prendergast (2000, p. 481): "Why was such a meaning culturally unintelligible given the framework Heath was working within [. . .]" (pp. 481–482); Schultz (2002): "What are the meanings of this writing in students' lives?" (p. 363); Stark (1999): "But with Romanticism comes the aesthetically and economically motivated idea that the original expression is, in fact, original meaning or knowledge, meaning that was never thought or owned before" (p. 460); Trimbur (2000a): "The meanings and values that characterize a structure of feeling supply the motives that bump up against formally held, systematic beliefs" (p. 287); West and Olson (1999): "Because subjects and meanings exist before negotiation, because they are anterior to it, does not mean that they are 'pregiven.' Subjects and meanings in part emerge in enunciative, co-constructive moments" (p. 246); et cetera.

[3] I owe this observation to an anonymous review of an earlier version of this material (K. Porter, 2003).

[4] Consider, for example, the contested invention of the calculus (cf. Kramer, 1970, pp. 171–172), with Newton eventually victorious over Leibniz.

[5] Foucault (1963/1977d) describes the memorial role of the Greek epic, and of language in general, as a struggle against death: So long as we keep talking, or are talked about, we cannot be entirely dead (cf. Niles, 1998). And Ratcliffe (2000), drawing on Heidegger, claims that if "we do not deal with the past, it saps our strength, relegating us either to emotional prisonhouses [. . .] or to endless repetitions of the moments that landed us here" (p. 95).

[6] The ideal survey, of course, would be the one that could see and comprehend everything at the same time, thus fulfilling the dream of "an infinite understanding (intellectus infinitus) for which everything exists simultane-

ously (omnia simul)" (Gadamer, 1960/1997, p. 210), but there is no Archimedean point to enable a panoptic gaze, no mind that is omnipresent. Perfect maps also lead to paradoxes. For example, there is Borgés and Cesares's (1946/1972) famous short story of the folly of cartographers whose perfect map of a kingdom had to be exactly as large as the kingdom itself. And Russell recounts two paradoxes proposed by the philosopher Josiah Royce: a perfect map that therefore contains a map of the map, ad infinitum (1919/1948, p. 80), and a bottle with a label on which there is a picture of the bottle and its label, ad infinitum (1940, p. 86).

[7] Thomas Miller (1997) offers a similar criticism of historians of English literature who overemphasize the influence of famous theorists and prestigious institutions in the founding and development of English studies, ignoring the pressures for change exerted by students entering the academy from the cultural margins or from the work of members of academic institutions that are, for a variety of reasons, of little prestige in relation to other academic institutions. Following Canagarajah (1996), we might call these people "periphery scholars."

[8] Essentially, Nystrand, Greene, and Wiemelt are complaining about the lack of a historical sense in their predecessors. But we might wonder why it is possible for people *not* to have a historical sense—that is, why it is possible to engage texts as if they were without history, or at least as contemporaneous. Part of the answer lies, I think, in the fact that each taxonomizer, through his or her essay, attempts to synchronize for readers the texts he or she cites, and can cite only those texts with which he or she is synchronized at the time of writing. Another part of the answer lies in the preservation and resulting accumulation of texts, texts that do not have to be read in chronological order. No one reads this way, nor do texts carry their history in ways that ensure they can only be meaningful if read chronologically. For example, despite the antecedence of the latter before the former, I may read Derrida before Descartes, Putnam before Plato, and synchronize through juxtaposition (as I have just done) all of them in a single footnote; and it seems to make little difference from the vantage point of thirteen years after the fact whether Knoblauch's essay appeared in 1988 or 1992. Derrida, Descartes, Putnam, Plato, and Knoblauch alike belong to the vastness of the already written, and alike they remain meaningful only to the extent that they remain consequential in the finitude of the present.

[9] But, pace Phelps (1999), the past is not an "inexhaustible [. . .] source of alternate futures" (p. 52); meaning consequentialism rejects her claim that "in principle nothing can finally be lost from history as a path to an alternate future" (p. 52). Of course, my claim cannot be empirically demonstrated, for the desire prove something in particular is permanently lost requires that that something cannot be "lost" (cf. Heidegger's position, in *Being and Time*, on the interconnections between questions/questioning and answers/answer-

ing); otherwise, we would not know what to look for it. But the lack of empirical confirmation does not embarrass me, for Phelps's claim is no more demonstrable than my own. Consequently, whichever claim one chooses, then, must be determined by how likely or reasonable one finds the respective claims.

[10] The notion of a "small world" was first proposed by sociologist Stanley Milgram in 1967 and was immediately embraced by researchers and people at large, despite, as Kleinfeld (2000/2002) observes, (a) Milgram's limited data set; (b) his questionable methods of analyzing and reporting that data (e.g., ignoring disconfirming findings and calculating links between individual in ways skewed toward finding or manufacturing those links); (c) his easy assumption that the fact that a person may be "connected" to another person through a few acquaintances is a significant connection; (d) the non-randomness of Milgram's sample; and (e) the relative dearth of replication studies—and the poor quality of what studies have been conducted—with findings that support the hypothesis (cf. Pool and Kochen, 1978/1989, p. 4). Kleinfeld suggests that the "astonishing degree of acceptance of the notion that we are inter-connected is in itself a phenomenon important to investigate."

[11] And, frankly, it would be a dreary exercise simply to point out, for example, how Kent (1993a, 1993b, 1993c) invokes Davidson, Cooper (1982), Grice; Phelps (1998), Gadamer; Bruffee (1984/1996), Rorty; Spellmeyer (1993b), Foucault; Berthoff (1978), Richards; Steinmann (1982), Searle; ad infinitum.

[12] I agree with Waismann (1956/1959) that philosophers can offer only arguments with varying degrees of persuasiveness, not conclusive proofs deductively derived from certain premises: "No philosophic argument ends with a Q.E.D. However forceful, it never forces" (p. 372). For Waismann, the philosopher "*builds up a case.* First, he makes you see all the weaknesses, disadvantages, shortcomings of a position; he brings to light inconsistencies in it or points out how unnatural some of the ideas underlying the whole theory are by pushing them to their farthest consequences [. . .]. On the other hand, he offers you a new way of looking at things not exposed to those objections" (pp. 372–373). The goal of the activity of philosophy, then, is "vision" (p. 374) an "attempt to unfreeze habits of thinking, to replace them by less stiff and restricting ones" (p. 376). Compare Rorty (1979, 1989).

[13] Sanford (1985) and Barry Smith (1996) have independently argued that theory-building should not be primarily concerned with the reduction of that theory to a single principle or axiom. As Smith contends, "systems capable of describing real-world phenomena will require large numbers of non-logical primitives, no group of which will be capable of being eliminated formally in favour of any other group" (p. 288). Thus, I am not disappointed by the fact, and hope that readers will similarly not find it disappointing, that

my account of meaning apriorism isn't reducible to a single principle—one cannot deduce, say, the principle of empiricism from meaning apriorism as I have formulated it—or that no single principle subsumes all of the others.

[14] As Barthes (1971/1977i) puts it, "If I have chanced to mention certain possible meanings, the purpose has not been to discuss the probability of those meanings but rather to show how the structure "disseminates" contents—which each reading can make its own. My object is not the philological or historical document, custodian of a truth to be discovered, but the volume, the *signifiance* of the text" (pp. 136–137).

[15] For example, within rhetoric and composition studies: Bernard-Donals and Glejzer (1998); Bizzell (1986/1992b); Gale (2000); Vitanza (1991); Yarbrough, 1999). And beyond it: Barthes (1968/1977b); Condillac (1792/1982a); Derrida (1967/1976); Foucault (1971/1977e); Quine (1950/1961a); and Rorty (1979, 1989).

[16] If language and meaning are always already social, then social formations must exist prior to them. This position was articulated by the eighteenth-century philosopher Lord Monboddo (James Burnett), who argued that language was not a natural or essential ability of human beings, but an acquired one. Monboddo believed that the development of even the simplest languages in human history prove that they could not precede, but must presuppose, the existence of prior "rational and social structures" that provide their "intellectual content" (Land, 1985, p. 161).

[17] As my list indicates, many of these notions are not unprecedented: My thinking through of meanings in terms of consequences would not be possible without my having found consequential the work of many philosophers, rhetoricians, literary theorists, linguistics, and so on.

Chapter 2

[1] According to Benedict Anderson (1983/1996), for the "great global communities of the past"—i.e., Christendom, the Islamic Ummah, the Middle Kingdom—the specific languages of Church Latin, Qur'anic Arabic, and Examination Chinese were thought to be "emanations of reality, not randomly fabricated representations of it," so that one did not know the world unless one spoke the proper language (p. 14). Of course, *which* language is the *proper language* is disputed—e.g., Latin, as John of Salisbury thought, French, as Rivarol (1782/1919) proposed, etc.

[2] This myth of the constitutive powers of divine language is not limited to Judeo-Christianity. For example, Heraclitus (or Hèracleitus) "held [the divine word, the Logos] to be the origin and first principle of all things, of the cosmic and moral order" (Cassirer, 1944/1972, p. 113); and Gusdorf (1965) claims that the major religions of the world agree that the divine Word brought the world into existence.

[3] Cf. Aquinas (trans. 1947), who argues that "the author of Holy Writ is God, in whose power it is to signify His meaning, not by words only (as man also can do), but also by things themselves" (I.1.10).

[4] According to Newton-Smith (1987/1988, p. 29), Newton's interests in alchemy and theology have been generally neglected in order to preserve his stature as a giant of science, and his sizable corpus of "mystical" papers have yet to be published.

[5] In his *Discourse on Metaphysics*, Leibniz (1840/1968b) writes: "[E]very substance is like an entire world and like a mirror of God, or indeed of the whole world which it portrays, each one in its own fashion [. . .]. It can indeed be said that every substance bears in some sort the character of God's infinite wisdom and omnipotence, and imitates him as much as it is able to; for it expresses, although confusedly, all that happens in the universe, past, present and future, deriving thus a certain resemblance to an infinite perception or power of knowing" (p. 15).

[6] Although Einstein (1922/1956) formulated a theory of relativity, he is careful to point out that this relativity extends only to space and time considered separately—space-time is "absolute" (pp. 30–31). This point has been lost on theorists, such as Whorf (1940/1956b, 1940/1956c), who are enamored with relativism and perhaps overeager to enlist Einstein as an illustrious fellow traveler of sorts. Schryer (1999), too, might wish to reconsider her claim, following Holquist (1990), that Bakhtin is attempting to apply and extend Einstein's insights about space-time into considerations about language and discourse—if, that is, she believes that Bakhtin's philosophy resists spatialized conceptions of time. We will consider more carefully questions surrounding Bakhtin's conception of time, particularly *great time,* in Chapter 6.

[7] According to Davies (1995), "Just as we can survey space as a landscape spread before us, so we can survey time (in our mind's eye, at least) as a timescape timelessly laid out" (p. 72).

[8] Cf. Murphy (1974, p. 49). Notice that Luther is already attempting to protect his own claims about Biblical infallibility by arguing that such infallibility extends only to the original Biblical texts; if passages of Biblical texts throw into doubt the consistency or unity of the Bible, then such problems can be explained away as corruptions introduced after the fact by human redactors.

[9] In the Book of Judges (11:1–40), Jephthah, an Israeli warrior, vows that he shall offer as sacrifice the first person he sees in his household if the Lord grants him a victory over the Ammonites; ironically, his only child, unnamed in the Bible, is the one who first greets Jephthah after his triumph. Instead of struggling against the barbarous vow, the daughter meekly accepts her fate and, after a brief period of mourning, is sacrificed to God.

[10] Even when *interference* or *noise* is accepted as an unavoidable feature of communicative systems (cf. Shannon, 1948/1959), its function is wholly negative—a subtraction from the content of the message, something to be ameliorated as best one can. Misinterpretation occurs because, like any other physical process, communication is subject to the inexorable laws of entropy.

[11] In his *Tractatus Theologico-Politicus,* Spinoza (1670/1951b) excoriated what he called the "diseased imagination" of mystics who "dream that most profound mysteries lie hid in the Bible, and weary themselves out in the investigation of these absurdities, to the neglect of what is useful" (p. 99). As we shall see later, Spinoza preferred a more scholarly, historicist approach to interpreting the Bible that resembles the erudite hermeneutic of Erasmus (cf. Aldridge, 1966).

St. Paul, too, worried about the corrosive effects to the community of the Church of people who believed they spoke in "tongues" directly with God:

> If anyone speaks in tongues he is talking with God, not with men and women; no one understands him, for he speaks divine mysteries in the Spirit. On the other hand, if anyone prophesies, he is talking to men and women, and his words have power to build; they stimulate and they encourage. Speaking in tongues may build up the speaker himself, but it is prophecy that builds up a Christian community [. . .]. The prophet is worth more than one who speaks in tongues—unless indeed he can explain its meaning, and so help to build up the community [. . .]. If what you say in tongues yields no precise meaning, how can anyone tell what is being said? You will be talking to empty air. There are any number of languages in the world; nowhere is without language. If I do not know the speaker's language, his words will be gibberish to me, and mine to him [. . .]. Thank God, I am more gifted in tongues than any of you, but in the congregation I would rather speak five intelligible words, for the benefit of others as well as myself, than thousands of words in the language of ecstasy. (1 Cor. 14: 2–4, 9–11, 18–19)

[12] We should not think of the Catholic Church, even in its earliest periods of development, as a single, unified entity, but in terms of a colloidal laminate as described in Chapter 1. For example, during the latter part of the second century, there were many doctrinal disputes between local synods and the three main churches of Rome, Antioch, and Alexandria. For St. Iranaeus, the Church of Rome was "pre-eminent" because its "apostolic suc-

cession could be traced back to St Peter and St Paul" (Twomey, 1995, p. 89); Rome's eventual preeminence was never a given, but an always contingent result of a sustained effort to secure that preeminence.

[13] Divinity can be identified with rationality, as in the Platonic scheme of the Logos, in which the substance of the universal mind, man's mind, reason, and language are identified with each other (Scott, 1967). Theologian Johannes Piscator (1546–1625), influenced by Ramist logic, argued that "in effect, Christ's message took the form of a syllogism and that the accounts of his message were concatenations of syllogisms" (Conley, 1990, p. 133). Of course, some theologians, despite their respect for dialectic, worried about treating sermons as logical arguments; for example, in the thirteenth century, Richard of Thetford warned that "preaching is not a form of disputation; thus it does not lead from proposition to conclusion" (Murphy, 1974, p. 328).

[14] The contempt for—or at least distrust of—natural language as a source of confusion, ambiguity, and deception is especially strong in the work of empiricist philosophers (e.g., F. Bacon, 1605/1900b; Condillac, 1746/1982a; Hobbes 1668/1994; Locke 1689/1987) and logical positivists (e.g., Carnap, 1932/1959a; Frege, 1924–1925/1979c; Russell, 1919/1948; Schlick, 1930–1931/1959); but it also is manifest in, for example, the work of Spinoza (1677/1951a), Nietzsche (1887/1992b), Peirce (1878/1991b), J. L. Austin (1950/1979e, 1961/1979a), and Churchland (1986/2000, p. ix). To "fix" the imperfections of language, theorists dream of artificial languages with "precise, consistent rules" (Ayer, 1946/1952, p. 70), generating statements that attain the "degree zero" of logic—a language without aesthetic interest or persuasive force (Barilli, 1983/1989, pp. 49, 51), a language without flaw whose logical syntax prevents the formation of meaningless statements (e.g., statements that cannot be verified through empirical means, statements that contain terms without referents, statements in which descriptions fail to refer to only one descriptum). And some theorists, such as Barthes (1957/1982), Richards (1936/1950), and Ricoeur (1969/1974), dream that, at least in mathematics or other highly formalized discourses, such perfect univocity has been achieved.

Not all theorists dream, of course: Some have actually constructed full-fledged artificial languages, such as Esperanto, Ido, Interlingua, and Volapük (cf. G. Miller, 1951, pp. 113–117)—only to be disappointed by the failure of people to embrace them, or even know of their existence! The logician Hans Freudenthal (1960) has even dreamed on a larger scale, constructing the artificial language "Lincos" as a medium of possible "cosmic intercourse" between humans and extraterrestrials.

[15] Similarly, Vygotsky (1962/1986) envisions "the totality of concepts as distributed over the surface of a globe" (p. 199), in which "the location of every concept may be defined by means of a system of coordinates, cor-

responding to longitude and latitude of geography. One of these coordinates will indicate the location of a concept between the extremes of maximally generalized abstract conceptualization and the immediate sensory grasp of an object—i.e., its degree of concreteness and abstraction. The second coordinate will represent the objective reference of the concept, the locus within reality to which it applies" (p. 199).

[16] Nystrand (2001, p. 256) assures us that "any lingering fantasies that texts can be autonomous" are "long gone"—at least, it should be hedged, within current research in rhetoric and composition studies; but if this is true, why do we repeatedly need to exorcise the ghost of autonomous meaning, to persuade ourselves that we, in fact, aren't haunted by it any longer?

[17] The source of the quotation cited by Hirsch is Marhenke (1950/1952, p. 146).

[18] According to Foucault (1969/1972a),

> The history of ideas usually credits the discourse that it analyses with coherence. If it happens to notice an irregularity in the use of words, several incompatible propositions, a set of meanings that do not adjust to one another, concepts that cannot be systematized together, then it regards it as a duty to find, at a deeper level, a principle of cohesion that organizes the discourse and restores to it its hidden unity. This law of coherence is a heuristic rule, a procedural obligation, almost a moral constraint of research [. . .]. But this same coherence is also the result of research [. . .]. In order to reconstitute it, it must first be presupposed, and one will only be sure of finding it if one has pursued it far enough and for long enough. (p. 149)

[19] Cf. D'Angelo (1975), who argues that a methodologically sound analysis of texts need not account for or explain the presence of every sentence, but only "key" sentences (pp. 79–80), thus ensuring that analysis can "regularize" (p. 80) or "normalize" (p. 87) otherwise intransigent or problematic texts.

[20] Barthes (1973/1977c) writes of Diderot's tableau as an attempt to fashion a *perfect instant* for a work of art: "Necessarily total, this instant will be artificial (unreal; this is not a realist art), a hieroglyph in which can be read at a single glance (at one grasp, if we think in terms of theatre and cinema) the present, the past and the future; that is, the historical meaning of the represented action. This crucial instant, totally concrete and totally abstract, is what Lessing subsequently calls (in the *Laocoon*), the pregnant moment" (p. 73).

Chapter 3

[1] Derrida (1988a; cf. G. Olson, 1990/1991) has repeatedly disavowed interpretations and applications of his deconstructive method that treat reading as an undisciplined activity of imposing whatever meanings one wishes onto texts. On the contrary, he emphasizes the importance of erudite, close readings of texts and respect for the texts of the past. For Derrida (1988a, pp. 144–148), semantic indeterminacy does not result from the impossibility of assigning a determinate meaning, for example, to a sentence, but the impossibility of assigning the determinate meaning to the exclusion of all others for that same sentence. In other words, we have determinate options, but cannot make or, better, enforce a single choice. In the tradition of analytic philosophy, Davidson (1986a) declares that semantic indeterminacy is no more threatening than the fact that some people use the Fahrenheit scale and others the Celsius scale to measure temperature; it if this true, then it would be absurd to ask which scale more accurately measures temperature.

[2] Derrida (1967/1978) argues that "simultaneity is the myth of a total reading or description, promoted to the status of a regulatory ideal [. . .]. By saying 'simultaneity,' instead of space, one attempts to concentrate time instead of forgetting it" (pp. 24–25).

[3] This plenum, of course, must be an *actual* plenum, not a *potential* plenum; that is, as I discuss (or will discuss, or have already discussed) in Chapter 6, we must not overemphasize the consequentiality of texts or utterances. Meaning consequentialism, as I now conceive of it, requires me to recognize that meanings do not proliferate ceaselessly without effort, but may be forgotten; that meanings do not necessarily refract or disjoin, but may perdure; that most utterances and texts have only limited consequences. My current effort to think through meanings in terms of consequences does not require me to embrace or celebrate the propagation of meanings for its own sake (e.g., because such propagation may be liberatory); I wish only to explain why such propagation occurs.

[4] I am close here to the work of theorist Avital Ronell, who insists not only that writing involves surrendering to the risks of writing (i.e., accepting that one is not in control of the effects of one's texts), but it also requires assuming responsibility, as the signatory of the text, for those effects (Davis, 2000, p. 246). (Cf. my discussion of the "Samoan theory of meaning" in Chapter 6.)

Chapter 4

[1] Had I time and space enough to discuss the principle of empiricism, I would critique the verificationist theory of meaning espoused here by Einstein. But, for present purposes, I must pass over this remark in silence.

[2] This, of course, is the *time dilation effect,* in which the closer the speed of an object is to the speed of light, the slower it appears to pass through time from the perspective of an object moving at a slower speed. Readers are likely familiar with the famous "Twins Paradox," in which one twin boards a spacecraft, zooms away at near light speeds, and returns to find that her twin has aged considerably more than she has in the interval between departure and return (Davies, 1995, pp. 55–67). Neither twin experienced the passage of time any differently (i.e., moving at near-light speeds does not slow one's sense of the passage of time), but they will disagree about the duration of the trip (i.e., the interval of time between departure and return will not be the same for each twin).

[3] As Adam (1990, p. 11) points out, one of the most vocal critics of absolute conceptions of time in the sociological theories is Giddens (1979, 1984). According to Giddens, social patterns emerge only through time—i.e., that looking a single snapshot of society would not reveal any patterns at all. However, I think that Giddens is mistaking epistemic constraints on what an observer could deduce from such a snapshot from the ontological properties of the society represented by the snapshot: That is, it does not seem to follow from an observer's inability to find patterns that the patterns aren't there. And what Giddens proposes instead—to track a society through a span of time—simply converts the absolute "snapshot" without structure into a panchronic or a durational "movie" with structure.

[4] These efforts, of course, continued in twentieth century, whether in the guise of the handbook "boom" in early twentieth-century America (Connors, 1985) or Stalin's personal interest in language as a tool "to unify a majority of the Soviet people (Newmeyer, 1986, p. 118), and continue still. Cf. Linell's (1982) discussion of the role of twentieth-century linguists, especially in post-colonial countries, to construct standardized languages to serve political and economic goals.

[5] Dummett (1973/1996d) argues that lexicographers are only fooling themselves if they think they merely describe linguistic practices because linguistic practices, like all social practices, are inherently normative: "to take the social character of language seriously is to recognise that, in using language, a speaker intends to be taken as responsible to, and only to, those linguistic practices agreed on by all members of the linguistic community, or at least to those held as correct by whatever members or group of members of it he takes as having authority over usage, save for any ad hoc conventions of which he gives explicit notice" (p. 403). As should be clear by now, I reject the spatialism of Dummett's model of language and society (i.e., "all members of the linguistic community"); but at least Dummett does not, pace Campbell, contradict himself.

[6] Thus, even in contemporary research, linguists such as Pearson (1996) classify languages in biological categories, such as *language phyla* (p. 91), lin-

guistic *stock* (p. 90), language *family* (p. 90), linguistic *ancestors* (p. 94), *genetic subgrouping* (p. 95), etc., so that all languages may be said to comprise only the differentiation and diversification of a primal language. Cf. Marr's discredited theory of *stadialism,* in which the origin of all languages is to be found in four primordial morphemes: *sal, ber, yon,* and *ro* (L. Thomas, 1957, p. 63).

[7] Cf. Ervin's (1999, p. 461) discussion of what she terms *discursive entrenchment.*

[8] For example, theorists (e.g., Augustine, trans. 1997; Grice, 1948/1991a; Peirce, 1868/1991c) often divide signs into *natural* signs, the meanings of which are causally or essentially connected to them, from *non-natural* or *conventional* signs, the meanings of which are assigned by prior social agreements.

[9] Cf. Bakhtin (1986/1996, p. 108); Foucault (1969/1972a, p. 102); Quine (1960, p. 191); Ricoeur (1969/1974, p. 92); Russell (1940, pp. 42–430); Saussure, (1916/1959, pp. 10, 13); and Vološinov (1929/1986, pp. 99–100).

[10] Cf. Gerbner (1956, pp. 180–181), who makes a similar distinction between *unintended consequences* and *intended effects.*

[11] Researchers in cultural and media studies, such as Brunsdon and Morley (1978), Hartley (1987), and Graeme Turner (1990), have demonstrated how the producers of television programs and other media imagine their audiences, but, at the same time, feel a profound sense of disconnection from them. Hartley in particular argues that the *television audience* is an invention of and an exchangeable commodity for producers, network executives, media critics, media regulators, and polling organizations.

[12] See also Iser's (1972/1978) "implied reader."

[13] Hirsch and Harrington (1981) also too easily pass over the question of intended audience: How is the extension of the audience determined? Is it a static conception (i.e., the audience consists of a_1, a_2, a_3, a_n, ..., a_{n+1} at time t)? Or does it change—and if so, how could the author's intention at time t "contain" the audience of $t + 1$?

[14] Derrida (1967/1976) makes the similar claim that "the names of authors or of doctrines here have no substantial value. They indicate neither identities nor causes. It would be frivolous to think that 'Descartes,' 'Leibniz,' 'Rousseau,' 'Hegel,' etc., are names of authors, of authors of movements or displacements that we thus designate. The indicative value that I attribute to them is first the name of a problem" (p. 99).

[15] Linell (1982) has argued that these visual metaphors represent the spatializing influence of writing on conceptions of language (and mind):

> most of the knowledge structures postulated in artificial
> intelligence and cognitive science seem to display some
> fundamental properties of written or pictorial representa-
> tion, cf. networks or graphs with nodes containing propo-

sitions, and analogical "mental models" respectively. This in turn suggests an interpretation according to which a knowledge structure is conceived of as a more or less fixed, static and context-free object, which is exploited in thinking and communication, where various parts of it would be retrieved, displayed, combined or otherwise manipulated, and finally perhaps transferred in communication [. . .]. (p. 122)

Chapter 5

[1] Hirsch's (1977, p. 121) puzzle of reconciling seemingly atemporal structures of meaning to the temporality of consciousness is a puzzle only if one assumes that meanings have atemporal structures.

[2] Here I refer to notions of *ideas* that are "clear," "distinct," or "determinate" (e.g., Descartes, 1701/1970c, pp. 7, 19–22; Locke, 1689/1987, II.xi.3; Spinoza, 1677/1951a, p. 23) or *thoughts* whose simultaneity language, necessarily analytic, cannot adequately represent (e.g., Chafe, 1970/1975, p. 51; Condillac, 1792/1982a, p. 354; Hirsch, 1977, pp. 120–121; F. Smith, 1971, p. 194; Vygotsky, 1962/1986, p. 251).

[3] For example, Iser (1989b, p. 53); Wulf (1996/2001).

[4] For example, Kant (1781–1787/1996); Husserl (1931/1970a).

[5] Cf. Levinas (1961/1969), who argues that the "interiority" of the subject prevents totalization because it "institutes an order different from historical time in which totality is constituted, an order where everything is pending, where what is no longer possible historically remains always possible" (p. 55). Interiority, then, is a deferral or "postponement" (p. 55).

[6] Cf. Levinas (1961/1969), who contends that the "being that thinks at first seems to present itself, to a gaze that conceives it, as integrated into a whole. In reality it is so integrated only once it is dead" (p. 55).

[7] Blind spots are the not-insignificant absences in our visual field that occur because our retinas do not have light-receptor cones or rods at the place where the retina is joined to the optic nerve. Notice that the blind spot is not a positive area of blackness (i.e., we don't see a *hole* in our visual field), which would be a visual perception of some sort, but an imperceptible void. The brain does not notice these gaps because it is not wired to process information about what is occurring within them (i.e., the brain isn't *curious* about what happens in those gaps) (Dennett, 1991, pp. 323–324).

[8] Scotomata are voids in the perceptual field caused by damage to the cerebral cortex. As with normal blind spots, scotomata are invisible to those who suffer from them; however, unlike what occurs with normal blind spots, a person who has a scotoma feels that her visual field is incomplete, for, having been wired to process information in certain places, her brain expects

information about them and therefore is "curious" about what is occurring there (Dennett, 1991, pp. 322–333).

⁹ Dennett (1991) uses as an example the "absences" in consciousness produced by petit mal epileptic seizures: "These are noticeable by the sufferer, but only by inference: they can't 'see the edges' any more than you can see the edges of your blind spot, but they can be struck, retrospectively, by discontinuities in the events they have experienced" (p. 356).

¹⁰ Levinas's (1961/1969) conception of time as death and resurrection, and its bearing on a consequentialist account of time, will be discussed in much more detail in Chapter 7.

¹¹ The difference between *communal* or *private* meanings is not so much a question of the *priority* of the one or the other or of their *incommensurability*, but a question of *scope* (cf. Dewey, 1927/1985, p. 15; Geisler, 2001, pp. 299–301): Communal meanings would be comprised of the consequences of an utterance that extends beyond an individual speaker, whereas private meanings would be comprised of the subset of those consequences for that speaker.

¹² Cf. Yarbrough (1999, pp. 5–6).

¹³ Cf. Mathieu (1999), who argues that people often neglect the ideological implications of advertisements by engaging in what he calls "scotosis"—"rationalized acts of selective blindness that occur by allowing certain information to be discounted or unexamined" (pp. 114–115).

¹⁴ Cf. Paul Drew (1990), who, in his discussion of "knowledge asymmetries" between interlocutors, asserts that

> participants' knowledge asymmetries in conversation are not necessarily associated with one party not knowing something, or with one being at any disadvantage relative to the other. Where, however, one is put at some disadvantage by the other, that is achieved interactionally. Furthermore, the ways in which knowledge asymmetries are *consequential* for conversational interaction arise from speakers' orientations to such asymmetry. Thus we are looking for ways in which asymmetries of knowledge are demonstrably relevant to the participants in the design of their talk. (p. 26, emphasis added)

¹⁵ I cannot here enter into a lengthy digression about attempts to theorize whether communication as transmission is possible in principle (e.g., Dewey, 1927/1985, p. 155; Dretske, 1981, p. 17; Ogden and Richards, 1923/1946, p. 19), necessarily partial (e.g., Chafe, 1970/1975, p. 17; Dillon, 1981, p. 53; Hardy, 1998, p. 181; Alfred Schutz, 1962/1990, p. 322; Vygotsky, 1962/1986, p. 252; Witte, 1992, p. 288), or wholly illusory (e.g., Davis, 1999, pp. 645–646; Nancy and Smock, 1993, pp. 314–315), and whether

the very act of entering into conversation depends upon an already existing solidarity with one's interlocutors (e.g., Fish, 1980d, p. 303; Ong, 1982, pp. 176–177; Searle, 1979/1985, p. 418) or is prompted by a sense of distance from them (e.g., Emerson, 1841/1985a, p. 232; Iser, 1980/1989a, p. 33; Levinas, 1961/1969, p. 73; Rommetveit, 1974, p. 29).

Chapter 6

[1] Cf. Francis Bacon (1605/1900b), who affirms as an indisputable axiom of physics and theology that "all things change, but nothing is lost" (p. 77).

[2] Bergson (1946) also appeals as proof to anecdotal accounts of "seeing one's life pass before one's eyes" at the moment of death (pp. 152–153).

[3] Following Derrida (1967/1976), I would argue that a discontinuity that is always incorporated into a wider continuity cannot actually be, from the perspective of that continuity, a discontinuity.

[4] Cf. Kripke (1972/1996, p. 96), who describes the effort required to sustain the continuity of reference.

[5] Which assumes, of course, that there is only a single person who has been, is, or ever will be named *Aristotle* and that *gold* does not also refer, for example, to a segment of the visible spectrum of light.

[6] Cf. Jean-Luc Nancy (1991/2001):

> I start out from the idea that such a thinking—the thinking of community as essence—is in effect the closure of the political. Such a thinking constitutes closure because it assigns to community a common being, whereas community is a matter of something quite different, namely, of existence inasmuch as it is in common, but without letting itself be absorbed into a common substance. Being in common has nothing to do with communion, with fusion into a body, into a unique and ultimate identity that would no longer be exposed. Being in common means, to the contrary, no longer having, in any form, in any empirical or ideal place, such a substantial identity, and sharing this (narcissistic) 'lack of identity.' (p. xxxviii)

[7] Theorists often appeal to the notion of enlightened self-interest. For example, David Lewis (1969) posits that conventions are mutually beneficial solutions to "coordination problems," which are "situations of interdependent decision by two or more agents in which coincidence of interest predominates and in which there are two or more proper coordination equilibria" (p. 24). These coordination equilibria are combinations of choices between two or more individuals in which "no one would have been better off had any one agent acted otherwise, either himself or someone else" (p. 14). Thus, because

it is in everyone's interest to ensure polite greetings, "we" solve the problem by conforming to certain forms of address; over time, these solutions become institutionalized and, therefore, obligatory (Luckmann, 1992, p. 228).

[8] Cf. Vitanza (1997), who argues, "I do not believe it is possible to have an uncoerced consensus based on a communicative model of rationality as warranted assertability; such a model is, though ever so subtle, the very epitome of the negative itself, that is, of exclusion as effected by logic and of purgation as effected by politics" (p. 60).

[9] Even if this argument were valid (which it is not), I do not understand, unless it assumes that all linguistic expressions are representations of already existing entities and events, how it would constitute a description of the workings of language in general.

[10] Cf. Nystrand's (1986, pp. 65–71) discussion of the work of researchers with the so-called Prague School, such as Firbas (1964) and Daneš (1964), on "communicative dynamism" and the "functional sentence perspective."

[11] Cf. my argument (2000) that change can be as conservative as stasis if everything is made to change at the same rate—i.e., that an immobilized world, for all intents and purposes, is the same as a "thoroughly and uniformly" mobilized world (p. 71).

[12] One can accept Duranti's observations about particular people identified as "Samoans" without accepting that there is a "Samoan culture" which is spatialized and pre-given. Whether all Samoans treat meaning in this way is not as important as whether there are, in fact, some who do (or at least did).

[13] As J. L. Austin (1956–1957/1979c) writes in his classic paper, "A Plea for Excuses"—a paper that would be impossible for one of Duranti's Samoans to write!—"it has always to be remembered that few excuses get us out of it completely: the average excuse, in a poor situation, gets us only out of the fire into the frying pan—but still, of course, any frying pan in a fire. If I have broken your disk or your romance, maybe the best defence I can find will be clumsiness" (p. 177).

[14] Meaning consequentialism would accept the premise of countless propagating chains, but would reject that these chains contain an infallible memory of prior meanings, that each link of the chain it itself stable *a priori*, or that all chains run "concurrently" in the sense that each shares a temporal viscosity that allows for them to be usefully situated on a plane of simultaneity.

[15] Perhaps the most extreme form of the worship of past wisdom is that practiced by the Ciceronians of the fifteenth and sixteenth centuries, who limited their lexicon to the words used by Cicero (G. Kennedy, 1980, p. 214).

[16] These changes need not be deliberate, however, no more than Darwin's principle of natural selection depends upon deliberate mutations. For

example, Rorty (1989, p. 16) argues that one may subscribe to linguistic evolutionism without subscribing to a teleology for language. The "improvement" of language is not measured by its nearing an ideal state, but rather by our sense that changes to our language, whether accidental or purposive, make our language increasingly useful for meeting our needs and desires at a certain point in time.

[17] Ruskin (1865/1886) provides a classic (and classist!) statement of the doctrine; he observes that the "well-educated gentleman" is "learned in the *peerage* of words; knows the words of true descent and ancient blood at a glance, from words of modern canaille; remembers all their ancestry—their intermarriages, distant relationships, and the extent to which they were admitted, and the offices they held, among the national noblesse of words at any time, and in any country" (p. 23).

[18] In this respect, J. L. Austin defies suspicions of etymology dating back at least as far as Plato (trans. 1871/1964a, 414c-d) and Quintilian (trans. 1987, I.vi.32–38).

[19] These examples, of course, hardly exhaust manifestations of linguistic evolution: See also, for example, Jespersen (1925, p. 61); Ong (1982, pp. 66–67); Polanyi (1958/1974, p. 113); Quine (1960, p. 7), Saussure (1916/1959, p. 168); Spencer (1852/1933, p. 12); and Mark Turner (1994, p. 93).

[20] For example, Virginia Anderson (2000), Cox (1998, p. 150), Gramsci (1948–1951/1971, p. 324), and Thomas Miller and Bowdon (1999, p. 596).

[21] For example, Bazerman (1988, pp. 224, 252, 309); de Certeau et al.(1994/1998, p. 135); Heath (1983, pp. 155, 362); Hobbs (1998, pp. 174, 178); Myers (1996, p. 13); Read (1981, p. 108); Kathleen Welch (1990, pp. 3–4); Raymond Williams (1961, pp. 47, 50); and Worsham (1998, p. 219).

[22] Indubitable, but not intrinsic, for a thoroughly intertextual theory of meaning cannot account for the first utterance or text.

[23] Besides a "seamless textual fabric," the intertext also appears as a "semantic universe" (Medway, 1996, p. 477), a "semantic encyclopedia" (Eco, 1979, p. 24), a "gigantic semiosic web" (Sebeok, 1991c, p. 96), etc.

[24] For example, Fleckenstein (1999, p. 296), Hardy (1998, p. 16), and Schwebke and Medway (2001, p. 351).

[25] Cf. Bakhtin (1986/1996, p. 105), Cherwitz and Darwin (1995, pp. 18–21), Fleckenstein (1999, p. 296), and Hikins (1990, pp. 52–53).

[26] For example, Bolinger (1976, pp. 1–2); Dummett (1973/1996c, pp. 303–305); Fodor (1987, pp. 56–61); Russell (1940, p. 390); and James Williams (1993, pp. 543–544).

[27] According to Leibniz, there are no causal relations between a nonmaterial mind and material body (e.g., the fact that I wish to raise my arm does not cause my arm to be raised, even though my arm is raised after I wish it), but an illusion of causality that results from a "preestablished harmony" between mind and body (Kim, 1996/1998, p. 51). Recall that, for Leibniz,

monads "sympathize with one another" (1720/1968c, p. 212) in such a way that they "correspond" without "acting upon one another" (1840/1968b, p. 23).

[28] Cf. Flower (1994, p. 77), Fiske (1989, p. 84), Errol Harris (1988, p. 103).

[29] Similarly, Greene (1990) argues that "as students read and write, they invoke a unique sociolinguistic past, enacting a process that has been shaped by a legacy of schooling and diverse cultural background that dictates how they fulfill the tasks we give them" (p. 163).

[30] Cf. Levinas (1972/1987), who argues that "every sign is a trace [. . .] [for i]n addition to what the sign signifies, it is the past of him who delivered the sign," even if it is a past that is "absolutely bygone" (p. 105).

[31] Cf. Ogden and Richards (1923/1946), who contend that "the effects upon the organism due to any sign, which may be any stimulus from without, or any process taking place within, depend upon the past history of the organism, both generally and in a more precise fashion. In a sense, no doubt, the whole past history is relevant: but there will be some among the past events in that history which more directly determine the nature of the present agitation than others" (p. 52). See also Sapir (1921/1949), who asserts that "the single impression which I have had of a particular house must be identified with all my other impressions of it" (p. 13).

[32] A point conceded by Bloomfield (1933/1961), who nevertheless retains as an *article of faith* that

> Every speaker's language, except for personal factors that we must ignore here, is a composite result of what he has heard other people say.

> > Imagine a huge chart with a dot for every speaker in the community, and imagine that every time any speaker uttered a sentence, an arrow were drawn into the chart pointing from his dot to the dot representing each one of his hearers [. . .]. The chart we have imagined is impossible of construction. An insurmountable difficulty, and the most important one, would be the factor of time: starting with persons now alive, we should be compelled to put in a dot for every speaker whose voice had ever reached anyone now living, and then a dot for every speaker whom these speakers had ever heard, and so on, back beyond the days of King Alfred the Great, and beyond earliest history, back indefinitely into the primeval dawn of mankind: our speech depends entirely upon the speech of the past. (pp. 46–47)

[33] As I will argue later, I am distinguishing here between the notion of the utterance or text as a carrier of meaning potentials (i.e., the utterance or text is a carrier of structured information that limits the possible or acceptable meanings of the utterance or text) from the notion of an utterance's or text's having a potential for meaningfulness (i.e., having a potential to propagate consequences) (cf. Nystrand, 1982b, p. 25; 1986, p. 102; 1989, p. 76).

[34] Cf. Neitzsche (1887/1992b), who writes:

> The concept "punishment" possesses in fact not *one* meaning but a whole synthesis of "meanings": the previous history of punishment in general, the history of its employment for the most various purposes, finally crystallizes into a kind of unity that is hard to disentangle, hard to analyze and, as must be emphasized especially, totally *indefinable* [. . .]. At an earlier stage, on the contrary, this synthesis of "meanings" can still be disentangled, as well as changed; one can still perceive how in each individual case the elements of the synthesis undergo a shift in value and rearrange themselves accordingly, so that now this, now that element comes to the fore and dominates at the expense of the others; and under certain circumstances (the purpose of deterrence perhaps) appears to overcome all the remaining elements. (p. 516)

[35] Cf. Shannon (1948/1959) and Sebeok (1991a, p. 28).
[36] Cf. George Miller's (1951) discussion of "frequencies" or "tendencies" of meaning (p. 112).
[37] Cf. Derrida (1967/1978), who argues that meaning is an "infinite implication, the indefinite referral of signifier to signifier" (p. 25), that can "overflow signification" (p. 12).
[38] Barthes (1970/1977j) argues that "the obtuse meaning is not in the language-system (even that of symbols). Take away the obtuse meaning and communication and signification still remain, still circulate, still come through: without it, I can still state and read" (p. 60).
[39] According to Barthes (1970/1977j), "The obtuse meaning, then, has something to do with disguise [. . .]. a multi-layering of meanings which always lets the previous meaning continue, as in a geological formation, saying the opposite without giving up the contrary" (p. 58).

Chapter 7

[1] A physics founded upon the symmetry of past and future is a physics whose laws are essentially timeless because (a) the ordering of a sequence of events *A, B,* and *C* could be reversed without any violation of those laws and

(b) there is no priority of the past over of the future in causal explanations (H. Price, 1991, p. 39; cf. Chapter 2). A paradigm example of symmetry would be watching a video recording of billiard balls colliding with one another; if the balls are already in motion when the recording starts, then it would be impossible to discern from the recording alone whether one is watching the "objective" sequence of events (i.e., the 9-ball collides with the 4-ball, which then collides with the 7-ball) or those events being played in reverse order (i.e., the 7-ball strikes the 4-ball which then strikes the 9-ball). If one could describe with absolute precision the state of the balls on the pool table at any given moment, one would not only be able to state where the balls will go, but also where they have been. And, more importantly, *where they "will go" or where they "have been" simply depends only upon the imposition of a particular direction to time that time itself does not have*—or at least does not seem to have any good physical reasons for having—because, for a physics of symmetry, the directionality of time makes no difference to the outcomes of interactions of physical processes.

Of course, as Dummett (1954/1996a, p. 321) would point out, if our videotaped event included the action that started the billiard balls moving, symmetry would disappear—the physical theory required to explain how all of the varied interactions of the billiard balls *resulted* in the conservation of forces into a single ball that then strikes the cue would, in order to explain the improbability of the behavior of the billiard balls, have to be infinitely more complicated than a physics that would explain the sequence of events run in the opposite, expected direction.

[2] But not the only ones. Theorists as diverse as Grice (1948/1991b, pp. 220–222), Halliday (1978, p. 2), Humboldt (1836/1988, p. 154), and Searle (1965/1991, p. 254) have emphasized the central role played by the use of linguistic tokens.

[3] The term *congruent* in reference to sentences would be more appropriate here than *identical,* especially when one considers how rarely inked letter forms or verbal sound waves overlap so perfectly as to be indistinguishable. Cf. the discussion of *congruence* in Chapter 5.

[4] For example, Vološinov (1929/1986) claims that "Meaning, in essence, means nothing; it only possesses potentiality—the possibility of having a meaning within a concrete theme" (p. 101). But this position fails to cohere with Vološinov's claim on the preceding page that

> The meaning of the utterance 'What time is it?'—*a meaning that, of course, remains the same in all historical instances of its enunciation* [italics added]—is made up of the meanings of the words, forms of morphological and syntactic union, interrogative intonations, etc., that form the construction of the utterance. (p. 100)

Here, Vološinov is articulating the entirely separate view of meaning as meaning potential that I critique in Chapter 6. Note also that, as I mentioned in my discussion of Vande Kopple (1994) in Chapter 1, Vološinov is smuggling in categories, such as *morphological* and *syntactic,* that are not separable from semantics and so are not purely formal.

[5] A sentence is also not a geometric figure, for sentences could only map onto each other precisely if, say, the same font and font-size were used. See note 3.

[6] The example is Davidson's (1968–1969/1984b, p. 98). Notice that the assumption that *leaped* and *liebt* are different words because they belong to different *languages* is simply the converse of the assumption that the *bear* and *bear* of (3) and (4) are the same word because they belong to the same *language*. But what constitutes a language—the apparent self-evidence of language—is precisely what I have been calling into question throughout this book.

[7] Prediction would be impossible not because events occur unlawfully, but because each event would be the result of its own particular and necessarily non-generalizable law. Cf. Davidson (1970/1980d, 1974/1980e), who argues that mental events may in fact be fully determined by physical laws yet still resist the attempts of materialists to construct generalized laws about cognition.

[8] Even if a being, such as the demon imagined by Laplace (1814/1995, pp. 2–3), could possess perfect knowledge of the state of the entire universe (which assumes, of course, that the universe has such a simultaneous state), that knowledge would not suffice to predict the future because physical reality is riddled with instabilities (Prigogine and Stengers, 1996/1997, p. 38).

[9] A *chronon* is the hypothesized fundamental unit of time, calculated to be 10^{-23} seconds (i.e., the length of time required for light to travel a hypothesized minimum spatial length of 10^{-13} millimeters) (Whitrow, 1972/1975, pp. 140–141)—a conclusion that, according to Rees (1997, p. 275), is no longer supported by experimental findings, which place the fundamental unit of time at at least 10^{-26} seconds (p. 275). However, there are theoretical reasons, derived from quantum mechanics, for positing the fundamental interval to be at 10^{-43} seconds, called *Planck time:*

> Heisenberg's uncertainty relationship tells us that, to measure a time interval with increasing precision, we need to use quanta of shorter wavelength (and thus higher energy). Because the light quanta move at finite speed, this increasing amount of energy must be focused into smaller dimensions (smaller than the interval being measured multiplied by the speed of light). A limit arises when the require energy is so high, and so tightly concentrated, that it would collapse to a black hole. Quantifying this argument sug-

gests that there is a minimum timescale of 10^{-43} seconds, commonly called the Planck time. Events cannot be timed or ordered more precisely than this. (Rees, 1997, p. 210)

Chronon seems to a clearer and more concise term for this fundamental unit, so I employ that term rather than *Planck time* throughout.

[10] It seems to me that, pace Böhlen et al. (1998, p. 376) and Bettini et al. (1998, p. 408), it is important to distinguish between granules and chronons, rather than conflating them. A chronon is necessarily a granule because it is a discrete span of time, but not every granule is a chronon.

[11] What the extent of that spatial extension might be is beyond the scope of this project; for present purposes, the important thing is not so much the calculation of those boundaries, but to think through the implications of the boundedness of time.

[12] Cf. Docherty (1993, p. 19), Dunmire (2000, pp. 97–99), Prigogine and Stengers (1996/1997, p. 161), and Virilio (1984/1989, pp. 1–4).

[13] The definition of the chronon in note 9 neglects the effects of velocity on space and time. For example, if we think of a chronon as the time required for light to pass from point B to point C, an observer traveling in the opposite direction from BC will not agree with an observer traveling toward BC on either the length of time it took for light to pass from B to C or the distance traveled by the light from B to C (assuming, of course, that both observers have instruments capable of detecting these minute differences).

[14] There can be no interval of time smaller than a chronon, so the gap between granules must either be comprised of smaller granules of time or, in the case of the smallest granules, *literally no time at all*. The gap between maximally contiguous granules of time cannot itself be a granule of time.

[15] For example, the discredited *steady-state theory* of cosmology, advanced by Fred Hoyle, Hermann Bondi, and Thomas Gold in the late 1940s, postulated that an expanding universe could be reconciled with an eternal universe (i.e., a universe without a big bang) if minute amounts of matter could be spontaneously created (Rees, 1997, pp. 36–42). More recently, the work of Prigogine and others on chaos theory has attempted to demonstrate the self-organization of matter into patterns of increasing complexity.

[16] Unlike Heidegger, for whom primordial temporality is finite because Dasein is finite, Levinas (1961/1969) asserts that primordial temporality is necessarily a relation of exteriority (i.e., a relation to an Other) and, therefore, necessarily infinite because the Other cannot be totalized (p. 80).

Chapter 8

[1] Instances of *interpretation* or *interpreters* in this chapter should not be read as my advocating the continued use of these terms, but an acknowledgment of how those terms have been used (cf. Chapter 3). That is, I refer to

interpretation in reference to the principle of charity, not because I believe in the notion of interpretation, but because Davidson uses that term in relation to the principle of charity.

[2]It should be noted that Davidson is hardly alone in making this assumption; concepts similar to charity are guiding tenets of research in dialogism (e.g., Blakar, 1992, p. 241), discourse analysis (e.g., Blum-Kulka, 1997), hermeneutics (e.g., Apel, 1972–1973/1980, pp. 158–159, 258–262), and philosophy of language (e.g., Grice, 1967/1991a). The importance of Davidson's contribution, however, is its thorough articulation of why charity is necessary (a point that is often assumed to be self-evidently true) and its connection of philosophy of language with a philosophy of action.

[3] Cf. Foucault (1971/1972b), who writes that "the analysis of discourse thus understood, does not reveal the universality of a meaning, but brings to light the action of imposed rarity, with a fundamental power of affirmation" (p. 234).

[4] Flower's (1994) complaint that school writing tasks are *arhetorical* seems infelicitous—the word itself looks odd—when we consider the importance of practice that included formal exercises in the history of rhetorical theory and instruction (Isocrates, trans. 2000; pseudo-Cicero, trans. 1939/1989; cf. Murphy, 1974, 1990; Fleming, 1998, pp. 183–184). But even were that not the case, I suggest that if school writing were really non-rhetorical, then it would be a kind of writing unaccountable for by rhetorical theory, a discourse without rhetoric.

[5] Critics have argued that unless students are convinced that their texts will be circulated to people other than their instructor, they will write texts tailored to meet their perceptions of what the instructor wants, even if the assignment requires them to pretend that their texts have some other targeted readership (e.g., N. Bacon, 2000; Freedman, Adam, and Smart, 1994; Clark, 1998; K. Lunsford, 2002).

[6] Herzberg's configuration of the problem as one of translation—i.e., converting the academic arguments one already has on hand into arguments that will persuade public audiences—is problematic in at least two ways. First, it neglects the fact that whatever text a student produces in order to effect this conversion will be a new text, not the original text in a new skin. An earlier text cannot be transmuted or reincarnated into a new one, so the new text does not contain in some hidden depths the Meaning of the old text, even if it in fact produces similar consequences to the earlier text. And second, such a conception implies an aprioristic view of discourse production, reminiscent of Flower and Hayes's (1981a, 1981b) early work—critiqued by, among others, Bizzell (1982/1992a) and Nystrand (1986)—in which one first has thoughts, then one translates them into appropriate forms for a particular audience.

[7] In other words, a person's actions in the world are causally related to their beliefs about the world, which are themselves *causally related to,* but not *justified by,* the world (cf. Davidson, 1986a). Davidson adds this important proviso because of his holistic conception of mind and language: Beliefs can be justified only by other beliefs, and utterances can only be justified by other utterances:

> The relation between a sensation and a belief cannot be logical, since sensations are not beliefs or other propositional attitudes. What then is the relation? The answer is, I think, obvious: the relation is causal. Sensations cause some beliefs and in this sense are the basis or ground of those beliefs. But a causal explanation of a belief does not show how or why the belief is justified [. . .].
>
> All beliefs are justified in this sense: they are supported by numerous other beliefs (otherwise they wouldn't be the beliefs they are), and have a presumption in favor of their truth. The presumption increases the larger and more significant the body of beliefs with which a belief coheres, and there being no such thing as an isolated belief, there is no belief without a presumption in its favor. (pp. 311–319)

Like Sellars (1956/1997), Davidson rejects the claims of logical empiricists that at least some beliefs can be given to us singly by experience (i.e., that some beliefs do not need justification but are self-justifying).

[8] Davidson (1985) equates rationality with the possession of a language and language with propositional structures, so that thought can be formulated in, and only in, propositions. Consequently, Davidson is unwilling to extend the label of *rational* to animals without language—which, for Davidson, are at present all of them aside from human beings,—or, presumably, even human infants.

[9] I am not suggesting that signs must be interpreted in the same way—in fact, as I argue in Chapter 3, I reject the notion of *interpretation* entirely—as if an aural sign must be registered in the same way as a tactile sign, but only that different methods of interpretation—or whatever we wish to call it—should be subsumable under an explanation capable of accounting for all of them. And similarly for meanings, which are manifold and polyform yet subsumable under the notion of *consequences.*

References

Aarsleff, H. (1988). Introduction. In W. V. Humboldt, *On language: The diversity of human language structure and its influence on the mental development of mankind* (P. Heath, Trans.; pp. vii-lxv). Cambridge, UK: Cambridge University Press.

Abbott, D. P. (1990). Rhetoric and writing in Renaissance Europe and England. In J. J. Murphy (Ed.), *A short history of writing instruction: From ancient Greece to twentieth-century America* (pp. 95–120). Davis, CA: Hermagoras Press.

Abrams, M. H. (1953). *The mirror and the lamp: Romantic theory and the critical tradition.* New York: Norton.

Ackerman, J., & Oates, S. (1996). Image, text, and power in architectural design and workplace writing. In A. H. Duin & C. J. Hansen (Eds.), *Nonacademic writing: Social theory and technology* (pp. 81–121). Mahwah, NJ: Erlbaum.

Adam, B. (1990). *Time and social theory.* Philadelphia: Temple University Press.

Adler-Kassner, L. (1998). Ownership revisited: An exploration in progressive era and expressivist composition scholarship. *College Composition and Communication, 49,* 208–233.

Aitcheson, J. (1991). *Language change: Progress or decay?* Cambridge, UK: Cambridge University Press.

Aldridge, J. W. (1969). *The hermeneutic of Erasmus.* Richmond, VA: John Knox Press.

Alexander, S. (1920). *Space, time and deity.* London: Macmillan.

Althusser, L. (1989). Ideology and ideological state apparatuses. In D. Latimer (Ed.), *Contemporary critical theory* (pp. 60–102). San Diego, CA: Harcourt Brace Javanovich. (Original work published in 1970)

Anderson, B. (1996). *Imagined communities: Reflections on the origin and spread of nationalism* (Rev. ed.). London: Verso. (Original work published in 1983)

Anderson, V. (2000). Property rights: Exclusion as moral action in "The battle of Texas." *College English, 62,* 445–472.

Anson, C. M. (1999). Distant voices: Teaching writing in a culture of technology. *College English, 61*, 261–280.

Apel, K.-O. (1980). *Towards a transformation of philosophy* (G. Adey & D. Frisby, Trans.). London: Routledge & Kegan Paul. (Original work published in 1972–1973)

Applebee, A. N. (1981). *Writing in the secondary schools: English and the content areas.* Urbana, IL: NCTE.

Aquinas, T. (trans. 1947). *Summa theologica* (Vols. 1–2). New York: Benzinger.

Arendt, H. (1958). *The human condition.* Chicago: University of Chicago Press.

Aristotle. (trans. 1991). *On rhetoric* (G. A. Kennedy, Trans.). New York: Oxford University Press.

—. (trans. 2001). *On the soul* (*De anima*) (J. A. Smith, Trans. [On-line] Available: http://ccat.sas.upenn.edu/jod/texts/aristotle.soul.html

Ashcroft, B. (1994). Excess: Post-colonialism and the verandahs of meaning. In C. Tiffin & A. Lawson (Eds.), *De-scribing empire: Post-colonialism and textuality* (pp. 33–44). London: Routledge.

Augustine. (trans. 1992). *Confessions* (H. Chadwick, Trans.). Oxford: Oxford University Press.

—. (trans. 1997). *On Christian teaching* (R. P. H. Green, Trans.). Oxford: Oxford University Press.

Austin, G. (1806). *Chironomia: Or, a treatise on rhetorical delivery.* London: Bulmer & Company.

Austin, J. L. (1962). *How to do things with words.* Oxford: Clarendon.

—. (1979a). The meaning of a word. In J. O. Urmson & G. J. Warnock (Eds.), *Philosophical papers* (3rd ed.; pp. 55–75). Oxford: Oxford University Press. (Original work published in 1961)

—. (1979b). Performative utterances. In J. O. Urmson & G. J. Warnock (Eds.), *Philosophical papers* (3rd ed.; pp. 233–252). Oxford: Oxford University Press. (Original work published in 1961)

—. (1979c). A plea for excuses. In J. O Urmson & G. J. Warnock (Eds.), *Philosophical papers* (3rd ed.; pp. 175–204). Oxford: Oxford University Press. (Original work published in 1956–1957)

—. (1979d). Three ways of spilling ink. In J. O. Urmson & G. J. Warnock (Eds.), *Philosophical papers* (3rd ed.; pp. 272–287). Oxford: Oxford University Press. (Original work published in 1966)

—. (1979e). Truth. In J. O. Urmson & G. J. Warnock (Eds.), *Philosophical papers* (3rd ed.; pp. 117–133). Oxford: Oxford University Press. (Original work published in 1950)

Ayer, A. J. (1952). *Language, truth and logic.* New York: Dover. (Original work published in 1946)

Bacon, F. (1900a). *Novum organum.* In J. McCarthy et al. (Series Eds.), *Advancement of learning and novum organum* (pp. 309–470). Oxford: Clarendon. (Original work published in 1620)

—. (1900b). *On the dignity and advancement of learning.* In J. McCarthy et al. (Series Eds.), *Advancement of learning and novum organum* (pp. 1–307). Oxford: Clarendon. (Original work published in 1605)

—. (1997). Community service writing: Problems, challenges, questions. In L. Adler-Kassner, R. Crooks, & A. Watters (Eds.), *Writing the community: Concepts and models for service-learning in composition* (pp. 39–56). Washington, DC: AAHE.

—. (2000). Building a swan's nest for instruction in rhetoric. *College Composition and Communication, 51,* 589–609.

Bailey, G., Tillery, J., & Wikle, T. (1997). Methodology of a survey of Oklahoma dialects. *The SECOL Review, 21,* 1–30.

Bakhtin, M. M. (1981). *The dialogic imagination* (M. Holquist, Ed.; C. Emerson & M. Holquist, Trans.). Austin: University of Texas Press. (Original work published in 1975)

—. (1996). *Speech genres and other late essays* (C. Emerson & M. Holquist, Eds.; V. W. McGee, Trans.). Austin: University of Texas Press. (Original work published in 1986)

Banner, J. M., Jr., & Cannon, H. C. (1998). Teachers: Missionaries for learning. *American Educator, 21.4,* 8–11, 46. (Original work published in 1997)

Barbour, J. (1999). *The end of time: The next revolution in our understanding of the universe.* London: Westfield & Nicolson.

Barilli, R. (1989). *Rhetoric* (G. Menozzi, Trans.). Minneapolis: University of Minnesota Press. (Original work published in 1983)

Barthes, R. (1977a). Change in the object itself. In S. Heath (Ed. & Trans.), *Image, music, text* (pp. 165–169). New York: Hill & Wang. (Original work published in 1971)

—. (1977b). The death of the author. In S. Heath (Ed. & Trans.), *Image, music, text* (pp. 142–148). New York: Hill & Wang. (Original work published in 1968)

—. (1977c). Diderot, Brecht, Eisenstein. In S. Heath (Ed. & Trans.), *Image, music, text* (pp. 69–78). New York: Hill & Wang. (Original work published in 1973)

—. (1977d). From work to text. In S. Heath (Ed. & Trans.), *Image, music, text* (pp. 155–164). New York: Hill & Wang. (Original work published in 1971)

—. (1977e). The grain of the voice. In S. Heath (Ed. & Trans.), *Image, music, text* (pp. 179–189). New York: Hill & Wang. (Original work published in 1972)

—. (1977f). Introduction to the structural analysis of narratives. In S. Heath (Ed. & Trans.), *Image, music, text* (pp. 79–124). New York: Hill & Wang. (Original work published in 1966)

—. (1977g). The photographic message. In S. Heath (Ed. & Trans.), Image, music, text (pp. 15–31). New York: Hill & Wang. (Original work published in 1961)

—. (1977h). Rhetoric of the image. In S. Heath (Ed. & Trans.), *Image, music, text* (pp. 32–51). New York: Hill & Wang. (Original work published in 1964)

—. (1977i). The struggle with the angel: Textual analysis of Genesis 32:22–32. In S. Heath (Ed. & Trans.), *Image, music, text* (pp. 125–141). New York: Hill & Wang. (Original work published in 1971)

—. (1977j). The third meaning. In S. Heath (Ed. & Trans.), *Image, music, text* (pp. 52–68). New York: Hill & Wang. (Original work published in 1970)

—. (1977k). Writers, intellectuals, teachers. In S. Heath (Ed. & Trans.), *Image, music, text* (pp. 190–215). New York: Hill & Wang. (Original work published in 1971)

—. (1982). Myth today. In S. Sontag (Ed.), *A Barthes reader* (pp. 93–149). New York: Hill & Wang. (Original work published in 1957)

Bartholomae, D. (1995). Writing with teachers: A conversation with Peter Elbow. *College Composition and Communication, 46,* 62–71.

—. (1996). Inventing the university. In M. Wiley, B. Gleason, & L. W. Phelps (Eds.), *Composition in four keys: Inquiring into the field* (pp. 460–479). Mountain View, CA: Mayfield. (Original work published in 1985)

Barton, E. L. (1995). Contrastive and non-contrastive connectives: Metadiscourse functions in argumentation. *Written Communication, 12,* 219–239.

Baudrillard, J. (1983). *Simulations* (P. Foss, P. Patton, & P. Beitchman, Trans.). New York: Semiotext[e].

Bawarshi, A. (2000). The genre function. *College English, 62,* 335–360.

Bazerman, C. (1988). *Shaping written knowledge: The genre and activity of the experimental article in science.* Madison: University of Wisconsin Press.

Beardsley, M. C. (1976). *Writing with reason.* Englewood Cliffs, NJ: Prentice Hall.

Beidler, P. G., & Mackes, M. (1986). Writing the alumni career profile: A real-world assignment for composition students. *College Composition and Communication, 37,* 351–353.

Berger, P. L., & Luckmann, T. (1967). *The social construction of reality: A treatise in the sociology of knowledge.* New York: Anchor. (Original work published in 1966)

References 353

Bergmann, M. (1991). Metaphorical assertions. In S. Davis (Ed.), *Pragmatics: A reader* (pp. 231–241). Oxford: Oxford University Press. (Original work published in 1982)

Bergson, H. (1946). *The creative mind: An introduction to metaphysics.* New York: Wisdom Library.

Berkenkotter, C., & Huckin, T. N. (1993). You are what you cite: Novelty and intertextuality in a biologist's experimental article. In N. R. Blyler & C. Thralls (Eds.), *Professional communication: The social perspective* (pp. 109–127). Newbury Park, CA: Sage.

Berlin, J. (1987). *Rhetoric and reality: Writing instruction in American colleges, 1900–1985.* Carbondale: Southern Illinois University Press.

—. (1988). Rhetoric and ideology in the writing class. *College English, 50,* 477–494.

—.(1993). Composition studies and cultural studies: Collapsing boundaries. In A. R. Gere (Ed.), *Into the field: Sites of composition studies* (pp. 99–116). New York: MLA.

—. (1996). Contemporary composition: The major pedagogical theories. In M. Wiley, B. Gleason, & L. W. Phelps (Eds.), *Composition in four keys: Inquiring into the field* (pp. 556–566). Mountain View, CA: Mayfield. (Original work published in 1982)

Bernard-Donals, M., & Glejzer, R. R. (Eds.). (1998). *Rhetoric in an antifoundational world: Language, culture, and pedagogy.* New Haven, CT: Yale University Press.

Bernstein, B. (1971–1975). *Class, codes and control* (Vols. 1–3). London: Routledge & Kegan Paul.

Berthoff, A. E. (1978). *Forming/thinking/writing: The composing imagination.* Rochelle Park, NJ: Hayden.

—. (1999). Reclaiming the active mind. *College English, 61,* 671–680.

Berthoff, A., Daniell, B., Campbell, J., Swearingen, C. J., & Moffett, J. (1994). Interchanges: Spiritual sites of composing. *College Composition and Communication, 45,* 237–263.

Bettini, C., Dyreson, C. E., Evans, W. S., Snodgrass, R. T., & Wang, X. S. (1998). A glossary of time granularity concepts. In O. Etzion, S. Jajodia, S. Sripada (Eds.), *Temporal databases: Research and practice* (pp. 406–413). Berlin: Springer-Verlag.

Bhaktivedanta, A C. (Trans.). (1972). *Bhagavad-Gītā as it is.* New York: Bhaktivedanta Book Trust.

Bitzer, L. (1968). The rhetorical situation. *Philosophy and Rhetoric, 1,* 1–14.

Bizzell, P. (1991). Power, authority, and critical pedagogy. *Journal of Basic Writing, 10,* 54–70.

—. (1992a). Cognition, context, and certainty. In P. Bizzell, *Academic discourse and critical consciousness* (pp. 75–104). Pittsburgh, PA: University of Pittsburgh Press. (Original work published in 1982)

—. (1992b). Foundationalism and anti-foundationalism in composition studies. In P. Bizzell, *Academic discourse and critical consciousness* (pp. 202–221). Pittsburgh, PA: University of Pittsburgh Press. (Original work published in 1986)

—. (1992c). Thomas Kuhn, scientism, and English studies. In P. Bizzell, *Academic discourse and critical consciousness* (pp. 39–50). Pittsburgh, PA: University of Pittsburgh Press. (Original work published in 1979)

—. (1992d). What is a discourse community? In P. Bizzell, *Academic discourse and critical consciousness* (pp. 222–237). Pittsburgh: University of Pittsburgh Press.

Black, E. (1999). The second persona. In J. L. Lucaites, C. M. Condit, & S. Caudill (Eds.), *Contemporary rhetorical theory: A reader* (pp. 331–340). New York: Guilford Press. (Original work published in 1970).

Blakar, R. M. (1992). Towards an identification of preconditions for communication. In A. H. Wold (Ed.), *The dialogic alternative: Towards a theory of language and mind* (pp. 235–252). Oslo: Scandinavian University Press.

Bleich, D. (1990). Literacy citizenship: Resisting social issues. In A. Lunsford, H. Moglen, & J. Slevin (Eds.), *The right to literacy* (pp. 163–169). New York: MLA.

Bloom, H. (1973). *The anxiety of influence.* New York: Oxford University Press.

Bloom, Lois. (1994). Meaning and expression. In W. F. Overton & D. S. Palermo (Eds.), *The nature and ontogenesis of meaning* (pp. 215–235). Hillsdale, NJ: Erlbaum.

Bloom, Lynn. (1999). The essay canon. *College English, 61,* 401–430.

Bloomfield, L. (1961). *Language.* New York: Holt, Rinehart & Winston. (Original work published in 1933)

Blum-Kulka, S. (1997). Discourse pragmatics. In T. A. van Dijk (Ed.), *Discourse studies: A multidisciplinary introduction: Vol. 2. Discourse as social interaction* (pp. 38–63). London: Sage.

Böhlen, M. H., et al. (1998). The consensus glossary of temporal database concepts—February 1998 version (S. J. Jensen & C. E. Dyreson, Eds.). In O. Etzion, S. Jajodia, S. Sripada (Eds.), *Temporal databases: Research and practice* (pp. 367–405). Berlin: Springer-Verlag.

Bolinger, D. (1976). Meaning and memory. *Forum Linguisticum, 1,* 1–14.

Borgés, J. L., & Casares, A. B. (1972). Of exactitude in science. In J. L. Borgés, *A universal history of infamy* (N. T. di Giovanni, Trans.; p. 141). New York: Dutton. (Original work published in 1946)

Bormann, E. G. (1972). Fantasy and rhetorical vision: The rhetorical criticism of social reality. *Quarterly Journal of Speech, 58,* 396–407.

Bourdieu, P. (1990). *The logic of practice* (R. Nice, Trans.). Stanford, CA: Stanford University Press. (Original work published in 1980)

—. (1991). *Language and symbolic power* (J. B. Thompson, Ed.; G. Raymond & M. Adamson, Trans.). Cambridge, MA: Harvard University Press. (Original work published in 1982)

Bowers, F. (1959). *Textual and literary criticism.* Cambridge, UK: Cambridge University Press.

Bracewell, R. J. (1999). Objects of study in situated literacy: The role of representations in moving from data to explanation. *Written Communication, 16,* 76–92.

Branch, K. (1998). From the margins at the center: Literary, authority, and the great divide. *College Composition and Communication, 50,* 206–231.

Brandom, R. (1994). *Making it explicit: Reasoning, representing, and discursive commitment.* Cambridge, MA: Harvard University Press.

Brandt, D. (1998). Sponsors of literacy. *College Composition and Communication, 49,* 165–185.

—. (2001). Protecting the personal. In D. Brandt, E. Cushman, A. R. Gere, A. Herrington, R. E. Miller, V. Villanueva, M.-Z. Lu, G. Kirsch, The politics of the personal: Storying our lives against the grain (pp. 42–44). *College English, 64,* 41–62.

Bridgman, P. W. (1966). *The way things are.* Cambridge, MA: Harvard University Press. (Original work published in 1959)

Britton, J. (1992). *Language and learning* (2nd ed.). London: Penguin. (Original work published in 1970)

Britton, J., Burgess, T., Martin, N., McLeod, A., & Rosen, H. (1975). *The development of writing abilities (11–18).* London: Macmillan Education.

Bruffee, K. A. (1996). Collaborative learning and the "conversation of mankind." In M. Wiley, B. Gleason, & L. W. Phelps (Eds.), *Composition in four keys: Inquiring into the field* (pp. 84–97). Mountain View, CA: Mayfield. (Original work published in 1984)

Bruner, J. (1986). *Actual minds, possible worlds.* Cambridge, MA: Harvard University Press.

Bruns, G. L. (1992). *Hermeneutics ancient and modern.* New Haven, CT: Yale University Press.

Brunsdon, C., & Morley, D. (1978). *Everyday television: 'Nationwide.'* London: British Film Institute.

Buber, M. (1966). *I and thou* (2nd ed.; R. G. Smith, Trans.). Edinburgh: Clark. (Original work published in 1923)

Burke, K. (1945). *A grammar of motives.* New York: Prentice-Hall.

—. (1966a). Terministic screens. In K. Burke, *Language as symbolic action: Essays on life, literature, and method* (pp. 44–62). Berkeley: University of California Press. (Original work published in 1965)

—. (1966b). What are the signs of what? (A theory of "entitlement"). In K. Burke, *Language as symbolic action: Essays on life, literature, and method* (pp. 359–379). Berkeley: University of California Press. (Original work published in 1962)

—. (1969). *A rhetoric of motives.* Berkeley: University of California Press. (Original work published in 1950)

Burnett, R. E. (1996). "Some people weren't able to contribute anything but their technical knowledge": The anatomy of a dysfunctional team. In A. H. Duin & C. J. Hansen (Eds.), *Nonacademic writing: Social theory and technology* (pp. 123–156). Mahwah, NJ: Erlbaum.

Butterworth, G., & Grover, L. (1988). The origins of referential communication in human infancy. In L. Weiskrantz (Ed.), *Thought without language* (pp. 5–24). Oxford: Clarendon.

Cain, M. A. (1999). Problematizing formalism: A double-cross of genre boundaries. *College Composition and Communication, 51,* 89–95.

Campbell, G. (1988). *The philosophy of rhetoric* (L. F. Bitzer, Ed.). Carbondale: Southern Illinois University Press. (Original work published in 1776)

Canagarajah, A. S. (1996). "Non-discursive" requirements in academic publishing, material resources of periphery scholars, and the politics of knowledge production. *Written Communication, 13,* 435–472.

Carnap, R. (1959a). The elimination of metaphysics through logical analysis of language (A. Pap, Trans.). In A. J. Ayer (Ed.), *Logical positivism* (pp. 60–81). New York: Free Press. (Original work published in 1932)

—. (1959b). Psychology in physical language. In A J. Ayer (Ed.), *Logical positivism* (pp. 165–198). New York: Free Press. (Original work published in 1932–1933)

—. (1988). *Meaning and necessity: A study in semantics and modal logic* (2nd ed.). Chicago: University of Chicago Press. (Original work published in 1947)

Carter, M. (1990). The idea of expertise: An exploration of cognitive and social dimensions of writing. *College Composition and Communication, 41,* 265–286.

Cassirer, E. (1972). *An essay on man.* New Haven, CT: Yale University Press. (Original work published in 1944)

Certeau, M. de. (1984). *The practice of everyday life* (S. F. Rendall, Trans.). Berkeley: University of California Press. (Original work published in 1974)

Certeau, M. de., Giard, L., & Mayol, P. (1998). *The practice of everyday life: Vol. 2. Living and cooking* (T. J. Tomasik, Trans.). Minneapolis: University of Minnesota Press. (Original work published in 1994)

Chafe, W. L. (1975). *Meaning and the structure of language.* Chicago: University of Chicago Press. (Original work published in 1970)

—. (1994). *Discourse, consciousness, and time: The flow and displacement of conscious experience in speaking and writing.* Chicago: University of Chicago Press.

Chaput, C. (2000). Identity, postmodernity, and an ethics of activism. *JAC, 20,* 43–72.

Chase, W. J. (1926). Introduction. In Donatus (trans. 1926), *Ars minor* (W. J. Chase, Trans.; pp. 3–26). Madison: University of Wisconsin Press.

Chenowith, N. A., Hayes, J. R., Gripp, P., Littleton, E. B., Steinberg, E. R., & van Every, D. (1999). Are our courses working? Measuring student learning. *Written Communication, 16,* 29–50.

Cherwitz, R. A., & Darwin, T. J. (1995). Toward a relational theory of meaning. *Philosophy and Rhetoric, 28,* 17–29.

Chomsky, N. (1969). *Syntactic structures.* The Hague, the Netherlands: Mouton. (Original work published in 1957)

—. (1972). *Language and mind* (Enlarged ed.). New York: Harcourt Brace Jovanovich. (Original work published in 1968)

—. (1986). *Knowledge of language: Its nature, origin, and use.* New York: Praeger.

Chown, M. (2001, March 10). The omega man. *The New Scientist.* [Online]. Available: www.newscientist.com/features/features.jsp?id=ns22811

Churchland, P. S. (2000). *Neurophilosophy: Toward a unified science of the mind/brain.* Cambridge, MA: MIT Press. (Original work published in 1986)

[Cicero]. (trans. 1989). *De ratione dicendi (rhetorica ad Herennium)* (H. Caplan, Trans.). Cambridge, MA: Harvard University Press. (Original work published in 1939)

Cicero. (trans. 1970). *On oratory and orators* (J. S. Watson, Ed. & Trans.). Carbondale: Southern Illinois University Press.

Cintron, R. (1997). *Angel's town: Chero ways, gang life, and the rhetorics of the everyday.* Boston: Beacon.

Clark, G. (1998). Writing as travel, or rhetoric on the road. *College Composition and Communication, 49,* 9–23.

Clifford, C. (1999). St. Athanasius. In *The Catholic encyclopedia* (Vol. 2). [On-line]. Available: www.newadvent.org/cathen/02035a.htm (Original work published in 1907).

Coles, W. E., Jr. (1978). *The plural I: The teaching of writing.* New York: Holt, Rinehart, and Winston.

Collins, V. T. (1999). The speaker respoken: Material rhetoric as feminist methodology. *College English, 61,* 545–573.

Cohen, L. J. (1962). *The diversity of meaning.* London: Methuen.

Comfort, J. R. (2000). Becoming a writerly self: College writers engaging black feminist essays. *College Composition and Communication, 51,* 540–559.

Condillac, E. T., de. (1982a). *Logic, or the first developments of the art of thinking.* In F. Philip & H. Lane (Trans.), *Philosophical writings of Etienne*

Bonnot, abbe de Condillac (pp. 341–422). Hillsdale: Erlbaum. (Original work published in 1792)

—. (1982b). *A treatise on the sensations.* In F. Philip & H. Lane (Trans.), *Philosophical writings of Etienne Bonnot, abbe de Condillac* (pp. 155–339). Hillsdale: Erlbaum. (Original work published in 1754)

—. (1982c). *A treatise on systems.* In F. Philip & H. Lane (Trans.), *Philosophical writings of Etienne Bonnot, abbe de Condillac* (pp. 1–153). Hillsdale: Erlbaum. (Original work published in 1746)

Condit, C. M. (1999). The rhetorical limits of polysemy. In J. L. Lucaites, C. M. Condit, & S. Caudill (Eds.), *Contemporary rhetorical theory* (pp. 494–511). New York: Guilford Press. (Original work published in 1989)

Conley, T. M. (1990). *Rhetoric in the European tradition.* Chicago: University of Chicago Press.

Connors, R. J. (1985). Mechanical correctness as a focus in composition instruction. *College Composition and Communication, 36,* 61–72.

—. (1998). The rhetoric of citation systems—part one: The development of annotation structures from the Renaissance to 1900. *Rhetoric Review, 17,* 6–48.

—. (1999). The rhetoric of citation systems—part two: Competing epistemic values in citation. *Rhetoric Review, 17,* 219–245.

Cooper, M. M. (1982). Context as vehicle: Implicatures in writing. In M. Nystrand (Ed.), *What writers know: The language, process, and structure of written discourse* (pp. 105–128). New York: Academic Press.

Corbett, E. P. J. (1965). *Classical rhetoric for the modern student.* New York: Oxford University Press.

—. (1981). The status of writing in our society. In M. F. Whiteman (Ed.), *Writing: The nature, development, and teaching of written communication: Vol. 1. Variation in writing: Functional and linguistic-cultural differences* (pp. 47–52). Hillsdale, NJ: Erlbaum.

Corner, M. (1990). Responding to the word: Problems and pitfalls in interpreting the Bible. In G. McGregor & R. S. White (Eds.), *Reception and response: Hearer creativity and the analysis of spoken and written texts* (pp. 216–241). London: Routledge.

Coupland, N., & Giles, H. (1988). Communicative accommodation: Recent developments. *Language and Communication, 8,* 175–327.

Couture, B. (1999). Modeling and emulating: Rethinking agency in the writing process. In T. Kent (Ed.), *Post-process theory: Beyond the writing process paradigm* (pp. 30–48). Carbondale: Southern Illinois University Press.

Cox, K. C. (1998). Magic and memory in the contemporary story cycle: Gloria Naylor and Louise Erdrich. *College English, 60,* 150–172.

Crosswhite, J. (1996). *The rhetoric of reason: Writing and the attractions of argument.* Madison: University of Wisconsin Press.

D'Angelo, F. J. (1975). *A conceptual theory of rhetoric.* Cambridge, MA: Winthrop.

Daneš, F. (1964). A three-level approach to syntax. *Travaux Linguistiques de Prague, 1,* 225–240.

Daniel, S. H. (1994). *The philosophy of Jonathan Edwards: A study in divine semiotics.* Bloomington: Indiana University Press.

Dasenbrock, R. W. (1993). Do we write the text we read? In R. W. Dasenbrock (Ed.), *Literary theory after Davidson* (pp. 18–36). University Park: Pennsylvania State University Press. (Original work published in 1991)

—. (1995). Truth and methods. *College English, 57,* 546–561.

—. (1999). Why read multicultural literature? An Arnoldian perspective. *College English, 61,* 691–701.

—. (2001). *Truth and consequences: Intentions, conventions, and the new thematics.* University Park: Pennsylvania State University Press.

Davidson, D. (1980a). Hempel on explaining action. In D. Davidson, *Essays on actions and events* (pp. 261–275). Oxford: Clarendon. (Original work published in 1976)

—. (1980b). Hume's cognitive theory of pride. In D. Davidson, *Essays on actions and events* (pp. 277–290). Oxford: Clarendon. (Original work published in 1976)

—. (1980c). The material mind. In D. Davidson, *Essays on actions and events* (pp. 245–259). Oxford: Clarendon. (Original work published in 1973)

—. (1980d). Mental events. In D. Davidson, *Essays on actions and events* (pp. 207–225). Oxford: Clarendon. (Original work published in 1970)

—. (1980e). Psychology as philosophy. In D. Davidson, *Essays on actions and events* (pp. 229–239). Oxford: Clarendon. (Original work published in 1974)

—. (1984a). Belief and the basis of meaning. In D. Davidson, *Inquiries into truth and interpretation* (pp. 141–154). Oxford: Clarendon. (Original work published in 1974)

—. (1984b). On saying that. In D. Davidson, *Inquiries into truth and interpretation* (pp. 93–108). Oxford: Clarendon. (Original work published in 1968–1969)

—. (1984c). On the very idea of a conceptual scheme. In D. Davidson, *Inquiries into truth and interpretation* (pp. 183–198). Oxford: Clarendon. (Original work published in 1974)

—. (1984d). Radical interpretation. In D. Davidson, *Inquiries into truth and interpretation* (pp. 125–139). Oxford: Clarendon. (Original work published in 1973)

—. (1985). Rational animals. In E. Lepore & B. P. McLaughlin (Eds.), *Actions and events: Perspectives on the philosophy of Donald Davidson* (pp. 473–480). Oxford: Blackwell.

—. (1986a). A coherence theory of truth and knowledge. In E. Lepore (Ed.), *Truth and interpretation: Perspectives on the philosophy of Donald Davidson* (pp. 307–319). Oxford: Basil Blackwell.

—. (1986b). A nice derangement of epitaphs. In E. Lepore (Ed.), Truth and interpretation: Perspectives on the philosophy of Donald Davidson (pp. 443–446). Oxford: Basil Blackwell.

—. (1993a). Locating literary language. In R. W. Dasenbrock (Ed.), Literary theory after Davidson (pp. 295–308). University Park: Pennsylvania State University Press.

—. (1993b). Reply to Andreas Kemmerling. In R. Stoecker (Ed.), *Reflecting Davidson: Donald Davidson responding to an international forum of philosophers* (pp. 117–119). New York: de Gruyter.

—. (1993c). Reply to Felix Mühlhölzer. In R. Stoecker (Ed.), *Reflecting Davidson: Donald Davidson responding to an international forum of philosophers* (pp. 54–55). New York: de Gruyter.

Davies, P. (1995). *About time: Einstein's unfinished revolution.* New York: Simon & Schuster.

Davis, D. D. (1999). "Addicted to love": Or, toward an inessential solidarity. *JAC, 19,* 633–656.

—. (2000). Confessions of an anacoluthon: Avital Ronell on writing, technology, pedagogy, politics. *JAC, 20,* 243–281.

Deleuze, G. (1990). *The logic of sense* (C. V. Boundas & D. Mitchell, Ed.; M. Lester & C. Stivale, Trans.). New York: Columbia University Press. (Original work published 1969)

—. (1994). *Difference and repetition* (P. Patton, Trans.). New York: Columbia University Press. (Original work published in 1968)

Delpit, L. D. (1986). Skills and other dilemmas of a progressive black educator. *Harvard Educational Review, 56,* 379–385.

—. (1988). The silenced dialogue: Power and pedagogy in educating other people's children. *Harvard Educational Review, 58,* 280–298.

Dennett, D. C. (1978). Skinner skinned. In D. C. Dennett, *Brainstorms: Philosophical essays on mind and psychology* (pp. 51–70). Montgomery, VT: Bradford Books.

—. (1991). *Consciousness explained.* Boston: Little, Brown.

Derrida, J. (1976). *Of grammatology* (G. C. Spivak, Trans.). Baltimore: Johns Hopkins University Press. (Original work published in 1967)

—. (1978). *Writing and difference* (A. Bass, Trans.). Chicago: University of Chicago Press. (Original work published in 1967)

—. (1981). *Dissemination* (B. Johnson, Trans.) Chicago: University of Chicago Press. (Original work published in 1972)

—. (1988a). Afterword (S. Weber, Trans.). In J. Derrida, *Limited Inc* (pp. 111–160). Evanston, IL: Northwestern University Press.

—. (1988b). Limited Inc a b c... (S. Weber, Trans.). In J. Derrida, *Limited Inc* (pp. 29–110). Evanston, IL: Northwestern University Press. (Original work published in 1977)

—. (1988c). Signature event context (S. Weber & J. Mehlman, Trans.). In J. Derrida, *Limited Inc* (pp. 1–23). Evanston, IL: Northwestern University Press. (Original work published in 1972)

Descartes, R. (1970a). *Discourse on the method of rightly conducting the reason and seeking for truth in the sciences.* In E. S. Haldane & G. R. T. Ross (Eds. & Trans.), *The philosophical works of Descartes* (Vol. 1; pp. 79–130). Cambridge, UK: Cambridge University Press. (Original work published in 1637)

—. (1970b). *Meditations on the first philosophy in which the existence of God and the distinction between mind and body are demonstrated.* In E. S. Haldane & G. R. T. Ross (Eds. & Trans.), *The philosophical works of Descartes* (Vol. 1; pp. 131–199). Cambridge, UK: Cambridge University Press. (Original work published in 1641)

—. (1970c). *Rules for the direction of the mind.* In E. S. Haldane & G. R. T. Ross (Eds. & Trans.), *The philosophical works of Descartes* (Vol. 1; pp. 1–77). Cambridge, UK: Cambridge University Press. (Original work published in 1701)

Devitt, A. J. (2000). Integrating rhetorical and literary theories of genre. *College English, 62,* 696–718.

Dewey, J. (1985). *The public and its problems.* Athens, OH: Swallow Press. (Original work published in 1927)

Dillon, G. L. (1981). *Constructing texts: Elements of a theory of composition and style.* Bloomington: Indiana University Press.

Docherty, T. (1993). Postmodernism: An introduction. In T. Docherty (Ed.), *Postmodernism: A reader* (pp. 1–31). New York: Columbia University Press.

Donahue, M., J. (2002). An introduction to chaos theory and fractal geometry. [On-line] Available: www.duke.edu/~mjd/chaos/chaosp.html (Original work published in 1997)

Donatus. (trans. 1926). *The ars minor of Donatus* (W. J. Chase, Trans.). Madison: University of Wisconsin Press.

Donnellan, K. (1966). Reference and definite descriptions. *Philosophical Review, 75,* 281–304.

Dorman, W., & Dorman, S. F. (1997). Service-learning: Bridging the gap between the real world and the composition classroom. In L. Adler-Kassner, R. Crooks, & A. Watters (Eds.), *Writing the community: Concepts and models for service-learning in composition* (pp. 119–132). Washington, DC: AAHE.

Douglas, W. (1996). Rhetoric for the meritocracy: Composition at Harvard. In R. Ohmann, *English in America: A radical view of the profession* (pp.

97–132). Middletown, CT: Wesleyan University Press. (Original work published in 1976)

Dretske, F. I. (1981). *Knowledge and the flow of information.* Cambridge, MA: MIT Press.

Drew, J. (1998). Cultural composition: Stuart Hall on ethnicity and the discursive turn. *JAC, 18,* 171–196.

Drew, P. (1990). Asymmetries of knowledge in conversational interactions. In I. Marková & K. Foppa (Eds.), *Asymmetries in dialogue* (pp. 21–48). Savage, MD: Barnes & Noble.

Dummett, M. (1986). Comments on Davidson and Hacking. In E. Lepore (Ed.), *Truth and interpretation: Perspectives on the philosophy of Donald Davidson* (pp. 459–476). Oxford: Blackwell.

—. (1996a). Can an effect precede its cause? In M. Dummett, *Truth and other enigmas* (pp. 319–332). Cambridge, MA: Harvard University Press. (Original work published in 1954)

—. (1996b). Frege's distinction between sense and reference. In M. Dummett, *Truth and other enigmas* (pp. 116–144). Cambridge, MA: Harvard University Press. (Original work published in 1975)

—. (1996c). The justification of deduction. In M. Dummett, *Truth and other enigmas* (pp. 290–318). Cambridge, MA: Harvard University Press. (Original work published in 1973)

—. (1996d). The significance of Quine's indeterminacy thesis. In M. Dummett, *Truth and other enigmas* (pp. 375–419). Cambridge, MA: Harvard University Press. (Original work published in 1973)

Dunmire, P. (1997). Naturalizing the future in factual discourse: A critical linguistic analysis of a projected event. *Written Communication, 14,* 221–264.

—. (2000). Genre as temporally situated social action: A study of temporality and genre activity. *Written Communication, 17,* 93–138.

Duranti, A. (1985). Famous theories and local theories: The Samoans and Wittgenstein. *The Quarterly Newsletter of the Laboratory of Comparative Human Cognition,* 7.2, 46–51.

—. (1990). Doing things with words: Conflict, understanding, and change in a Samoan *fono.* In K. A. Watson-Gegeo & G. M. White (Eds.), *Disentangling: Conflict discourse in Pacific societies* (pp. 459–489). Stanford, CA: Stanford University Press.

—. (1997). *Linguistic anthropology.* Cambridge, UK: Cambridge University Press.

Durkheim, E. (1982). *The rules of sociological method.* In E. Durkheim, *The rules of sociological method and selected texts on sociology and its metheod* (pp. 29–163; S. Lukes, Ed.; W. D. Halls, Trans.). New York: Free Press. (Original work published in 1895)

Dyreson, C. E., Evans, W. S., Lin, H., & Snodgrass, R. T. (2000). Efficiently supporting temporal granularities. *IEEE Transactions on Knowledge and Data Engineering, 12,* 568–587.

Dyson, A. H. (1989). *Multiple worlds of child writers: Friends learning to write.* New York: Teachers College Press.

—. (1992). The case of the singing scientist: A performance perspective on the "stages" of school literacy. *Written Communication, 9,* 3–47.

—. (1997). Rewriting for, and by, the children: The social and ideological fate of a media miss in an urban classroom. *Written Communication, 14,* 275–312.

Earman, J. (1989). *World enough and space-time: Absolute versus relational theories of space and time.* Cambridge, MA: MIT Press.

Eckford-Prossor, M., & Clifford, M. (1998). Language obscures social change. In M. Bernard-Donals & R. R. Glejzer (Eds.), *Rhetoric in an antifoundational world: Language, culture, and pedagogy* (pp. 101–127). New Haven, CT: Yale University Press.

Eco, U. (1979). Introduction: The role of the reader. In U. Eco, *The role of the reader: Explorations in the semiotics of texts* (pp. 3–43). Bloomington: Indiana University Press.

Ede, L., & Lunsford, A. (1996). Audience addressed/audience invoked: The role of audience in composition theory and pedagogy. In M. Wiley, B. Gleason, & L. W. Phelps (Eds.), *Composition in four keys: Inquiring into the field* (pp. 198–210). Mountain View, CA: Mayfield. (Original work published in 1984)

Edelman, G M. (1989). *The remembered present: A biological theory of consciousness.* New York: Basic Books.

—. (1992). *Bright air, brilliant fire: On the matter of mind.* New York: Basic Books.

Einstein, A. (1956). *The meaning of relativity* (5th ed.). Princeton, NJ: Princeton University Press. (Original work published in 1922)

—. (1961). *Relativity: The special and the general theory* (R. W. Lawson, Trans.). New York: Three Rivers Press. (Original work published in 1916)

Elbow, P. (1973). *Writing without teachers.* London: Oxford University Press.

—. (1981). *Writing with power: Teachings for mastering the writing process.* New York: Oxford University Press.

—. (1986). *Embracing contraries: Explorations in learning and teaching.* New York: Oxford University Press.

—. (1999a). In defense of private writing: Consequences for theory and research. *Written Communication, 16,* 139–170.

—. (1999b). Inviting the mother tongue: Beyond "mistakes," "bad English," and "wrong language." *JAC, 19,* 359–388.

Eliot, T. S. (1999a). Ben Jonson. In T. S. Eliot, *Selected essays* (pp. 147–160). London: Faber & Faber. (Original work published in 1919)

—. (1999b). Dante. In T. S. Eliot, *Selected essays* (pp. 237–277). London: Faber & Faber. (Original work published in 1919)

—. (1999c). Tradition and the individual talent. In T. S. Eliot, *Selected essays* (pp. 13–22). London: Faber & Faber. (Original work published in 1919)

Ellis, S. M. (1999). Up close and personal: A real-world audience awareness assignment. *Teaching English in the Two-Year College, 26,* 286–290.

Emerson, R. W. (1985a). Circles. In L. Ziff (Ed.), *Selected essays* (pp. 225–238). New York: Penguin. (Original work published in 1841)

—. (1985b). Experience. In L. Ziff (Ed.), *Selected essays* (pp. 285–311). New York: Penguin. (Original work published in 1844)

—. (1985c). Nature. In L. Ziff (Ed.), *Selected essays* (pp. 35–82). New York: Penguin. (Original work published in 1836)

—. (1985d). The poet. In L. Ziff (Ed.), *Selected essays* (pp. 259–284). New York: Penguin. (Original work published in 1844)

Emig, J. (1971). *The composing processes of twelfth graders.* Urbana, IL: NCTE.

Ervin, E. (1999). Academics and the negotiation of local knowledge. *College English, 61,* 448–470.

Eubanks, P. (1999). Conceptual metaphor as rhetorical response: A reconsideration of metaphor. *Written Communication, 16,* 171–199.

Faigley, L. (1985). Nonacademic writing: The social perspective. In L. Odell & D. Goswami (Eds.), *Writing in nonacademic settings* (pp. 231–248). New York: Guilford.

—. (1994). Competing theories of process: A critique and a proposal. In S. Perl (Ed.), *Landmark essays on writing process* (pp. 149–164). Davis, CA: Hermagoras Press. (Original work published in 1986)

Fearghail, F. Ó. (1995). Philo and the Fathers: The letter and the spirit. In T. Finan & V. Twomey (Eds.), *Spiritual interpretation in the Fathers: Letter and spirit* (pp. 39–59). Dublin, Ireland: Four Courts Press.

Feyerabend, P. (1993). *Against method* (3rd ed.). London: Verso. (Original work published in 1975)

Finn, S. (1995). Measuring effective writing: Cloze procedure and anaphoric "this." *Written Communication, 12,* 240–266.

Firbas, J. (1964). On defining the theme in functional sentence perspective. *Travaux Linguistiques de Prague, 1,* 267–280.

Fischer, M. M., & Abedi, M. (1990). Qur'anic dialogues: Islamic poetics and politics for Muslims and for us. In T. Maranhão (Ed.), *The interpretation of dialogue* (pp. 120–153). Chicago: University of Chicago Press.

Fish, S. (1980a). How to recognize a poem when you see one. In S. Fish, *Is there a text in this class? The authority of interpretive communities* (pp.

322–337). Cambridge, MA: Harvard University Press. (Original work published in 1970)

—. (1980b). Interpreting the *Variorum*. In S. Fish, *Is there a text in this class? The authority of interpretive communities* (pp. 147–173). Cambridge, MA: Harvard University Press. (Original work published in 1976)

—. (1980c). Introduction, or how I stopped worrying and learned to love interpretation. In S. Fish, *Is there a text in this class? The authority of interpretive communities* (pp. 1–17). Cambridge, MA: Harvard University Press.

—. (1980d). Is there a text in this class? In S. Fish, *Is there a text in this class? The authority of interpretive communities* (pp. 303–321). Cambridge, MA: Harvard University Press.

—. (1980e). Literature in the reader: Affective stylistics. In S. Fish, *Is there a text in this class? The authority of interpretive communities* (pp. 21–67). Cambridge, MA: Harvard University Press. (Original work published in 1970)

—. (1980f). What is stylistics and why are they saying such terrible things about it? In S. Fish, *Is there a text in this class? The authority of interpretive communities* (pp. 68–96). Cambridge, MA: Harvard University Press. (Original work published in 1970)

—. (1980g). What makes an interpretation acceptable? In S. Fish, *Is there a text in this class? The authority of interpretive communities* (pp. 338–355). Cambridge, MA: Harvard University Press.

Fishman, S. M., & McCarthy, L. (2001). An ESL writer and her discipline-based professor. *Written Communication, 18*, 180–228.

Fiske, J. (1989). *Reading the popular*. Boston: Unwin Hyman.

Fleckenstein, K. S. (1999). Writing bodies: Somatic mind in composition studies. *College English, 61*, 281–306.

Fleming, D. (1998). Rhetoric as a course of study. *College English, 61*, 169–191.

Flory, D. (1994). Stoic psychology, classical rhetoric, and theories of imagination in western philosophy. *Philosophy and Rhetoric, 29*, 147–167.

Flower, L. (1988). The construction of purpose in writing and reading. *College English, 50*, 528–550.

—. (1994). *The construction of negotiated meaning: A social cognitive theory of writing*. Carbondale: Southern Illinois University Press.

Flower, L., & Hayes, J. R. (1981a). A cognitive process theory of writing. *College Composition and Communication, 32*, 365–387.

—. (1981b). Plans that guide the composing process. In C. H. Frederiksen & J. F. Dominic (Eds.), *Writing: The nature, development, and teaching of written communication: Vol. 2: Writing: Process, development and communication* (pp. 39–58). Hillsdale, NJ: Erlbaum.

Fodor, J. A. (1971). On knowing what we would say. In J. F. Rosenberg & C. Travis (Eds.), *Readings in the philosophy of language* (pp. 126–136). Englewood Cliffs, NJ: Prentice-Hall. (Original work published in 1964)

—. (1987). *Psychosemantics: The problem of meaning in the philosophy of mind.* Cambridge, MA: MIT Press.

—. (1990). Semantics, Wisconsin style. In J. A. Fodor, *A theory of content and other essays* (pp. 31–49). Cambridge, MA: MIT Press. (Original work published in 1984)

Fodor, J., & Lepore, E. (1993). Is radical interpretation possible? In R. Stoecker (Ed.), *Reflecting Davidson: Donald Davidson responding to an international forum of philosophers* (pp. 57–76). New York: Walter de Gruyter.

Fortescue, A. (1999). Iconoclasm. In *The Catholic encyclopedia* (Vol. 7). [Online] Available: www.newadvent.org/cathen/07620a.htm (Original work published in 1910)

Foucault, M. (1970). *The order of things: An archaeology of the human sciences* (A. Sheridan, Trans.). New York: Vintage. (Original work published in 1966)

—. (1972a). *The archaeology of knowledge* (A. M. Sheridan Smith, Trans.). New York: Pantheon. (Original work published in 1969)

—. (1972b). The discourse on language. In M. Foucault, *The archaeology of knowledge* (A. M. Sheridan Smith, Trans.; pp. 215–237). New York: Pantheon. (Original work published in 1971)

—. (1977a). Fantasia of the library. In D. F. Bouchard (Ed.), *Language, counter-memory, practice: Selected essays and interviews* (D. F. Bouchard & S. Simon, Trans.; pp. 87–109). Ithaca, NY: Cornell University Press. (Original work published in 1967)

—. (1977b). History of systems of thought. In D. F. Bouchard (Ed.), *Language, counter-memory, practice: Selected essays and interviews* (D. F. Bouchard & S. Simon, Trans; pp. 199–204). Ithaca, NY: Cornell University Press.

—. (1977c). Intellectuals and power. In D. F. Bouchard (Ed.), *Language, counter-memory, practice: Selected essays and interviews* (D. F. Bouchard & S. Simon, Trans.; pp. 205–217). Ithaca, NY: Cornell University Press. (Original work published in 1972)

—. (1977d). Language to infinity. In D. F. Bouchard (Ed.), *Language, counter-memory, practice: Selected essays and interviews* (D. F. Bouchard & S. Simon, Trans; pp. 53–67). Ithaca, NY: Cornell University Press. (Original work published in 1963)

—. (1977e). Nietzsche, genealogy, history. In D. F. Bouchard (Ed.), *Language, counter-memory, practice: Selected essays and interviews* (D. F. Bouchard & S. Simon, Trans; pp. 139–164). Ithaca, NY: Cornell University Press. (Original work published in 1971)

—. (1977f). A preface to transgression. In D. F. Bouchard (Ed.), *Language, counter-memory, practice: Selected essays and interviews* (D. F. Bouchard & S. Simon, Trans; pp. 29–52). Ithaca, NY: Cornell University Press. (Original work published in 1963)

—. (1977g). Revolutionary action: "Until now." In D. F. Bouchard (Ed.), *Language, counter-memory, practice: Selected essays and interviews* (D. F. Bouchard & S. Simon, Trans; pp. 218–233). Ithaca, NY: Cornell University Press. (Original work published in 1971)

—. (1977h). Theatrum philosophicum. In D. F. Bouchard (Ed.), *Language, counter-memory, practice: Selected essays and interviews* (D. F. Bouchard & S. Simon, Trans; pp. 165–196). Ithaca, NY: Cornell University Press. (Original work published in 1970)

—. (1987). Maurice Blanchot: The thought from the outside. In M. Foucault & M. Blanchot, *Foucault/Blanchot* (pp. 7–58; B. Massumi, Trans.). New York: Zone Books.

—. (1995). *Discipline and punish: The birth of the prison* (A. Sheridan, Trans.). New York: Vintage. (Original work published in 1975)

Freadman, A. (1998, January). *Uptake.* Paper presented at the International Symposium on Genre, Vancouver, Canada.

Freedman, A., Adam, C., & Smart, G. (1994). Wearing suits to class: Simulating genres and simulations as genre. *Written Communication, 11,* 193–226.

Frege, G. (1979a). Logic [1897]. In H. Hermes et al. (Eds.), *Posthumous writings* (P. Long, R. White, & R. Hargreaves, Trans.; pp. 126–151). Oxford: Blackwell.

—. (1979b). 17 key sentences on logic [1906 or earlier]. In H. Hermes et al. (Eds.), *Posthumous writings* (P. Long, R. White, & R. Hargreaves, Trans.; pp. 174–175). Oxford: Blackwell.

—. (1979c). Sources of knowledge of mathematics and the mathematical natural sciences [1924–1925]. In H. Hermes et al. (Eds.), *Posthumous writings* (P. Long, R. White, & R. Hargreaves, Trans.; pp. 267–274). Oxford: Blackwell.

—. (1984a). Logical investigations: Part 1: Thoughts (P. Geach & R. H. Stoothoff, Trans.). In B. McGuinness (Ed.), *Collected papers on mathematics, logic, and philosophy* (pp. 351–372). Oxford: Blackwell. (Original work published in 1918–1919)

—. (1984b). Logical investigations: Part 2: Negation (P. Geach & R. H. Stoothoff, Trans.). In B. McGuinness (Ed.), *Collected papers on mathematics, logic, and philosophy* (pp. 373–389). Oxford: Blackwell. (Original work published in 1918–1919)

—. (1984c). Logical investigations: Part 3: Compound thoughts (P. Geach & R. H. Stoothoff, Trans.). In B. McGuinness (Ed.), *Collected papers on mathematics, logic, and philosophy* (pp. 390–406). Oxford: Blackwell. (Original work published in 1923–1926)

—. (1984d). On sense and meaning (M. Black, Trans.). In B. McGuinness (Ed.), *Collected papers on mathematics, logic, and philosophy* (pp. 157–177). Oxford: Blackwell. (Original work published in 1892)

—. (1984e). Review of E. G. Husserl, *Philosophie der arithmetik I [Philosophy of arithmetic I]* (H. Kaal, Trans.). In B. McGuinness (Ed.), *Collected papers on mathematics, logic, and philosophy* (pp. 195–209). Oxford: Blackwell. (Original work published in 1894)

Freire, P. (1971). *Pedagogy of the oppressed* (M. B. Ramos, Trans.). New York: Herder & Herder.

Freudenthal, H. (1960). *Lincos: Design of a language for cosmic intercourse.* Amsterdam: North-Holland.

Friend, C. (1999). From the contact zone to the city: Iris Marion Young and composition theory. *JAC, 19,* 657–676.

Fulkerson, M. M. (1994). *Changing the subject: Women's discourses and feminist theology.* Minneapolis, MN: Fortress Press.

Fulkerson, R. (1996). Four philosophies of composition. In M. Wiley, B. Gleason, & L. W. Phelps (Eds.), *Composition in four keys: Inquiring into the field* (pp. 551–555). Mountain View, CA: Mayfield. (Original work published in 1979)

Funk, R. W. (1969). *Language, hermeneutic, and word of God: The problem of language in the New Testament and contemporary theology.* New York: Harper and Row.

Gadamer, H.-G. (1977a). Aesthetics and hermeneutics (D. E. Linge, Trans.). In H.-G. Gadamer, *Philosophical hermeneutics* (D. E. Linge, Ed.; pp. 95–104). Berkeley: University of California Press. (Original work published in 1964)

—. (1977b). Heidegger's later philosophy (D. E. Linge, Trans.). In H.-G. Gadamer, *Philosophical hermeneutics* (D. E. Linge, Ed.; pp. 213–228). Berkeley: University of California Press. (Original work published in 1960)

—. (1977c). Man and language (D. E. Linge, Trans.). In H.-G. Gadamer, *Philosophical hermeneutics* (D. E. Linge, Ed.; pp. 59–68). Berkeley: University of California Press. (Original work published in 1966)

—. (1977d). On the scope and function of hermeneutical reflection (G. B. Hess & R. E. Palmer, Trans.). In H.-G. Gadamer, *Philosophical hermeneutics* (D. E. Linge, Ed.; pp. 18–43). Berkeley: University of California Press. (Original work published in 1967)

—. (1997). *Truth and method* (2nd rev. ed.). New York: Continuum. (Original work published in 1960)

Gale, X. L. (2000). Historical studies and postmodernism: Rereading Aspasia of Miletus. *College English, 62,* 361–386.

Gates, R. (1993). Creativity and insight: Toward a poetics of composition. In A. R. Gere (Ed.), *Into the field: Sites of composition studies* (pp. 147–158). New York: MLA.

Geisler, C. (1996). Toward a sociocognitive model of literacy: Constructing mental models in a philosophical conversation. In M. Wiley, B. Gleason, & L. W. Phelps (Eds.), *Composition in four keys: Inquiring into the field* (pp. 375–387). Mountain View, CA: Mayfield. (Original work published in 1991)

—. (2001). Textual objects: Accounting for the role of texts in the everyday life of complex organizations. *Written Communication, 18*, 296–325.

George, R. (1997). Psychologism in logic: Bacon to Balzano. *Philosophy and Rhetoric, 30*, 213–242.

Gerbner, G. (1956). Toward a general model of communication. *Audio-Visual Communication Review, 4*, 171–199.

Gergen, K. J. (1994). The communal creation of meaning. In W. F. Overton & D. S. Palermo (Eds.), *The nature and ontogenesis of meaning* (pp. 19–39). Hillsdale, NK: Erlbaum.

Gibbs, R. W., Jr. (1999). *Intentions in the experience of meaning.* Cambridge, UK: Cambridge University Press.

Giddens, A. (1979). *Central problems in social theory: Action, structure, and causation in social analysis.* Berkeley: University of California Press.

—. (1984). *The constitution of society: Outline of the theory of structuration.* Cambridge, UK: Polity Press.

Gilmore, W. J. (1992). *Reading becomes a necessity of life: Material and cultural life in rural New England, 1780–1835.* Knoxville: University of Tennessee Press. (Original work published in 1989)

Giroux, H. A. (2000). Public pedagogy and the responsibility of intellectuals: Youth, Littleton, and the loss of innocence. *JAC, 20*, 9–42.

Glejzer, R. R. (1998). The subject of invention: Antifoundationalism and medieval hermeneutics. In M. Bernard-Donals & R. R. Glejzer (Eds.), *Rhetoric in an antifoundational world: Language, culture, and pedagogy* (pp. 318–340). New Haven, CT: Yale University Press.

Golumb, C. (1974). *Young children's sculpture and drawing: A study in representational development.* Cambridge, MA: Harvard University Press.

Goodburn, A. (1998). It's a question of faith: Discourse of fundamentalism and critical pedagogy in the writing classroom. *JAC, 18*, 333–353.

Goodwin, C. (1994). Professional vision. *American Anthropologist, 93*, 606–633.

Goodwin, D. (1999). Toward a grammar and rhetoric of visual opposition. *Rhetoric Review, 18*, 92–111.

Gramsci, A. (1971). *Selections from the prison notebooks* (Q. Hoare & G. N. Smith, Eds. & Trans.). New York: International. (Original work published in 1948–1951)

Greene, S. (1990). Toward a dialectical theory of composing. *Rhetoric Review, 9,* 149–172.

Grice, P. (1991a). *Logic and conversation.* In P. Grice, *Studies in the way of words* (pp. 3–143). Cambridge, MA: Harvard University Press. (Original work published in 1967)

—. (1991b). Meaning. In P. Grice, *Studies in the way of words* (pp. 213–223). Cambridge, MA: Harvard University Press. (Original work published in 1948)

—. (1991c). Meaning revisited. In P. Grice, *Studies in the way of words* (pp. 283–303). Cambridge, MA: Harvard University Press. (Original work published in 1976)

Gusdorf, G. (1965). *Speaking* (P. T. Brockelman, Trans.). Evanston, IL: Northwestern University Press.

Habermas, J. (1975). *Legitimation crisis* (T. McCarthy, Trans.). Boston: Beacon Press. (Original work published in 1973)

Hacking, I. (1986). A parody of conversation. In E. Lepore (Ed.), *Truth and interpretation: Perspectives on the philosophy of Donald Davidson* (pp. 447–458). Oxford: Blackwell.

Halasek, K. (1999). *A pedagogy of possibility: Bakhtinian perspectives on composition studies.* Carbondale: Southern Illinois University Press.

Hall, D. G., & Nelson, B. A. (1987). Initiating students into professionalism: Teaching the letter of inquiry. *Technical Writing Teacher, 14,* 86–89.

Hall, S. (1982). The rediscovery of "ideology": Return of the repressed in media studies. In M. Gurevitch et al. (Eds.), *Culture, society and the media* (pp. 56–90). London: Methuen.

—. (1986). Gramsci's relevance for the study of race and ethnicity. *Journal of Communication Inquiry, 10.2,* 5–27.

Halliday, M. A. K. (1973). *Explorations in the functions of language.* New York: Arnold.

—. (1975). *Learning how to mean: Explorations in the development of language.* New York: Elsevier.

—. (1978). *Language as social semiotic: The social interpretation of language and meaning.* London: Edward Arnold.

—. (1987). Language and the order of nature. In M. Fabb, D. Attridge, A. Durant, & C. McCabe (Eds.), *The linguistics of writing: Arguments between language and literature* (pp. 135–154). Manchester, UK: Manchester University Press.

Hardy, C. (1998). *Networks of meaning: A bridge between mind and matter.* Westport, CT: Praeger.

Harris, E. E. (1988). *The reality of time.* Albany: State University of New York Press.

Harris, J. (1989). The idea of community in the study of writing. *College Composition and Communication, 40,* 11–22.

Harris, R. (1998). *Introduction to integrational linguistics.* Oxford: Elsevier.

Harris, W. V. (1996). Reflections on the peculiar status of the personal essay. *College English, 58,* 934–953.

Hartley, J. (1987). Invisible fictions: Television audiences, paedocracy, pleasure. *Textual Practice, 1,* 121–138.

Harvey, G. (1994). Presence in the essay. *College English, 56,* 642–654.

Hassan, W. S. (2000). World literature in the age of globalization: Reflections on an anthology. *College English, 63,* 38–47.

Hawking, S. (1990). *A brief history of time: From the big bang to black holes.* New York: Bantam. (Original work published in 1988)

Hayes, J. R., Hatch, J. A., & Silk, C. M. (2000). Does holistic assessment predict writing performance? Estimating the consistency of student performance on holistically scored writing assignments. *Written Communication, 17,* 3–26.

Heath, S. B. (1983). *Ways with words: Language, life, and work in communities and classrooms.* Cambridge, UK: Cambridge University Press.

Heidegger, M. (1962). *Being and time* (J. Macquarrie & E. Robinson, Trans.). New York: Harper & Row. (Original work published in 1927)

—. (1993a). The origin of the work of art (A. Hofstadter, Trans.). In D. F. Krell (Ed.), *Basic writings* (pp. 139–212). New York: HarperCollins. (Original work published in 1960)

—. (1993b). The way to language (A. Hofstadter, Trans.). In D. F. Krell (Ed.), *Basic writings* (pp. 393–426). New York: HarperCollins. (Original work published in 1959)

Heilker, P. (1997). Rhetoric made real: Civic discourse and writing beyond the curriculum. In L. Adler-Kassner, R. Crooks, & A. Watters (Eds.), *Writing the community: Concepts and models for service-learning in composition* (pp. 71–77). Washington, DC: AAHE.

Heilker, P., & Vandenberg, P. (Eds.). *Keywords in composition studies.* Portsmouth, NH: Boynton/Cook.

Heine, H. (1950). *Poems and ballads* (E. Lazarus, Trans.). New York: Perma Giants.

Hêracleitus. (trans. 1996). Hêracleitus of Ephesus. In K. Freeman (Trans.), *Ancilla to the pre-Socratic philosophers* (pp. 24–34). Cambridge, MA: Harvard University Press. (Original work published in 1948)

Herrington, A. (2001). When is my business your business? In D. Brandt, E. Cushman, A. R. Gere, A. Herrington, R. E. Miller, V. Villanueva, M.-Z. Lu, G. Kirsch, The politics of the personal: Storying our lives against the grain (pp. 47–49). *College English, 64,* 41–62.

Herrington, A., & Moran, C. (2001). What happens when machines read our students' writing. *College English, 63,* 480–499.

Herzberg, B. (2000). Service learning and public discourse. *JAC, 20,* 391–404.

Hikins, J. W. (1990). Realism and its implications for rhetorical theory. In R. A. Cherwitz (Ed.), *Rhetoric and philosophy* (pp. 21–77). Hillsdale, NJ: Erlbaum.

Hilosky, A., Moore, M. E., & Reynolds, P. (1999). Service learning: Brochure writing for basic level college students. *College Teaching, 47,* 143–147.

Hindman, J. E. (2001). Making writing matter: Using "the personal" to recover[y] an essential[ist] tension in academic discourse. *College English, 64,* 88–108.

Hirsch, E. D., Jr. (1967). *Validity in interpretation.* New Haven, CT: Yale University Press.

—. (1976). *The aims of interpretation.* Chicago: University of Chicago Press.

—. (1977). *The philosophy of composition.* Chicago: University of Chicago Press.

Hirsch, E. D., Jr., & Harrington, D. P. (1981). Measuring the communicative effectiveness of prose. In C. H. Frederiksen & J. F. Dominic (Eds.), *Writing: The nature, development, and teaching of written communication: Vol. 4. Writing: Process, development and communication* (pp. 189–207). Hillsdale, NJ: Erlbaum.

Hirsh-Pasek, K., Golinkoff, R. M., & Reeves, L. (1994). Constructivist explanations for language acquisition may be insufficient: The case for language-specific principles. In W. F. Overton & D. S. Palermo (Eds.), *The nature and ontogenesis of meaning* (pp. 237–254). Hillsdale, NJ: Lawrence Erlbaum.

Hobbes, T. (1994). *Leviathan* (E. Curley, Ed.). Indianapolis, IN: Hackett. (Original work published in 1668)

Hobbs, C. (1998). Review. *Rhetoric Review, 17,* 174–178.

Hobsbaum, P. (1970). *Theory of criticism.* Bloomington: Indiana University Press.

Holquist, M. (1981). Introduction. In M. M. Bakhtin, *The dialogic imagination* (M. Holquist, Ed.; C. Emerson & M. Holquist, Trans.; pp. xv-xxxiv). Austin: University of Texas Press. (Original work published in 1975)

—. (1990). *Dialogism: Bakhtin and his world.* London: Routledge.

—. (1996). Introduction. In M. M. Bakhtin, *Speech genres and other late essays* (C. Emerson & M. Holquist, Eds.; V. W. McGee, Trans.; pp. ix-xxiii). Austin: University of Texas Press. (Original work published in 1986)

hooks, b. (2000). Remembered rapture: Dancing with words. *JAC, 20,* 1–8. (Original work published in 1999)

Hoopes, J. (1991). Introduction. In J. Hoopes (Ed.), *Peirce on signs* (pp. 1–13). Chapel Hill: University of North Carolina Press.

Hoover, M. R., & Politzer, R. L. (1981). Bias in composition tests with suggestions for a culturally appropriate assessment technique. In M. F. Whiteman (Ed.), *Writing: The nature, development, and teaching of writ-*

ten communication: Vol. 1. Variation in writing: Functional and linguistic-cultural differences (pp. 197–207). Hillsdale, NJ: Erlbaum.

Horkheimer, M., & Adorno, T. W. (1988). *Dialectic of enlightenment* (J. Cumming, Trans.). New York: Seabury. (Original work published in 1947)

Horner, B. (2001). "Students' rights," English only, and re-imagining the politics of language. *College English, 63,* 741–758.

Huckin, T. N. (1997). Technical writing and community service. *Journal of Business and Technical Communication, 11,* 49–59.

Humboldt, W. V. (1988). *On language: The diversity of human language structure and its influence on the mental development of mankind* (P. Heath, Trans.). Cambridge, UK: Cambridge University Press. (Original work published in 1836)

Hume, D. (1977). *An enquiry concerning human understanding.* In E. Steinberg (Ed.), *An enquiry concerning human understanding/A letter from a gentleman to his friend in Edinburgh* (pp. 1–114). Indianapolis, IN: Hackett. (Original work published in 1748)

Husserl, E. (1970a). *Cartesian meditations: An introduction to phenomenology* (D. Cairns, Trans.). The Hague: Martinus Nijhoff. (Original work published in 1931)

—. (1970b). *Logical investigations* (J. N. Findlay, Trans.). London: Routledge & Kegan Paul. (Original work published in 1900–1901)

Hymes, D. (1974). *Foundations in sociolinguistics: An ethnographic approach.* Philadelphia: University of Pennsylvania Press.

Iser, W. (1978). *The implied reader: Patterns of communication in prose fiction from Bunyan to Beckett.* Baltimore, MD: Johns Hopkins University Press. (Original work published in 1972)

—. (1989a). Interaction between text and reader. In W. Iser, *Prospecting: From reader response to literary anthropology* (pp. 31–41). Baltimore, MD: Johns Hopkins University Press. (Original work published in 1980)

—. (1989b). Interview. In W. Iser, *Prospecting: From reader response to literary anthropology* (pp. 42–69). Baltimore, MD: Johns Hopkins University Press.

Isocrates. (trans. 2000). *Against the sophists* (D. C. Mirhady, Trans.). In D. C. Mirhady & Y. L. Too (Trans.), *Isocrates* (vol. 1; pp 61–66). Austin: University of Texas Press.

Jackendoff, R. (1994). Word meanings and what it takes to learn them: Reflections on the Piaget-Chomsky debate. In W. F. Overton & D. S. Palermo (Eds.), *The nature and ontogenesis of meaning* (pp. 129–144). Hillsdale, NJ: Erlbaum.

James, W. (1981). *Pragmatism* (B. Kuklick, Ed.). Indianapolis, IN: Hackett. (Original work published in 1907)

Janangelo, J. (1998). Joseph Cornell and the artistry of composing persuasive hypertexts. *College Composition and Communication, 48,* 24–44.

Janet, P. (1968). Introduction. In G. W. V. Leibniz, *Basic writings* (pp. vii-xxiii; E. Freeman, Series Ed.; G. R. Montgomery, Trans.). LaSalle, IL: Open Court. (Original work published in 1902)

Jarratt, S., & Reynolds, N. (1994). The splitting image: Contemporary feminisms and the ethics of ethos. In J. S. Baumlin & T. F. Baumlin (Eds.), *Ethos: New essays in rhetorical and critical theory* (pp. 37–63). Dallas, TX: Southern Methodist University Press.

Jespersen, O. (1925). *Mankind, nation, and individual from a linguistic point of view.* Cambridge, MA: Harvard University Press.

Johnson, R. L., Penny, J., & Gordon, B. (2001). Score resolution an the interrater reliability of holistic scores in rating essays. *Written Communication, 18,* 229–249.

Johnson, S. (1755). *A dictionary of the English language.* London: Strahan.

Johnson, T. R. (1999). Discipline and pleasure: "Magic" and sound. *JAC, 19,* 431–452.

—. (2001). School sucks. *College Composition and Communication, 52,* 620–650.

Jourdain, P. E. B. (1956). *The nature of mathematics.* In J. R. Newman (Ed.), *The world of mathematics* (Vol. 1; pp. 4–72). New York: Simon & Schuster. (Original work published in 1913)

Journet, D. (1993). Interdisciplinary discourse and "boundary rhetoric": The case of S. E. Jelliffe. *Written Communication, 10,* 510–541.

—. (1999). Writing within (and between) disciplinary genres: The "adaptive landscape" as a case study in interdisciplinary rhetoric. In T. Kent (Ed.), *Post-process theory: Beyond the writing-process paradigm* (pp. 96–115). Carbondale: Southern Illinois University Press.

Kant, I. (1996). *Critique of pure reason* (W. S. Pluhar, Trans.; Unified edition). Indianapolis, IN: Hackett. (Original work published in 1781–1787)

Kastely, J. L. (1999). From formalism to inquiry: A model of argument in Antigone. *College English, 62,* 222–241.

Katz, J. J. (1977). *Propositional structure and illocutionary force: A study of the contribution of sentence meaning to speech acts.* New York: Crowell.

Kaufer, D. S., & Butler, B. S. (1996). *Rhetoric and the arts of design.* Mahwah, NJ: Erlbaum.

Kaufer, D. S., & Carley, K. (1994). Some concepts and axioms about communication: Proximate and at a distance. *Written Communication, 11,* 8–42.

Kemmerling, A. (1993). The philosophical significance of a shared language. In R. Stoecker (Ed.), *Reflecting Davidson: Donald Davidson responding to an international forum of philosophers* (pp. 85–116). New York: de Gruyter.

Kennedy, G. A. (1980). *Classical rhetoric and its Christian and secular tradition.* Chapel Hill: University of North Carolina Press.

Kennedy, K. (1999). Cynic rhetoric: The ethics and tactics of resistance. *Rhetoric Review, 18,* 26–45.

Kent, T. (1992). Externalism and the production of discourse. *JAC, 12,* 57–74.

—. (1993a). Formalism, social construction, and the problem of interpretative authority. In N. R. Blyler & C. Thralls (Eds.), *Professional communication: The social perspective* (pp. 79–91). Newbury Park, CA: Sage.

—.(1993b). Interpretation and triangulation: A Davidsonian critique of reader-oriented literary theory. In R. W. Dasenbrock (Ed.), *Literary theory after Davidson* (pp. 37–58). University Park: Penn State University Press.

—.(1993c). *Paralogic rhetoric: A theory of communicative interaction.* Lewisburg, PA: Bucknell University Press.

—.(1999). Introduction. In T. Kent (Ed.), *Post-process theory: Beyond the writing-process paradigm* (pp. 1–6). Carbondale: Southern Illinois University Press.

Keynes, J. M. (1956). Newton, the man. In J. R. Newman (Ed.), *The world of mathematics* (Vol. 1; pp. 277–285). New York: Simon & Schuster. (Original work published in 1947)

Kim, J. (1998). *Philosophy of mind.* Boulder, CO: Westview Press. (Original work published in 1996)

Kinneavy, J. L. (1996). *Kairos:* A neglected concept in classical rhetoric. In M. Wiley, B. Gleason, & L. W. Phelps (Eds.), *Composition in four keys: Inquiring into the field* (pp. 211–224). Mountain View, CA: Mayfield. (Original work published in 1986)

Kintsch, W., & Vipond, D. (1979). Reading comprehension and readability in educational practice and psychological theory. In L.-G. Nilsson (Ed.), *Perspectives on memory research* (pp. 329–365). Hillsdale, NJ: Erlbaum.

Kixmiller, L. S. A. (2004). Standards without sacrifice: The case for authentic writing. *English Journal, 94,* 29–33.

Kleinfeld, J. (2002). Could it be a big world after all? What the Milgram papers in the Yale archives reveal about the original small world study. [On-line]. Available: //smallworld.sociology.columbia.edu/history.html

Knoblauch, C. H. (1996). Rhetorical constructions: Dialogue and commitment. In M. Wiley, B. Gleason, & L. W. Phelps (Eds.), *Composition in four keys: Inquiring into the field* (pp. 582–593). Mountain View, CA: Mayfield. (Original work published in 1988)

Knoblauch, C. H., & Brannon, L. (1984). *Rhetorical traditions and the teaching of writing.* Portsmouth, NH: Boynton/Cook.

Kramer, E. E. (1970). *The nature and growth of modern mathematics.* New York: Hawthorn Books.

Kress, G. (1997). *Before writing: Rethinking the paths to literacy.* London: Routledge.

Kripke, S. A. (1996). *Naming and necessity.* Cambridge, MA: Harvard University Press. (Original work published in 1972)

Kristeva, J. (1986). Psychoanalysis and the polis (M. Waller, Trans.). In T. Moi (Ed.), *The Kristeva reader* (pp. 301–320). New York: Columbia University Press. (Original work published in 1982)

Lamb, C. E. (1991). Beyond argument in feminist composition. *College Composition and Communication, 42,* 11–24.

Land, S. K. (1985). *The philosophy of language in Britain: Major theories from Hobbes to Thomas Reid.* New York: AMS Press.

Laplace, P.-S. (1995). *Philosophical essay on probabilities* (A. I. Dale, Trans.). New York: Springer-Verlag. (Original work published in 1814)

Le Bon, G. (1995). *The crowd: A study of the popular mind.* New Brunswick, NJ: Transaction Publications. (Original work published in 1895)

Leibniz, G. W. V. (1968a). *Correspondence relating to the metaphysics.* In G. W. V. Leibniz, *Basic writings* (pp. 65–248; E. Freeman, Series Ed.; G. R. Montgomery, Trans.). LaSalle, IL: Open Court. (Original work published in 1840)

—. (1968b). *The discourse on metaphysics.* In G. W. V. Leibniz, *Basic writings* (pp. 1–63; E. Freeman, Series Ed.; G. R. Montgomery, Trans.). LaSalle, IL: Open Court. (Original work published in 1840)

—. (1968c). *The monadology.* In G. W. V. Leibniz, *Basic writings* (pp. 249–272; E. Freeman, Series Ed.; G. R. Montgomery, Trans.). LaSalle, IL: Open Court. (Original work published in 1720)

Lentine, G., & Shuy, R. (1990). Mc-: Meaning in the marketplace. *American Speech, 65,* 349–366.

Levinas, E. (1969). *Totality and infinity: An essay on exteriority* (A. Lingis, Trans.). Pittsburgh, PA: Duquesne University Press. (Original work published in 1961)

—. (1987). Meaning and sense. In A. Lingis (Trans.), *Collected philosophical papers* (pp. 75–107). Dordrecht, The Netherlands: Martinus Nijhoff. (Original work published in 1972)

Lewis, C. I. (1956). *Mind and the world order: Outline of a theory of knowledge.* New York: Dover. (Original work published in 1929)

Lewis, D. (1969). *Convention: A philosophical study.* Cambridge, MA: Harvard University Press.

Lewontin, R. C. (1991). *Biology as ideology: The doctrine of DNA.* New York: HarperPerennial.

Lindemann, E. (1995). *A rhetoric for writing teachers* (3rd ed.). New York: Oxford University Press.

Linell, P. (1982). *The written language bias in linguistics.* Linköping, Sweden: University of Linköping Press.

Locke, J. (1987). *An essay concerning human understanding* (P. H. Nidditch, Ed.). Oxford: Clarendon. (Original work published in 1689)

Luckmann, T. (1990). Social communication, dialogue and conversation. In I. Marková & K. Foppa (Eds.), *The dynamics of dialogue* (pp. 45–61). New York: Harvester Wheatsheaf.

—. (1991). The constitution of human life in time. In J. Bender & D. E. Wellbery (Eds.), *Chronotypes: The construction of time* (pp. 151–166). Stanford, CA: Stanford University Press.

—. (1992). On the communicative adjustment of perspectives, dialogue and communicative genres. In A. H. Wold (Ed.), *The dialogic alternative: Towards a theory of language and mind* (pp. 219–234). Oslo: Scandinavian University Press.

Lunsford, A. A. (1991). The nature of composition studies. In E. Lindemann & G. Tate (Eds.), *An introduction to composition studies* (pp. 3–14). New York: Oxford University Press.

Lunsford, K. J. (2002). Contextualizing Toulmin's model in the writing class: A case study. *Written Communication, 19*, 109–174.

Luther, M. (1982). The righteousness of God—Ps. 71. *First lectures on the Psalms.* In H. C. Oswald & G. S. Robbert (Eds.), *Luther as interpreter of scripture* (pp. 9–16). St. Louis, MO: Concordia Publishing House. (Original work published in 1513–1515)

Lynch, D., & Jukuri, S. (1998). Beyond master and slave: Reconciling our fears of power in the writing classroom. *Rhetoric Review, 16*, 270–288.

Lyons, J. (1995). *Linguistic semantics: An introduction.* Cambridge, UK: Cambridge University Press.

Lyons, S. R. (2000). Rhetorical sovereignty: What do American Indians want from writing? *College Composition and Communication, 51*, 447–468.

Lyotard, J.-F. (1993). *The postmodern condition: A report on knowledge* (G. Bennington & B. Masumi, Trans.). Minneapolis: University of Minnesota Press. (Original work published in 1979)

Macrorie, K. (1970). *Telling writing.* Rochelle Park, NJ: Hayden.

Madden, N. (1995). Maximus Confessor: On the Lord's Prayer. In T. Finan & V. Twomey (Eds.), *Spiritual interpretation in the Fathers: Letter and spirit* (pp. 119–141). Dublin, Ireland: Four Courts Press.

Mailloux, S. (1982). *Interpretive conventions: The reader in the study of American fiction.* Ithaca, NY: Cornell University Press.

Malinowitz, H. (1999). Textual trouble in River City: Literary, rhetoric, and consumerism in *The music man. College English, 62*, 58–82.

Malkki, L. (1994). Citizens of humanity: Internationalism and the imagined community of nations. *Diaspora, 3*, 41–68.

Mansfield, M. A. (1993). Real world writing and the English curriculum. *College Composition and Communication, 44*, 69–83.

Maranhão, T. (1990). Introduction. In T. Maranhão (Ed.), *The interpretation of dialogue* (pp. 1–22). Chicago: University of Chicago Press.

Marhenke, P. (1952). The criterion of significance. In L. Linsky (Ed.), *Semantics and the philosophy of language: A collection of readings* (pp. 137–159). Urbana: University of Illinois Press. (Original work published in 1950)

Marková, I. (1992). On structure and dialogicity in Prague semiotics. In A. H. Wold (Ed.), *The dialogic alternative: Towards a theory of language and mind* (pp. 45–63). Oslo: Scandinavian University Press.

Martin, B. (1983, March). *Making it real: The student as working writer.* Paper presented at the annual meeting of the Conference on College Composition and Communication, Detroit, MI. (ERIC Document Reproduction Service No. ED.230959)

Mather, S. (1969). *The figures or types of the Old Testament.* New York: Johnson Reprint Corporation. (Original work published in 1705)

Mathieu, P. (1999). Economic citizenship and the rhetoric of gourmet coffee. *Rhetoric Review, 18,* 112–127.

McEvoy, J. (1995). The patristic hermeneutic of spiritual freedom and its Biblical origins. In T. Finan & V. Twomey (Eds.), *Spiritual interpretation in the Fathers: Letter and spirit* (pp. 1–25). Dublin, Ireland: Four Courts Press.

McGee, M. C. (1999a). In search of "the people": A rhetorical alternative. In J. L. Lucaites, C. M. Condit, & S. Caudill (Eds.), *Contemporary rhetorical theory* (pp. 341–356). New York: Guilford Press. (Original work published in 1975)

—. (1999b). Text, context, and the fragmentation of contemporary culture. In J. L. Lucaites, C. M. Condit, & S. Caudill (Eds.), *Contemporary rhetorical theory* (pp. 65–78). New York: Guilford Press. (Original work published in 1990)

McGoldrick, P. (1995). Liturgy: The context of patristic exegesis. In T. Finan & V. Twomey (Eds.), *Spiritual interpretation in the Fathers: Letter and spirit* (pp. 27–37). Dublin, Ireland: Four Courts Press.

Mecke, J. (1990). Dialogue in narration (the narrative principle). In T. Maranhão (Ed.), *The interpretation of dialogue* (pp. 195–215). Chicago: University of Chicago Press.

Medway, P. (1996). Virtual and material buildings: Construction and constructivism in architecture and writing. *Written Communication, 13,* 473–514.

Meyer, M. (1995). *Of problematology: Philosophy, science, and language* (D. Jamison & A. Hart, Trans.). Chicago: University of Chicago Press.

Milgram, S. (1967). The small-world problem. *Psychology Today, 1,* 61–67.

Mill, J. S. (1949). *A system of logic* (8th ed.). London: Longmans. (Original work published in 1843)

Miller, C. R. (1984). Genre as social action. *Quarterly Journal of Speech, 70,* 151–167.

—. (1994). Rhetorical community: The cultural basis of genre. In A. Freedman & P. Medway (Eds.), *Genre and the new rhetoric* (pp. 67–78). London: Taylor & Francis.

Miller, G. A. (1951). *Language and communication.* New York: McGraw-Hill.

—. (1956). The magical number seven, plus or minus two: Some limits on our capacity for processing information. *The Psychological Review, 63,* 81–97.

Miller, R. E. (1994). Fault lines in the contact zone. *College English, 56,* 389–408.

—. (1996). The nervous system. *College English, 58,* 265–286.

—. (1998). The arts of complicity: Pragmatism and the culture of schooling. *College English, 61,* 10–28.

Miller, S. (1989). *Rescuing the subject: A critical introduction to rhetoric and the writer.* Carbondale: Southern Illinois University Press.

—. (1991). *Textual carnivals: The politics of composition.* Carbondale: Southern Illinois University Press.

Miller, T. P. (1997). *The formation of college English: Rhetoric and belles lettres in the British cultural provinces.* Pittsburgh: University of Pittsburgh Press.

Miller, T. P., & Bowdon, M. (1999). Archivists with an attitude: A rhetorical stance on the archives of civic action. *College English, 61,* 591–598.

Milton, J. (1957). On time. In J. Milton, *Complete poems and major prose* (M. Y. Hughes, ed.; p. 80). New York: Macmillan. (Original work published in 1645)

Minsky, M. (1985). *The society of mind.* New York: Simon & Schuster.

Minter, D. W., Gere, A. R., & Keller-Cohen, D. (1995). Learning literacies. *College English, 57,* 669–687.

Moffett, J. (1968). *Teaching the universe of discourse.* Boston: Houghton-Mifflin.

—. (1994). *The universal schoolhouse: Spiritual awakening through education.* San Francisco, CA: Jossey-Bass.

Molière, J.-B. (1950). *The would-be invalid (Le malade imaginaire)* (M. Bishop, Ed. & Trans.). New York: Appleton-Century-Crofts. (Original work published in 1673)

Montgomery, M. (2000). Isolation as a linguistic construct. *Southern Journal of Linguistics, 24,* 41–53.

Moran, C. (1998). Review: English and emerging technologies. *College English, 60,* 202–209.

Morson, G. S., & Emerson, C. (1990). *Mikhail Bakhtin: Creation of a prosaics.* Stanford, CA: Stanford University Press.

Moss, B. J. (1996). Ethnography and composition: Studying language at home. In M. Wiley, B. Gleason, & L. W. Phelps (Eds.), *Composition in four keys: Inquiring into the field* (pp. 388–397). Mountain View, CA: Mayfield. (Original work published in 1992)

Muckelbauer, J. (2000). On reading differently: Through Foucault's resistance. *College English, 63,* 71–94.

Mühlhölzer, F. (1993). Quine and Davidson on reference and evidence. In R. Stoecker (Ed.), *Reflecting Davidson: Donald Davidson responding to an international forum of philosophers* (pp. 41–53). New York: de Gruyter.

Murphy, J. J. (1974). *Rhetoric in the middle ages: A history of rhetorical theory from Saint Augustine to the renaissance.* Berkeley: University of California Press.

—. (1990). Roman writing instruction as described by Quintilian. In J. J. Murphy (Ed.), *A short history of writing instruction: From ancient Greece to twentieth-century America* (pp. 19–75). Davis, CA: Hermagoras Press.

Murray, D. M. (1994). All writing is autobiographical. In S. Perl (Ed.), *Landmark essays on writing process* (pp. 207–216). Davis, CA: Hermagoras Press. (Original work published in 1991)

—. (1996). Teaching the other self: The writer's first reader. In M. Wiley, B. Gleason, & L. W. Phelps (Eds.), *Composition in four keys: Inquiring into the field* (pp. 50–55). Mountain View, CA: Mayfield. (Original work published in 1982)

Myers, G. (1990). *Writing biology: Texts in the social construction of scientific knowledge.* Madison: University of Wisconsin Press.

—. (1996). Out of the laboratory and down to the bay: Writing in science and technology studies. *Written Communication, 13,* 5–43.

Nancy, J.-L. (2001). *The inoperative community* (P. Connor, Ed.; P. Connor, L. Garbus, M. Holland & S. Sawhney, Trans.). Minneapolis: University of Minnesota Press. (Original work published 1991)

Nancy, J.-L., & Smock, A. (1993). Speaking without being able to. In J.-L. Nancy, *The birth to presence* (B. Holmes et al., Trans.; pp. 310–318). Stanford, CA: Stanford University Press.

Neumann, O. (1990, May). *Some aspects of phenomenal consciousness and their possible functional correlates.* Paper presented at a conference hosted by the Zentrum für Interdisziplinäre Foschung, Bielefeld, Germany.

Newkirk, T. (1984a). Direction and misdirection in peer response. *College Composition and Communication, 35,* 301–311.

—. (1984b). How students read student papers. *Written Communication, 1,* 283–305.

Newmeyer, F. J. (1986). *The politics of linguistics.* Chicago: University of Chicago Press.

Newton, I. (1962). *Mathematical principles of natural philosophy* (A. Motte & F. Cajori, Trans.). Berkeley: University of California Press. (Original work published in 1729)

Newton-Smith, W. H. (1988). Science, rationality, and Newton. In M. Sweet Stayer (Ed.), *Newton's dream* (pp. 19–35). Kingston, Ontario: McGill-Queen's University Press. (Original work published in 1987)

Nietzsche, F. (1992a). *Beyond good and evil.* In W. Kaufmann (Ed. & Trans.), *Basic writings of Nietzsche* (pp. 191–435). New York: Modern Library. (Original work published in 1886)

—. (1992b). *On the genealogy of morals.* In W. Kaufmann (Ed. & Trans.), *Basic writings of Nietzsche* (pp. 449–599). New York: Modern Library. (Original work published in 1887)

Niles, J. D. (1998). Reconceiving *Beowulf:* Poetry as social praxis. *College English, 61,* 143–166.

Nold, E. W. (1981). Revising. In C. H. Frederiksen & J. F. Dominic (Eds.), *Writing: The nature, development, and teaching of written communication: Vol. 2: Writing: Process, development and communication* (pp. 67–79). Hillsdale, NJ: Erlbaum.

Novikov, I. D. (1998). *The river of time* (V. Kisin, Trans.). Cambridge, UK: Cambridge University Press.

Nystrand, M. (1982a). An analysis of errors in written communication. In M. Nystrand (Ed.), *What writers know: The language, process, and structure of written discourse* (pp. 57–74). New York: Academic.

—. (1982b). Introduction: Rhetoric's "audience" and linguistics' "speech community." In M. Nystrand (Ed.), *What writers know: The language, process, and structure of written discourse* (pp. 1–28). New York: Academic.

—. (1982c). The structure of textual space. In M. Nystrand (Ed.), *What writers know: The language, process, and structure of written discourse* (pp. 75–86). New York: Academic.

—. (1986). *The structure of written communication: Studies in reciprocity between writers and readers.* Orlando, FL: Academic Press.

—. (1989). A social-interactive model of writing. *Written Communication, 6,* 66–85.

—. (2001). Introduction: On writing and rhetoric in everyday life. *Written Communication, 18,* 255–258.

Nystrand, M., & Duffy, J. (2003). The sociocultural context for the new discourse about writing: Towards a rhetoric of everyday life. In M. Nystrand & J. Duffy (Eds.), *Towards a rhetoric of everyday life: New directions in research on writing, text, and discourse* (pp. xv–xxxiv). Madison: University of Wisconsin Press.

Nystrand, M., Gamoran, A., Kachur, R., & Prendergast, C. (1997). *Opening dialogue: Understanding the dynamics of language and learning in the English classroom.* New York: Teachers College Press.

Nystrand, M, Greene, S., & Wiemelt, J. (1993). Where did composition studies come from? An intellectual history. *Written Communication, 10,* 267–333.

Oakeshott, M. (1962). The voice of poetry in the conversation of mankind. In M. Oakeshott, *Rationalism in politics and other essays* (pp. 197–247). New York: Basic Books. (Original work published in 1959)

Oaklander, L. N. (2004). On the experience of tenseless time. In L. N. Oaklander, *The ontology of time* (pp. 227–234). Amherst, NY: Prometheus Books. (Original work published in 1993)

Oakley, T. V. (1999). The human rhetorical potential. *Written Communication, 16,* 93–128.

Ogden, C. K., & Richards, I. A. (1946). *The meaning of meaning: A study of the influence of language upon thought and of the science of symbolism* (8th ed.). New York: Harcourt, Brace & World. (Original work published in 1923)

O'Grady, W., Dobrovolsky, M., & Aronoff, M. (1993). *Contemporary linguistics: An introduction* (2nd ed.). New York: St. Martin's Press.

Ohmann, R. M. (1996). *English in America: A radical view of the profession.* Middletown, CT: Wesleyan University Press. (Original work published in 1976)

Olson, D. R. (1977). From utterance to text: The bias of language in speech and writing. *The Harvard Educational Review, 47,* 257–281.

—. (1994). *The world on paper: The conceptual and cognitive implications of writing and reading.* Cambridge, UK: Cambridge University Press.

Olson, D. R., & Torrance, N. (1981). Learning to meet the requirements of written text: Language development in the school years. In C. H. Frederiksen & J. F. Dominic (Eds.), *Writing: The nature, development, and teaching of written communication: Vol. 2: Writing: Process, development and communication* (pp. 235–255). Hillsdale, NJ: Erlbaum.

Olson, G. A. (1991). Jacques Derrida on rhetoric and composition: A conversation. In G. A. Olson & I. Gale (Eds.), *(Inter)views: Cross-disciplinary perspectives on rhetoric and literary* (pp. 121–141). Carbondale: Southern Illinois University Press. (Original work published in 1990)

Ong, W. J. (1977). The writer's audience is always a fiction. *PMLA, 90,* 9–21.

—. (1982). *Orality and literacy: The technologizing of the word.* London: Methuen.

Orr, C. J. (1990). Critical rationalism: Rhetoric and the voice of reason. In R. A. Cherwitz (Ed.), *Rhetoric and philosophy* (pp. 105–147). Hillsdale, NJ: Erlbaum.

Ortega y Gassett, J. (1957). *Man and people* (W. R. Trask, Trans.). New York: Norton.

Papoulis, I. (1993). Subjectivity and its role in "constructed" knowledge: Composition, feminist theory, and psychoanalysis. In A. R. Gere (Ed.), *Into the field: Sites of composition studies* (pp. 133–146). New York: MLA.

Parks, S., & Goldblatt, E. (2000). Writing beyond the curriculum: Fostering new collaborations in literacy. *College English, 62,* 584–606.

Parsons, T. (1951). *The social system.* Glencoe, IL: Free Press.

Pascal, B. (1941). *Pensées* (W. F. Trotter, Trans.). New York: Modern Library. (Original work published in 1660)

Pattison, R. (1982). *On literacy: The politics of the word from Homer to the age of rock.* New York: Oxford University Press.

Pearson, J. K. (1996). Linguistic evidence for population movement in North America. *The SECOL Review, 20,* 88–100.

Peck, W. C., Flower, L., & Higgins, L. (1995). Community literacy. *College Composition and Communication, 46,* 199–222.

Peirce, C. S. (1960). *Collected papers of Charles Sanders Peirce: Vols. 1–2* (C. Hartshorne & P. Weiss, Eds.). Cambridge, MA: Harvard University Press. (Original work published in 1931)

——. (1991a). The fixation of belief. In J. Hoopes (Ed.), *Peirce on signs* (pp. 144-159). Chapel Hill: University of North Carolina Press. (Original work published in 1869)

——. (1991b). How to make our ideas clear. In J. Hoopes (Ed.), *Peirce on signs* (pp. 160–177). Chapel Hill: University of North Carolina Press. (Original work published in 1878)

——. (1991c). Some consequences of four incapacities. In J. Hoopes (Ed.), *Peirce on signs* (pp. 54–84). Chapel Hill: University of North Carolina Press. (Original work published in 1868)

Perelman, C. (1982). *The realm of rhetoric* (W. Kluback, Trans.). Notre Dame, IN: University of Notre Dame. (Original work published in 1977)

Petraglia, J. (1995). Spinning like a kite: A closer look at the pseudotransactional function of writing. *JAC, 15,* 19–33.

Phelps, L. W. (1998). Surprised by response: Student, teacher, editor, reviewer. *JAC, 18,* 247–273.

——. (1999). Paths not taken: Recovering history as alternative future. In M. Rosner, B. Boehm & D. Journet (Eds.), *History, reflection, and narrative: The professionalization of composition, 1963–1983* (pp. 39–58). Stamford, CT: Ablex.

Pinker, S. (1995). *The language instinct.* New York: Harper Perennial.

Plato. (trans. 1964a). *Cratylus* (B. Jowett, Trans.). In E. Hamilton & H. Cairns (Eds.), *The collected dialogues of Plato* (pp. 421–474). New York: Pantheon. (Original work published in 1871)

—. (trans. 1964b). *Meno* (W. K. C. Guthrie, Trans.). In In E. Hamilton & H. Cairns (Eds.), *The collected dialogues of Plato* (pp. 353–384). New York: Pantheon. (Original work published in 1956)

—. (trans. 1964c). *Philebus* (R. Hackforth, Trans.). In E. Hamilton & H. Cairns (Eds.), *The collected dialogues of Plato* (pp. 1086–1150). New York: Pantheon. (Original work published in 1945)

Plotinus. (trans. 2000). *Ennead III* (S. MacKenna & B. J. Page, Trans.). [Online]. Available: www.spiritweb.org/Plotinus/part-25.html (Original work published in 1956)

Poe, E. A. (1987). The purloined letter. In D. McQuade et al. (Eds.), *The Harper American literature* (Vol. 1; pp. 1601–1614). New York: Harper & Row. (Original work published in 1844)

Polanyi, M. (1974). *Personal knowledge: Towards a post-critical philosophy.* Chicago: University of Chicago Press. (Original work published in 1958)

Pool, I. de S., & Kochen, M. (1989). Contacts and influence. In M. Kochen (Ed.), The small world (pp. 3–51). Norwood, NJ: Ablex. (Original work published in 1978)

Popper, K. R. (1959). *The logic of scientific discovery.* New York: Basic Books. (Original work published in 1934)

—. (1962). *Conjectures and refutations: The growth of scientific knowledge.* New York: Basic Books.

Porter, J. E. (1996). Intertextuality and the discourse community. In M. Wiley, B. Gleason, & L. W. Phelps (Eds.), *Composition in four keys: Inquiring into the field* (pp. 225–233). Mountain View, CA: Mayfield. (Original work published in 1986)

Porter, K. J. (1998). Methods, truths, reasons. *College English, 60,* 426–440.

—. (2000). Terror and emancipation: The disciplinarity and mythology of computers. *Cultural Critique, 44,* 43–83.

—. (2001). A pedagogy of charity: Donald Davidson and the student-negotiated composition classroom. *College Composition and Communication, 52,* 574–611.

—. (2003). Literature reviews re-viewed: Toward a consequentialist account of surveys, surveyors, and the surveyed. *JAC, 23,* 351–377.

Pratt, M. L. (1987). Linguistic utopias. In M. Fabb, D. Attridge, A. Durant, & C. McCabe (Eds.), *The linguistics of writing: Arguments between language and literature* (pp. 103–122). Manchester, UK: Manchester University Press.

—. (1991). Arts of the contact zone. *Profession, 91,* 33–40.

Prendergast, C. (1998). Race: The absent presence in composition studies. *College Composition and Communication, 50,* 36–53.

—. (2000). The water in the fishbowl: Historicizing *Ways with words. Written Communication, 17,* 452–490.

Preus, J. S. (1969). *From shadow to promise: Old Testament interpretation from Augustine to the young Luther.* Cambridge, MA: Harvard University Press.

Price, H. (1996). *Time's arrow and Archimedes' point: New directions for the physics of time.* New York: Oxford University Press.

Price, R. G. (1996). A refutative demonstration in *Metaphysics* gamma. *Philosophy and Rhetoric, 29,* 93–102.

Prigogine, I., & Stengers, I. (1984). *Order out of chaos: Man's new dialogue with nature.* Toronto: Bantam Books. (Original work published in 1979)

—. (1997). *The end of certainty: Time, chaos, and the new laws of nature.* New York: Free Press. (Original work published in 1996)

Putnam, H. (1975a). Language and reality. In H. Putnam, *Philosophical papers: Vol. 2. Mind, language and reality* (pp. 272–290). Cambridge, UK: Cambridge University Press.

—. (1975b). The meaning of 'meaning.' In H. Putnam, *Philosophical papers: Vol. 2. Mind, language and reality* (pp. 215–271). Cambridge, UK: Cambridge University Press. (Original work published in 1975)

—. (1983a). Models and reality. In H. Putnam, *Philosophical papers: Vol. 3. Realism and reason* (pp. 1–25). Cambridge, UK: Cambridge University Press. (Original work published in 1980)

—. (1983b). There is at least one *a priori* truth. In H. Putnam, *Philosophical papers: Vol. 3. Realism and reason* (pp. 98–114). Cambridge, UK: Cambridge University Press. (Original work published in 1978)

—. (1983c). 'Two dogmas' revisited. In H. Putnam, *Philosophical papers: Vol. 3. Realism and reason* (pp. 87–97). Cambridge, UK: Cambridge University Press. (Original work published in 1976)

—. (1983d). Reference and truth. In H. Putnam, *Philosophical papers: Vol. 3. Realism and reason* (pp. 69–86). Cambridge, UK: Cambridge University Press. (Original work published in 1980)

Quine, W. V. O. (1960). *Word and object.* Cambridge, MA: MIT Press.

—. (1961a). Identity, ostension, and hypostasis. In W. V. Quine, *From a logical point of view* (2nd ed.; pp. 65–79). (Original work published in 1950)

—. (1961b). The problem of meaning in linguistics. In W. V. Quine, *From a logical point of view* (2nd ed.; pp. 47–64). (Original work published in 1953)

—. (1961c). Two dogmas of empiricism. In W. V. Quine, *From a logical point of view* (2nd ed.; pp. 20–46). (Original work published in 1951)

—. (1966). Carnap and logical truth. In W. V. Quine, *The ways of paradox and other essays* (pp. 100–125). New York: Random House. (Original work published in 1956)

Quintilian. (trans. 1987). *On the teaching of speaking and writing: Translations from books one, two, and ten of the* Institutio oratoria (J. J. Murphy, Ed.). Carbondale: Southern Illinois University Press.

Ramberg, B. T. (1989). *Donald Davidson's philosophy of language: An introduction.* Oxford, UK: Blackwell.

Rand, L. (2001). Enacting faith: Evangelical discourse and the discipline of composition studies. *College Composition and Communication, 52,* 349–367.

Ratcliffe, K. (2000). Eavesdropping as rhetorical tactic: History, whiteness, and rhetoric. *JAC, 20,* 87–119.

Ray, C. (1991). *Time, space and philosophy.* London: Routledge.

Read, C. (1981). Writing is not the inverse of reading for young children. In C. H. Frederiksen & J. F. Dominic (Eds.), *Writing: The nature, development, and teaching of written communication: Vol. 2: Writing: Process, development and communication* (pp. 105–118). Hillsdale, NJ: Erlbaum.

Read, R., & Guetti, J. (1999). Meaningful consequences. *The Philosophical Forum, 30,* 289–315.

Redish, J. C., Battison, R. M., & Gold, E. S. (1985). Making information accessible to readers. In L. Odell & D. Goswami (Eds.), *Writing in nonacademic settings* (pp. 129–153). New York: Guilford Press.

Reed, Carol E. (1981). Teaching teachers about teaching writing to students from varied linguistic social and cultural groups. In M. F. Whiteman (Ed.), *Writing: The nature, development, and teaching of written communication: Vol. 1. Variation in writing: Functional and linguistic-cultural differences* (pp. 139–152). Hillsdale, NJ: Erlbaum.

Reed, Cheryl. (1996). Projecting real world audiences. *Writing Instructor, 15,* 131–139.

Rees, M. (1997). *Before the beginning: Our universe and others.* Reading, MA: Perseus Books.

Reichenbach, H. (1947). *Elements of symbolic logic.* New York: Macmillan.

Reid, T. (1989). Oration II. In D. D. Todd (Ed.), *The philosophical orations of Thomas Reid: Delivered at graduation ceremonies in King's College, Aberdeen, 1753, 1756, 1759, 1762* (S. D. Sullivan, Trans.; pp. 41–51). Carbondale: Southern Illinois University Press. (Original work published in 1937)

Reither, J. A. (1994). Writing and knowing: Toward redefining the writing process. In S. Perl (Ed.), *Landmark essays on writing process* (pp. 141–148). Davis, CA: Hermagoras Press. (Original work published in 1985)

The revised English Bible with the Apocrypha. (1989). Oxford: Oxford University Press.

Richards, I. A. (1950). *The philosophy of rhetoric.* New York: Oxford University Press. (Original work published in 1936)

Ricouer, P. (1974). *The conflict of interpretations: Essays in hermeneutics* (D. Ihde, Ed.). Evanston, IL: Northwestern University Press. (Original work published in 1969)

Rivarol, A. (1919). *De l'universalite de la langue française* (W. W. Comfort, Ed.). Boston: Ginn & Company. (Original work published in 1782)

Roberts, P. (1998). Habermas's rational-critical sphere and the problem of criteria. In M. Bernard-Donals & R. R. Glejzer (Eds.), *Rhetoric in an antifoundational world: Language, culture, and pedagogy* (pp. 170–194). New Haven, CT: Yale University Press.

Roemer, M., Schultz, L. M., & Durst, R. K. (1999). Reframing the great debate on first-year writing. *College Composition and Communication, 50,* 377–392.

Rommetveit, R. (1974). *On message structure: A framework for the study of language and communication.* London: Wiley.

Rorty, R. (1979). *Philosophy and the mirror of nature.* Princeton, NJ: Princeton University Press.

—. (1989). *Contingency, irony, and solidarity.* Cambridge, UK: Cambridge University Press.

Rosaldo, M. Z. (1982). The things we do with words: Ilongot speech acts and speech act theory in philosophy. *Language in Society, 11,* 203–237.

Rosenblatt, L. M. (1978). *The reader, the text, the poem.* Carbondale: Southern Illinois University Press.

Ross, S. D. (1994). *The limits of language.* New York: Fordham University Press.

Rudinow, J., & Barry, V. E. (1999). *Invitation to critical thinking* (4th ed.). Fort Worth, TX: Harcourt Brace College.

Ruskin, J. (1886). *Sesame and lilies.* New York: Wiley & Sons. (Original work published in 1865)

Russell, B. (1940). *An inquiry into meaning and truth.* New York: Norton.

—. (1948). *Introduction to mathematical philosophy* (2nd ed.). London: Allen. (Original work published in 1919)

—. (1981). Introduction. In L. Wittgenstein, *Tractatus logico-philosophicus* (pp. 7–23). London: Routledge. (Original work published in 1922)

Ryan, S. (1994). Inscribing the emptiness: Cartography, exploration and the construction of Australia. In C. Tiffin & A. Lawson (Eds.), *De-scribing empire: Post-colonialism and textuality* (pp. 115–130). London: Routledge.

Ryle, G. (1959). Philosophical arguments. In A. J. Ayer (Ed.), *Logical positivism* (pp. 327–344). New York: Free Press. (Original work published in 1946)

—. (1962). *The concept of mind.* New York: Barnes & Noble.

—. (1963). The theory of meaning. In C. E. Caton (Ed.), *Philosophy and ordinary language* (pp. 128–153). Urbana: University of Illinois Press. (Original work published in 1957)

Said, E. (1983). *The world, the text, and the critic.* Cambridge, MA: Harvard University Press.

Sanford, D. H. (1985). Causal relata. In E. Lepore & B. P. McLaughlin (Eds.), *Actions and events: Perspectives on the philosophy of Donald Davidson* (pp. 282–293). Oxford: Blackwell.

Sapir, E. (1949). *Language: An introduction to the study of speech.* New York: Harcourt, Brace. (Original work published in 1921)

Sartre, J.-P. (1956). *Being and nothingness: An essay on phenomenological ontology* (H. E. Barnes, Trans.). New York: Philosophical Library. (Original work published in 1943)

—. (1965a). The emotions: Outline of a theory. In W. Baskin (Ed.), *The philosophy of existentialism* (B. Frechtman, Trans.; pp. 189–254). New York: Philosophical Library. (Original work published in 1948)

—. (1965b). What is writing? In W. Baskin (Ed.), *The philosophy of existentialism* (B. Frechtman, Trans.; pp. 303–331). New York: Philosophical Library. (Original work published in 1948)

Saussure, F. de. (1959). *Course in general linguistics* (C. Bally, A. Sechehaye, & A. Riedlinger, Ed.; W. Baskin, Trans.). New York: McGraw-Hill. (Original work published in 1916)

Savage, G. J. (1997). Doing unto others through technical communication internship programs. *Journal of Technical Writing and Communication, 27,* 401–415.

Schegloff, E. A. (1996). Turn organization: One intersection of grammar and interaction. In E. Ochs, E. A. Schegloff, & S. A. Thompson (Eds.), *Interaction and grammar* (pp. 52–134. Cambridge, UK: Cambridge University Press.

Schilb, J. (1999). Reprocessing the essay. In T. Kent (Ed.), *Post-process theory: Beyond the writing process paradigm* (pp. 198–214). Carbondale: Southern Illinois University Press.

Schildgen, B. D. (1993). Reconnecting rhetoric and philosophy in the composition classroom. In A. R. Gere (Ed.), *Into the field: Sites of composition studies* (pp. 30–43). New York: MLA.

Schlick, M. (1959). The turning point in philosophy (D. Rynin, Trans.). In A. J. Ayer (Ed.), *Logical positivism* (pp. 53–59). New York: Free Press. (Original work published in 1930–1931)

Schryer, C. F. (1999). Genre time/space: Chronotopic strategies in the experimental article. *JAC, 19,* 81–89.

Schultz, K. (2002). Looking across space and time: Reconceptualizing literacy learning in and out of school. *Research in the Teaching of English, 36,* 356–390.

Schutz, Aaron, & Gere, A. R. (1998). Service learning and English studies: Rethinking 'public' service. *College English, 60,* 129–149.

Schutz, Alfred. (1990). *Collected papers: Vol. 1. The problem of social reality* (M. Natanson, Ed.). Dordrecht, the Netherlands: Kluwer Academic. (Original work published in 1962)

Schwebke, L., & Medway, P. (2001). The reader written: Successive constructions of self and text in encounters with everyday writing. *Written Communication, 18,* 350–389.

Scott, R. L. (1967). On viewing rhetoric as epistemic. *Central States Speech Journal, 18,* 9–16.

—. (1976). On viewing rhetoric as epistemic: Ten years later. *Central States Speech Journal, 27,* 258–266.

Searle, J. R. (1969). *Speech acts: An essay in the philosophy of language.* Cambridge, UK: Cambridge University Press.

—. (1985). Metaphor. In A. P. Martinich (Ed.), *Philosophy of language* (pp. 416–437). Oxford: Oxford University Press. (Original work published in 1979)

—. (1991). What is a speech act? In S. Davis (Ed.), *Pragmatics: A reader* (pp. 254–264). Oxford: Oxford University Press. (Original work published in 1965)

—. (1995). *The construction of social reality.* New York: Free Press.

Searle, J. R., & Vanderveken, D. (1985). *Foundations of illocutionary logic.* Cambridge, UK: Cambridge University Press.

Sebeok, T. A. (1991a). Communication. In T. A. Sebeok, *A sign is just a sign* (pp. 22–35). Bloomington: Indiana University Press.

—. (1991b). The evolution of semiosis. In T. A. Sebeok, *A sign is just a sign* (pp. 83–96). Bloomington: Indiana University Press.

—. (1991c). Indexicality. In T. A. Sebeok, *A sign is just a sign* (pp. 128–143). Bloomington: Indiana University Press.

Segal, E. (2000). *Mishnah.* [On-line]. Available: www.acs.ucalgary.ca/~elsegal/TalmudMap/Mishnah.html

Segal, J., Paré, A., Brent, D., & Vipond, D. (1998). The researcher as missionary: Problems with rhetoric and reform in the disciplines. *College Composition and Communication, 50,* 71–90.

Selfe, C. L. (1999). Technology and literacy: A story about the perils of not paying attention. *College Composition and Communication, 50,* 411–436.

Selfe, C. L., & Selfe, R. J. (1994). The politics of the interface: Power and its exercise in electronic contact zones. *College Composition and Communication, 45,* 480–504.

—. (1996). Writing as democratic social action in a technological world: Politicizing and inhabiting virtual landscapes. In A. H. Duin & C. J. Hansen (Eds.), *Nonacademic writing: Social theory and technology* (pp. 325–358). Mahwah, NJ: Erlbaum.

Sellars, W. (1997). *Empiricism and the philosophy of mind.* Cambridge, MA: Harvard University Press. (Original work published in 1956)

Serres, M. (1979). The algebra of literature: The wolf's game. In J. V. Harari (Ed.), *Textual strategies: Perspectives in post-structuralist criticism* (pp. 260–276). Ithaca, NY: Cornell University Press.

Shannon, C. E. (1959). The mathematical theory of communication. In C. E. Shannon & W. Weaver (Eds.), *The mathematical theory of communication* (pp. 3–91). Urbana: University of Illinois Press. (Original work published in 1948)

—. (1951). Prediction and entropy of printed English. *Bell Systems Technical Journal, 30*, 50–64.

Sharov, A. (2001). Analysis of Meyen's typological concept of time. [On-line]. Available: http://www.gypsymoth.ento.vt.edu/~sharov/biosem/time/time.html (Original work published in 1995)

Shaughnessy, M. (1977). *Errors and expectations.* London: Oxford University Press.

Shaw, C. L. M. (1997). Personal narrative: Revealing self and reflecting other. *Human Communication Research, 24*, 302–319.

Shelley, P. B. (2002). Ozymandius. [On-line]. Available: www.tomki.com/poetry/ozymandius.html (Original work published in 1817)

Shelton, J. H. (1996). *Handbook for technical writing.* Lincolnwood, IL: NTC Business.

Sidgwick, A. (1921). Statements and meaning. *Mind, 30*, 271–286.

Silva, T., Leki, I., & Carson, J. (1997). Broadening the perspective of mainstream composition studies: Some thoughts from the disciplinary margins. *Written Communication, 14*, 398–428.

Siorvanes, L. (1996). *Proclus: Neo-platonic philosophy and science.* New Haven, CT: Yale University Press.

Skinner, B. F. (1957). *Verbal behavior.* Englewood Cliffs: Prentice-Hall.

Smagorinsky, P. (1997). Personal growth in social context: A high school senior's search for meaning in an through writing. *Written Communication, 13*, 291–313.

Smith, B. (1996). Mereotopology: A theory of parts and boundaries. *Data & Knowledge Engineering, 20*, 287–303.

Smith, B., & Brogaard, B. (2002). Quantum mereotopology. [On-line] Available: //ontology.buffalo.edu/smith//articles/QM.htm (Original work published in 2000)

Smith, F. (1971). *Understanding reading: A psycholinguistic analysis of reading and learning to read.* New York: Holt, Rinehart & Winston.

Smith, J. (1997). Students' goals, gatekeeping, and some questions of ethics. *College English, 59*, 299–320.

Smith, R. E. (1998). Hymes, Rorty, and the social-rhetorical construction of meaning. In M. Bernard-Donals & R. R. Glejzer (Eds.), *Rhetoric in an antifoundational world: Language, culture, and pedagogy* (pp. 227–253). New Haven, CT: Yale University Press. (Original work published in 1992)

Smitherman, G. (1999). CCCC's role in the struggle for language rights. *College Composition and Communication, 50*, 349–376.

Sorel, G. (1999). *Reflections on violence* (J. Jennings, Trans.). Cambridge, UK: Cambridge University Press. (Original work published in 1912)

Spellmeyer, K. (1993a). Being philosophical about composition: Hermeneutics and the teaching of writing. In A. R. Gere (Ed.), *Into the field: Sites of composition studies* (pp. 9–29). New York: MLA.

—. (1993b). *Common ground: Dialogue, understanding, and the teaching of composition.* Englewood Cliffs, NJ: Prentice Hall.

—. (1998). "Too little care": Language, politics, and embodiment in the life-world. In M. Bernard-Donals & R. R. Glejzer (Eds.), *Rhetoric in an anti-foundational world: Language, culture, and pedagogy* (pp. 254–291). New Haven, CT: Yale University Press. (Original work published in 1993)

Spencer, H. (1933). *The philosophy of style.* New York: Appleton-Century. (Original work published in 1852).

Sperber, D., & Wilson, D. (1986). *Relevance: Communication and cognition.* Oxford: Blackwell.

Spigelman, C. (2001). Argument and evidence in the case of the personal. *College English, 64,* 63–87.

Spinoza, B. de. (1951a). *On the improvement of the understanding.* In R. H. M. Elwes (Trans.), *Chief works of Spinoza* (Vol. 2; pp. 1–41). New York: Dover. (Original work published in 1677)

—. (1951b). *A theologico-political treatise.* In R. H. M. Elwes (Trans.), *Chief works of Spinoza* (Vol. 1; pp. 1–278). New York: Dover. (Original work published in 1670)

Spivak, G. C. (1976). Translator's preface. In J. Derrida, *Of grammatology* (pp. ix–lxxxvii). Baltimore: Johns Hopkins University Press.

Stampe, D. (1968). Toward a grammar of meaning. *The Philosophical Review, 77,* 137–174.

—. (1975). Meaning and truth in the theory of speech acts. In P. Cole & J. L. Morgan (Eds.), *Syntax and Semantics: Vol. 3. Speech acts* (pp. 1–39). New York: Academic Press.

—. (1977). Toward a causal theory of linguistic representation. *Midwest Studies in Philosophy, 2,* 42–63.

Stark, R. (1999). Clichés and composition theory. *JAC, 19,* 453–464.

Staten, H. (1989). The secret name of cats: Deconstruction, intentional meaning, and the new theory of reference. In R. W. Dasenbrock (Ed.), *Redrawing the lines: Analytic philosophy, deconstruction, and literary theory* (pp. 3–26). Minneapolis: University of Minnesota Press.

Steinmann, M., Jr. (1982). Speech-act theory and writing. In M. Nystrand (Ed.), *What writers know: The language, process, and structure of written discourse* (pp. 291–323). New York: Academic Press.

Stevens, E. W., Jr. (1988). *Literacy, law, and social order.* DeKalb, IL: Northern Illinois University Press. (Original work published in 1987)

Stevenson, D. W. (1985). The writing teacher in the workplace: Some questions and answers about consulting. In L. Odell & D. Goswami (Eds.), *Writing in nonacademic settings* (pp. 345–389). New York: Guilford.

Stewart, D. C. (1972). *The authentic voice: A pre-writing approach to student writing.* Dubuque, IA: W. C. Brown.

Stoddard, T. D. (1985). My favorite assignment. *Bulletin of the Association for Business Communication, 48.2,* 28–29.

Stratman, J. (2000). Readers' perception of bias in public education documents: The case of ballot booklets. *Written Communication, 17,* 520–578.

Strawson, P. F. (1971). On referring. In J. F. Rosenberg & C. Travis (Eds.), *Readings in the philosophy of language* (pp. 175–195). Englewood Cliffs, NJ: Prentice-Hall. (Original work published in 1950)

——. (1994). Intention and convention in speech acts. In R. M. Harnish (Ed.), *Basic topics in the philosophy of language* (pp. 40–56). Englewood Cliffs, NJ: Prentice Hall. (Original work published in 1964)

Struever, N. S. (1985). Historical discourse. In T. A. van Dijk (Ed.), *Handbook of discourse analysis: Vol. 1: Disciplines of discourse* (pp. 249–271). London: Academic Press.

Sullivan, D. L. (1999). Identification and dissociation in rhetorical exposé: An analysis of St. Ireneaus's *Against heresies. Rhetoric Society Quarterly, 29,* 49–76.

Suppes, P. (1992a). Congruence of meaning. In P. Suppes, *Language for humans and robots* (pp. 3–18). Oxford: Blackwell. (Original work published in 1973)

——. (1992b). The primacy of utterer's meaning. In P. Suppes, *Language for humans and robots* (pp. 47–66). Oxford: Blackwell. (Original work published in 1986)

——. (1992c). A puzzle about responses and congruence of meaning. In P. Suppes, *Language for humans and robots* (pp. 19–29). Oxford: Blackwell. (Original work published in 1984)

Suppes, P., & Crangle, C. (1992). Context-fixing semantics for the language of action. In P. Suppes, *Language for humans and robots* (pp. 317–343). Oxford: Blackwell. (Original work published in 1988)

Tamor, L., & Bond, J. T. (1983). Text analysis: Inferring process from product. In P. Mosenthal, L. Tamor, & G. Walmsley (Eds.), *Research on writing: Principles and methods* (pp. 99–138). New York: Longman.

Tanselle, G. T. (1989). *A rationale of textual criticism.* Philadelphia: University of Pennsylvania Press.

Tarski, A. (1956). *Logic, semantics, metamathematics: Papers from 1923 to 1938* (J. H. Woodger, Trans.). Oxford: Clarendon Press.

Taylor, C. (1991). *The ethics of authenticity.* Cambridge, MA: Harvard University Press.

Thomas, L. L. (1957). *The linguistic theories of N. Ja. Marr.* Berkeley: University of California Press.

Thomas, W. I., & Thomas, D. S. (1928). *The child in America: Behavior problems and programs.* New York: Knopf.

Tobin, L. (1993). *Writing relationships: What really happens in the composition classroom.* Portsmouth, NH: Heinemann-Boynton/Cook.

Trimbur, J. (1989). Consensus and difference in collaborative learning. *College English, 51,* 602–616.

—. (2000a). Agency and the death of the author: A partial defense of modernism. *JAC, 20,* 283–298.

—. (2000b). Composition and the circulation of writing. *College Composition and Communication, 52,* 188–219.

Trimmer, J. F. (1999). Real world writing assignments. *JAC, 19,* 35–49.

Turner, G. (1990). *British cultural studies: An introduction.* Boston: Unwin Hyman.

Turner, M. (1994). Design for a theory of meaning. In W. F. Overton & D. S. Palermo (Eds.), *The nature and ontogenesis of meaning* (pp. 91–107). Hillsdale, NJ: Erlbaum.

Twomey, V. (1995). St Athanasius: *De synodis* and the sense of scripture. In T. Finan & V. Twomey (Eds.), *Spiritual interpretation in the Fathers: Letter and spirit* (pp. 85–118). Dublin, Ireland: Four Courts Press.

Uexküll, J. V. (1982). The theory of meaning (T. V. Uexküll, Trans.). *Semiotica, 42,* 25–82.

Uexküll, T. V. (1982). Introduction: Meaning and science in Jakob von Uexküll's concept of biology. *Semiotica, 42,* 1–24.

Valdés, G. (1992). Bilingual minorities and language issues in writing: Toward professionwide responses to a new challenge. *Written Communication, 9,* 85–136.

van Wijk, C., & Sanders, T. (1999). Identifying writing strategies through text analysis. *Written Communication, 16,* 51–75.

Vande Kopple, W. J. (1985). Some exploratory discourse on metadiscourse. *College Composition and Communication, 36,* 82–93.

—. (1994). Some characteristics and functions of grammatical subjects in scientific discourse. *Written Communication, 11,* 534–564.

Verscheuren, J. (1983). On Boguslawski on promise. *Journal of Pragmatics, 7,* 629–632.

Villanueva, V. (1999). On the rhetoric and precedents of racism. *College Composition and Communication, 50,* 645–661.

Virilio, P. (1989). *War and cinema: The logistics of perception* (P. Camiller, Trans.). New York: Verso. (Original work published in 1984)

Vitanza, V. J. (1991). Three countertheses: Or, a critical in(ter)vention into composition theories and pedagogies. In P. Harkin & J. Schilb (Eds.),

Contending with words: Composition and rhetoric in a postmodern age (pp. 139–172). New York: MLA.

— (1997). *Negation, subjectivity, and the history of rhetoric.* Albany: State University of New York Press.

Vološinov, V. N. (1986). *Marxism and the philosophy of language* (L. Matejka & I. R. Titunik, Trans.). Cambridge, MA: Harvard University Press. (Original work published in 1929)

Vygotsky, L. (1986). *Thought and language* (A. Kozulin, Trans.). Cambridge, MA: MIT Press. (Original work published in 1962)

Waismann, F. (1959). How I see philosophy. In A. J. Ayer (Ed.), *Logical positivism* (pp. 345–380). New York: Free Press. (Original work published in 1956)

Wander, P. (1999). The third persona: An ideological turn in rhetorical theory. In J. L. Lucaites, C. M. Condit, & S. Caudill (Eds.), *Contemporary rhetorical theory: A reader* (pp. 357–379). New York: Guilford Press. (Original work published in 1984)

Wardhaugh, R. (1999). *Proper English: Myths and misunderstandings about language.* Malden, MA: Blackwell.

Welch, K. (1990). Writing instruction in ancient Athens after 450 B.C. In J. J. Murphy (Ed.), *A short history of writing instruction: From ancient Greece to twentieth-century America* (pp. 1–17). Davis, CA: Hermagoras Press.

Welch, N. (1998). Sideshadowing teacher response. *College English, 60,* 374–395.

Wells, S. (1996). Rogue cops and health care: What do we want from public writing? *College Composition and Communication, 47,* 325–341.

West, T., & Olson, G. A. (1999). Rethinking negotiation in composition studies. *JAC, 19,* 241–251.

White, E. M. (1995). *Assigning, responding, evaluating: A writing teacher's guide* (3rd ed.). New York: St. Martin's Press.

Whitrow, G. J. (1975). *The nature of time.* Harmondsworth, UK: Penguin. (Original work published in 1972)

Whorf, B. L. (1956a). A linguistic consideration of thinking in primitive communities. In J. B. Carroll (Ed.), *Language, thought, and reality: Selected writings of Benjamin Lee Whorf* (pp. 65–86). Cambridge, MA: MIT Press.

—. (1956b). Linguistics as an exact science. In J. B. Carroll (Ed.), *Language, thought, and reality: Selected writings of Benjamin Lee Whorf* (pp. 220–232). Cambridge, MA: MIT Press. (Original work published in 1940)

—. (1956c). Science and linguistics. In J. B. Carroll (Ed.), *Language, thought, and reality: Selected writings of Benjamin Lee Whorf* (pp. 207–219). Cambridge, MA: MIT Press. (Original work published in 1940)

Williams, J. D. (1993). Rule-governed approaches to language and composition. *Written Communication, 10,* 542–568.

Williams, R. (1961). *The long revolution*. London: Chatto & Windus.

Wimsatt, W. K., Jr., & Beardsley, M. C. (1954). The affective fallacy. In W. K. Wimsatt, Jr., *The verbal icon: Studies in the meaning of poetry* (pp. 21–39). Lexington: University of Kentucky Press. (Original work published in 1946)

Winsor, D. (1994). Invention and writing in technical work: Representing the object. *Written Communication, 11*, 227–250.

Winspur, S. (1989). Text acts: Recasting performatives with Austin and Derrida. In R. W. Dasenbrock (Ed.), *Redrawing the lines: Analytic philosophy, deconstruction, and literary theory* (pp. 169–188). Minneapolis: University of Minnesota Press.

Winterowd, W. R. (1996). The rhetorical transaction of reading. In M. Wiley, B. Gleason, & L. W. Phelps (Eds.), *Composition in four keys: Inquiring into the field* (pp. 157–162). Mountain View, CA: Mayfield. (Original work published in 1976)

—. (2000). Where the action is: *Doing* versus *being* in the academy. *JAC, 20*, 299–309.

Witte, S. P. (1992). Context, text, intertext: Toward a constructivist semiotic of writing. *Written Communication, 9*, 237–308.

Wittgenstein, L. (1968). *Philosophical investigations* (3rd ed.; G. E. M. Anscombe, Trans.). New York: Macmillan. (Original work published in 1953)

—. (1972). *On certainty* (G. E. M. Anscombe & G. H. von Wright, Eds.; D. Paul & G. E. M. Anscombe, Trans.). New York: Harper & Row. (Original work published in 1969)

—. (1978). *Philosophical grammar* (R. Rhees, Ed.; A. Kenny, Trans.). Berkeley: University of California Press. (Original work published in 1974)

—. (1981). *Tractatus logico-philosophicus* (G. E. M. Anscombe, Trans.). London: Routledge. (Original work published in 1922)

Wood, A. S. (1969). *Captive to the word: Martin Luther: Doctor of sacred scripture*. Devon, UK: Paternoster Press.

Worsham, L. (1991). Writing against writing: The predicament of *écriture féminine* in composition studies. In P. Harkin & J. Schilb (Eds.), *Contending with words: Composition and rhetoric in a postmodern age* (pp. 82–104). New York: MLA.

—. (1998). Going postal: Pedagogic violence and the schooling of emotion. *JAC, 18*, 213–245.

—. (1999). Critical interference and the postmodern turn in composition studies: An agenda for theory. *Composition Forum, 10*(1), 1–15.

Worsham, L., & Olson, G. A. (1999a). Hegemony and the future of democracy: Ernesto Laclau's political philosophy. *JAC, 19*, 1–34.

—. (1999b). Rethinking political community: Chantal Mouffe's liberal socialism. *JAC, 19*, 163–199.

Wulf, R. (2001). The historical roots of gestalt theory theory. [On-line]. Available: www.gestalt.org/wulf.htm (Original work published in 1996)

Yarbrough, S. R. (1999). *After rhetoric: The study of discourse beyond language and culture.* Carbondale: Southern Illinois University Press.

Yeats, W. B. (1988a). Among school children. In R. Ellmann & R. O'Clair (Eds.), *The Norton anthology of modern poetry* (2nd ed.; pp. 167–169). New York: Norton. (Original work published in 1927)

—. (1988b). Sailing to Byzantium. In R. Ellmann & R. O'Clair (Eds.), *The Norton anthology of modern poetry* (2nd ed.; pp. 161–162). New York: Norton. (Original work published in 1928)

Zawacki, T. M. (1998, April). *Telling stories: The subject is never just me.* Paper presented at the annual meeting of the Conference on College Composition and Communication, Chicago, IL.

Index

Jackendoff, R., 179, 239
James, W., 51, 68, 77, 161, 170, 295, 329n, 341n
Janangelo, J., 298
Janet, P., 131
Jarratt, S., 326n
Jerome, Saint, 78
Jespersen, O., 138, 341n
John of Salisbury, 68, 329n
Johnson, R. L., 278
Johnson, S., 139
Johnson, T. R., 56, 161
Jourdain, P. E. B., 92
Journet, D., 28, 161
Jukuri, S., 278
Kachur, R., 278
Kant, I., 92, 337n
Kastely, J. L., 295
Katz, J. J., 166
Kaufer, D. S., 55, 65, 136-137, 299-300
Keller-Cohen, D., 220, 238, 298
Kemmerling, A., 110
Kennedy, G. A., 67-68, 71, 80-84, 98, 340n
Kennedy, K., 155
Kent, T., 33-34, 165, 185, 204, 279, 293, 328n
Keynes, J. M., 70
Kim, J., 314, 341n
Kinneavy, J. L., 230
Kintsch, W., 100
Kixmiller, L. S. A., 295
Kleinfeld, J. 328n
Knoblauch, C. H., 33, 37, 239, 278, 316, 327n
knowledge, 21, 23-24, 28, 31, 33, 67, 69-70, 75, 82, 85-86, 89, 101, 103, 122, 146-147, 159, 168-170, 172, 176, 178-179, 226-228, 236, 261, 284, 286, 301, 314, 316, 326n, 336n, 338n, 345n

Kochen, M., 328n
Kramer, E. E., 326n
Kress, G., 176, 185, 236
Kripke, S. A., 65, 121, 133, 215-216, 220, 275, 322, 339n
Kristeva, J., 8
Lamb, C. E., 278
Land, S. K., 68, 70, 329n
language, 4-8, 15-19, 28, 30-31, 33-34, 36, 40-41, 43-45, 50, 52, 55, 59-60, 64, 68-71, 77, 85, 90, 100, 104, 107-110, 116-117, 119, 121, 123, 126, 130, 132, 134, 137-150, 152-155, 158-159, 161-164, 166-170, 173-176, 181-183, 185, 202-203, 208, 212, 214-215, 217-219, 221-223, 225-228, 231, 233-235, 239-245, 247, 249-254, 256-258, 264, 266, 294, 295-296, 298, 304, 306, 320, 325n, 326n, 329n, 330n, 331n, 332n, 335n, 336n, 337n, 340n, 341n, 342n, 343n, 345n, 347n, 348n; artificial, 135, 332n; common, 19, 138, 141, 174, 216; competence, 45, 126; conventions/conventionalism, 17, 31, 33-34, 45, 109, 126, 130, 158, 160-162, 164-165, 167-168, 172, 185, 217, 335n, 339n; established, 138; evolution of, 153; grapholect, 139, 279; idiolect, 64, 126, 130, 176, 181-183, 202, 208, 242, 244; *langue*, 45, 47, 152-153, 164, 222, 225, 239, 242, 257; legitimate, 142; *lingua adamica*, 69; linguistic evolutionism, 226-227, 341n; linguistic isolation, 156, 325n; mother tongue, 138; national, 55, 138, 141, 160, 174, 235;

137, 163, 166-168, 171, 173,
183-187, 190, 192-193, 201-
204, 206-207, 214, 222-223,
225, 228-231, 234, 240, 243,
250, 254-255, 259-261, 266,
268-269, 273-275, 277-281,
283, 285-294, 296-299, 302-
303, 307-313, 315-316, 320-
324, 327n, 328n, 329n, 334n,
336n, 338n, 343n, 347n, 348n;
defined, 56
meaninglessness, 17, 61, 70, 184,
332n
Mecke, J., 219, 253-254
mediations, 115, 118-119, 125,
201, 255, 261-262, 314, 323
Medway, P., 238, 341n
metaphor, 39, 48, 92, 138-139,
153, 163, 169, 220
Meyer, M., 219
Milgram, S., 328n
Mill, J. S., 116, 228
Miller, C. R., 15, 161
Miller, G. A., 114, 139, 239, 332n,
343n
Miller, R. E., 137
Miller, S., 7, 108, 123, 229
Miller, T. P., 23, 78, 139, 140,
230, 327n, 341n
Milton, J., 66, 175
mind, 4, 10, 13, 18, 30-31, 33,
34, 42, 44, 46, 48, 64-65, 68,
72, 88, 97, 112, 119, 126, 130,
133, 136, 141, 159, 164, 176-
181, 185-188, 190-193, 201-
203, 207-208, 212, 214, 225,
227, 235-236, 281-282, 288,
306, 308, 311, 313, 323-324,
327n, 330n, 332n, 336n, 341n,
348n; Cartesian Theater, 193;
consciousness, 46, 116, 130,
164, 176-179, 187, 192-197,
200-203, 210-212, 214, 222,

235-236, 261-262, 323, 337n,
338n; distension, 186; interiority, 163-164, 274, 321, 337n;
memory, 17, 72, 178, 180, 195-
196, 200, 213, 222, 225, 229,
269, 340n; monothetic, 187,
322; Multiple Drafts Theory
of, 193-195; noo-field, 177;
polythetic, 187, 322; representation of time, 114; stream of
consciousness, 178, 193-195,
214, 235-236; umwelten, 176,
181; unconscious, 178, 195,
201
Minsky, M., 198
Minter, D. W., 220, 238, 298
Mishnah, 87
Moffett, J., 98, 138, 143
Molière, J.-B., 5
Montgomery, M., 156
Moore, M. E., 298
Moran, C., 132, 278
Morley, D., 132, 336n
Morson, G. S., 219-220
Moss, B. J., 326n
movies of the mind, 310-311, 313
Muckelbauer, J., 25-26
Mühlhölzer, F., 215
Murphy, J. J., 69, 82, 87, 98, 123,
284, 330n, 332n, 347n
Murray, D. M., 185, 314
Myers, G., 143, 231, 341n
myth, 38, 49, 122, 133, 152, 182,
250, 293, 313, 329n, 334n
Nancy, J.-L., 339n
Nelson, B. A., 298
Neumann, O., 198
Newkirk, T., 278
Newmeyer, F. J., 174, 227, 335n
Newton, I., 70, 127, 326n, 330n
Newton-Smith, W. H., 330n
Nietzsche, F., 56, 78, 106, 115,
238, 332n

About the Author

Kevin J. Porter (PhD, Wisconsin) is Assistant Professor of English at the University of Texas at Arlington, where he teaches courses in rhetoric and composition studies with an emphasis on its collisions and collusions with critical theory, hermeneutics, literary theory, philosophy, and semiotics. His essays have appeared in, among other places, *College Composition and Communication, College English, Cultural Critique, JAC,* and *SubStance.*

CPSIA information can be obtained at www.ICGtesting.com
Printed in the USA
LVOW041349290112

266019LV00001B/336/A